Just Add Water

Just Add Water

Solving the World's Problems Using
Its Most Precious Resource

RHETT B. LARSON

OXFORD
UNIVERSITY PRESS

OXFORD
UNIVERSITY PRESS

Oxford University Press is a department of the University of Oxford. It furthers the University's objective of excellence in research, scholarship, and education by publishing worldwide. Oxford is a registered trademark of Oxford University Press in the UK and certain other countries.

Published in the United States of America by Oxford University Press
198 Madison Avenue, New York, NY 10016, United States of America.

© Oxford University Press 2020

Library of Congress Cataloging-in-Publication Data
Names: Larson, Rhett, author.
Title: Just add water : solving the world's problems using its most precious resource / Rhett B. Larson.
Description: New York, NY : Oxford University Press, [2020] | Includes bibliographical references and index.
Identifiers: LCCN 2019047239 (print) | LCCN 2019047240 (ebook) | ISBN 9780190948009 (hardback) | ISBN 9780190948030 (epub) | ISBN 9780190948016 (online) | ISBN 9780190948023 (updf)
Subjects: LCSH: Water security—Social aspects. | Water-supply—Social aspects. | Social problems.
Classification: LCC HD1691 .L37 2020 (print) | LCC HD1691 (ebook) | DDC 333.91—dc23
LC record available at https://lccn.loc.gov/2019047239
LC ebook record available at https://lccn.loc.gov/2019047240

1 3 5 7 9 8 6 4 2

Printed by Integrated Books International, United States of America

Note to Readers
This publication is designed to provide accurate and authoritative information in regard to the subject matter covered. It is based upon sources believed to be accurate and reliable and is intended to be current as of the time it was written. It is sold with the understanding that the publisher is not engaged in rendering legal, accounting, or other professional services. If legal advice or other expert assistance is required, the services of a competent professional person should be sought. Also, to confirm that the information has not been affected or changed by recent developments, traditional legal research techniques should be used, including checking primary sources where appropriate.

(Based on the Declaration of Principles jointly adopted by a Committee of the American Bar Association and a Committee of Publishers and Associations.)

You may order this or any other Oxford University Press publication by visiting the Oxford University Press website at www.oup.com.

For Becky, my oasis.

Contents

Contents

Foreword

The turning point of my life began with one drop of water. My family has lived, farmed, ranched, mined, and built in the arid southwestern United States for generations. I grew up in Yuma, Arizona—a farming community located where California, Arizona, and Mexico meet, and where the Colorado River crosses the border between the United States and Mexico. I was raised in communities where we constantly talked of, worried about, and prayed for water. But the drop of water that changed the life of this desert dweller fell on my head on a tropical island, on September 22, 1998, in the Dominican Republic.

I was a nineteen-year-old missionary living in Santo Domingo. I had been living in the Dominican Republic for nearly eight months, but most of that time was spent in a small fishing village in the northern part of the island. I had only been in Santo Domingo for a few weeks when we heard rumors of an approaching hurricane on September 21. A friend and fellow missionary had watched the news and stopped by our small apartment to warn us. The apartment was on the bottom floor of a three-story cinder-block building that lay at the foot of large cliffs. Built in and around these caves were hundreds of small colorful homes made of wood, tin, and dried palm bark.

We climbed through the cliffs of our barrio. We warned people to leave their homes and go to the school or the church, which were located on higher ground and made of solid concrete and cinder block. People said they would not leave their homes, either out of fear of abandoning their home to looters or because of confidence that hurricanes always just brushed the island but rarely made landfall. The last major hurricane to have made landfall in the Dominican Republic had been Hurricane David, twenty years earlier.

We walked to a small market run out of a neighbor's home. As a teenager from the desert, I had no experience with anything like a hurricane or how to prepare for it. I bought a one-liter carton of orange juice and one small package of animal crackers as my emergency supplies. As we walked back to our apartment that evening, I felt the first drop of water on my head. It was quickly followed by another. And another.

Within a short time, four young missionaries were huddled in our small apartment as a storm unlike anything I could have imagined raged outside. The wind screamed ceaselessly through the whole night, louder even than the pounding rain. We had no electricity, which was not uncommon, but the darkness was so profound that it was somehow more all-encompassing than the noise. We wrapped a few belongings in plastic trash bags as the water in our apartment rose, from inches to feet. We debated trying to run to the church or school through the storm. We debated trying to climb onto the roof. We debated in voices yelling above the din and yelling out our panic. And then we yelled suddenly into complete silence and sunlight.

We waded our way out of the door and blinked away the dazzling bright tropical sky. Animal carcasses floated down the rivers that had been streets the day before. We climbed our way up the hills in our barrio to help our friends and neighbors as they began to repair roofs and salvage belongings. As we climbed, I look up and around. Above us was an azure sky of Caribbean perfection. Around us on all horizons were black curtains streaked with lightning.

We were in the eye. We ran through the flooded streets, trying to help as many of our neighbors as possible make it to the church or the school before the storm came back. Before we reached safety, the wind hit from the other direction with the force of a bomb. The rain fell in torrents again. The sun was blocked out, and we crashed and slid our way toward the rushing waters of the street below. We never made it to safety. The rest of the storm was spent in panic—combating the deluge.

That night, as the waters began to slowly recede, I lay down and sobbed. I sobbed until my ribs hurt. Then, out of the night and from somewhere in the city, an epically huge car sound system began to play. The music echoed over the whole city. It was Bob Marley's "No Woman, No Cry." As he reached the chorus and chanted "Everything's gonna be alright," I sat up and wrapped my arms around my knees. I wiped my eyes and mastered myself.

In the coming days and weeks, we worked in rescue and rebuilding. We had problems I could have expected—homelessness, sickness, injuries, theft. But the most difficult problem was how to prioritize which problems to address first. One thing I knew for certain was that the harder I worked, the sicker and thirstier I got. I felt like I was dying of thirst in water up to my waist. One day, we cut apart a large tree that had crushed a home. When we finished, the family said, "Please let us give you something for helping us." All I thought was: "Water, please let it be water." They returned with plates full of boiled yucca, which must be the driest food on Earth. I gratefully choked it down. And I really regretted buying animal crackers and orange juice instead of water.

As we continued our rebuilding efforts, we were constantly evaluating our priorities. As we did so, I sounded like some absurd parody of an infomercial in responding to these questions. "What should we do?" "How can we help?" "What's next?" I felt like my answer was always the voice of the guy hawking Chia Pets, or miracle cleaners, or dinosaur-shaped sponges on late-night TV. *"Just add water!"*

It seemed like the answer to every problem was to think about water first. Every other problem would disappear, or at least be more manageable, if we could just get rid of excess dirty water and get our hands on enough clean water. And that is what changed everything for me. Since then, I have devoted my professional life to solving water problems. I worked as a water lawyer, representing towns, tribes, cities, mines, utility companies, chemical companies, environmental protection organizations, farmers, golf course resorts, and individuals. I have worked as a professor, teaching and researching on issues of water law and policy. I have worked to resolve large water resource disputes between tribes, cities, towns, farms, ranches, mines, and nations. I've worked in water resource development projects on five continents. And no matter where I go, and no matter what problem needs to be solved, my instinctive response is: "Just add water."

I hesitate to use the words "solve" or "solution" because so many problems (like water scarcity in the desert) are not solveable, but instead are challenges to be managed. While there are perhaps more accurate descriptors for the aim of this book than to provide "solutions," I've decided to use that word and its derivations because they are aspirational and more evocative of water itself, given the double meaning of "solution." Perhaps rather than perfectly and permanently resolving our problems, focusing on water allows them to be dissolved, diluted, and clarified.

I am aiming to engage water policy experts across disciplines with my proposals, but more importantly I am hoping to demonstrate to a general readership the critical and often under-appreciated role water policy plays in our lives. It is difficult to write a broad book about such complex and technical issues that can engage both experts and the general public. I have done my best to explain technical concepts and provide background and context, but it is nearly impossible to discuss water policy without encountering a veritable alphabet soup of acronyms. When I was just starting out as a young water lawyer, my boss came into my office and said, "Rhett, have you seen the Smurfs?" Thinking he meant the cartoon about little blue creatures who lived in mushrooms, I responded, "Yes, I've seen the Smurfs." He then said, "Well, they were on my desk yesterday, and now I can't find them." I thought my boss had cracked under the stress. It wasn't until later that day that I learned he was referring to "Self-Monitoring Reporting Forms." Hopefully, I have avoided such confusion for a general readership.

In this book, I argue that no other challenge is more fundamental to more global problems that water security—achieving a sufficient quantity and quality of water for people and the environment with acceptable costs and risks. And I suggest measures we can take to promote global water security. But I confess to another, more personal, agenda in writing this book. As a water lawyer and scholar and teacher of water law and policy, I am regularly asked questions like "What type of a law do you practice?" or "What do you teach and write about?" When I answer, "water law," I often hear responses along the lines of "Oh . . . that's a very narrow, niche field." I do not understand this response, particularly as I have never heard a similar response to those who answer "criminal law" or "bankruptcy law." I have to restrain myself from saying, "Compare the number of people who declare bankruptcy or are arrested for committing a crime to the number of people who drink water. Why is my field the narrow one?"

In addition to arguing for greater prioritization of measures to achieve global water security, this book is my effort to demonstrate that water law is at least as broad and important as any other field of law. Indeed, my greatest concern in writing this book is not the inevitable criticism I will receive that I am biased in my argument of the importance of water policy. I cheerfully plead guilty to being overly enthusiastic about my field. I know that all of the problems I address in this book are far more complicated than Chia Pets or dinosaur sponges, and that issues such as poverty, discrimination, or war will not dissolve with the simple addition of water, any more than adding clean water would have rebuilt destroyed homes or repaired demolished infrastructure following the hurricane in the Dominican Republic. But in my experience, water is a good place to start and has frequently further-reaching benefits than many other worthy contenders for the top public policy priority.

Rather than my bias in favor of water policy, my biggest concern in writing this book is that in attempting to demonstrate the breadth and significance of the scope of the role water policy plays in all sorts of social problems, I will fail to adequately demonstrate its depth and complexity. Entire books can be (and have been) written about water policy in the context of war, immigration, discrimination, and public health. In this book I spend only short chapters on these and other issues. I hope the many experts I cite and learn from will forgive me for failing to fully convey the nuance they have in more focused works. I comfort myself in this concern by noting that a book about human rights will inevitably be less nuanced in its discussion of freedom of expression than a book devoted solely to that topic, but that does not mean the broader book does not have a role to play in connecting, comparing, summarizing, and synthesizing narrower aspects of the field. My hope is that this book launches readers upon an exploration into water policy's role in addressing seemingly disparate and unrelated social problems and that readers will dive more deeply into the ocean of water policy after I have described its vastness. Like water seeping into the soil, water law and policy permeate—in ways seen and unseen—virtually every social challenge we confront. A basic understanding of the scope and significance of water law and policy is essential not only for policymakers but for any engaged citizen. Hopefully, for many readers, this book is the first drop of water.

Acknowledgments

Thanks so much to Merel Alstein, Meera Seth, David Lipp, Blake Ratcliff, and everyone at Oxford University Press for making this book possible. I am grateful as well for feedback, criticism, and encouragement from friends and colleagues: Ram Aviram, Bret Birdsong, Dan Bodansky, Di Bowman, Karen Bradshaw, Tomer Broude, Dave Brown, Vanessa Casado Pérez, Adam Chodorow, Alvar Closas, Kevin Cluff, Laura Coordes, David Cordero Heredia, Barbara Cosens, Robin Kundis Craig, Joseph Dellapenna, David DePianto, Holly Doremus, Joya Douaihy, Gabriel Eckstein, Monika Ehrman, Kathy Ferris, Grady Gammage, Jr., Dustin Garrick, Robert Glennon, David Gay, Amit Gross, Zack Gubler, Joyeeta Gupta, Noah Hall, Emily Hammond, Michael Hanemann, Andy Hessick, Carissa Hessick, Cameron Holley, Bruce Huber, Wendy Jepson, Eric Johnson, Kit Johnson, Nate Johnson, Kelsey Leonard, Erik Luna, Andrés Martínez Moscoso, Othman Al Mashaqbeh, Kaipo Matsumura, Assad Mawad, Stephen McCaffrey, Mark McGinnis, Anthonio Moawad, Nabil Moawad, Nayla Moawad, Richard Morrison, Sarah Porter, Trevor Reed, J.B. Ruhl, Troy Rule, Richard Rushforth, Erin Ryan, Robbie Sabel, Victoria Sahani, Salman Salman, James Salzman, Shelley Ross Saxer, Erin Scharff, Josh Sellers, Bijal Shah, Darren Sinclair, Kathryn Sorenson, Bill Staudenmaier, Doug Sylvester, Dan Tarlock, Buzz Thompson, Patrick Thomson, Justin Weinstein-Tull, and Lisa Whelan. Zak Kramer—thank you so much for everything. Mary Sigler—I miss you, and thanks.

Thanks go as well to all my teachers and mentors, including David Bradley, Ignacio Garcia, Yvette Garcia, David Grey, Michael Hanemann, Bernard Harcourt, Rob Hope, David Johnstone, Rachael McDonnell, Bernard Meltzer, Mark New, Michael Rouse, Anna Russell, Jeff Shumway, and Geoffrey Stone. I am grateful to all of my students, especially Jeramy Moschonas and Alex Ronchetti for their work as research assistants. I am so grateful for feedback and research support from Andrea Gass, whose help has been invaluable. I appreciate the support from Arizona State University, the Kyl Center for Water Policy, the Weidenfeld-Hoffmann Scholarship and Leadership Programme, the Fulbright Scholar Program, the Lady Davis Fellowship Trust, the University of New South Wales and the PLuS Alliance, the Hebrew University of Jerusalem, and the Pontifical Catholic University of Ecuador. I am grateful to the U.S. Agency for International Development (USAID) and my partners and friends in the Holistic Water Solutions Initiative: the René Moawad Foundation, Mercy Corps, GreenCo, and H2O for Humanity. The views and information contained in this book are solely my responsibility and do not necessarily reflect the views of any partners of the Holistic Water Solutions Initiative, Arizona State University, USAID, or the U.S. government.

Finally, this book would not be possible without all of my family. When I was young, and I earned a treat, my mom would say, "You can pick out any book you want." She instilled in me a love of books. My dad taught me hard work, and he worked hard as my first editor on every chapter of this book. Thanks, Mom and Dad—I love you both. My kids enjoy the old Walt Disney animated *Robin Hood* movie, in which all of the characters are animals. There is a part in the movie when a turtle is in an archery contest, and his son waves a little flag and cheers, "Yay, Dad!" My kids say that to me a lot, from little things like opening a mayonnaise jar to big things like finishing a book. Thanks, Annie, Brig, Camille, and Lizzy, for cheering me on even when I feel like a turtle trying to shoot an arrow. And I am so grateful to my amazing wife, Becky. I love you. Home Team.

Introduction

Understanding Water Security

Scientists have long been searching for a unified field theory—one answer to all of the questions about the physical universe.[1] What if one theory could explain everything, from gravity to quantum mechanics?[2] Philosophers have pursued something similar in metaphysics in attempting to describe being and substance, with the ancient Greek philosopher Thales of Miletus arguing that everything is water.[3] In this book, I take a similar approach to social policy questions. What if we could find a unified social policy theory—the answer to every question from how to prevent war to how to promote gender equality? And like Thales of Miletus, the answer I am suggesting is water.

Most serious global challenges are "wicked problems," meaning they are complex, multifaceted, and resistant to resolution because they are ever-changing and because our knowledge about the problem is incomplete or contradictory.[4] But perhaps the first step in solving the wicked problems of terrorism, racism, climate change, global pandemics, mass immigration, and a host of other challenges is the same: We should reform our laws, policies, and priorities to achieve global water security. Global water security means reasonable access to water of acceptable quantity and quality with acceptable costs and risks for people and the environment.[5] Water security integrates policies aimed at water supply (both in terms of drought and flood), water quality (both for human use and in the natural environment), and water distribution (including consideration of both intragenerational and intergenerational equity). A water-secure society is a safer society, a fairer society, a healthier society, and a more prosperous society.

In setting forth such an ambitious proposal, I do not mean to oversimplify multifaceted problems, and I do not claim to solve all of the world's problems with a drop or two of water. But I am arguing that prioritizing solving one problem—water insecurity—may be the best place to start solving all our problems. Relatedly, I argue that water plays an underappreciated role in many disparate aspects of public policy, and that it behooves all citizens, leaders, and scholars to understand that role. Each chapter of this book examines a complex social challenge, many of which may on the surface seem unrelated to water policy, but in fact can be understood as significantly tied to water insecurity. I argue that advancing water security will help address each of these wicked problems. In the final chapter, I set out a framework of proposals to advance global water security, and I make recommendations for what individuals, companies, organizations, and governments can do to promote water security. Along the way, I hope to also introduce the core concepts and concerns underlying water law and policy. My goal in this book is to convince the reader that the answer, or at least one part of the answer, to our most serious problems is the oft-repeated late-night infomercial exhortation: "Just add water."

For some problems, the addition of water is an obvious solution, as in the case of drought, famine, or improved public health through improved sanitation and hygiene. Indeed, water, by itself, represents one of the most pressing global challenges. Currently, 2.3 billion people live without access to adequate water supplies, and approximately 6,000 children under the age of five die every day from water-related diseases.[6] Two-thirds of the world's population, or 5.5 billion people, are predicted to live in areas of "water stress" by 2025 due to climate change, population growth, and economic development leading to increased consumption.[7] Because water is required to produce all goods, the costs associated with water are embedded in all goods, a concept called "virtual water."[8] The production of one kilogram of grain requires approximately one thousand liters of water, and as much as sixty gallons of water are used for every ton of coal mined. The role of water in achieving food and energy security is obvious. But the relationship between other social challenges and water security is less obvious.

For example, the issue of religious freedom and tolerance is one of tremendous significance. Wars have been fought over religious freedom or due to religious intolerance, and we have seen in recent years violent attacks on places of worship and discrimination against, and oppression of, religious minorities. At first glance, this important issue appears to have little to do with water policy. But upon closer examination, issues of religious freedom and intolerance intersect with water policy in important ways.[9]

Consider, for example, the case of *Navajo Nation v. U.S. Forest Service*.[10] The San Francisco Peaks in Northern Arizona are owned by the U.S. federal government, managed through the U.S. Forest Service, and operated, in part, as the Snow Bowl ski resort. The San Francisco Peaks are also sacred land to the Navajo Nation and several other tribes indigenous to the region. The Snow Bowl ski resort operators, during a year of low snow pack, proposed to use artificial snow to keep the resort open. The artificial snow would be made from recycled waste water—essentially, treated sewage. The Navajo and other tribes objected, arguing that permitting application of this recycled water constituted a substantial burden on their free exercise of religion because it amounted to a desecration of sacred land. In reviewing the lower court's rejection of this argument, the Ninth Circuit Court of Appeals held that government action does not substantially burden the free exercise of religion unless it punishes or denies benefits based on that exercise. The dissent in the appellate court's decision, however, noted: "I do not think that the majority would accept that the burden on a Christian's exercise of religion would be insubstantial if the government permitted only treated sewage effluent for use as baptismal water."[11] How water and its uses are valued, and the perceived extent to which its management impacts social, aesthetic, and spiritual considerations, depend on cultural perspectives. Protections of religious freedom are most important for minority religious groups less able to protect their beliefs and practices through the political process.

But there are water management questions that must be confronted when evaluating how much any law or policy could be permitted to interfere with religious practices, which so often include ceremonial water use. For example, should a minority religious group be able to complicate the use of recycled water in an arid region with limited freshwater resources? Should the Navajo's religious concern outweigh the need to conserve freshwater? All water is recycled water. Every drop of water we drink has passed through some animal at some point and is recycled through the hydrologic cycle. On the other hand, the Navajo's objection is not purely religious, even if largely expressed in religious terms. To treat and transport that much wastewater requires a lot of energy, with inherent environmental impacts, and even though the wastewater is treated, it is not drinking-water quality. If you knew the snow on the mountain on which you were skiing was recycled wastewater, you'd close your mouth a little tighter when you fell, right? The recycled water contains some fecal bacteria and will certainly contain some chemical contaminants, including pharmaceuticals that could not be removed through treatment. Contaminants in the artificial snow will reach streams, whose flow has been conserved by the use of recycled water. There are potential environmental and sustainability concerns with the application of recycled wastewater that weigh both against and in its favor, but that policy—like so many water policies—is complicated by the unique sociocultural value of water.

The Water Protectors opposing the Dakota Access Pipeline in North Dakota similarly grounded a broad movement aimed at protecting water supplies on a foundation of religious sentiment and rhetoric.[12] The oil pipeline project was viewed as a threat to both surface water and groundwater supplies for several indigenous communities, in particular the Standing Rock Sioux. A common refrain from Water Protectors protesting the pipeline was "Defend the Sacred." While the aim of the movement remains the rather concrete goal of protecting water supplies and ecosystems from contamination, that aim is framed and motivated by the sacred character of the water. Just like the Navajo, legal opposition to government approvals that threaten the sacred, such as the Dakota Access Pipeline, have similarly been framed in terms of religious freedom.[13]

The Navajo Nation's objection to the use of recycled water on sacred land, and the Water Protectors' opposition to the Dakota Access Pipeline as a threat to sacred waters, are hardly the only examples of the intersection of water policy and religion. Indeed, similar to the Navajos' objections, some Muslim communities have opposed using treated sewage effluent in ablution rituals (wudhu) as ceremonially impure, despite freshwater's scarcity in many Muslim-majority countries.[14] These religious concerns can relate to majority beliefs spanning entire river basins (as is the case of the sacred nature of the Ganges River for Hindus in India) or for a small indigenous minority within a larger river system (as is the case of certain indigenous communities within the Amazon River Basin).[15] The Ganges provides water to millions and is Mother Ganga to the Hindus—a goddess associated with purity.[16] Yet the Ganges River is one of the most polluted rivers in the world. The sacred nature of the Ganges can complicate or facilitate efforts to address contamination, with some Hindus seeing decontamination as a religious obligation and encouraging grassroots efforts to protect the river, and others seeing the assertion of contamination as tantamount to blasphemy.[17]

The Jordan River, shared by Israel, Jordan, and Palestine, is one of the most complex river basins, and features as part of the broader regional conflict. Its religious character—as the traditional site of the baptism of Jesus Christ—brings pilgrims to the region, which encourages maintenance of some minimal in-stream flow.[18] In a river basin shared by countries with a history of religious conflict and scarce water resources for growing populations, religion may provide a common reason for countries to preserve environmental flows so pilgrims can continue to visit the river for ceremonial and spiritual reasons. Where water policies interfere with water purity or availability in ways that impact its religious use or meaning, human rights protecting the free practice of religion at the national and international level could be asserted not only as a means of protecting religious expression but also of promoting water security.[19]

Beyond illustrating the kind of discussion contained in each chapter, these examples of the intersection of water policy and religion demonstrate how water is an utterly unique resource. Water is everything that commodities like coal, or oil, or uranium are—a valuable resource and a private property right in many jurisdictions. But water is also unique. We do not throw lumps of coal at one another in the wintertime or squirt one another with gasoline in the summertime, and we do not baptize our children in pools of uranium. Water is also everything that faith, health, and art are—an essential aspect of individual and communal liberty recognized as fundamental human rights in many jurisdictions. The challenge of water management is not simply one of resource management, but of how we live with one another and relate to the natural environment. This dual nature of water perhaps partially explains the "water-diamond paradox" discussed by Adam Smith in his seminal work on economics—*The Wealth of Nations*.[20] Smith notes that water has a very high use value (indeed, it is used for virtually everything), but a very low exchange value (we are generally not willing to pay much for water), whereas diamonds are the opposite—very high exchange value (we'll pay a lot for diamonds), but relatively low use value. Plato formulated the issue similarly, observing that "only what is rare is valuable, and water, which is the best of all things . . . is also the cheapest."[21] This paradox exists, perhaps, because we struggle to draw a line between water as an economic resource and water as a sociocultural resource.

The unique challenge specific to the law in enhancing global water security is one of line drawing. Law is often a line-drawing exercise. On this side of the line is your property, and on the other side is mine. On this side of the line is one jurisdiction, on the other side another authority controls. On this side of the line is lawful activity, on the other unlawful. On this side of the line is private property rights, and on the other a universal human right. But water defies lines. It flies above them, sinks below them, absorbs through them, flows across them, or washes them away. The history of water law is a frustrating effort to impose lines on water—to define where the banks of a river end and the abutting wetland begins, or where water ceases to be surface water and becomes groundwater. Perhaps even more difficult is the effort water lawyers make in determining where individual property rights in water end and a fundamental human right to water begins. And most frustrating of all is when water itself is the line—a river or lake dividing property owners or nations who must share the resource as it is constantly moving between them and changing the boundary that separates them.

How these lines are drawn is a political question, answered by examining where power resides and why it resides there.[22] And those political questions are often answered through conflict, as political scientist Raul Pacheco-Vega states, "[c]onflict about who gets to consume water, who gets to extract it and commodify it, and who is excluded from its consumption . . . therefore, facing water insecurity."[23] The power dynamics in these conflicts are often about disparate economic means and influence, with the oft-repeated refrain in water policy that water does not flow downhill: water flows to money.

Despite this connection between money and water, there is no "Water Security and Poverty" chapter in this book. Economically disadvantaged people struggle to pay for water services, people living in less-developed countries often face poor water quality and poorly maintained water infrastructure, and people without financial means struggle to gain access to courts and institutions that might protect their rights and interests in water. But poverty is often the result of multiple, intersecting challenges, like political instability, war, racial or ethnic discrimination, gender inequality, inadequate education systems, and failures of civil society and the protection of basic human rights. These intersecting issues can be better addressed in separate chapters that will collectively demonstrate the role of water security in addressing the global challenge of poverty.

Disparate political influence and corruption are social issues that, like poverty, are difficult to adequately frame in a single chapter because an imbalance in political power, like poverty, is a complex function of many intersecting challenges. Water politics, in my experience, do not generally break down along traditional conceptions of conservative versus progressive ideologies. Instead, water politics, and its related conflicts, are often between rural and urban interests. The rural communities express something like: "This is where the water comes from—where we grow your food, produce your energy, mine your metals, and where the mountains, rivers, lakes, and wildlife you claim to love either thrive or are threatened. Yet cities want to take more than their fair share, without regard to our needs." The urban communities respond along the lines of: "You have disproportionate power and control over resources like water, because more than 70 percent of the global water supplies go to agriculture, which means you have disproportionate political power. Our cities are where most of the people live and work, where the money and innovations are made, where a diversity of people live together, and our more sustainable lifestyle bears the costs of pollution from rural areas due to mining, oil and gas development, deforestation, and farming." I used to think that water politics were unique in this way. But increasingly, the national politics of many countries resembles less the dynamics between conservatives and progressives, and increasingly the dynamics of water politics. In this book, each chapter will focus on social challenges that, unlike food and energy, have a less-than-obvious connection to water policy, and unlike poverty and politics, can conceivably be introduced and discussed in a single chapter.

I explore the role of the law in promoting global water security as the answer, at least in part, to a variety of social challenges. I argue that water security should take a higher priority in public policy, and propose legal reforms to facilitate achieving water security. Each chapter will address the role of law to promote water security as a response to a broad social challenge—from climate change, to various forms of discrimination and inequality, disease epidemics, and space exploration—with the conclusion proposing legal reforms to achieve water security. Each one of these chapters could easily occupy entire volumes, but my hope here is that a better understanding of how water security connects these disparate challenges is worth the sacrifice in nuance. While water policy is inherently interdisciplinary, and requires some foundational understanding in a variety of fields, including economics, hydrology, ecology, water-treatment engineering, and geography, this book focuses on law as a tool for advancing water security.

Ultimately, the only reason the blue rock we are currently spinning on matters is because it is blue. Life has found a way to survive on this planet without air, without light, at the absolute heights and the most profound depths. But nothing has yet found a way to survive without water. Water is essential to life, and it is essential to civilization. It is no coincidence that the earliest human civilizations were born along the banks of desert rivers like the Nile, the Tigris and Euphrates, and the Indus. The desert was the great incubator of human ingenuity, and water was the locus of our earliest lessons in intertribal cooperation and collective innovation. But while water has historically been a catalyst for cooperation, it can also be the cause of conflict. Indeed, the word "rival," comes from the Latin word *rivalis*—meaning people who share a river.[24] Just as the essential element to all life is water, so water is often the essential element to both the cause and solution to many of life's challenges.

The political philosopher John Rawls argued that if human beings were placed in an "original position" behind the "veil of ignorance" (meaning starting the world all over again, without knowing what our individual circumstances would be in the new world), they would agree to the provision of certain "primary goods" to each person.[25] Primary goods are those rights and resources necessary for the realization of all other rights and responsibilities. Water is perhaps the quintessential Rawlsian primary good—nothing else will matter if you don't have water.

Isaiah Berlin thought along similar lines, writing: "First things come first: there are situations in which—to use a saying satirically attributed to the nihilists by Dostoevsky—boots are superior to Pushkin; individual freedom is not everyone's primary need."[26] Like Rawls, Berlin recognized that the provision of primary goods, like water, is a foundation upon which to build a society capable of protecting individual freedom.[27] Berlin's argument, rephrased in the water context, would be "water before freedom of religion," rather than "boots before Pushkin." My argument is effectively to extend Rawls and Berlin's point. In a world of wicked problems so overwhelming in their number and complexity, we struggle to know where to begin. Let us begin by putting first things first—water security.

But while water security may seem like a reasonable place to begin, achieving water security is incredibly difficult. Farhana Sultana, a professor of geography and water policy expert, said, "Water complicates social processes. . . . [It] seeps through everything, the social, the economic, the political, the ecological, technological, cultural and spiritual."[28] One reason why water uniquely complicates social process is that water is the only primary good a government is capable of providing for which there is no substitute.[29] There are different kinds of food, energy, shelter, education, employment, and health care. There are many different forms of government and approaches to achieving safety and prosperity. But only water is water. There is no person, industry, or nation that does not depend on it, and it is embedded in every product and service. Moreover, unlike other primary goods, water moves— it moves through the air, through rivers, and underground without regard to political borders, and moves through goods, such as food or clothing, in international commerce.[30] Water transports energy, nutrients, minerals, diseases, and toxins around the world. It is essential to all life on Earth and is one of the leading causes of death on the planet, whether directly through floods or disease, or indirectly through famine or conflict.[31]

Water is life and death, droughts and floods, food and famine, poverty and prosperity, sickness and health, war and peace. Its centrality is evident in the ruins of our most ancient civilizations and in our hopes for a future among the stars. It is a cause of, and solution for, our most serious problems. Water is not just an important thing. Water is everything.

1

Water Security and Climate Change

Climate change is one social problem with a clear connection to water security. Discussions about climate change in the media are often centered on hurricanes, floods, droughts, and rising sea levels—all problems squarely within the purview of water security. But this chapter is not about water security as a means of addressing climate change. Instead, this chapter is about water security supplanting climate change.[1] Climate change is obsolete. Not because the science behind climate change is bad (it's not).[2] And not because climate change isn't important (it is—very).[3] Climate change has become obsolete because, as a policy paradigm, it is both incomplete and not sufficiently effective.

Climate change is obsolete because it has not resonated well enough with the general public to provoke the kind of immediate collective action needed to address the problem.[4] The dialogue between climate change experts and much of the general public too frequently sounds like this exchange:

CLIMATE SCIENTIST: "You should really worry about climate change."

GENERAL PUBLIC: "Why? I love climate change—leaves changing colors, flowers blooming . . ."

CLIMATE SCIENTIST: "No, I mean global warming."

GENERAL PUBLIC: "I would love a warmer globe—stupid arctic vortex."

CLIMATE SCIENTIST: "No, I mean it could get two, maybe four degrees warmer over the next couple of decades."

GENERAL PUBLIC: "It's going to get that much warmer over the next few hours, Dr. Oblivious."

CLIMATE SCIENTIST: "No, this could cause sea-level rise—"

GENERAL PUBLIC: "I'll be closer to the beach!"

CLIMATE SCIENTIST: "No, polar ice caps will melt, polar bears will—"

GENERAL PUBLIC: "Never seen a polar ice cap or a polar bear, and don't really want to."

CLIMATE SCIENTIST: "But greenhouse gases, including carbon emissions from—"
GENERAL PUBLIC: "You lost me, Professor."

To the average person, a problem framed in terms of a few degrees Celsius or a few feet of sea-level rise does not sound very serious, and a problem framed in terms of ice caps or polar bears does not sound very relevant. Furthermore, carbon footprints and greenhouse gas emissions are metrics so unfamiliar to most people that they struggle to assess both the severity of the problem and the likelihood of success of proposed solutions. Efforts to make climate change more accessible have been moderately successful, and the climate change paradigm has advanced important goals of sustainability and resiliency.[5] Some will certainly argue that climate change has been much more resonant in certain parts of the world, particularly developing countries and small island nations, and that it is beginning to gain greater traction. I agree. But I doubt many would argue that we have made adequate progress in responding to the threat of climate change, and that warrants asking whether we have been talking about the problem in the right way, and if there is a better way going forward. Much more is necessary to broadly engage and educate people regarding the impacts and importance of adapting to changing global climate patterns.[6]

Furthermore, "climate change," as a policy brand, has become so politicized in some jurisdictions as to frequently be paralyzed. Something that should have been as controversial as carrying an umbrella when the forecast is rainy has somehow taken its place next to abortion as a topic not to be discussed in mixed company. The election of Donald Trump has strengthened the political position of climate change deniers in the United States and beyond, and put those who do not highly prioritize climate change mitigation and adaption in positions of influence over federal natural resource policies.[7] These issues are hardly unique to the United States, as recent national elections in countries like Brazil and Australia have also placed power in the hands of those who do not prioritize climate change mitigation.[8] If the aims of sustainable natural resource policies are to be advanced in coming administrations, then scholars, activists, and policy entrepreneurs may find it necessary to talk about climate change without saying "climate change."

The second reason the climate change paradigm is obsolete is because it is incomplete. Climate change is not the main problem. Climate change makes the main problem worse. The main problem is that, by 2035, global population growth and economic development will increase the demand for food, water, and energy by 50 percent, whether or not the climate continues to change.[9] Much has been done to demonstrate the scope of climate change causes and effects.[10] However, the dominance of climate change thinking results in narrowly defining "sustainability" or "green" policies in terms of low-carbon footprint. That narrow conception fails to account for the myriad ways such low-carbon policies or technologies might be otherwise harmful—for example, nuclear and hydroelectric energy may have relatively low-carbon footprints, but are not obviously "green" or "sustainable."[11]

Our sustainability challenges should be rebranded in a way that makes sense to, and motivates, the general public, and integrates the human and environmental impacts of rising food, water, and energy demands with related concerns associated with climate change. The current narrow and inaccessible climate change paradigm should be replaced by the water-security paradigm. As defined in the introduction to this book, water security means achieving a sustainable and acceptable quantity and quality of water at acceptable costs and risks.

Natural Resource Policy Paradigms

Before reorienting the aims of natural resource law and policy away from climate change and toward the rising water-security paradigm, it is essential to first understand how and why policy paradigms rise and fall in prominence.

A policy paradigm is a distinct conceptual framework within which policy decisions are made and justified.[12] A policy paradigm includes shared assumptions about problems and solutions, and is often reinforced by having those problems and proposed solutions framed within the context of that existing paradigm.[13] Policy paradigms evolve, often beginning as a reaction to challenge existing modes of thinking when those modes prove inadequate or unsatisfactory. Initially, policymakers resist new paradigms because they do not fit within the existing paradigm. As the nascent paradigm proves effective at explaining or solving problems better than the existing paradigm, it gains acceptance and legitimacy. Dominant paradigms give way as their limitations are exposed by policy implementation or the paradigm becomes obsolete because of improved information or technology, and are replaced by a rising paradigm that accounts for new technology and information and addresses the ebbing paradigm's limitations. As policy paradigms rise and fall, multiple paradigms may exist simultaneously within the same policy sphere, or even lose and gain acceptance over time. But typically, in any given policy sphere, one particular paradigm will dominate perspectives.

Take education policy, for example. I am not an education policy expert, but I am a university professor and a father. And over the years, I have noticed the paradigm that drove my education giving way to a rising paradigm in the education of my children and my students. My education was driven by a particular paradigm, with a focus on standardized age cohorts, classroom interactions, and courses and majors divided by traditional subjects and disciplines. But my children and students appear to be transitioning into a new paradigm, with greater focus on interdisciplinary training, online learning platforms, and customized courses and teaching methods to accommodate special needs. Whether this new paradigm will, or should, supplant the old is a question parents, educators, and policymakers will struggle to answer.

Early leaders and advocates of a paradigm establish the paradigm's aims and frequently its limitations, so understanding why paradigms succeed and fail requires an examination of the actors who influenced the movement. A new paradigm is often characterized and distinguished by the identity of the policy advocates who develop and rely on its framework. Some policy paradigms are top-down, driven by initiatives at the national or even supranational governmental level. These are hierarchical paradigms, characterized by high-level government leadership, or hierarchists. Other policy paradigms are bottom-up initiatives, characterized as civil movements and distinguished by the leadership of ethicists concerned primarily with social justice. Some policy paradigms are led by entrepreneurs and are characterized by leadership from the private, for-profit sector and a focus on wealth maximization and efficiency. Of course, it is possible that a paradigm is driven by multiple different advocates—ethicists, entrepreneurs, and hierarchists all working together. Still, it can be helpful to look to the earliest and most dominant advocates of a particular paradigm as a means of categorizing paradigms and examining how their main advocates influence the trajectory of a paradigm's development.[14] Early or dominant advocates not only set the course, but are often disproportionately influential in outlining the goals of a paradigm's policies and defining success.

Natural resource policy paradigms ebb and flow like any other and can also be characterized by whether they are advocated by hierarchists, ethicists, or entrepreneurs. The earliest broad frameworks for the management of natural resources emerged with the industrial revolution. The industrial paradigm was characterized by the leadership of entrepreneurs, a paradigm driven by reliance on market incentives. These incentives encouraged the development of natural resources and improved efficiencies in natural resource exploitation and in technological innovation, but also led to many instances of negative externalities—meaning costs imposed on third parties not engaged in an economic transaction. For example, a cosmetics manufacturer discharges air and water pollution that impacts the health of downstream and downwind communities, most of whom do not purchase those cosmetics. Those health impacts are negative externalities and are characteristic of one of the main problems with the industrial paradigm for natural resource policy.

In the context of water law and policy, the era of the industrial paradigm is sometimes referred to as the "hydraulic mission."[15] The hydraulic mission is characterized by an ethos that any water that reaches the ocean is water wasted and that every drop should be put to beneficial economic use. As part of the hydraulic mission, water was dammed and polluted in pursuit of economic development; water was treated as a commodity with economic, but not necessarily inherent, value. Furthermore, water is a symbol of political legitimacy, with operation of large water infrastructure perceived as essential to political power. The subjugation and exploitation of natural resources in pursuit of political legitimacy and economic development is the hallmark of the hydraulic mission and the industrial paradigm of natural resource policy. As with any paradigm, the earliest advocates set the trajectory of the hydraulic mission and defined what success means. In the case of the hydraulic mission, the trajectory was one of resource development and exploitation, wringing the maximum amount of economic value from each drop of water.

The limitations of the industrial paradigm were exposed by its failure to integrate consideration of externalities, such as pollution and resource depletion. Because of these limitations, the industrial paradigm was ultimately challenged and supplanted by the green paradigm.[16] The green paradigm is characterized by its focus on Pigovian taxes to encourage internalization of costs like pollution. A Pigovian tax is a policy mechanism to encourage or require cost internalization—for example, by requiring the cosmetics manufacturer to obtain a permit for pollution discharge and to pay for the cleanup of any contamination it causes. The green paradigm also focuses policies toward greater transparency in natural resource management, as is the case with environmental impact assessments under the National Environmental Protection Act and the listing and consultation requirements under the Endangered Species Act.

The green paradigm was marked by the leadership of ethicists, or non-governmental, grassroots advocacy.[17] Rachel Carson's book—*Silent Spring*—and the leadership of Lois Gibbs in responding to the Love Canal crisis are examples of how ethicists initiated and facilitated the green movement at the grassroots level in response to the threat of environmental contamination.[18] Beyond the legal reforms discussed above, the green paradigm led to Earth Day, recycling programs, and generally broader awareness of human impacts on the environment. Ethicists set the green paradigm on a trajectory favoring bottom-up advocacy for interventions focused on the prevention of environmental harms, the protection of public health and ecosystems, and a broader and stronger public environmental ethos.

However, the green paradigm failed to fully account for the growing threat of global climate change and did not adequately address concerns of intergenerational equity.[19] For example, the green agenda's focus on pollution prevention and remediation aimed to achieve acceptable resource quality for current generations, but not necessarily resource sustainability for future generations. Furthermore, the green paradigm's aims were diffuse and not integrated, with efforts to address air pollution, hazardous waste, clean water, and endangered species often operating in independent legal and policy spheres. What was needed, then, was a new paradigm that found ways to connect the disparate aspects of the green movement and raise the priority of climate change adaptation and mitigation relative to those other disparate environmental concerns, like pollution or endangered species.

The climate change paradigm followed the green paradigm. Climate change is about more than just impacts from changing climate patterns brought on by anthropogenic greenhouse gases. This paradigm is distinct from the green paradigm in many ways, in particular in its focus on adaptation and resiliency rather than establishing minimum standards of environmental quality. The climate change paradigm is a direct response to the green paradigm's limitations. The climate change paradigm attempts to integrate broader concerns for intergenerational and intragenerational equity with the narrower issue, environmental degradation. Climate change also prioritizes natural resource policies around the adaptation or resilience to changing climate patterns and the mitigation of those impacts through the reduction of greenhouse gas emissions. The metric that is frequently used to integrate these concerns is the concept of carbon footprints. Carbon footprints, as a metric and policy tool, potentially integrate concerns of resource overexploitation, income inequities in resource allocation, defor-estation, and sustainable development.

The climate change paradigm has been largely led by hierarchists, that is, government officials at the national or supranational levels engaged in top-down regulation. Given the sheer geographic scope of the challenge of mit-igating anthropogenic climate change, and the inevitable spillover effects of greenhouse gas emissions, the movement began with seeking intervention by the United Nations to cooperatively address climate change through an international framework convention.[20] Climate change regulation is effec-tively the regulation of the global commons, and thus a cooperative interna-tional framework was seen as the ideal approach. Such an approach arguably requires a hierarchical, top-down approach within a supranational organi-zation. The nature of the problem of climate change, and thus the climate change paradigm, is to be more integrated. Climate change is a problem of planetary scope, involving the entire atmosphere, oceans, mountains, forests, energy, and food. As such, the climate change paradigm—unlike the green paradigm—pursues policies that consider the relationship between air, land, water, food, energy, economic development, and wildlife protection.

Such a hierarchical, integrated approach can spread quickly, penetrating different industries, levels of government, and policy arenas, and then go on to become a dominant paradigm because its sine qua non is top-down regulation developed through political and scientific consensus with broad economic and geographic scope. Given the implications of global cli-mate change, it arguably should dominate all other natural resource policy paradigms out of sheer necessity. Its scope and significance inevitably have resulted in debates about how best to characterize the paradigm and its goals, including the deployment of descriptive terms or goals such as sustainability, resilience, or adaptation. Similarly, the scope of the challenges of climate change also includes debates regarding environmental justice, including the role of human rights and the disproportionate impact climate change has on economically or politically marginalized communities.

While the climate change paradigm has replaced the green paradigm as the dominant paradigm in environmental and natural resource law and policy, its dominant position in the scholarly debate has not absolutely crowded out other paradigms.[21] Prior paradigms have not disappeared, and they continue to influence the current climate change paradigm. Both the industrial paradigm and the green paradigm persist and even affect the cli-mate change paradigm itself. For example, market incentives and private governance approaches to address greenhouse gas emissions derive from the industrial paradigm's entrepreneurial approach.[22] Grassroots advocacy in climate change, Pigovian carbon taxes, and the view of greenhouse gas emissions as "pollution" to be regulated under command-and-control statutes like the Clean Air Act have their roots in the green paradigm.[23]

Additionally, it is necessary to point out that the climate change paradigm has not been entirely hierarchical. Climate change has a "multiscalar character," wherein activists, entrepreneurs, and regulators function at different jurisdictional scales from the local to the supranational.[24] As larger-scale national and supranational jurisdictions leave niches unfilled in addressing climate change, smaller-scale jurisdictions may step in to fill these policy niches. These efforts of state and local governments in the United States to respond to greenhouse gas emissions are examples of nonhierarchical approaches to climate change.[25] Still, these more localized approaches are responses to the limitation of the general hierarchical character of the climate change paradigm.

Climate change has not necessarily dominated policy discussions at all levels and all instances, and vestiges of the green paradigm and industrial paradigm continue to dictate policy choices. And there remain many, even in positions of influence, who are skeptical of climate change science and the importance of addressing climate change for future generations.[26] But among scholars and advocates within the natural resources and environmental policy spheres, climate change dominates the discourse, particularly if one accepts that debates about resilience, sustainability, adaptation, and environmental justice are conducted within the context of climate change.[27] The dominance of the climate change paradigm has facilitated critical advances in environmental and natural resource policy, including raising public awareness of the threat of global climate change, reforming laws and regulations to better address anthropogenic greenhouse gases, increasing investment in adaptation and resiliency, greater focus on the disparate impacts of climate change upon the poor, and greater integration of environmental and natural resource issues under the rubric of carbon footprints and sustainable development.

The Limitations of the Climate Change Paradigm

Despite improving on the green paradigm, the climate change paradigm is nevertheless incomplete, inadequately framed, and ultimately obsolete.

Perhaps because it is a hierarchist paradigm, the climate change paradigm frames the discussion in terms inaccessible to, and remote from, most people. The general public is regularly assured by advocates and scholars of the scientific consensus regarding global climate change.[28] But this consensus, while certainly broad and strong, is built upon jargon-laden scholarly exchanges regarding complex mathematical models.[29] And even that consensus is really about accepted degrees of uncertainty. It does not lend itself well to simple transmission to typical voters and consumers. Additionally, the deficiencies of the climate change paradigm have arisen because it is being led by the wrong people. The early development of the climate change paradigm was largely hierarchical, meaning its trajectory was set by a top-down national and supranational agenda.[30] While this approach made sense for a global challenge like climate change, it has resulted in decision-making that is frequently attenuated from the uniquely local cultural, economic, and natural conditions of the resources implicated by climate change. Localized leadership is necessary to take this more nuanced approach and is more likely to be achieved in a paradigm that focuses on localized resources rather than a global commons problem like climate change.

Attempts to make the research underlying climate change more accessible often oversimplify, and the general public is left wondering how its local weatherman can continually be wrong about the next day's weather, but thousands of scientists can be so confident about the planet's climate in the coming decades and centuries. Even in instances where the science is adequately conveyed, the relevance and significance are often lost on the general public.[31] The initial framing of the challenge was often in terms of "global warming," but this frame failed to raise the concerns of many people busy shoveling snow from their driveways, and who are not terribly familiar with polar ice caps or glaciers.[32] The pitch changed to "climate change" because global warming did not adequately describe a problem that was instead about increased extreme climate events and altered climate patterns.[33] But while public awareness and understanding of climate change causes and impacts have increased, efforts to mobilize both individuals and nations to respond to the threat have not resulted in adequate responsive measures.[34] Efforts to mobilize responses to climate change by framing the challenge in terms of either low-probability or temporally remote catastrophic events instead arguably generated apathy or a wave of skeptics or deniers.[35]

Furthermore, the climate change paradigm fails to adequately address the primary concern of natural resource policy (increasing global demand for food, energy, and water) by focusing too much on greenhouse gas emissions and carbon footprints. Despite the strong science underlying anthropogenic climate change, there has been decades of public debate about the reality of the threat, its significance, and its salience.[36] The climate change paradigm has sought to move past this debate through education or improved messaging.[37] But perhaps it would have been better to abandon the debate as an expensive drag on progress by recognizing that the central issue in question—anthropogenic climate change—is not in fact the greatest or most pressing natural resource problem facing humanity. Indeed, though climate change is enormously important, it is ultimately an aggravating factor of a more fundamental and proximal concern. As noted earlier, by 2030, the planet will need 50 percent more food, water, and energy, regardless of climate change, as a result of population growth and increased consumption patterns.[38]

The climate change paradigm's focus on two versus four degrees Celsius, carbon footprints, and greenhouse gas emissions fails to address the challenge of meeting increasing energy, food, and water demands. Its relatively narrow focus inevitably fails to fully integrate critical considerations into natural resource policy decisions. For example, developments of nuclear or hydroelectric energy are low carbon emitting energy sources, and may be necessary to meet rising energy demands, but they may not ultimately be best for environmental stewardship. Solar and wind energy require extraction of natural resources like copper and silicon that also may adversely impact the environment. But if the paradigm focuses on carbon and climate change, it may not adequately consider the environmental costs associated with these energy sources.

Additionally, regulatory measures aimed at addressing climate change may not integrate other natural resource considerations. For example, if U.S. federal government regulations impose more stringent emissions standards on coal-fired power plants, with associated compliance costs potentially passed on to energy consumers, this could impact water supplies to indigenous peoples. The Navajo Generating Station (NGS) is a coal-fired power plant that provides the necessary energy to bring Arizona's allocation of Colorado River water from the river through the Central Arizona Project (CAP) canal system and to water users throughout the state.[39] The CAP is critical infrastructure for delivering water to Native American tribes in Arizona who have settled their water rights claims to central Arizona rivers in exchange for the more reliable CAP water.[40] Tribes typically agree to pay for the power costs to transport the water. But increased power costs associated with more stringent emissions standards on a facility like NGS, or even the closure of such facilities and replacement with more costly energy sources, could make water provision through CAP unaffordable for some tribes, effectively depriving the tribes of the water rights they agreed to in settlement.[41] Regulators with the best of intentions to address climate change thus may inadvertently make water unaffordable for thousands of Native Americans in Arizona.[42] The challenge for natural resource law and policy is to move away from the narrow climate change paradigm and toward a new approach that integrates the broader and more pressing concerns of water, food, and energy demands.

An understandable response to the claim that the climate change paradigm is inadequate would be to note recent success in moving the climate change agenda forward, including the commitments of major greenhouse gas emissions reductions under the Paris Accords by most nations, despite wavering U.S. support.[43] The reductions agreed to under the United Nations Framework Convention on Climate Change in the Conference of the Parties (COP) 21 in Paris represent important progress in international cooperation in addressing climate change and one of the true success stories of the climate change paradigm.[44] Each natural resource paradigm has made important contributions and likely will endure as part of the paradigm portfolio of natural resource law and policy in some form. The industrial paradigm encouraged resource development and infrastructure investment. The green paradigm encouraged cost internalization and a public environmental ethos. The climate change paradigm has encouraged international cooperation to address a pressing global crisis. I am not arguing that the climate change paradigm is a failure or that it was unnecessary or counterproductive. I am arguing that the climate change paradigm has played its important role, but in doing so has exposed its limitations. And while the climate change paradigm, like previous paradigms, will remain influential, a new paradigm should now assume primacy in natural resource policy to address those limitations by integrating climate change concerns with increasing resource demands in a way that is relatable to the general public.

Given the climate change paradigm's limitations, a new paradigm is needed, one that is more integrated, accessible, and focused, and one not characterized by the limitations and trajectories of past paradigms set by hierarchists, entrepreneurs, or ethicists. Water security should be the new preeminent paradigm in environmental and natural resource law and policy.

Toward a Water-Security Paradigm

The water-security paradigm reorients all of natural resource and environmental law and policy around achieving an acceptable quantity and quality of water with acceptable costs and risks. The specific quantity and quality to be achieved, and at what cost and risks, should be determined at the river basin level and be tailored to the unique cultural characteristics and physical conditions of each basin. The water-security paradigm should be led by regional experts because they will be more successful than the entrepreneurs, ethicists, or hierarchists of previous natural resource policy paradigms. Entrepreneurs encourage development and investment, but externalize costs. Ethicists encourage cost-internalization and grassroots engagement, but lack expertise and an integrated, holistic agenda. Hierarchists encourage reliance on expertise and policy integration, but lack familiarity with local conditions and nuance in policy formulation and implementation. The water-security paradigm should be led by regionalists—norm advocates embedded within the river basin and familiar with the unique sociocultural, economic, hydrologic, and climatologic characteristics of that geographic unit, defined by the limits of the watershed. Water security is the more integrated and accessible paradigm needed to address the limitations of the climate change paradigm and move natural resource law and policy forward.

The water-security paradigm is the way forward because it addresses the two fundamental limitations of the current climate change paradigm. First, unlike the climate change paradigm, water security deals directly with the growing demand for food and energy, because the energy and agriculture sectors are our largest water consumers. Water is embedded in virtually all products, a concept called virtual water, with significant virtual water embedded in energy and food. For example, the production of a single kilogram of wheat requires approximately one thousand liters of water.[45] Just as virtual water is embedded in food and other agricultural products, virtual water is embedded in our energy.

Nearly everything humans do, for better and for worse, can be expressed in terms of quantity of water. Water is essential in all parts of energy production and generation: it is used as a reactor coolant in nuclear energy; it produces steam to turn turbines in coal power plants; it is used in oil and gas production, in the growth of biofuels, in the mining of coal, uranium, and minerals used in components for wind and solar energy sources. Coal mining, for example, uses around sixty gallons of water for every ton of coal mined.[46] To complicate matters, virtual energy is similarly embedded in the treatment and distribution of water. The energy required to run a faucet for five minutes is equal to the energy used in a 60-watt light bulb for fourteen hours.

If we move water security to the forefront in our discussions about sustainability, we will integrate climate change concerns with the problems associated with increasing global consumption patterns because we will account for water throughout the chain of production in agriculture and energy. Because of the role emissions of greenhouse gases play in monitoring and assessing climate change impacts and interventions, reducing those emissions (particularly in the form of carbon dioxide equivalent [CO_2e]) has played a central role in the climate change paradigm.[47] The measuring, reporting, and reducing of "carbon footprints" (or the amount of CO_2 emitted to produce a given product or provide a given service) has become a central goal of policymakers and the indispensable signal of good environmental stewardship. The centrality of carbon footprints has been one of the major policy features of both food and energy security. This focus on carbon footprints creates incentives to deploy low- carbon energy sources, like nuclear, solar, wind, and hydroelectric energy.

The current climate change paradigm's focus on greenhouse gas emissions and carbon footprints fails to account for environmental impacts from these so-called "green" or "clean" energy sources. Carbon footprint measurements do not account for environmental concerns associated with low-carbon energy sources, like nuclear energy, hydroelectric, or solar and wind energy, which include water consumption and contamination in the production and transmission of energy. Carbon footprints do not fully integrate the environmental impacts of extractive industries associated with the energy sector, like coal mining or oil and gas exploration and extraction, including fracking. Carbon footprints also fail to include the environmental impacts of climate change mitigation measures, like geologic carbon sequestration (which can cause groundwater pollution), "green" building codes, smart grids, or hybrid cars (which can require increased uses of copper and other mined materials).

For example, a state seeks to reduce its carbon footprint as part of the climate change paradigm. It replaces its coal-fired power plants with a nuclear power plant, solar cell arrays, and wind turbines. The state retrofits another power plant to run on natural gas (which has a lower carbon footprint than coal) and geologically sequesters the emitted carbon from its use of natural gas. The state also builds a large hydroelectric dam and a smart grid for its electricity transmission. Additionally, it passes a green building code to improve energy efficiency and provides subsidies for purchases of hybrid cars or cars using biofuels. These efforts would reduce the state's carbon footprint and advance the climate change paradigm.

But that reduction would not account for the environmental impacts from mining silicon, copper, gold, tungsten, and other minerals necessary for the solar cells, wind turbines, dams, "green" buildings, hybrid cars, or smart grids. It would not account for the increased water needed to cool the nuclear reactors, to grow the biofuels, to replace the water lost to evaporation behind the dam, or to supply the fracking operations that recover natural gas. It would also not account for the water pollution from nuclear waste disposal, fracking, geologic sequestration, or hydroelectric dams. In short, the monitoring and reporting regime of the climate change paradigm is incomplete and provides an inadequate assessment of sustainable and environmentally responsible practices.

A water footprint metric addresses fossil fuel energy production like a carbon footprint, because it would account for the water used in that energy production. Just as carbon footprints quantify the amount of carbon dioxide emitted in the production and transportation of a certain good or service, so a water footprint quantifies the amount of water consumed for each good and service. Water footprints would also integrate the impacts of pollution and water consumption from across the entire chain of production of no- or low-carbon energy sources. Water contaminated through mining, nuclear waste disposal, deforestation to support biofuel production, or geologic carbon sequestration would similarly be accounted for in water footprints, thereby providing information on environmental impacts not otherwise captured by the carbon footprint. Water footprints also provide necessary information on sustainability challenges arising from increased consumption attributable to population growth and economic development.

Furthermore, water footprints would provide a better understanding of how countries could face water insecurity through virtual water exports. For example, fracking fluid frequently includes an emulsifier produced from the guar plant's seed. The rapid global expansion of fracking has increased demand for guar seeds, with the international price of guar seed rising from $4 per kilogram to $30 per kilogram in an eighteen-month period.[48] Thousands of acres formerly used for food crops have been converted to the production of guar in India and Pakistan. Guar, however, is frequently a less drought-resilient and more water-intensive crop than the food crops it replaces, and such replacement has the potential to raise food prices. Guar production may facilitate a shift to cleaner natural gas in some nations with fracking opera-tions, but increase water insecurity in nations replacing food crops with guar. A shift to a water footprint metric will capture the impacts of these kinds of policies as virtual water moves around the world in global trade, determining whether exports have the net effect of achieving water security in one nation at the expense of the water security in another.

In addition to the focus on water footprints, a second way the water-security paradigm improves upon the climate change paradigm is by making sustainability issues more salient and accessible to the general public. One of the most significant challenges to responding to climate change is to en-gage with and educate the general public, who often perceive climate change impacts to be uncertain, temporally and spatially attenuated, and not per-sonally relevant. Even if citizens accept climate change as relevant and important, it still must compete with other issues for an individual's atten-tion. Psychological research suggests that as temporal and spatial distance increases, mental representations become more abstract and mental prioriti-zation less likely.[49] To more effectively convey sustainability concerns, these concerns must be framed in ways that are proximal in both time and space.[50]

In other words, people are unlikely to understand or prioritize sustaina-bility issues unless they immediately hit home. And the message of climate change that hits most immediately and closest to home is a message of water variability and extreme weather events (drought and flood) at the local and regional level. The water-security paradigm speaks directly in these terms, and indeed will reform laws to govern on the more local and regional level, rather than the hierarchical governance model of the climate change para-digm, which often involves policy choices made by people and in places remote from where the actual costs and benefits of those choices will be ex-perienced. Ultimately, any person can intuitively understand water waste and water pollution and the challenge of water scarcity. But the concept of carbon emissions, greenhouse gases, and their impacts on global climate patterns are far from intuitive, accessible, or even spatially and temporally proximal to most people. The water footprint metric focuses sustainability on the more intuitive concept of water use. Furthermore, a water footprint metric can be tailored to be understood and monitored within the specific geographic and cultural context in which it is used. Climate change's reliance on carbon footprints requires broader monitoring of sources and impacts divorced from geographic or cultural context. The regionalist governance of water se-curity, using water footprints as its tool for monitoring and measuring, would therefore provide a more nuanced and understandable governance approach than the hierarchical climate change paradigm.

The water-security paradigm should not be led by hierarchists, entrepreneurs, or ethicists. It should be led by regionalists. Localism is a governance approach marked by partnerships between water users within a given drainage basin familiar with the region's unique economic, ecologic, and cultural conditions. Top-down, hierarchical governance approaches are frequently ineffective because they depend on "thin simplifications" to explain complex systems.[51] Hierarchists are too far removed from the locus of most actual policy implementation and thus frequently fail to understand how communities organize themselves and respond to social problems. For purposes of water security, the world is like a golf ball—a sphere pocked with dimples. Each dimple on the golf ball is a drainage basin, or catchment, and the boundaries between the dimples are called watersheds. All water within a basin drains into a common point, which could naturally internalize the costs associated with water scarcity and quality.

The water-security paradigm should be led by regionalists and grounded geographically at the basin level for two reasons. First, the chemistry, ecology, uses, and cultural meaning of water vary not only from one river to another but even between stretches of the same river. Those most familiar with the unique climate, geology, hydrology, economy, and culture of water should be those who advance the water-security paradigm. Water changes in its ecologic and economic character as it flows from mountains, valleys, deserts, and deltas, and through farms, cities, and indigenous communities. Water also changes its cultural character in a way unique in natural resources. Water is different from other resources, not only because of its cultural, aesthetic, and religious significance, but because that significance changes as water flows through different communities. The regionalist approach follows the arguments of Friedrich Hayek regarding the inability of top-down planning to capture the dispersed knowledge of individuals.[52] Regionalists are best situated to appreciate how nuanced water management must be to achieve water security because they represent that dispersed knowledge.

Second, water is a spillover common pool resource, meaning that it often crosses jurisdictional boundaries. Under the "internalization prescription" for spillover commons, jurisdiction over spillover commons should be assigned at the smallest scale that internalizes the effects of management decisions.[53] In the case of spillover commons, jurisdictional boundaries must be redrawn, wherever possible, to conform to the geographic contours of the resource. The watershed is thus the natural jurisdictional boundary, and the catchment the appropriate scale of jurisdiction.[54] By basing governance boundaries on the watershed, the costs of water management will be internalized. Unfortunately, governance institutions have historically taken the opposite approach, using rivers as political boundaries to frustrating, and sometimes disastrous, results.

The shift from the climate change paradigm to the water security paradigm is fundamentally about governance—indeed, it addresses the "Goldilocks governance challenge." The Goldilocks governance challenge wrestles with how to scale governance so that jurisdiction is neither too big nor too small. The scope of governance must be just right. If the scope of jurisdiction is too big, there will be too many stakeholders who are too remote from one another and unfamiliar with local conditions, thus unnecessarily increasing the costs associated with policy development.[55] If the scope of jurisdiction is too small, it will likely produce negative externalities to neighboring jurisdictions.[56] For example, if two jurisdictions share a river and the jurisdictional boundaries do not correspond to the watershed, one jurisdiction can dam or pollute a river and externalize the costs of water scarcity or water contamination to its neighbor. If those states share a river and the boundaries incorporate many basins at a national or supranational level, water management will be inefficient because it will be attenuated from the stakeholders, and managers will be less familiar with unique regional conditions associated with the river.[57] Going back to the golf ball comparison—if a there are many jurisdictions within each divot of the golf ball (river basin), they will dam and pollute rivers and externalize the costs of water use to their neighbors. If a jurisdiction contains too many divots (river basins), then the people in charge won't know the unique character of the water and its use, and there will be too many people with whom to engage and educate in developing a coherent, adaptive, and nuanced water policy.

The Goldilocks governance challenge partially explains the failures of previous natural resource policy paradigms. Entrepreneurs tended to operate on smaller scales in the industrial paradigm, resulting in resource exploitation that generated negative externalities, like polluted rivers.[58] Hierarchists advance a top-down, global governance approach in the climate change paradigm, but this approach has advanced slowly in large part because the transaction costs of negotiating with so many diverse jurisdictions are simply too high.[59] The water security paradigm's focus on basin-level governance helps limit transactions costs by narrowing the field of stakeholders to those most familiar with and interested in the shared commons.[60] Basin-level governance facilitates cost internalization and avoids negative externalities by redrawing jurisdictional boundaries to correspond to the geographic contours of the spillover commons—the basin.[61] The water security paradigm's focus on basin-level governance by regionalists thus strikes the right balance in the Goldilocks governance challenge by making the scope of jurisdiction just the right size to limit transaction costs while avoiding externalities.

Conclusion

Of course, most jurisdictional boundaries do not correspond to the geographic contours of basins. Indeed, in 1868, explorer John Wesley Powell recommended to the U.S. Congress that state boundaries in the western territories of the United States be based on river basins.[62] The Congress ignored his recommendations, and even in some instances made the river itself the state boundary.[63] Indeed, the great irony of Powell's legacy is that, despite his revolutionary prescriptions regarding rivers, the reservoir that bears his name—Lake Powell—sits astride the Arizona-Utah border. And what has resulted has either been high transaction costs associated with federal control of water resources (such as the Clean Water Act) or the externalities associated with state control of water resources (such as water rights disputes over shared rivers). But sovereignty concerns make redrawing the boundaries to correspond to the basin politically problematic, if not impossible. Yet certain legal reforms can help to facilitate basin-level, interjurisdictional governance. At the international level, river treaties often establish international river basin commissions. At the domestic level, in the United States, interstate compacts can establish interstate river basin commissions.

Often, these transboundary river commissions lack meaningful regulatory authority, or even sufficient resources to facilitate cooperation and information exchange, in part because member jurisdictions fear turning over sovereignty to the commission. To alleviate this concern, such commissions should be subject to a judicially enforceable fiduciary duty to manage the basin for the benefit of all jurisdictions sharing the water. This would help avoid one jurisdiction co-opting the commission to its sole benefit and ensure adequate legal leverage for individual commission members to influence the commission and ensure that they have not sacrificed sovereignty, while still empowering the commission to avoid negative externalities and minimize transaction costs. Commission membership should also reflect the major industries, ethnic groups, utilities, and municipalities in the basin, thereby ensuring that transboundary commissions are led by regionalists in an effort to achieve water security.

Regionalists frequently have knowledge about social norms adapted over generations to unique regional conditions—including norms critical to natural resource development like cooperation and dispute resolution—that will not be captured by a hierarchist regime like climate change.[64] Rivers like the Ganges or the Jordan have unique religious significance best understood by regionalists. A river like the Colorado River Basin or Murray-Darling Basin can have one thousand days of reservoir storage to serve their respective populations, but one thousand days of reservoir storage to serve the population relying on the Brahmaputra River would flood an area the size of Pakistan.[65] Top-down, attenuated supranational management tends toward the one-size-fits-all approach to governance, and that approach is inappropriate when rivers require solutions tailor-made to their unique geographies. Interstate compacts and regional international treaties should effectively redraw jurisdictional boundaries to correspond to the geographic contours of river basins. Interbasin jurisdiction will be too remote from such adapted social norms, so treaties and compacts, granting basin-level jurisdiction to commissions, should redraw jurisdictional boundaries to empower regionalists. While political obstacles, in particular concerns of sovereignty, will be significant, these obstacles may erode in the face of the realities of water insecurity caused by growing populations, economic development, natural resources conflicts, plagues, and droughts and floods brought on by climate change.

The importance of climate change and its associated paradigm would remain even with a shift to water security as the dominant paradigm. Water security reorients how we think about our sustainability problems. Water insecurity is not part of the climate change problem. Climate change is a part of the water security problem.

2

Water Security and Public Health

In an epic example of insight and courage, John Snow saved countless lives and forged a heroic legacy.[1] His triumph in the face of crisis represented a turning point in history, tipping the balance in the ongoing battle between mankind and one of mankind's greatest threats.[2] And no, this is not a reference to *Game of Thrones*. John Snow was the father of epidemiology and the germ theory of disease. In 1848, one of a series of massive outbreaks of cholera in the nineteenth century swept through London.[3] Snow observed that the patterns of the outbreak were not consistent with the then-prominent miasma theory of disease transmission—the theory that "bad air" was the cause of epidemics like cholera and bubonic plague.[4] Snow theorized that the mode of transmission was water and distributed a pamphlet advising handwashing and boiling drinking water.[5]

In 1854, another cholera epidemic struck London.[6] Snow observed that competing distribution companies delivered water within the Soho neighborhood of London.[7] One of these companies, Vauxhall, derived its water supply downstream of major sewer discharges into the Thames River.[8] The other obtained its water supply upstream of the sewer discharges.[9] Snow, in what is called the "Grand Experiment," compared data on households consuming water supplied from these two companies.[10] Snow noted that the cholera rate was 8.5 times higher in households supplied by Vauxhall than its competitor.[11] He further noted that nearly a quarter of all cholera deaths in London occurred within a short distance of a hand pump on Broad Street, which was installed on top of a cesspit.[12] After speaking with families near the pump, he discovered that most had lost multiple members of their households to cholera, and all had taken water from the pump.[13] Legend has it that Snow removed the handle from the Broad Street pump, and saved the city.[14] You can visit the John Snow pub on Broad Street and see the pump handle.

John Snow's work also began the integration of epidemiology with the development and implementation of law.[15] In March 1855, Snow testified before Parliament regarding the development of laws to address sanitation.[16] At the time, a bill was proposed to regulate "offensive trades," including bone boiling and gasworks, which many believed contributed to the miasma of bad air and thus to disease transmission. Merchants within those trades called on Snow to testify as an expert witness. Snow argued in favor of increased investment in public sanitation projects and protection of drinking-water sources rather than regulation of offensive trades that impacted air quality. In 1866, after opposition from political and professional opponents and following another devastating outbreak of cholera, Snow's proposals were finally enacted into law, resulting in regulation of sewage discharges and treatment requirements for drinking water.[17]

Greater integration of epidemiology and water law is still required, including in ex ante procedural rules for the prevention of epidemics, and improved ex post rules to ensure adequate care for infected persons and containment of outbreaks.[18] In Haiti, for example, an ongoing cholera epidemic has killed over 8,500 people and sickened over 600,000.[19] In the wake of the catastrophic earthquake of 2010, U.N. relief workers from Nepal brought a particularly virulent form of cholera into Haiti.[20] The disease was introduced into the Haitian population by poor waste management at the U.N. camp.[21] A U.S. district court judge recently dismissed a lawsuit against the United Nations, stating that the United Nations is immune from liability associated with the cholera outbreak in Haiti.[22] The United Nations came to restore and improve Haiti's water infrastructure and protect its water resources, and such immunity arguably facilitates the efforts of the United Nations.[23] But because of a failure to integrate epidemiology into water planning, the United Nations introduced a fatal outbreak to an already reeling nation, an outbreak that has potentially shifted from an epidemic to an endemic crisis (meaning the disease now requires no external input to remain active in a community).[24]

The cholera outbreak in Haiti illustrates only one way in which law can fail to integrate epidemiology.[25] Water is both a major avenue through which pathogens infect people, either directly by ingestion or indirectly by vectors like mosquitoes, and a major factor in the prevention and treatment of infectious diseases, including through improved hygiene and sanitation.[26] Currently, 2.3 billion people live without access to adequate clean-water supplies, and approximately six thousand children under the age of five die every day from waterborne diseases.[27] Officials throughout the Western Hemisphere struggled to contain the Zika virus outbreak that began in 2015, spread by mosquitoes and resulting in serious birth defects and death.[28]

Cholera has infected nearly one million people in Yemen, with four thousand reported cases each day in 2017.[29] The deadly and ongoing water crisis in Flint, Michigan, has included a spike in legionnaires' disease.[30] The serious threat to human health posed by such diseases is likely to be aggravated by global climate change.[31] As such, water law should have a heightened emphasis on the prevention and mitigation of disease epidemics.

Nevertheless, water law largely concentrates on two agendas that are not directly related to disease prevention or mitigation—what I call the "Blue Agenda" and the "Green Agenda." The Blue Agenda is concerned with water quantity and drought resiliency.[32] In particular, the Blue Agenda deals with the allocation of water rights, the development of water-delivery infrastructure, the sustainable management of water consumption, and the apportionment of water resources between people and jurisdictions.[33] The Green Agenda is concerned with water quality.[34] In particular, the Green Agenda deals with the prevention of water pollution, the protection of aquatic ecosystems, and the effective treatment of toxic or carcinogenic chemicals in drinking water.[35] While both of these agendas have important implications for human health, they may at times be pursued in ways that interfere with the prevention of epidemics or that aggravate disease outbreaks.[36]

For example, the Green Agenda may prioritize pollution prevention in a way that interferes with the expeditious application of pesticides to kill mosquito larvae to mitigate a malaria or West Nile virus outbreak.[37] The Blue Agenda may prioritize bringing a reservoir or irrigation infrastructure into a community, but in doing so, may also bring mosquito breeding habitats closer to that community.[38] In such instances, the Green and Blue Agendas conflict with the aim to prevent and mitigate disease outbreaks, what I call the "Red Agenda." The Red Agenda deals with the control of habitats of disease vectors, like mosquitoes and snails, and the effective treatment of drinking water to address waterborne pathogens, like cholera or typhoid.[39] Additionally, the Red Agenda concentrates on the development of sanitation infrastructure to prevent diseases related to fecal contamination, like cryptosporidium and E. coli, and improved access to water to prevent hygiene-related epidemics, like Ebola.[40] The three agendas overlap and are mutually reinforcing in important ways, as shown in Figure 2.1. However, water law practitioners and scholars, and water policymakers, tend to be focused on Green and Blue. The tricolored framework seeks to make water law and policy more holistic and integrated by bringing more attention to the Red Agenda.

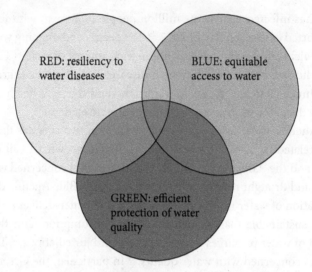

Figure 2.1 The Tricolored Agenda Framework. Source: Rhett B. Larson, *Law in the Time of Cholera*, 92 NOTRE DAME L. REV. 1271 (2017).[1]

[1]This figure was originally published in Vol. 92 NOTRE DAME LAW REVIEW, page 1271 (2017). © Notre Dame Law Review, University of Notre Dame. The publisher bears the responsibility for any errors that might have occurred in reprinting or editing.

Water law and policy should more highly prioritize, and more effectively integrate, the Red Agenda. The Red Agenda orients domestic and international water law toward preventing and mitigating the outbreak of communicable diseases.[41] The Red Agenda focuses on managing the interaction between human communities and the aquatic habitats of disease vectors in the development of water-delivery infrastructure, and prioritizes prevention, treatment, and mitigation of waterborne pathogens in the development of drinking-water systems.[42] While the Green Agenda focuses on protecting human health from contaminants, the Red Agenda focuses on protection from pathogens.

To the extent the Red Agenda is already part of water law and policy, it is only in two small ways. First, the Red Agenda is arguably a minor appendage to the Green Agenda's general protection of human health and its pursuit of "clean water" by, for example, establishing drinking-water standards for fecal coliforms or discharge permits for wastewater treatment plants.[43] Second, the Red Agenda is incidentally pursued along with the Blue Agenda's goal of sufficient water quantity, in which case human health is improved through access to water for hygiene and sanitation.[44] Nevertheless, these minor nods toward the Red Agenda are not only inadequate to address the massive global problem of communicable disease epidemics, but frequently, the pursuit of the Blue and Green Agendas interfere with the Red Agenda.

Understanding the Red Agenda of Water Security

Advancing the Red Agenda and more effectively integrating it within water law and policy requires understanding the inexorable link between communicable disease and water management.[45] One of the most important ways in which this connection between water and communicable diseases has been framed is in the functional classification of diseases by route of transmission, commonly referred to as Bradley Classifications in epidemiology.[46] The Bradley Classifications divide communicable diseases into four classes depending on the type of agent and transmission route, all of which are associated with water.[47] What is striking about the Bradley Classification system is how many major communicable diseases fit into one of these four water-related classes.

The first class includes waterborne infections.[48] Waterborne infections are those that occur by directly ingesting the microbial pathogen.[49] Waterborne infections include cholera, typhoid, cryptosporidium, giardia, E. coli, and other pathogens that can survive in water and can be transmitted through ingestion.[50] Typically, these pathogens are enteric microorganisms introduced to the aquatic environment by fecal contamination.[51] Symptoms of such diseases include abdominal pain, diarrhea, dehydration, and fever.[52] Transmission and ultimate infection depend on the degree of contamination, the survival of the pathogen in the aquatic environment, infectivity of the pathogen, and the degree of individual exposure to the contaminated water.[53] Preventive measures include improved sanitation infrastructure to prevent fecal contamination and improved treatment of drinking water (including disinfection by chlorine or chlorine dioxide).[54] Because of generally poor sanitation and inadequate treatment, waterborne disease outbreaks are particular deadly in the developing world.[55] At least 1.8 million people die annually from waterborne diseases like cholera, with children under the age of five constituting 90 percent of those deaths.[56] Waterborne diseases constitute 80 percent of all illnesses in the developing world.[57]

Outbreaks of cryptosporidium, however, are relatively common even in developed countries.[58] One outbreak in Wisconsin in 1993 infected over 400,000 people and resulted in over 100 deaths.[59] Unlike bacterial pathogens like cholera and typhoid, cryptosporidium is a protozoon that, during the oocyst stage of its lifecycle, is remarkably resilient to traditional means of disinfection, including by chlorine.[60] Addressing cryptosporidium outbreaks has required innovative approaches to drinking-water treatment, including increased and improved reliance on membrane filtration and implementation of ultraviolet radiation treatment.[61]

The second class includes water-washed infections. Such infections arise due to inadequate water for personal and domestic hygiene.[62] Water-washed infections include shigella, trachoma, and scabies.[63] Shigella is a bacterium closely related to salmonella and one of the leading causes of dysentery in the world.[64] Trachoma is caused by chlamydia bacteria in the eye and is an extreme form of conjunctivitis that can result in blindness.[65] Scabies is a skin infestation of mites, and infects over one hundred million people worldwide.[66] In each case, infection results in part from the lack of available water resources to promote adequate hygiene. One of the seminal longitudinal studies associated with water-washed diseases is called *Drawers of Water*.[67] That study demonstrated marked improvement in the health of communities in Uganda, including a significant decline in the prevalence of water-washed infections, when water-gathering containers changed from small peanut oil cans to larger plastic jugs.[68]

One of the implications of *Drawers of Water* is the prioritization of access to clean water for hygiene purposes in public health policy.[69] The importance of water access for hygiene can be seen in the 2014 Ebola outbreak.[70] One of the most significant aggravating factors of the Ebola outbreak in West Africa was the lack of water for hygiene, and one of the reasons Ebola was effectively contained within developed countries was the ready availability of clean water and flushing toilets.[71] The lawsuit against the United Nations seeking damages associated with the Haitian cholera outbreak blamed the United Nations for failing to screen workers for infectious diseases.[72] But just as important a factor in the ultimate severity of the epidemic was the lack of adequate sanitation infrastructure and clean water in Haiti.[73] Had there been flushing toilets and plenty of water for washing hands and food, cholera would likely have flared and burned out quickly in Haiti, as it does whenever it emerges in developed countries.[74] Instead, cholera is likely now an endemic disease in Haiti and costs much more in terms of loss of life than the cost of adequate sanitation.[75]

The third class includes water-based infections.[76] Water-based infections are those in which the pathogen spends part of its life inside vectors whose primary habitat is aquatic, like a snail or a water flea (a small crustacean).[77] This aquatic vector is the primary transmission pathway into human populations.[78] Water-based infections include guinea worm and schistosomiasis.[79] A person is infected by guinea worm diseases, also called dracunculiasis, by ingesting water containing water fleas, which carry the guinea worm larvae.[80] Schistosomiasis is a disease caused by flatworms that are released from freshwater snails and burrow through human skin.[81] Once in the human body, the lifecycle of the worm proceeds, with the worm traveling to the lungs, liver, kidneys, bladder, and even the brain.[82] Symptoms can include abdominal pain, diarrhea, and blood in the stool and urine, and infection can lead to liver damage, kidney failure, infertility, cancer, learning disabilities, and death.[83] Humans are generally infected by swimming or wading in freshwater infested with infected snails. Schistosomiasis affects nearly 210 million people worldwide, with as many as two hundred thousand deaths annually.[84] Like guinea worm, it is considered by the World Health (WHO) to be a neglected tropical disease in terms of invested research in treatment and prevention.[85]

The fourth class includes water-related infections.[86] Water-related infections are those in which the pathogen spends part of its life in a vector that breeds in aquatic environments, like mosquitoes or flies.[87] With these diseases, the problem is not being in the water, or ingesting the water, but is often about proximity to water. Water-related infections include malaria, West Nile virus, dengue fever, yellow fever, chikungunya, sleeping sickness, and filariasis.[88] The pathogen in each case is carried by the vector and transmitted to humans by the vector's bite.[89] These vectors breed, and have their larval stage, in aquatic environments.[90] The health effects of the different water-related infections vary. Malaria is the infection of a protozoan carried by mosquitoes and results in fever, fatigue, aches, vomiting, and in severe cases, seizures, coma, and death.[91] The West Nile, Zika, dengue, yellow fever, and chikungunya viral infections have malaria-like symptoms.[92]

These water-related infections have varying levels of effective treatments.[93] However, they represent collectively one of the greatest threats to human life.[94] Malaria alone kills between six hundred thousand and nine hundred thousand people each year.[95] While the majority of water-related infections occur in developing countries, small West Nile outbreaks are increasingly common in the developed world.[96] For each of these water-related infections, and regardless of location, vector control remains a critical measure for the prevention of epidemics.[97]

A review of the Bradley Classifications emphasizes the importance of the Red Agenda and orients its aims. First, the Red Agenda promotes improved drinking-water treatment and prioritizes microbial pathogen disinfection in the treatment and distribution of drinking water and in the establishment of drinking-water standards. The Red Agenda also emphasizes the role of water law in making water available for hygiene and sanitation and encourages investment in sanitation infrastructure. Additionally, the Red Agenda focuses on disease prevention, and in particular, the role of law in influencing land use, pesticide applications, and water-resource development to prevent or mitigate the increased intersection of disease-vector habitats and human communities.

There are few instances in water law where the Red Agenda takes prominence. For example, the Safe Drinking Water Act's (SDWA's) maximum contaminant levels (MCLs) and the WHO's drinking-water standards set limits on fecal coliforms and impose disinfectant requirements to ensure adequate treatment for pathogens.[98] Discharge permits for treated wastewater are generally designed to establish effluent limits for fecal coliforms, and surface-water quality standards typically address bacteria.[99] These, however, are only a few narrow instances in which water law explicitly and directly advances the Red Agenda, and even then, it does so as part of the broader standards and permitting scheme of the Green Agenda and only in the context of waterborne pathogens.

The litigation relating to the role of the United Nations in the Haitian cholera epidemic is illustrative of one possible approach to advancing the Red Agenda in international water law in the context of waterborne outbreaks.[100] International law could require the screening of aid workers and establish minimum sanitation practices to avoid the introduction of pathogens into an environment in ways that would risk outbreaks.[101] While the immunity claimed by the United Nations from liability associated with the outbreak would encourage investment by the international community in humanitarian response, the United Nations could establish a trust fund comparable to the compensation regimes used in black lung cases in the United States to compensate victims of epidemics that originate from international humanitarian projects.[102] Countries investing in humanitarian aid could be required to invest a minimum percentage in a trust fund or insurance policy aimed at compensating potential victims of disease epidemics and toward disease treatment, containment, and prevention.

The Zika virus outbreak that begin in 2015 and spread rapidly throughout the Western Hemisphere also provides helpful context for understanding the role of the Red Agenda in domestic water law in the context of water-related outbreaks.[103] Zika is a mosquito-borne virus similar to the dengue, West Nile, and yellow fever viruses.[104] The virus was likely brought into Brazil during the 2014 World Cup.[105] Since 2015, there have been over 2,400 cases (compared to 147 previously reported cases), and as many as 40 deaths.[106] More alarming, however, has been the first documented cases connecting Zika infection of pregnant women with microcephaly in infants.[107] Microcephaly is a birth defect resulting in an undersized head and underdeveloped brain, leading to development issues and premature death.[108] The current Zika outbreak is the largest recorded, and the first to suggest a connection between Zika infection and microcephaly.[109]

The response from the Brazilian government has ranged from advising citizens against becoming pregnant to establishing a task force to eliminate stagnant-water bodies where mosquitoes might breed.[110] When the wet season begins in Brazil, management of surface-water resources to limit mosquito breeding becomes the nation's best option, as there are no vaccines or cures for Zika. The Zika outbreak raised difficult international concerns as well, given the 2016 Summer Olympics in Rio. The Zika epidemic appears to be following the same epidemiological path as recent outbreaks of a similar mosquito-borne virus, chikungunya.[111] That virus has extended throughout much of Latin America[112] and the southwest United States.[113] Water law may ultimately play the most significant role in containing the disease, by facilitating pesticide applications to breeding habitats, limiting development projects that result in standing water, and regulating the development of irrigation, wetland, sewage, and storage infrastructure. Water law, in pursuing the Red Agenda, seeks to make communities resilient to these kinds of epidemics, while still meeting its goals of equitable water apportionment and efficient water quality protection.

The Red, Green, and Blue Agendas of water law interact in a myriad of ways. The Venn diagram in Figure 2.2 provides an illustration upon which a discussion of these interactions can be based.

As illustrated in this diagram, the three agendas of water law interact in important ways. For example, in Area A of the diagram, all three agendas are integrated. An example of a water law that integrates all three agendas might be legal incentives for water efficiency, like irrigation duties or minimum water efficiencies for appliances. In that case, more water is available for the environment to protect aquatic habitats and to dilute pollution, thus advancing the Green Agenda. More water is available for domestic, industrial,

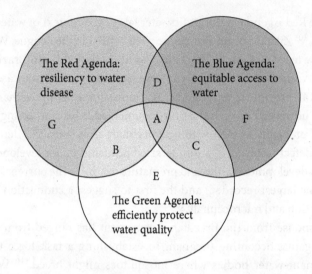

Figure 2.2　Venn Diagram of the Three Water Law Agendas. Source: Rhett B. Larson, *Law in the Time of Cholera*, 92 NOTRE DAME L. REV. 1271 (2017).[2]

[2]This figure was originally published in Vol. 92 NOTRE DAME LAW REVIEW, page 1271 (2017). © Notre Dame Law Review, University of Notre Dame. The publisher bears the responsibility for any errors that might have occurred in reprinting or editing.

and agricultural uses, and for water banking, thus advancing the Blue Agenda. And more water is available for hygiene and sanitation, thus preventing water-washed and waterborne diseases and advancing the Red Agenda.

Area B of the diagram would include ways in which the Red and Green Agendas reinforce one another. For example, prohibitions against un-treated discharges from wastewater treatment plants to rivers would pro-tect rivers from nutrient pollution and also limit exposure to diseases resulting from fecal contamination, thus advancing both the Green and Red Agendas. Area C is the intersection of the Blue and Green Agendas, which could refer to improved irrigation techniques that would enhance water available for agriculture under the Blue Agenda while limiting pol-lution from irrigation runoff under the Green Agenda. Area D is the inter-section of the Red and Blue Agendas, which would include investments in water infrastructure to deliver treated drinking water to households. This diagram illustrates many ways in which water law's three agendas are mu-tually reinforcing.

Nevertheless, there are areas in which each of the water law's three agendas may ignore the aims of each of the other agendas, or even be implemented in ways that conflict with those aims. In Area G, for example, the dumping of enormous concentrations of disinfectants and pesticides into rivers and lakes in the name of preventing waterborne or water-related diseases might inappropriately prioritize the Red Agenda over the Green Agenda. A large rice irrigation project might advance the Blue Agenda in Area F, but bring disease vectors closer to humans and result in fertilizer and pesticide contamination, thus frustrating the aims of the Green and Red Agendas.

The ongoing water crisis in Flint, Michigan, can be better understood through this framework. To address resource contraints associated with water service, the city of Flint ceased purchasing water from Detroit and instead shifted its primary water source to the nearby Flint River.[114] Lowering water costs and shifting to a closer source is an example of Blue Agenda thinking. However, the shift has resulted in a major public health crisis in Flint, including a spike in legionnaires' disease, a waterborne bacterial infection.[115] Had water planners integrated the Red Agenda into planning, they might have been more likely to consider the status of the new water source in terms of the potential for waterborne pathogen outbreaks. Additionally, the Blue Agenda approach that led to reliance on the Flint River as a drinking-water source arguably failed to adequately integrate the Green Agenda by not considering the corrosive nature of the Flint River water caused by chloride contamination and the resulting lead contamination in the city's drinking water.[116]

The crisis in Flint is arguably an example of pure Blue Agenda thinking, lodged in Area F of Figure 2.2 and failing to adequately integrate the other agendas. The fundamental importance of the three agendas framework is to encourage an integrated approach to the development and implementation of water law and policy, and avoid or mitigate conflicts between these agendas, like that in Flint. This integrated approach should result in a water policy that efficiently protects water quality (Green Agenda), equitably apportions water quantity (Blue Agenda), and enhances resilience to water diseases (Red Agenda).

The tripartite aims of water law and policy are thus equity in water distribution and access (the Blue Agenda), efficiency in water-quality protection and remediation (the Green Agenda), and resiliency to diseases classified under the Bradley Classifications (the Red Agenda). The inherent breadth and ambiguity of these terms are a double-edged sword, making it both simple and complicated to reconcile these aims, depending on how one defines them.

There is nothing inevitably irreconcilable about the aims to promote equity, efficiency, and resiliency in the development and application of law.

Conflicts between the Red, Blue, and Green Agendas

The advancement of the Red Agenda in water law, however, is often incidental to the promotion of the other agendas. Furthermore, the Green and Blue Agendas are sometimes pursued in water law in ways that ignore, or even conflict with, the Red Agenda. I will discuss three ways which water law pursues the Green Agenda and the Blue Agenda to the detriment of the Red Agenda: (1) in the establishment of drinking-water quality standards; (2) in the development of water infrastructure, and (3) in the interpretation of the right to water and a clean environment.

Drinking-Water Quality Standards Conflicting with the Red Agenda

Drinking-water quality standards would appear to be one part of water law that explicitly advances the Red Agenda. After all, the express purpose of the SDWA and its primary drinking-water standards are the protection of public health.[117] As noted earlier, drinking-water standards often directly address issues such as disinfection, minimum treatment techniques, and maximum levels of total coliforms.[118] Nevertheless, even in the area of water law most obviously and directly connected to disease prevention, the Red Agenda can be stifled by the Green Agenda.

For example, drinking-water quality standards typically establish maximum levels for disinfectant byproducts (DBPs).[119] DBPs are compounds produced from the reaction of disinfectants (like chlorine or chlorine dioxide) with organic compounds in water.[120] For example, a reservoir may have elevated organic compounds like leaves and bark, resulting from storm runoff after a wildfire or bark beetle infestation in the surrounding forest. When that reservoir water is treated with chlorine to kill harmful bacteria, the chlorine will react with the organic compounds, producing DBPs like trihalomethane or haloacetic acid. Chronic ingestion of elevated levels of DBPs in drinking water has been demonstrated to increase risks of cancer and neurological disorders.[121]

Where maximum chronic DBP standards are applied to drinking water in developing countries, the result is often prioritization of concerns for chronic DBP toxicity at the expense of effective treatment of pathogens.[122] Countries tend to focus on compliance with DBP standards by reducing treatment with disinfectants.[123] This may be a rational trade-off in some developed countries where the risk of cholera or typhoid is minimal, effective treatment options are available, and improved sanitation and hygiene practices would limit any outbreak.[124] However, the threat posed by microbial pathogens in developing countries is far greater than the health effects of chronic elevated DBP concentrations.[125] In the case of DBP standards, the aims of the Green Agenda to efficiently protect water quality at reasonable costs interfere with improving community resilience to waterborne pathogens like cholera, and thus conflict with the Red Agenda.

Drinking-water quality standards fail to integrate the Red Agenda in other ways as well, and in ways that impact communities in both developed and developing nations. There is growing pressure on regulators to improve drinking-water quality by addressing possible chemical threats to human health, such as pharmaceuticals or pesticides.[126] This pressure for more stringent drinking-water standards, particularly in developed countries, results in increased costs to public water systems.[127] In some instances, however, more stringent drinking-water standards may result in greater risks to human health. Small drinking-water systems cannot achieve economies of scale, often have limited bonding capacity, less access to credit and capital, and a smaller customer base.[128] Such systems may not be able to afford more stringent standards aimed at constituent chemicals that are difficult to detect, much less effectively treat.[129]

These systems may be forced to allocate scarce resources that could go toward treatment of microbial pathogens or toward monitoring for chemical constituents that are expensive to detect and treat. This is part of the current challenge facing many water systems that want to be responsive to concerns over persistent chemical contaminants, like per- and polyfluoroalkyl substances (PFAS). PFAS are ubiquitous chemicals with potential serious health effects, but responding to the PFAS concern may mean diverting needed resources away from system maintenance and upgrades with potentially broader health benefits. Under the SDWA, small public water systems that rely on surface water or groundwater under the direct influence of surface water must only monitor for cryptosporidium if E. coli concentrations exceed a certain level.[130] For these systems, more stringent standards for chemical constituents may divert resources away from filtration or ultraviolet treatment needed to address cryptosporidium.[131] As noted earlier, cryptosporidium outbreaks are relatively common, even in developed countries, and notoriously difficult and expensive to treat.[132] There are unquestionably health concerns associated with the presence of pharmaceuticals and pesticides in drinking water.[133] But the question is whether the risks associated with monitoring and treating these contaminants is as imminent and serious to a given community as the threat of a waterborne disease outbreak like cryptosporidium, and how systems evaluating these risks should allocate costs to mitigate them.

Similar issues arise in another aspect of the Green Agenda, though this applies to intentional criminal contamination of drinking-water supplies rather than the more typical conception of pollution. Increased costs have been imposed on small systems in the wake of the terrorist attacks in the United States on September 11, 2001.[134] In an effort to protect drinking-water systems from terrorist attacks, the SDWA was amended to require all community water systems (i.e., those systems serving at least fifteen service connections or twenty-five people year-round)[135] to conduct vulnerability assessments to chemical or biological attacks and prepare emergency response plans.[136] The costs associated with these assessments and emergency plans can be significant, particularly for smaller systems with limited resources.

Increased regulatory compliance costs cannot be easily addressed by increasing rates, either, because these systems are typically regulated public utilities with a state agency setting their rates.[137] As such, small drinking-water systems may be forced to expend limited resources on the prevention of, and response to, terrorism attacks rather than improved monitoring, filtration, and ultraviolet treatment for cryptosporidium. A terrorist attack on any community's drinking-water system would be catastrophic, and systems are well advised to invest in the prevention of, and response to, such attacks. However, appropriate consideration of the Red Agenda would facilitate better assessment of the risks terrorism pose to a system as compared to cryptosporidium.

However, integration of the Red Agenda alongside the Green Agenda would require an evaluation of the resiliency of the community to pathogens of concern, regardless of system size, in addition to the cost-benefit analysis associated with the application of more stringent standards for potentially toxic chemicals like biological or chemical weapons or pharmaceutical or pesticides. Under the current approach, many small public-water systems are forced to prioritize addressing toxic chemical constituents without knowing for certain whether microbial pathogens pose a greater threat to their consumers. Proper consideration of the Red Agenda would compel an evaluation of the relative risks posed to a given community and how best to allocate scarce resources to address these risks.

Water Infrastructure Development Conflicting with the Red Agenda

Despite these conflicts between the Green and Red Agendas, there are ways—like fecal coliform standards—in which these two agendas reinforce each other. The Blue Agenda—the pursuit of equitable allocation of, and access to, water resources—can also reinforce the Red Agenda. The essential lesson from *Drawers of Water* is that simply providing adequate water quantity for hygiene purposes can have dramatic effects for the prevention of water-washed diseases, like scabies or trachoma.[138] Nevertheless, some efforts to improve access to water and equitably allocate water resources can aggravate public health issues related to microbial pathogens.[139] As with the Green Agenda and its emphasis on DBPs, the Blue Agenda can at times conflict with the Red Agenda.

The construction of reservoirs, man-made wetlands, irrigation systems, rice fields, and other infrastructure or built habitats could advance access to water and promote the Blue Agenda.[140] Indeed, there is a pressing need throughout the world for increased investment in water infrastructure.[141] The need for increased investment in water infrastructure has led to increasing funds available from international development banks, nongovernmental organizations, international development agencies, and incentives for private lenders and investors to support water projects like dams, water treatment plants, and irrigation systems.[142]

But these water projects could also frustrate the Red Agenda by bringing disease-vector habitats closer to human communities.[143] This conflict results from a combination of factors that would be better addressed with improved integration of the Red Agenda in water law. These factors include deforestation and replacement of forest with irrigated agriculture or with cattle grazing requiring stock ponds for watering.[144] When replacement of forests with agriculture is combined with rising temperatures associated with global climate change, the conditions necessary for tropical disease vectors, like mosquitoes, to thrive expand and intersect with human communities.[145]

The example of the development of the Diama Dam is illustrative of the potential conflict between the Blue and Red Agendas in water law and policy.[146] In 1987, the first of a series of dams was completed on a tributary of the Senegal River in Mali, and the total project created a reservoir storage capacity of 11.3 billion cubic meters of water for irrigation, hydroelectric power, flood control, and human domestic and industrial uses.[147] The project was the result of a \$150 million loan from the African Development Bank, motivated in part by obligations to meet water rights guarantees made to farmers in the 1960s and to regulate the navigability of rivers between Mali and Senegal.[148]

The reservoir created by the dam also allowed improved navigation and recreation in streams that were wadable year-round[149] because the dam allowed maintenance of minimum stream flows.[150] The dam allowed expansion of irrigation infrastructure, including in particular flood rice irrigation.[151] Within a year after the dam's completion, communities living near new irrigation projects in Senegal suffered a significant increase in waterborne, water-related, and water-based infections.[152] These included cholera epidemics and increased incidence of malaria.[153] Most significant, however, was a dramatic increase in schistosomiasis. Studies in 1988 and 1989 showed that 60 percent of the people living within the vicinity of the Diama Dam had intestinal schistosomiasis.[154]

In the case of the Diama Dam, legal rights to water for irrigation, international legal obligations to maintain navigability on an international river, and incentives created by international development bank loan programs facilitated the development of a large dam and irrigation project that ultimately advanced the Blue Agenda (greater access to water). However, in the case of the Diama Dam, the Blue Agenda significantly conflicted with the aims of the Red Agenda by expanding disease-vector habitats in rice fields, increasing human interaction with disease vectors by making wading possible year-round, and by bringing drinking-water sources closer to human habitation without corresponding improvements in sanitation, increasing the likelihood of fecal contamination. Integration of the Red Agenda in water project financing, water rights, international navigation treaties, and water treatment requirements could have harmonized the two aims of the two agendas.

The conflict between the Blue and Red Agendas is not unique to the Diama Dam case or to developing countries in general. The increased incidence of

West Nile virus in the United States has been linked to the development of large dam projects, and particularly, the connection between large dams and irrigation in warm weather environments.[155] In the arid western United States, large dams and irrigation systems, often funded and managed by federal agencies, are critical to satisfying prior appropriation water rights and managing the equitable apportionment of interstate rivers.[156]

Dams and irrigation infrastructure, furthermore, are not the only water projects that implicate a conflict between the Blue and Red Agendas. In Arizona, for example, regulations encourage, and in some cases effectively require, artificial groundwater recharge in order to avoid unsustainable groundwater pumping, called overdraft.[157] Artificial groundwater recharge typically involves large, standing surface-water impounds, sometimes of river water and sometimes of treated sewage effluent, which then percolates into the underlying aquifer.[158] It is possible that the development of artificial groundwater recharge facilities, aimed at advancing the Blue Agenda, could frustrate the Red Agenda in ways similar to that of large irrigation projects or dams. Dams, irrigation systems, and groundwater recharge and water distribution projects promote intergenerational and intragenerational equitable water allocation under the Blue Agenda, but may erode or limit resiliency to water-related epidemics under the Red Agenda.

Human Right to Water Conflicting with the Red Agenda

One way in which water law seeks to advance both the Blue and Green Agendas is through human rights. There are increasing calls for the recognition of a human right to water, including a recent U.N. General Assembly Resolution and in the codification of such rights in national constitutions.[159] The human right to water can be interpreted as requiring a country to provide a minimum amount of water at a minimum quality, at a maximum price and maximum distance from the point of use.[160] However, guaranteeing water access within a reasonable proximity of the point of use could require bringing water sources closer to human habitation. As such, complying with the human right to water could result in greater intersection of human communities and disease-vector habitats and increased interaction between human waste and drinking-water sources. The Blue Agenda component of the human right to water thus could interfere with the Red Agenda in much the same way as the incentives for water infrastructure development discussed earlier.

The Green Agenda component of human rights may similarly interfere with the Red Agenda. As with growing calls for the recognition of a human right to water, there are also increasing calls for recognizing a human right to a clean environment.[161] Such a human right would place an affirmative obligation on governments to protect the environment from contamination at a certain level and require remediation of pollution exceeding that level.[162] Preventing water pollution and facilitating remediation of water contamination have potential benefits to human health as well as to environmental protection. Toxic chemicals and elevated heavy metals in drinking water have serious detrimental effects on humans.[163] Pollution of aquatic ecosystems results in destruction of habitat, loss of biodiversity, and contamination of water resources with inherent diminishment of aesthetic, recreational, cultural, and ecosystem service values.[164] Laws aimed at preventing these harms, including the standards and permits schemes associated with the Green Agenda, play an important role in protecting and promoting healthy ecosystems and human communities.[165]

Nevertheless, as with the example of the regulation of DBP concentrations, pollution prevention regulation can be implemented in a way that interferes with equally important human health considerations. In *National Cotton Council v. EPA*, the Sixth Circuit Court of Appeals struck down a federal rule that exempted pesticide application to surface waters from Clean Water Act (CWA) permitting requirements.[166] The Environmental Protection Agency (EPA) had promulgated a rule in 2006 to exempt pesticide applications from CWA permitting requirements when such application was conducted in accordance with the Federal Insecticide, Fungicide, and Rodenticide Act (FIFRA).[167] The rule was an outgrowth of previous cases that held that CWA permitting requirements applied to pesticide discharges into jurisdictional waters.[168] In the wake of these earlier decisions, many states moved to establish general permits for pesticide discharges, in part motivated to prevent individual permitting requirements from delaying response to outbreaks of West Nile virus.[169] General permits are issued pursuant to notice and comment rulemaking requirements to apply to a broad category of discharges, with individual discharges filing a Notice of Intent to discharge pursuant to those permits, and thus avoid the costs and delays associated with individual permits.[170] EPA declined to pursue a general permit approach, and instead promulgated the rule exempting such discharges from CWA permitting requirements, under the theory that these discharges were not "pollutants" as defined under the CWA because they were chemical "products" and not chemical "wastes."[171]

The Sixth Circuit rejected EPA's rationale and struck down the rule as inconsistent with the CWA.[172] The court held that residual pesticides in the water constituted a "waste" for purposes of the definition of a CWA pollutant and that other pesticides that relied on bacteria, fungi, or viruses were clearly "biological materials" and thus pollutants under the CWA.[173] In response to the Sixth Circuit's decision, the EPA ultimately pursued the same course as state-permitting agencies had taken in response to previous court decisions, and issued a Pesticide General Permit to regulate discharges of pesticides to jurisdictional waters.[174] Nevertheless, despite the cost savings as compared to an individual permit process, general permits still require the submittal of a Notice of Intent (NOI) and other related compliance costs, including potentially the preparation of a pollution-prevention plan, internal compliance audits, and employee training.[175]

The compliance costs associated with permitting pesticide discharges to prevent water pollution are a prime example of the conflict between the Green and Red Agendas in the context of human rights. In an effort to protect the environment from water pollution, water law imposes costs that could interfere with an expeditious response to water-related disease outbreak. The human right to a clean environment may ultimately protect human communities from toxins or carcinogens, but at the expense of exposing the same community to the harmful effects of pathogens and vectors. Achieving efficient protection of the environment under the Green Agenda with a relatively inexpensive general permit may nevertheless prevent adequate resiliency to epidemics under the Red Agenda.

The examples of pesticide and DBP regulation illustrate why distinguishing between the Green and Red Agendas is helpful. At first, these two agendas can appear identical, if not largely overlapping. After all, protecting the environment from water pollution and preventing harmful chemicals in drinking water seems completely consistent with protecting human health. And these agendas certainly may be pursued in ways that are consistent in their approach and mutually reinforcing. However, the cases of DBP regulation and pesticide permitting suggest that focusing excessively on pollution and chemicals (the heart of the Green Agenda) can sometimes exclude effective consideration of pathogens and vectors (the heart of the Red Agenda).

While the examples provided earlier note the myriad ways in which the predominant Blue and Green Agendas of water law conflict with the Red Agenda, such conflicts are not inevitable or ubiquitous. Indeed, as already noted, there are important ways in which these agendas already function in harmony and are mutually reinforcing, such as the Blue Agenda's focus on water provision facilitating improved hygiene and the Green Agenda's drinking-water standards relating to fecal coliforms. Indeed, one lesson from the *Drawers of Water* study is the importance of water access—even to less-than-clean water—in promoting improved hygiene and sanitation. While conflicts between agendas occur, water law is not necessarily characterized generally by such conflicts, and these agendas overlap in important ways. Even the conflicts discussed earlier between these agendas can be avoided or mitigated by making reforms to water law.

There are several reasons why the three water agendas may come into conflict. I will discuss these possible reasons for conflict and propose three broad categories of legal reforms to avoid or mitigate conflicts between the Green and Blue Agendas and the Red Agenda: (1) increase the role of local stakeholders in the development of drinking-water standards; (2) integrate pathogen and disease-vector habitat considerations into environmental assessments conducted by governments and development banks; and (3) re-interpret the human rights to water and a clean environment to account for disease prevention, including an adaptive approach that allows for emergency response to epidemics associated with water resources.

Reconciling the Red Agenda with the Blue and Green Agendas

The examples discussed earlier provide some evidence that the pursuit of the Blue and Green Agendas in water law and policy can interfere in varying degrees with the pursuit of the Red Agenda. But these examples leave open the question of the cause of such conflicts. As already noted, such conflicts are not inevitable, and each of these agendas can be, and often are, pursued in ways that are mutually reinforcing. What then causes these agendas to some-times clash? Silo thinking and attenuated decision-making are two possible explanations.

The silo effect afflicts large departments or divisions of larger organi-zations, where an individual department develops its own "bureaucratic imperatives" that create obstacles to effective information sharing and co-operation.[176] For example, the Department of Homeland Security was cre-ated in the aftermath of the attacks of September 11, 2001, as a response to silo thinking in intelligence agencies that arguably precluded information sharing related to the terrorist threat between the National Security Agency (NSA), the Central Intelligence Agency (CIA), and the Federal Bureau of Investigation (FBI).[177] The NSA focuses on signals intelligence, the CIA on foreign human espionage, and the FBI on domestic criminal intelligence. Arguably, these separate silos and distinct imperatives prevented effective coordination in counterterrorism.[178]

A large organization—like a national government or the World Bank—may broadly desire to protect the environment and human health while equitably allocating water resources. But individual agencies or departments within those organizations tasked with distinct agendas pursue those agendas within their individual silos. Effectively, the silo effect "reflects a divergence of interests and incentives between a large organization (the principal) and a particular department or division within it (the agent)."[179] Furthermore, the distinct competencies and bureaucracies of each agent create transaction costs in integrating process, jargon, and disciplinary expertise that may frustrate efforts at coordination.[180]

So the U.S. government may desire to simultaneously pursue all three water policy agendas, but the EPA focuses on the prevention of pollution and the treatment of drinking water, while the U.S. Army Corps of Engineers or Bureau of Reclamation focuses on water infrastructure development and management, and the Centers for Disease Control and Prevention (CDC) concentrates on the prevention of, and response to, disease outbreaks. Each has distinct processes for the development and implementation of policy, and each has different competencies, such that communication and coordination requires overcoming differences in expertise and operation. Additionally, each has different incentives, as one agency primarily responsible for advancing one agenda would receive little reward for advancing other agendas, particularly at the expense of its own. This "silo thinking" impedes interagency coordination for purposes of water policy in the same way it did so for the intelligence community.

In addition to silo thinking, attenuated decision-making also partially explains the reason water law agendas sometimes clash. Attenuated decision-making occurs when policy is made at a jurisdictional level remote from the implementation level.[181] Organizations like the EPA, WHO, or World Bank may be attenuated from the geographic, sociocultural, or economic reality of the areas where their water policy is ultimately implemented. Thus, the concerns of the developed world with respect to water—carcinogens, pesticides, pharmaceuticals, recreation—reflected in some agency decision-making may take precedence over the greater concerns associated with the Red Agenda in the communities where water policy is implemented.

Localized Water Governance

The WHO and the EPA's drinking water standards can fail to properly account for local conditions, because standard-setting agencies have an attenuated relationship with the water and its unique local and regional conditions, including organic material in source water and the relative risks posed to a population from DBP concentrations or microbial pathogens. The SDWA has a structure that facilitates some degree of localized control over drinking-water standards.[182] The EPA can grant primacy to state agencies under the SDWA to establish standards, with EPA retaining oversight authority.[183] Furthermore, public water systems can petition agencies implementing the SDWA for a variance from applicable MCLs if localized conditions make MCL compliance infeasible.[184]

Nevertheless, states with SDWA primacy typically adopt the EPA's MCLs.[185] Even oversight from a state agency may fail to appropriately comply with the internalization prescription, because the jurisdictional boundary is still often broader than the applicable watershed boundaries, or else the watershed crosses state jurisdictional boundaries.[186] Many water-treatment projects financed by development banks like the World Bank require treatment to WHO standards, including DBP concentration limits, with limited input from local stakeholders.[187] To more fully integrate the Red Agenda into water law, drinking-water standards could be developed through a negotiated rulemaking process involving input from local stakeholders at the sub-basin level.

For drinking-water treatment projects in developing countries, standards could prioritize disinfection at early stages, with a focus on treatment for heavy metals and toxins phased in over a period of years as waterborne infections are reduced. Such stakeholder groups will require support from technical experts, which should be factored into budgets associated with loans from development banks. Localized participation in the development and implementation of drinking-water standards does not require less technical or scientific competency, but is intended to ensure that scientists, technicians, financiers, developers, and policymakers are sensitive to the concerns and priorities of the communities where water projects are implemented. With exceptions to unlawful or otherwise negligent operation of treatment systems, water project financing, construction, and operation in the developing world could be shielded from liability associated with the presence of harmful chemicals in drinking water where that presence is attributable to the prioritization of disinfection over treatment of potentially harmful chemicals like DBPs, pesticides, or pharmaceuticals. Such a liability shield may avoid disincentives to investment in the control of water-borne infections and appropriately focus initial resources on disinfection of drinking water.

In the United States, a similar negotiated rulemaking process could apply to the development and implementation of MCLs. This process could be overseen by state agencies with SDWA primacy. Local stakeholder groups could also establish drinking-water standards for small water systems that do not fall within the jurisdiction of the SDWA. As a part of their application for Certificates of Convenience and Necessity (effectively, the granting of a monopoly over a certain area to a public utility by the state),[188] public water systems could pay into a trust administered by the state agency with SDWA primacy. The amount paid into the trust would be determined by the size of the customer base of the public water system and would create funds to support smaller drinking-water systems to conduct source water assessments for cryptosporidium and invest in filtration or ultraviolet treatment where necessary. Local stakeholder groups, adequately supported by resources from state and federal funds, should receive deference from EPA oversight and courts when reasonably prioritizing disinfection over investments in treatment for pharmaceuticals or other potentially harmful chemicals. This localized approach to the development of drinking-water quality standards and treatment requirements would ideally integrate the Green Agenda's concern with the efficient prevention and mitigation of water contamination with the Red Agenda's concern for community resilience to infection.

Pathogen and Vector Assessments in Water Development

A more localized approach to water governance may help overcome attenuated decision-making and thereby integrate the Red Agenda more effectively into water policy. However, additional reforms are necessary to overcome silo thinking. For example, ex ante water project assessments should require coordination between agencies tasked with promoting each agenda.

In environmental impact assessments made under the Espoo Treaty, the National Environmental Policy Act (NEPA), and similar programs, state-funded or state-conducted water projects should be required to consider disease-vector habitat issues as part of project assessment. Currently, disease-vector issues may be considered in these assessments, but no such consideration is explicitly required.[189] Such treaties and statutes could be amended to explicitly require the impact statement to address disease vectors, including the evaluation of project alternatives to mitigate possible intersection between expanded or enhanced disease-vector habitat and human communities. There is growing scholarship and increasing movement in policy implementation of Health Impact Assessments (HIAs) as a companion to environmental impact assessments to ensure adequate consideration of public health.[190]

Environment impact assessment requirements, like those of NEPA, have been criticized as toothless procedural hoops with little to no impact on substantive outcomes and improved environmental protection.[191] Nevertheless, these largely procedural statutes can improve project planning by at least requiring consideration of certain concerns and by imposing a transparency requirement on such consideration through a public release of the assessment report.[192] Furthermore, these statutes can have substantive components in the sense that agencies and companies may agree to enforceable obligations under memoranda of understanding incorporated into the record of decision as part of the assessment process.[193] An explicit requirement to consider microbial pathogens may have at least alerted the United Nations to the possible need to screen aid workers for cholera without having to impose liability on humanitarian efforts. The focus in water law on the Green and Blue Agendas may result in water projects moving forward without sufficient consideration being given to diseases under the Bradley Classifications. An improved environmental impact statement process would impose an obligation to at least evaluate the potential for water projects to impede advancing the Red Agenda. An express requirement in NEPA for the coordinated efforts of the EPA, CDC, and water-resource development agencies would mitigate the impacts of silo thinking in water policy development and implementation.

One of the ways in which environmental impact assessments could evaluate the concerns of the Red Agenda is by addressing how water projects might result in the loss of disability-adjusted life years (DALYs). The DALY is a measure of the burden of a disease, expressed in terms of the number of years of life lost due to poor health, disability, or premature death.[194] The

WHO relies on DALYs to make decisions on the allocation of resources for disease prevention.[195] Risk assessments made for water projects could be required to evaluate the potential health impacts from diseases under Bradley Classifications in terms of DALYs and subject those evaluations to public scrutiny in a public notice and comment process. While the DALY has its limits as a measurement of disease impact, an explicit requirement to model, measure, and evaluate health impacts in a widely accepted and relatively holistic metric would promote improved evaluation of issues central to the Red Agenda in environmental impact assessments.[196]

Environmental impact statements are not the only way in which water law could be reformed to require government agencies to more fully consider issues under the Red Agenda. For example, under prior appropriation regimes, applications for changes in diversion points on a stream, new appropriative rights, or transferring water rights typically require approval from a state agency.[197] State agencies may decline such applications for a number of reasons, including when such changes or transfers would be against the public welfare or a menace to public safety.[198] State agencies in such instances could use their authority to deny applications when and where changes in diversion points, new appropriative rights, or transfers of water rights might significantly enhance disease-vector habitat or substantially increase the likely intersection between disease-vector habitat and human communities, or human waste and drinking-water sources. Such an approach would integrate the concerns of the Red Agenda with the Blue Agenda's focus on the equitable apportionment of water resources between individuals, communities, and generations. State water rights agencies should have an explicit requirement to coordinate with state health agencies with relevant expertise in waterborne and water-related diseases to ensure that water rights transfers and changes in diversion points do not increases the risk of disease outbreaks.

An additional possible reform would be to create a water policy version of the Department of Homeland Security at the national level, and establish a system that integrates different water policy silos so that each water policy agenda is adequately considered. Water policy agents in the EPA, Bureau of Reclamation, U.S. Army Corps of Engineers, and CDC could have formalized interagency communication and collaboration in water-resource assessments. This integrated approach could be mirrored at the local level, with health, natural resource, and environmental agencies collaborating in water project assessments under a rigorous, participatory, and integrated HIA process.

Reinterpreting Rights to Account for the Red Agenda

Both silo thinking and attenuated decision-making are symptomatic in the reliance on human rights to advance water policy. Advocates pursuing both the Blue and Green Agendas have relied on human rights to advance equitable water apportionment and efficient water protection.[199] Although an international human right to water currently is of questionable efficacy and enforceability, the rhetoric of human rights raises the "lexical priority" of water issues at the international level.[200] Furthermore, domestic constitutional law has made advances in recent years in integrating express rights to water within an enforceable human rights framework.[201] Yet, as noted earlier, the human rights approach to the Blue and Green Agendas can be implemented in ways that interfere with the Red Agenda, including by preventing expeditious response to outbreaks through anti-vector pesticide application. These conflicts may arise in part when human rights organizations suffer from silo effects without proper coordination with health organizations, and when human rights advocates unfamiliar with local health concerns thereby improperly prioritize water access over disease prevention. These conflicts between water law agendas in the human rights sphere can be mitigated or reconciled by reinterpreting the human right to water and a clean environment in several ways.

First, advocating and formulating human rights to water and a clean environment, at both the national and international level, should tie such rights more directly to the right to life.[202] By so doing, these rights are placed within the context where protection of human life (perhaps measured by limiting loss of DALYs) is the primary goal of the right to water. Within that context, policymakers and courts may be more likely to interpret such human rights in terms that maximize human resilience to microbial diseases and water-related epidemics. Such an interpretation should encourage variances from water-quality standards and emergency waivers of permitting obligations to facilitate expeditious response to disease outbreaks, with such exceptions to the norm seen as consistent with the promotion and protection of human rights. When rights to water and a clean environment conflict with the right to life, such rights should be interpreted in favor of measures that minimize the loss of DALYs.

Second, the human right to water and a clean environment should consistently be tied to a human right to sanitation.[203] Fecal contamination of drinking-water sources is one of the primary causes of waterborne infections, including cholera and cryptosporidium.[204] Despite the importance of sanitation, progress in that area lags far behind improvements in access to water for drinking and domestic purposes. The U.N. Millennium Development Goals (MDGs) aimed to halve, by 2015, the proportion of the world's population lacking sustainable access to safe drinking water and basic sanitation.[205] Nevertheless, progress in the sanitation sector has lagged far behind progress in drinking-water provision since the MDGs were announced.[206] There are many possible explanations for this phenomenon. It could be because nongovernmental organizations, development banks, and nations can more easily and attractively publicize progress in drinking water than sanitation (glossy photographs of clean tap water, wells, and water treatment plants tend to be more aesthetically pleasing marketing and propaganda tools than photos of latrines). But part of the explanation may be a simple preference for investment in drinking water than sanitation, because sanitation is something people are less comfortable talking about than drinking water. Greater emphasis on sanitation within the human rights conversation, and interpretation of the right to water as including a right to sanitation, would facilitate this essential public conversation.

Third, a human rights approach to water provision and quality should be interpreted to include certain procedural rights associated with the development of water policy. A human right to water can be viewed as comprising two rights—a provision right and a participation right.[207] A provision right creates an affirmative obligation on the state to sustainably provide water of adequate quantity and quality.[208] Such a provision right is problematic because it is difficult to enforce and define and can reduce cost-recovery and incentives for water conservation.[209] The other right is a participation right, which involves a right to participate in the development of water policy and to procedural rights associated with water disconnection or rate increases.[210]

Conclusion

The recognition of the procedural component of a human right to water has an important connection with the integration of the Red Agenda into environmental impact statements. In 2013, California introduced and enacted its "Human Right to Water Bill."[211] That bill recognizes that "every human being has the right to safe, clean, affordable, and accessible water."[212] The most significant component of the law requires state agencies to consider the human right to water when "revising, adopting, or establishing policies, regulations, and grant criteria."[213] Under this approach, the human right to water imposes an obligation to factor water into all government actions. To the extent the right to water is reinterpreted to comprise all three agendas, then such a procedural or participation right approach would require a transparent and participatory stakeholder process in the development of water policy that included addressing the issues addressed in the Red Agenda. For developing countries, such procedural rights are likely most critically needed and most easily implemented in the internal processes of development banks.

Ultimately, a right can hardly be characterized as a "human right" if it is not primarily concerned with protecting humans. A human right to water and a clean environment is self-parody if it results in the state providing affordable water in close proximity to the point of use that meets WHO drinking-water standards to a population dying of cholera and malaria. Human rights involve prioritization of social concerns and should begin by putting first things first—the protection of human life.[214]

3

Water Security and Human Rights

In 1997, South Africa became the first country to include in its constitution an explicit right to water.[1] Under Section 27 of the South African Constitution, "[e]veryone has the right to have access to . . . sufficient food and water."[2] Importantly, Section 27 of South Africa's constitution conditions that right upon "progressive realization," meaning that the assurance of water access was not immediate, but a goal the government could strive to achieve over time. Initially, the city of Johannesburg attempted to comply with this constitutional requirement by providing an unlimited amount of water for a single flat rate. In Phiri, a historically black and poor township of about a million residents in Johannesburg, the flat rate approach resulted in only 1 percent of the water delivered to Phiri generating any revenue for the city, with no possibility of disconnecting anyone due to the constitutional water right. Under the flat fee approach, over six hundred billion liters a year were lost as a result of nonrevenue water in the city, at an annual total cost of $390 million. Phiri had the highest levels of nonrevenue water in the city, which includes water delivered to legal connections but without payment and water delivered to illegal water connections.[3]

In 2004, to address the problem of water sustainability, the Johannesburg municipal government implemented a new approach in a number of townships with problems involving cost recovery, including Phiri. The city would deliver "free basic water" to every household, at an amount of six kiloliters per household per month (which the city assumes would work out to about twenty-five liters per person per day), with additional water only delivered when paid for in advance through a household water meter.[4] Most Phiri households consumed the entire six kiloliters per month of free basic water within the first two weeks of the month, in part because the city grossly underestimated how many people lived in the average Phiri household. Other areas of the city continued to operate under the old flat rate system, or systems which allowed for water to be purchased on credit and not prepaid. Certain Phiri residents sued, claiming the "free basic water" program combined with the prepayment requirement violated their constitutionally guaranteed right to water. The limits of the policy approach were acutely demonstrated at one point when a fire broke out in Phiri and residents had to continue to pay the water meter in order to extinguish the fire.[5]

The court decision surrounding the Phiri residents' claim that the city violated their constitutional right to water, *Mazibuko v. City of Johannesburg*, became a landmark decision in human rights law.[6] The trial court ruled in favor of the residents of Phiri, holding that the prepaid meter system violated the right to water and ordered that fifty liters per person per day be established as the free basic water supply as soon as possible.[7] On appeal, a different court lowered the minimum free basic water supply to forty-two liters per person per day and emphasized the need for progressive realization given the city's resources.[8] The city then appealed to South Africa's Constitutional Court, the nation's highest court. The Constitutional Court reversed the appellate court's ruling and upheld the prepaid water program and minimum free basic water amounts established by the city. The Constitutional Court deferred to the expertise of agencies establishing the minimum amount of water as a reasonable determination and held that such technical determinations are not within the role of the judiciary. The Constitutional Court stated that courts are "ill-suited to adjudicate upon issues where Court orders could have multiple social and economic consequences for the community."[9]

In response to the concerns about water insecurity, including the water variability aggravated by climate change and threats to human health discussed in the previous two chapters, there is growing advocacy for a human rights–based approach to water law and policy at both the national and international levels, similar to the approach in South Africa. For example, the U.N. General Assembly adopted a resolution recognizing an international human right to water in 2010.[10] The 2010, U.N. Resolution declared that the "right to safe and clean drinking water . . . [is] a human right that is essential for the full enjoyment of life and all human rights."[11] More than forty national constitutions have incorporated language recognizing a right to water similar to that of the 2010 U.N. Resolution, including South Africa, Tunisia, Uganda, and Ecuador.[12]

But despite this seemingly obvious starting point for human rights, forty-one counties abstained from signing the 2010 U.N. Resolution when it was first introduced, and the vast majority of nations do not have a constitutionally protected right to water.[13] Reluctance to embrace a rights-based approach to water policy arguably stems from the uncertain effect of such an approach, including the challenges facing Johannesburg, the residents of Phiri, and the South African courts in the *Mazibuko* case. Formulations of the right to water often leave unanswered the most fundamental and important questions of water policy, including questions of who owns water, how to price water, whether and to what extent to subsidize water services, and whether such a right is sustainable and enforceable. Section 27 of the South African Constitution seems essential, wise, and compassionate on first reading, but on second reading, it's easy to see how many questions were left to the courts to answer. The challenge of a rights-based approach to water policy is how to frame such a right so as to effectively answer these fundamental questions.

Human rights are typically framed as either positive rights or negative rights.[14] Negative rights are guarantees against government interference, with certain rights—like freedom of expression, religious practice, or freedom from discrimination or arbitrary deprivations of life, liberty, and property by the government—without providing citizens due process and a demonstration of an adequate countervailing public interest.[15] The First and Fourteenth Amendments to the U.S. Constitution and the rights enumerated in the U.N. Covenant on Civil and Political Rights (the "CP Covenant," which includes freedom of religion and expression, among others) are examples of negative rights.[16] Positive rights are affirmative government duties to provide certain minimum quantity and quality of goods and services to each citizen, and may include rights to education, health care, or housing.[17] The right to an attorney for accused criminals in the United States or the rights enumerated in the U.N. Covenant on Economic, Social, and Cultural Rights (the "ESC Covenant," which includes rights to food and education, among others) are examples of positive rights.[18] The distinction between positive and negative rights, while in some ways intuitive, is problematic, because even negative rights impose an affirmative obligation on the state to provide some adjudicative and enforcement mechanisms.[19] For example, freedom from arbitrary deprivation of life, liberty, or property without due process is a negative right, but assumes the affirmative obligation on the government to provide the process.

National constitutions, legal scholars, and advocates of the human right to water typically frame the right to water as a positive right.[20] For example, the U.N. Human Rights Commission issued General Comment 15 to the ESC Covenant in 2002, which considers a positive right to water a prerequisite to the realization of other rights under the ESC Covenant, including the right to a standard of living and adequate food.[21] Furthermore, where the right to water is recognized by domestic courts or constitutions, it has been exclusively framed as a provision right.[22]

In one sense, the case for such a positive right seems simple and compelling. After all, if life depends on water, shouldn't that be where human rights begin? It would seem silly to pat someone on the shoulder who is suffering from dehydration or dying of cholera and say, "Don't worry—you have the right to a trial by jury!" Of course, implementing a positive right to water is not simple. In India, for instance, the Supreme Court inferred a positive right to water from the constitutional right to life under Article 21 of the Constitution of India.[23] The Court stated that "the right to access clean drinking water is fundamental to life and there is a duty on the state under Article 21 to provide clean drinking water to its citizens."[24] Despite the recognition of such a positive right, India struggles with water provision, with a small portion of its population having access to tapped, treated water, and many suffering from waterborne diseases.[25]

A positive right to water may fail to achieve effective and equitable water provision for many reasons. First, it is difficult for courts to enforce broadly worded positive rights. The judiciary, despite being the arbiter of rights, often lacks the competency as compared to other governmental entities to effectively establish minimum quantities and qualities and maximum and minimum prices of goods and services. Judges who are trained to think about freedom of speech or murder may not be familiar with the complex interplay of engineering, public finance, and hydrology necessary to adjudicate a positive right to water. In short, a positive right to water implicates the "familiar difficulties with judicial enforcement of affirmative duties."[26]

Second, the investments required for water and sanitation infrastructure are uniquely high, even compared to the capital requirements of other candidates for positive right status, like education or health care.[27] Schools and hospitals are costly, to be sure, but not nearly as costly as dams, reservoirs, well fields, pipes, treatment systems, and pumping stations. Because water infrastructure is uniquely capital intensive, the countries with the most apparent need to guarantee water provision are also often least able to afford it.[28] Furthermore, political pressure on government agencies that set water rates, and in some cases government corruption in granting contracts to private water utility companies, impact how water projects are financed, how water is priced, and how costs for water service are recovered.[29]

Third, because water is a common resource that falls for free out of the sky, and often carries cultural and religious meaning, people are generally more reluctant to pay full price for its provision than for other goods or services.[30] This hearkens back to Adam Smith's "water-diamond paradox." Water's unique characteristics combine to make water services underpriced in most of the world, leading to serious sustainability problems.[31] Underpriced water results in greater water consumption and water waste, with associated ecological and human health impacts. It also decreases recovery of water provision costs, thus decreasing investment in improving, expanding, and maintaining water infrastructure.[32] Policies leading to underpriced water, including in some instances a positive right to water, are often bad for the environment, bad for the economy, and bad for the poor. This chapter evaluates the human right to water in its common formulation as a positive right and proposes three considerations that should accompany any positive right to water.

The Purpose, History, and Formulation of the Right to Water

The Bolivian Water War of 2000 provides useful context to illustrate the different rationales for having a positive right to water. The Bolivian city of Cochabamba had been struggling with water supply quality and infrastructure problems for decades.[33] Most residents were not connected to the municipal water system, and many were paying as much as three times the municipal rate for water from private vendors.[34] In a deal to secure necessary financing for water system improvements from the World Bank, Cochabamba privatized its water supply and infrastructure.[35] The contract from the government to a private enterprise to own and operate the water system (a "concession contract") required increases in water tariffs and prohibition of alternative methods of water provision other than connection to the city system.[36] Cochabamba issued a concession contract to the sole bidder on its water project, a consortium called Aguas del Tunari (ADT). ADT signed a $2.5 billion, forty-year contract with the city, with a guaranteed 15 percent annual return on investment. The exigencies of meeting ADT's contractual rights resulted in an increase in water rates of 35 percent, with many in Cochabamba's poorest barrios paying one-third of their total annual income in water tariffs.

The public response to Cochabamba's increased water rates and prohibition against alternative water sources escalated into large-scale protests of the concession contract by early 2000. Following a prolonged and violent standoff, the government and protestors reached an agreement, nullifying the concession contract to the private water company, repealing the prohibitions on alternative water provision, and turning ownership and operation of the city's water services over to the municipal government.[37] Despite this response, water services problems remain in Cochabamba, with more than half of the city's population unconnected to the municipal system and water quality generally below World Health Organization (WHO) standards.[38]

The water conflict in Cochabamba illustrates three rationales often invoked for a positive human right to water. The first rationale is that such a positive right serves as a bulwark against inequity. Human rights advocates fear that water policy driven by profit will make water less affordable, particularly for the poor.[39] Studies show that water privatization often leads to increased water rates.[40] There are several reasons for such increases, including the political pressure on publicly owned systems to maintain low rates and the expectation of private water utilities to see a return on large upfront investments in infrastructure expansion and refurbishment before entering any government contract to assume ownership and operation of water systems. The concern, then, is that private water companies will neglect poorer communities because of the greater likelihood of cost recovery for improvements and services to wealthier areas—the concern that water will flow to money. A rights-based approach represents a possible counter to this risk of water privatization, whereby water is guaranteed as a right regardless of ability to pay.[41] Nevertheless, the Cochabamba example illustrates that inequity existed before, during, and after privatization.[42]

The second rationale relates to the idea of "putting first things first," as Isaiah Berlin suggests, and to political philosopher John Rawls' conception of primary goods. When the label "right" is attached to a public policy issue, the label gives that issue "lexical priority."[43] For policy activists, the label "human right" often has less to do with enforceable law and more to do with using rights rhetoric to emphasize the importance of the issue. Water is thus often characterized as a right to convey its essential nature to a dignified life.[44] The "putting first things first" rationale for rights-based water policy is evident in the Cochabamba example, both in favor of and opposing privatization. Advocates of privatization argued that it would attract investment in improving water quality and infrastructure, essential to prioritizing water services.[45] On the other hand, protestors argued that a right to water guaranteed provision of adequate water as a prerequisite to any other development goal, and high water rates driven by investors' expectation of profit threat-ened that right.[46]

The third rationale for a positive human right to water is to encourage ac-countability and transparency. This rationale speaks to a fundamental doc-trine of water law in many parts of the world—the public trust doctrine.[47] Under the public trust doctrine, the state holds title to water resources in trust with a fiduciary obligation to manage those resource for the benefit of all citizens.[48] The public trust doctrine, in various forms and applications, is rec-ognized in many legal systems, including in India, Pakistan, the Philippines, Uganda, the United States, Kenya, Nigeria, South Africa, Brazil, Ecuador, and Canada.[49] A human right to water may provide citizens with a clear legal ground on which to lay claim to a resource held in trust for their benefit. Opponents of water privatization in Cochabamba relied on the public trust doctrine in their arguments, noting that water is "a public trust to be guarded by all levels of government."[50]

These three rationales for recognizing a human right to water—equity, pri-ority, and accountability—have existed for as long as human civilization.[51] It is unsurprising, therefore, to see attempts to create a workable human right to water in different cultures and in different parts of the world throughout history. While the history of the development of the human right to water is wide-reaching, I will note two historical examples that have been particularly influential in how we understand the application of a human rights frame-work to water.

One of the earliest conceptions of a human right to water comes from one of the oldest and most broadly influential legal systems—Sharia law. Given Islam's roots in the arid Arabian Peninsula, the importance placed on water rights in Sharia law is perhaps unsurprising.[52] Sharia law recognizes a right to irrigate, called *shirb*, and a right for humans and animals to quench their thirst, called *shafa*. These rights are implemented in various ways depending on local laws and sectarian interpretations, but include certain generalizable principles, including a focus on equity in water distribution.[53] And while Sharia law is codified in only a few national legal systems, it remains influ-ential in many countries because it provides a foundation for the Ottoman water code, called the *Majalla*, which continues to inform water policy in areas formerly under Ottoman control.[54] In some instances, these Sharia water rights are interpreted as absolute prohibitions against charging for water services, as prohibiting charging for water but not for water delivery services, or, depending on distinctions between private and public water sources, in determining when, how, and how much to charge for water services.[55]

Similar to the role of the *Majalla* spreading Sharia human rights concepts through the Ottoman Empire, the Roman Empire also exported another early form of the human right to water into other nations' legal systems. In many modern nations that are former Roman colonies, property interests in water are allocated based on Roman riparian water rights.[56] Under a riparian water rights regime, landowners with property abutting a waterbody (called riparian land) have the right to make "reasonable use" of that water.[57] "Natural" uses are presumed reasonable, while "artificial" water uses are subject to a court's evaluation of the relative reasonableness of co-riparian landowners' water uses.[58] A natural use of water based on riparian rights satisfies basic needs and is typically limited to household-level drinking, sanitation, hygiene, and subsistence-level irrigation and livestock watering. All other water uses are considered artificial and therefore subject to the reasonableness evaluation. The ancient Roman riparian regime thus includes a legal recognition that water uses for basic human needs have higher priority than other uses, but these rights are limited to owners of riparian land.

Water rights under Sharia law and the prioritization of natural uses under riparian rights regimes illustrate one of the challenges in formulating and implementing a human right to water, which is delineating its boundaries. When we speak of a human right to water, is it a reference only to drinking water, to domestic water uses in general (including hygiene and sanitation), or to a broader right that incorporates access to water resources for the development of food and energy? More fundamentally, perhaps, each of these historic approaches reflect a major limitation to the human right to water—it is inherently anthropocentric. The human right to water is, unsurprisingly, concerned mainly with humans.

There are, of course, other examples of historic approaches to a human right to water beyond those of Sharia law and the Ottoman and Roman Empires, some of which will be discussed in coming chapters. These examples of imperial sowing of the seeds of the human right to water are not intended as an exhaustive list of early approaches to human rights to water, nor is referencing these approaches any kind of endorsement or defense of these empires nor of colonialism in general. But these seeds did take root in many parts of the world and influenced the development of the human right to water. The evaluation of the modern conception of a human right to water requires an understanding of the legal concepts from whence it has developed. Both of these examples illustrate two fundamental concerns at play in the human right to water—quantifying a minimum quantity and quality of water necessary to satisfy this right and ensuring that guaranteed water is affordable for all. Scholars, governments, nongovernmental organizations, and water policy advocates have generally framed the right to water, at both the international and domestic level, as a positive right, focused on addressing these two fundamental concerns.[59]

Currently, forty-one national constitutions enshrine a right to water, and they universally formulate that right as a positive one.[60] For example, Article 65 of the Constitution of Kenya provides that "[e]very person has the right to water in adequate quantities and reasonable quality."[61] Article 5 of the Constitution of Indonesia provides that the state must guarantee individual access and availability of water for everyone residing within the nation.[62] Article 23 of the Constitution of Ecuador recognizes the right to potable water.[63] In each case, however, the right is subject to progressive realization and available resources. For example, the constitutions of both Uganda and Zambia move even further from the rights-rhetoric to the "compelling interest" rhetoric, by framing the public interest in water as a government "objective" or "endeavor," subject to available resources.[64]

Often, nations may lack an express right to water, but infer such a right from other express rights on the grounds that the realization of any right depends on provision of a minimum core of primary needs.[65] As noted earlier, the Supreme Court of India inferred the right to water from other express constitutional rights.[66] A similar approach of judges inferring a provision right to water from other express rights has been arguably observed in Pakistan and Bangladesh.[67] The right to water under international law is similarly inferred from express rights.[68] For example, the U.N. Universal Declaration of Human Rights (HR Declaration) states: "Everyone has the right to a standard of living adequate for the health and well-being of himself and of his family."[69] A right to water is arguably implied within the right to a standard of living, because without water there is no living at all.[70] Indeed, on September 30, 2010, the U.N. Human Rights Council (UNHRC) inferred from the HR Declaration that a right to water was "inextricably related to . . . the right to life and human dignity."[71] Article 11 of the ESC Covenant recognizes a right to an adequate standard of living, health, food, and housing. The United Nations inferred a provision right to water from these guarantees in 2002, under General Comment 15 to the ESC Covenant.[72] The drafters of General Comment 15 draw the right to water from other express provision rights under the ESC Covenant, finding that the right to water is a "prerequisite for the realization of other human rights." The ESC Covenant, however, requires only that states "take steps . . . to the maximum of [their] available resources, with a view to achieving progressively the full realization of the rights recognized in the [ESC Covenant]."[73]

The international and national formulations of a positive right to water, whether express or implied, all leave open the questions of how much, how clean, at what cost, and when it must be achieved. These unanswered questions inevitably impact the enforceability and effectiveness of a rights-based approach to water provision.

The Limitations of a Positive Human Right to Water

If the rights-based approach is employed solely to secure the minimum quantity and quality of affordable water to sustain life, then such an approach has limited value. There are two kinds of people—people with enough water to stay alive and dead people. The right to water cannot mean only a guarantee of water sufficient to keep a person alive, because every living person already has that. The real challenge of the human right to water is guaranteeing an amount, quality, access, affordability, and allocation of water sufficient to achieve some standard of living, which may depend on varying social and hydrological conditions. The *Mazibuko* case in South Africa discussed at the beginning of this chapter illustrates three fundamental challenges of a provision right to water: (1) enforceability, (2) economic sustainability, and (3) ecologic sustainability.

There are serious economic and political forces limiting the capacity of courts to effectively enforce positive rights in general, and the human right to water in particular. In upholding Johannesburg's prepaid meter program that led residents of Phiri Township to sue, the Constitutional Court noted that, like positive rights in most contexts, South Africa's constitution guaranteed only the "progressive realization" of a right to water.[74] The Constitutional Court held that the city was required only to take reasonable steps to progressively realize the interests in water guaranteed under South Africa's constitution and that the constitution does not create "a self-standing and independent" positive right to water, enforceable irrespective of available resources.[75] Because positive rights are necessarily constrained in their realization by the ability of governments to take appropriate and effective action, governmental delays in realizing such rights are easily explained, and that explanation is not easily challenged.[76]

The nature of the judiciary is also a limitation on enforceability of a positive right to water. The Constitutional Court in *Mazibuko* upheld the city's established amount and reversed the lower court rulings based on what the Constitutional Court called "an understanding of the proper role of courts in our constitutional democracy."[77] The Constitutional Court stated that it is "institutionally inappropriate for a court to determine precisely what the achievement of any particular social and economic right entails and what steps government should take to ensure the progressive realization of the right. This is a matter, in the first place, for the legislature and executive, the institutions of government best placed to investigate social conditions in the light of available budgets and determine what targets are achievable in relation to social and economic rights."[78] The different opinions of what constitutes "sufficient water" of the three courts involved in adjudicating *Mazibuko* suggests that courts often are not well equipped for making the kind of technical determinations best left to expert executive agencies nor in determining how to prioritize expenditures of public resources perhaps best left to popularly elected legislatures.

Executive agencies or legislatures could take two different approaches to more effectively guide judicial enforcement of positive rights, each equally problematic. The first would be to establish a broad, guiding principle in the formulation of the right ("sufficient and affordable clean water") and allow courts to enforce that principle on a case-by-case basis. However, such ambiguity raises serious challenges in terms of enforcement. Where courts lack information and expertise relative to government budgets and revenue, the judicial enforcement of positive rights requiring government expenditures can create serious fiscal problems. Where courts lack information and expertise regarding local conditions, including population density, consumption patterns, and demographics, judicial enforcement of positive rights may prove inadequate or overreaching.

To avoid such indeterminacy, legislatures may take a second approach by quantifying the amount and quality of water required to meet a provision right. The City of Johannesburg attempted such an approach by establishing the six kiloliters per month per household standard. This standard, however, proved unworkable, partially because the government did not understand that households were much larger in Phiri than in other townships in the city. As such, in order to avoid the challenge of indeterminacy in judicial enforcement, codification of the provision right to water often forces a rigid legal establishment of minimum standards that cannot be easily adapted to unique local conditions. Such rigid standards may not prove workable as conditions differ both temporally and spatially.

Establishing causation of harm also poses an obstacle to judicial enforcement of a positive right to water. Droughts, floods, and waterborne epidemics impact human rights but are not necessarily human rights violations. The difficulty of establishing the government as the "cause," and therefore the liable party, of a failure to adequately provide sufficient water, when water availability is influenced by global climate patterns and other factors outside of any government's control, limits the enforceability of such rights.[79] Even when droughts, floods, or epidemics may be partially attributable to a failure of governance, courts are nevertheless incapable of evaluating where a natural disaster ends and governance failure begins in assessing causation, and thus enforcing a positive right to water.[80] Additionally, those citizens most likely to need the courts to enforce a positive right to water—the economically or socially disenfranchised—often lack the means to effectively assert that right.[81]

The challenge of enforcing a positive right to water is all the more complicated under international law. In addition to the problems of indeterminacy, progressive realization of minimum targets established by a positive right, rigidity, and limited resources, international law typically only applies to disputes between states.[82] To the extent a positive right to water exists under international law, it must be inferred from other express provision rights under the ESC Covenant, as noted in General Comment 15.[83] However, unlike the negative rights outlined in the CP Covenant, the ESC Covenant's Optional Protocol is not yet binding, as an insufficient number of states have acceded to the Optional Protocol.[84] Given the lack of a binding Optional Protocol, the ESC Covenant lacks adjudicative processes and enforcement mechanisms, making it "normatively and jurisprudentially underdeveloped" when compared to the negative human rights enshrined in international law.[85]

In addition to problems of enforceability, the positive right to water raises challenges of economic sustainability. Water is different from the objects of other provision rights regimes because treating water as an economic commodity has always been problematic—again, hearkening back to Adam Smith's "water-diamond paradox."[86] The price of water, influenced by actual or perceived notions of scarcity, does not accurately reflect the true value of water. Water is thus undervalued because consumers inaccurately perceive it has low production costs and greater supply than demand. This public perception influences political actors who set low water rates for water utilities, regulated as natural monopolies. The unique challenge of pricing water and recovery costs of water treatment and delivery can be aggravated by a provision right to water.

This aggravation results because the provision right to water is typically formulated in a way that either ignores, or is hostile to, the idea of water as a valuable commodity requiring expensive infrastructure to fully develop. For example, some have argued that full cost recovery for water services and effective water pricing are inconsistent with the idea of a right to water, arguing that water "must not be treated as a private commodity to be bought, sold, and traded . . . the global freshwater supply is . . . a fundamental human right."[87] But free or cheap water will likely mean wasted water and degrading infrastructure. Water in its natural state requires treatment to be safe for drinking, which is costly, and water is heavy and expensive to transport to places where it will be used. I once spoke with the head of a municipal water utility who said, "God has given us water. But He did not give us pipes and disinfectants—we have to pay for those things." Put somewhat differently, the head of a national water regulatory agency once told me, "If you believe water is a human right and should be free, then by all means, go hike up into the mountains and start filling buckets. But if you want someone to treat it and transport it to your house, you're going to have to pay those people." Placing economic value on water does not cheapen it as a right, but protects it and encourages its conservation.

A human right to water formulated as a pure positive right may be counterproductive for three primary reasons. First, many countries are reluctant to recognize any right to water because they are concerned that a positive right means free or cheap provision of clean water, which they simply cannot afford without recovering costs from consumers.[88] As such, positive right formulations of a human right to water hostile to cost recovery and appropriate pricing may discourage states from applying a rights framework to their water policy because they are understandably reluctant to assume obligations that they are unable to meet.[89]

Second, lack of cost recovery for water services due to guarantees of low- or no-cost water provision results in degraded treatment and delivery infrastructure and, ultimately, inadequate delivery of poor-quality water. There is a relationship between the economic sustainability of water provision, including consistent delivery and water quality, and the recovery of costs through consumer tariffs equitably based on the ability to pay.[90] The challenges faced by Bolivia and South Africa discussed in this chapter each illustrate how a positive rights approach to water may lead to a failure to properly price water and fully recover costs and ultimately undermine the rationales behind a right to water.

Third, where the positive right to water precludes or discourages cost recovery and water pricing, it may also discourage needed investment in water infrastructure.[91] The capital investment needed for "adequate" water and sanitation infrastructure over the next twenty years exceeds $100 billion per year globally, with regions in most need also least able to absorb those costs.[92] Much of the growing challenge of global water stress can be attributed to a dramatic shortfall in necessary capital to fund improvements in water infrastructure.[93] Africa has 38 percent of its population unserved by safe water, Asia 19 percent (52 percent without access to sanitation services), and Latin America and the Caribbean 15 percent without access to safe water (22 percent without sanitation services).[94] The annual shortfall of needed capital is estimated to be between $10 billion and $32 billion worldwide, with population growth in developing countries far outstripping efforts to make up lost ground. It is simply not possible to meaningfully implement a right to water without dramatic increases in capital expenditures in water infrastructure.[95] Such dramatic increases will not come unless there is support for effective water pricing and cost recovery.

Where the right to water is framed as guaranteed access to water "free of economic encumbrances," such a right is counterproductive to the development and expansion of affordable clean water supplies for all.[96] The challenge presented in formulating a right to water is to meet the purpose of such a right—protecting the disadvantaged, promoting transparency, and prioritizing water—while at the same time ensuring that water provision is economically sustainable by treating water as a valuable and often scarce resource.[97] The recent World Water Commission strongly advocated for full cost pricing of water services, noting that "the single most immediate and important measure that we can recommend is the systematic adoption of full-cost pricing of water services."[98] The concern, however, is the impact full-cost pricing of water will have on the poor in developing countries.[99]

The poor in developing countries often pay up to twenty-five times more for water from private water vendors than those who have access to a regular tap supply.[100] The charges imposed by water vendors are not only evidence of the inequity resulting from certain water policies, but are also evidence that expanding access to tapped and treated water can reduce expenditures on water by the poor. However, such expansion requires investment in infrastructure. When infrastructure for delivery and treatment go unfunded because of a failure to generate revenue and recover costs, water delivery becomes inconsistent, water quality decreases, and the poor suffer most.[101]

Two counterarguments could be made against policies aimed at water cost recovery and water pricing. The first is that large general governmental subsidies allow for payment of water services and infrastructure maintenance and upgrades without requiring consumers to pay water tariffs. Why not just tax big corporations and rich people, and use those taxes to make water free or cheap? Advocacy for the positive right to water is often coupled with arguments in favor of large general water subsidies as a means of ensuring expanded access and maintenance of water infrastructure to poor communities and avoiding rate increases often associated with a private water sector.[102] General water subsidies are motivated predominantly by social objectives, including ensuring water provision to the poor, under the assumption that the poor cannot afford to pay for piped, treated water.[103]

But if they are already paying twenty-five times more for clean water from water vendors, the poor may be better off paying higher rates for improved tap water.[104] Currently, cost recovery of drinking-water services in developing countries is about 35 percent on average.[105] The fiscal burden of underpricing water in developing countries can be conservatively estimated at $13 billion per year, with total subsidies for drinking water in developing countries reaching in excess of $45 billion per year.[106] Big general subsidies may not be helping either the poor or developing countries.

The challenge for a publicly financed, general subsidy approach to water provision is that water rates are set by regulators subject to political pressure.[107] Large water treatment and distribution utilities are natural monopolies.[108] If you do not like the prices charged or service provided by your water utility, you cannot just go to a competitor. The reason for this is that large water systems have high initial start-up costs, creating a barrier to entry into the market. If you don't like your hamburger from McDonald's, you can go to a different restaurant, or even start your own and compete. However, unlike making hamburgers, it is extremely expensive to compete with a water utility, which must build reservoirs, well fields, pipeline distribution systems, and treatment plants at enormous costs. These high costs stifle competitors. Additionally, natural monopolies like water utilities have low marginal costs, meaning once they have invested in those expensive initial costs, it's very cheap for them to provide service to one more customer. Since these enterprises do not have competitive market forces to keep their prices down, the government regulates their prices. Prices have to be set low enough for citizens to afford the services, but high enough to allow for cost recovery and maintenance—effectively, the rates should approximate what the price of water would be in a competitive market.[109]

But these regulators—in some instances, elected officials—face political pressure from the public to keep water rates low. As such, regulators keep rates low, if charged or collected at all, with the water sector receiving large general subsidies to offset lack of cost recovery. Large general subsidies and low rates and collection result in significant waste of water resources because there is no incentive for conservation.[110] Furthermore, public financing of the water sector has demonstrated costs associated with waste and ineffi- ciency. Such general subsidies for drinking water favor the rich, as the rich are more often connected to public water systems than the poor.[111]

The second argument against policies favoring full cost recovery and water pricing is based on concerns about the risks associated with privatization of water resources. Concerns over cost recovery, pricing, and capital investment in infrastructure are often conflated with advocacy for water resource and infrastructure privatization. Privatization of water services, supply, and in- frastructure is a global trend that has created challenges in many nations, in- cluding those illustrated earlier in the Cochabamba Water War in Bolivia.[112] Privatization is advocated on the one hand as a way of facilitating access to capital and technical expertise, promoting efficiency, reducing costs through competitive bidding, expanding access and improving quality.[113] On the other hand, some argue that privatization is a dereliction of the government's public trust in a shared, common resource and unduly burdens the poor as water rates are raised to ensure debts are repaid and profits secured.[114] Although the general merits of privatization are beyond the scope of this chapter (or indeed of this book), it is important to note that cost recovery and effective and reasonable pricing of water as a valuable commodity is not syn- onymous with privatization.[115]

A positive right to water framed in a manner opposed to water pricing and cost recovery is not only counterproductive to its presumed end of protecting disadvantaged communities but also poses risks to ecologic sustainability and human health. Appropriate water pricing encourages sustainable use.[116] According to a World Bank senior executive, "water pricing is an essential instrument to enhance the sustainability of the resource."[117] Free or heavily subsidized water services lead invariably to waste of water resources, with implications for human health, intergenerational equity, and the environment as water is withdrawn faster than it is naturally restored.[118] We waste the things we do not value. I confess I have no idea where I have left any of the free toys I found in cereal boxes over the years, but I know exactly where I parked my car. If we put a price on water that demonstrates how we value it, we are more likely to conserve it.

Large general water subsidies frequently produce waste that is not ecologically sustainable, and general subsidies for water are harmful in the long run to the environment.[119] Large general water subsidies are a major cause of overdevelopment and environmental degradation in arid regions.[120] In developing countries in particular, general water subsidies have been linked to severe environmental damage, such as salinity contamination of rivers, land subsidence, pollution from agricultural runoff, erosion, and loss of biodiversity.[121] Where drinking water is underpriced because of large general subsidies, the lack of incentive to avoid wasting water in domestic uses results in water mining or "overdraft," where water is withdrawn faster than it is naturally recharged, with reduced flow impacting wildlife and nutrient transport and cycling.[122]

The positive right to water often fails to satisfy the justifications for a rights-based approach—equity, priority, and accountability. Because positive rights are often effectively unenforceable, water may not be given high priority by policymakers and governments may not be held accountable for their failure to deliver sufficient quality water. Ultimately, a human right to water, no matter how theoretically appealing, must be evaluated for its pragmatic utility, and implemented in the same way. Without such pragmatism, the human right to water is grounded in nothing more than an altruistic desire to take a symbolic action without regard for the interests of the very people they purport to benefit, and reflect only "the conscience of the more privileged."[123]

Toward an Effective and Enforceable Positive Right to Water

To give effect to the admirable, if often unrealized, aims of the human right to water, I am suggesting three pragmatic reforms that could facilitate the equitable and sustainable implementation of a positive human right to water. Despite its limitations, a practical approach to the human right to water remains important and a tool with tremendous potential. Indeed, the challenges and potential for a human right to water are evident throughout the world, in ways that mirror both Cochabamba and Johannesburg.

The city of Detroit in the United States has faced these challenges as well. Detroit declared bankruptcy because of mounting debt and declining revenues, in part because of the difficult economic conditions faced by the city's residents.[124] Both the city and its residents were impacted in particular in water services, with delinquent water accounts costing the city millions of dollars.[125] Detroit began shutting off water services to these delinquent accounts, resulting in citywide protests that garnered national media attention.[126] As a result of the shutoffs, cost recovery improved as consumers paid overdue bills or entered into a repayment program.[127] Nevertheless, the city stopped shutting off water services after the judge in Detroit's bankruptcy proceedings, the United Nations, protestors, and commentators claimed that this approach violated a fundamental human right.[128] Similar large protests erupted in Dublin in late 2014 in response to Ireland's new water charges as part of the austerity program that formed part of its agreement with the European Union, with opponents arguing that increased water charges violated their human rights.[129]

How can Dublin, Cochabamba, Detroit, and Johannesburg, as well as many other cities, meet the aims of a positive human right to water while avoiding the pitfalls of unsustainable water policies? I propose three modest reforms that could facilitate an equitable and sustainable positive right to water: (1) the creation of specialized tribunals with expertise to adjudicate claims involving rate-setting, disconnection, scope of service, and sustainability; (2) a tariff structure where the largest consumers pay the highest rates, with that revenue then used for directed subsidies to indigent consumers based on their ability to pay; and (3) a transparent and participatory public concession contracting process.

Specialized Tribunals for Public Utilities Cases

Despite the flaws of the positive rights approach, the pursuit of a workable version of such a human right to water could prove invaluable in advancing global water security.[130] However, one of the main obstacles to an enforceable positive right is the relative lack of expertise of most courts in rate-setting, ecology, infrastructure finance, and public health relating to water services. To address this shortfall in institutional competence, states seeking to implement a positive right to water should institute specialized tribunals with relevant expertise to adjudicate these rights.[131]

A specialized court is one with jurisdiction, usually exclusive jurisdiction, in a single legal field.[132] This approach has been applied in the fields of bankruptcy, tax, corporate law, and patents.[133] The institutional competency of specialized courts does more than simply provide a better-informed adjudicator of a complicated dispute, it also better protects positive rights from arbitrary executive action.[134] When a court reviewing executive action lacks field-specific competence relative to the agency it reviews, it typically defers to that agency's expertise, as was the case when the Constitutional Court deferred to the City of Johannesburg in *Mazibuko*.[135] But when the reviewing court has sufficient expertise to effectively review de novo the actions of the executive, and particularly when those actions affect fundamental rights, the court is more likely to provide an effective bulwark against executive overreach.[136]

The use of specialized tribunals in deciding cases involving natural resources is not without precedent. Certain courts in the United States rely on special masters, often experts relied on to perform fact-finding functions for the court, in cases involving complex water rights disputes to review.[137] The state of Colorado relies on special water courts to adjudicate water disputes.[138] These systems involving expert adjudicators in water issues have commended it for their fairness, adaptability, and high levels of expertise.[139]

Specialized courts or judges generally cost more than generalized adjudicators.[140] However, procedural reforms can reduce costs, including required disclosures held in a public database, limits on participation of parties not directly involved in the dispute, and cost sharing for expert engineers and economists relied on as witnesses.[141] Despite the potentially higher costs of specialized courts, this approach has been successfully implemented in tax, bankruptcy, and intellectual property law, so these costs could be worth the investment in the context of the right to water. These courts should be independent of the executive and provide oversight of agency adjudication of disputes involving water services, including disconnection, rate increases, denial of service, or violation of water quality standards. By establishing specialized courts, the positive right to water will not simply be an aspirational statement, but will be a right that can be effectively overseen and enforced by expert judges.

Block Tariffs and Direct Subsidies in Public Utilities

A specialized court is a potentially important step in implementing a positive right to water but it does not address the issues of equity and sustainability. The implementation of a positive right to water must result in affordable water services, but still allow for cost recovery to encourage water conservation and allow for maintenance and reinvestment in water infrastructure. To balance these potentially competing aims, the implementation of a positive right to water requires careful consideration of how water rates are set and recovered.

One possible tariff reform is the adoption of block tariffs. Block tariffs are water rates that increase as consumption increases.[142] Block tariffs can help ensure access to a minimum amount of water at an affordable price, while still facilitating cost recovery and encouraging conservation, particularly among those that consume the most water.[143] The largest water consumers bear the greatest burden of ensuring cost recovery and have a correspondingly greater incentive for conservation.[144] On the other hand, indigent consumers who require only enough public utility service to meet a minimum standard of living would pay the lowest rate, with perhaps an initial block provided without charge.

This approach alone, however, still leaves open the question of whether that low- or no-cost initial block rate would still appropriately encourage conservation and how to subsidize that low rate. The block tariff approach should be coupled with direct public utilities subsidies to indigent consumers based on their ability to pay.[145] Chile has taken an innovative approach along these lines.[146] In 1998, Chile enacted a new law to encourage full cost recovery and equitable pricing.[147] Poor households would go to their local government, which would make an ability-to-pay determination. The household would then pay what it could afford based on the amount of its consumption (thus still encouraging conservation). The local government would then provide a direct subsidy in the form of a "water stamp" to cover the rest of the cost of water provision, similar to a food stamp program.[148]

Despite their promise, block tariffs can disproportionately burden poor households because water vendors may buy water in bulk from the public utility at the higher rate and then pass the cost on to the poor, who often rely on water vendors in developing countries because of a lack of trust in the public water system.[149] Additionally, wealthier households and businesses are more able to bear the cost of water-efficient technologies. By supplementing block tariffs with the Chilean direct subsidy approach, the poor would be able to afford water connections and not need to seek out water vendors. Revenues generated from higher rates charged to larger consumers would fund directed subsidies, the water stamps, at the local level, distributed based on customers' ability to pay as determined by the municipal authority.

This approach has potential risks and problems. The energy and agricultural industries are the largest water consumers, so would be charged the highest rates.[150] But if the costs of higher water rates are simply passed on to poorer households in the form of more expensive food and energy, then this policy would not be affordable or equitable. The embedded nature of water—virtual water—makes it difficult to establish equitable water pricing without any increased block rates being reflected in the costs of other goods and services. But ultimately, the essential role of household water for drinking, sanitation, and hygiene may weigh in favor of this combined block tariff–direct subsidy approach, despite these risks. Indeed, these risks are arguably smaller than those associated with policies favoring large general subsidies for the water sector.

Large general subsidies could allow for payment of public utility services without requiring consumers to pay high tariffs.[151] These general subsidies would be funded from general tax revenue.[152] Advocacy for positive rights is often coupled with arguments in favor of large general subsidies as a means of ensuring expanded access to poor communities and avoiding rate increases.[153] The economic burden of underpriced water in developing countries is approximately $13 billion per year, with total subsidies for drinking water in developing countries exceeding $45 billion per year.[154] The cost-recovery gap will ultimately harm the poor most. The rich will benefit from subsidized utility services, and the poor will be left without access, with poor quality, or with higher rates they must pay to vendors.[155] The ability-to-pay determination, combined with water stamps funded from revenues generated through block tariffs, facilitates both cost-internalization of all consumers and full cost recovery, while also providing affordable water services without excessive public debt.

Effective Concession Contracts for Public Utilities

The ultimate success or failure of tariff reforms may depend on the degree to which any private water provider partners with the state in facilitating a positive right to water. If water systems are going to be designed, owned, or operated by private enterprises, then water rates should be high enough to achieve cost recovery and encourage conservation, while also attracting capital, maintaining credit, and retaining expertise. But if water rates are set too high and the government fails to provide effective oversight, then any positive right to water is undermined by poor quality and unaffordable prices. Where there is little transparency or stakeholder involvement in water policy, corruption may prove the biggest threat to the prospect of an effective human right to water.

The process for contracting with a private enterprise to operate the water system in Cochabamba is a cautionary tale for any state attempting to implement a human right to water through privatization. Equitable and affordable pricing are impossible if the concession contract establishes a rate of return for the private enterprise that allows for monopolistic pricing. The process failed in Cochabamba because of a lack of transparency, legitimacy, and oversight of the concession contract. The return for the private enterprise in the concession must be large enough to attract good management and achieve economies of scale, and the length of the contract term should be long enough to encourage management commitment and continuity.[156] However, the term must also be short enough to provide for regular review and encourage performance to secure another contract.[157] Effective government oversight also requires performance reviews at regular intervals during the contract term, with underperformance resulting in penalties or contract rescission.[158] This approach facilitates public-private coordination and contract compliance.

This type of effective government oversight begins even before the contract, during the process of identifying and issuing the concession contract. The concession must be made through a transparent competitive bidding process.[159] The power of competition to achieve efficient pricing cannot be ignored even in the case of natural monopolies like water services. Competitive bidding processes avoid corruption and facilitate affordable rates by awarding concession contracts to the party able to achieve the objectives of a positive right to water. The contract itself must facilitate transparency by providing clear objectives and requiring the disclosure of essential information to consumers and regulators. Such requirements are essential to discourage corruption in concession contracting, so that governments do not reward poor performance and do not issue contracts based on bribes or personal relationships.[160]

The process for granting a concession contract must also be perceived as legitimate by water consumers. The concession contract should require a participatory stakeholder process and consumer consultation during the term of the contract.[161] Legitimacy, sustainability, and racial and gender equality in public utilities provision are achieved most effectively through community engagement and are the hallmarks of an effective positive right.[162] Equitable and affordable water services cannot be provided if consumer voices are ignored, marginalized, or silenced.

Conclusion

Of course, water privatization through concession contracts is not necessary in all instances to achieve a human right to water. Many arguments in favor of a human right to water are based on concerns about the risks associated with privatization of water services.[163] Privatization of water systems is a global trend that has created challenges in many nations, but it is also advocated as a response to the failure of public operation of water systems, with both arguments finding evidence in the example of the Cochabamba Water War. Privatization is advocated as a way of facilitating access to capital and technical expertise, promoting efficiency, reducing costs through competitive bidding, expanding access, and improving quality.[164] There are strong arguments, depending on the situation, for privatization, public ownership, and for a hybrid public-private partnership. However, where private enterprises are involved in water services, as seen in the Cochabamba example, corruption and a lack of transparency and public participation will frustrate efforts to secure a workable human right to water.

4

Water Security and Racial Discrimination

The water challenges in places like Flint, Michigan, and Johannesburg, South Africa, are often about something more than prioritizing water provision or protecting public health. In some instances, and in these two instances in particular, water policy is about confronting racial discrimination. There is no escaping the racial implications of the lead contamination in Flint. The water challenge confronting Flint was not unique.[1] A city struggles with declining revenues, so the city pursues a cheaper alternative water supply from a nearby river. The river water is contaminated, and when that water is run through the city's outdated infrastructure, the water leaches lead from the pipes and solder. This approach—effectively what happened in Flint involving a shift to a cheaper, but lower quality, water source—is not unheard of, and while obviously a serious problem, need not be a public health crisis. Flint is a public health crisis because the consequences of this approach were hidden from the community and the community's concerns were largely dismissed. And Flint is predominantly black.

A civil rights commission issued a 129-page report stating that civil rights violations involved in the Flint water crisis were, in part, attributable to "historical, structural and systemic racism combined with implicit bias."[2] The report was issued after a year-long investigation and concluded: "The people of Flint have been subjected to unprecedented harm and hardship, much of it caused by structural and system discrimination and racism that have corroded your city, your institutions, and your water pipes, for generations."[3] The problem of racism in water services in the United States is not limited to Flint, with communities like Campti, Louisiana, facing similar problems.[4] Even where there are not infrastructure and water quality failures and violations of public reporting requirements, protests in Detroit against water shutoffs predominantly impacting black citizens illustrate how water policies can have disproportionate racial impacts. The problems in Detroit, Flint, and Campti are unfortunately only examples of a broader challenge of racism in water policy in the United States.[5]

These problems are not limited to the United States. As in Flint, there is no escaping the racial implications in the "free basic water" program in

Johannesburg. The decision to provide a minimum amount of water for free, and then require prepayment to continue water services, was not established uniformly across the city. Instead, this "free basic water" program was implemented only in communities like Phiri—historically black and economically disadvantaged townships.[6] The South African Constitutional Court not only upheld the city's selective implementation of prepaid water services in predominantly black townships but also held that such facially race-neutral policies did not constitute unlawful discrimination.[7] However, the court did not consider how the legacy of apartheid has impacted the ability of many black residents in the city to pay for water services.[8] These disparate impacts of water policy decisions are evident around the world not only in racial discrimination but ethnic discrimination as well. The Romani are an ethnic group living in small communities around the world, and in Europe especially, and have faced discrimination and negligence in the provision of water services in many nations.[9] Evictions, water service disconnection, and contaminated water provision in Romani communities in Europe has resulted in claims that water polices in some nations violate the Romani's human rights.[10]

The racial and ethnic implications of water policies are often even more challenging in the context of indigenous communities. Frequently, indigenous communities face the same kinds of discriminatory policies or disparate impacts as other minority groups. But these impacts are magnified by the cultural or spiritual connection many indigenous communities have with their traditional water sources and the deep familiarity with these systems built over millennia.[11] This has resulted in complex water disputes, like the challenge the Navajo Nation brought against the U.S. government over the use of wastewater to make artificial snow on the San Francisco Peaks or opposition by the Standing Rock Sioux against the Dakota Access Pipeline.[12] The impacts of water policy often touch on the very nature of indigeneity. Water rights disputes between the Navajo and the Hopi people in the southwestern United States, or between Israelis, Jordanians, and Palestinians, are often framed in terms of who was here first and thus has the superior claim to the water.[13]

This chapter will address the more general challenge of racial and ethnic discrimination in water policy and the role of water insecurity in aggravating racial and ethnic inequality. I will also propose some measures governments and minority communities can take to address racial discrimination in water services. But I will also focus part of this chapter on the more specific challenge facing indigenous communities in asserting their unique claims to water resources.

Discrimination and Water Policy

Around the same time the Constitutional Court was hearing the claims of the residents of Phiri regarding South Africa's constitutional right to water, another case involving water was proceeding in neighboring Botswana. Matsipane was a member of the Basarwa, an indigenous community that has lived for generations in the Kalahari Desert. The government of Botswana created the Central Kalahari Game Reserve (CKGR) as a national park in Botswana in 1961, which included much of the Basarwa's traditional lands.[14] As part of an attempt to eliminate human impacts within the game reserve, the Botswanan government decommissioned the Basarwa wells within the CKGR.[15] These wells were the main source of water for the community, and their decommissioning resulted in serious health complications for the Basarwa.[16] The Court of Appeals of Botswana noted that the *Matsipane* case is "a harrowing story of human suffering and despair caused by a shortage of water in the harsh climatic conditions of the Kalahari Desert where the appellants and their Basarwa community live."[17] Unlike in South Africa and in Mazibuko and the Phiri community, there was no positive right to water under the Constitution of Botswana for Matsipane and the Basarwa to assert against the government.

The Basarwa, however, were able to use a negative right guaranteed under the Constitution of Botswana to secure access to water resources on their traditional lands.[18] The Basarwa relied on Section 7(1) of the Constitution of Botswana, which provides that "[n]o person shall be subjected to torture or to inhuman or degrading punishment or other treatment."[19] This negative rights approach to securing access to water has certain advantages over a positive rights approach, and particular advantages for marginalized communities facing racism in water policy implementation. Unlike South Africa's Constitutional Court decision in *Mazibuko*, and indeed most other positive rights to water conditioned upon water provision via "progressive realization," the appellate court in Botswana noted that the negative right constitutional guarantees, like the one at issue in *Matsipane*, are "absolute and unqualified."[20] The Botswanan court concluded, given how the Basarwa suffered from lack of water, that the denial of access to wells constituted a violation of the Basarwa's constitutional right to be free from degrading treatment.[21] The government subsequently recommissioned and maintained the wells, with the Basarwa paying tariffs to cover the costs of maintenance.[22] The court's decision immediately secured water resources for the Basarwa without requiring the court to make a technical determination of a minimum core of water quantity and quality to meet basic needs, and the decision did not require an unsustainable approach to water provision.

As I have already discussed, the positive rights approach to water policy raises potential problems associated with enforcement, economic and ecologic sustainability, and public health. An alternative approach, aimed at achieving appropriate prioritization of water, equitable water policies, and accountability in water management while avoiding problems of enforceability and sustainability, is reliance on existing negative rights. Such negative rights, unlike positive rights, would be immediately binding and enforceable and would not require courts to make technical determinations regarding the minimum quantity or quality of water required. Additionally, because negative rights are largely procedural or involve government forbearance rather than an affirmative obligation to expend resources (at least not at the level of capital-intensive water infrastructure), negative rights do not raise the same issues of economic and ecologic sustainability as positive rights. This negative rights approach is particularly relevant in the context of communities facing racism or other forms of discrimination, because a common negative right is the right to equal protection of the law.[23] For example, the U.N. Human Rights Committee commented on Israel's approach to water provision in Palestinian territories, arguing that the denial of water could constitute a violation of the right to equal protection under the law.[24] Under international law, the advantages of a negative rights approach to water policy are even more pronounced. Negative rights guaranteed under the U.N. Covenant on Civil and Political Rights (the "CP Covenant") are more jurisprudentially mature than positive rights under the U.N. Covenant on Economic, Social, and Cultural Rights (the "ESC Covenant"), and allow for claims to be brought by nonstate actors under a binding Optional Protocol, unlike the ESC Covenant.[25] One way to distinguish these two approaches is that the positive right is a "right to water" (meaning a right to receive a certain amount and quality of water at a certain price for a certain use), whereas the negative right is a "right in water" (meaning an interest in the management of the resource held equally by all citizens).

However, there are obvious limitations to these types of negative rights claims in the context of water. In *Matsipane*, in particular, the right at issue is a broad and rather uniquely formulated right and particularly well suited to the unique facts of the case.[26] Additionally, these claims are not necessarily aimed at water, but are fundamentally about addressing discrimination that is manifesting itself in water services, and likely in other ways. Furthermore, these claims assume the state is discriminating in its water provision or management, but in some instances, particularly in developing countries, the state's failure may have more to do with available resources than with racial or ethnic animus. A negative right in water should satisfy the three objectives of a positive right to water—equity, priority, and accountability. How such a right functions, the foundations upon which it can be built, and how it might achieve these objectives, are evident in the historic foundations of a negative right in water.

As I discussed previously, the human right to water has historic roots in many cultures and legal traditions. Some of these approaches have been spread around the world through empires, like the natural use concept in Roman riparian rights and *shafa*, or the right to quench thirst, under Sharia law as spread through the Ottoman water code, the *Majalla*. These approaches, however, are emblematic of a positive rights approach to the human right to water. The negative rights approach has a similar history and has similarly been spread by large empires. Under British law, the king could grant charters (monopolies) to certain enterprises, but these charters came with strict obligations.[27] These obligations function as a quid pro quo of sorts—the state grants a monopoly to an enterprise, and in return, the enterprise assumes certain duties. One is the duty to serve, which means to accept all customers without discrimination. This is a legal obligation on any public utility granted a natural monopoly by the state, including water utilities. The duty to serve is thus a proto-human right and bulwark against discrimination in the context of public services, in that it guarantees an affordable price and access to all similarly situated people served by the utility.[28]

The "public trust doctrine" is another legal doctrine, like the duty to serve, with roots in Roman and British law and is recognized in many countries that are former colonies of both empires. Under this doctrine, water is held in trust by the government, with the government having a fiduciary obligation to manage water for the benefit of all citizens.[29] While the public trust doctrine is interpreted and applied differently through the world, it is widely recognized legal doctrine in many parts of Africa, Asia, the Americas, and

Europe.[30] Furthermore, the public trust doctrine is increasingly recognized as customary international law.[31] The public trust doctrine constitutes both a negative limitation on the government inequitably managing water and an affirmative obligation on the government to protect water held in trust for all.[32]

These three broadly recognized legal doctrines—the right to equal protection under the law, the common law duty to serve for all public utilities, and the public trust doctrine—provide the foundation for a negative right in water. Where the government provides or prices water services in a way that discriminates on the basis of race or ethnicity, it violates these citizens' rights to equal protection under the law, the water utility violates its common law duty to serve, and the government violates its fiduciary duty under the public trust doctrine to manage water for the benefit of all citizens. This approach has the same primary objectives as the positive right to water—it prioritizes water as an essential right, it focuses on its equitable provision, and it facilitates government accountability by providing citizens with a cause of action against the government when it mismanages water resources.

South Africa and the *Mazibuko* case provide excellent context to understand how the negative right in water based on these three legal doctrines could operate to protect individuals and communities facing discriminatory water policies. The public trust doctrine is enshrined in South Africa's National Water Act and the National Environmental Management Act.[33] The South African Constitution provides that "[e]veryone is equal before the law and has the right to equal protection and the benefit of the law."[34] South Africa is a former British colony, and recognizes many aspects of British common law, including the common law duty to serve for public utilities.[35] In addition to pursuing a positive rights claim under the constitutional guaranty of water, Mazibuko and the residents of Phiri claimed that the prepaid water program violated their right to equal protection because it discriminated against them on the basis of race, as evidenced by the fact that predominantly white townships in Johannesburg did not have a prepaid water system. Additionally, though, Mazibuko could have claimed that, as beneficiaries of the water under the public trust doctrine, the city violated its fiduciary obligation to effectively include them as stakeholders in the development of the "free basic water" program on an equal basis. Finally, Mazibuko could have claimed that the city breached its duty to serve in discriminating against them as compared to other communities. A similar approach could be taken in other communities where these legal doctrines are recognized, including in Flint, Detroit, Botswana, and Bolivia.[36] This approach may also be viable in international tribunals that recognize these doctrines.[37]

This approach may not guarantee an actual quantity and quality of water at an affordable price, but it avoids some of the sustainability problems associated with the positive right to water while still advancing its main justifications—prioritizing water policy, requiring equitable water provision, and providing a means for disadvantaged or discriminated communities to hold the government accountable in water services and to have a voice in the development of water policy.

Despite its advantages over a positive right, the negative right in water is no panacea. A participation rights approach in water policy in general has several potential limitations. First, the successful assertion of such a right requires the recognition of one or more of these three legal doctrines, which while common due to their imperial origins, are by no means universal. Even where recognized, these doctrines may be underdeveloped or weakly enforced, and modes of interpreting and implementing these principles will vary widely between countries. Second, disadvantaged people facing discriminatory water policies are likely to face discrimination or marginalization in other aspects of civic affairs, including in access to courts and lawyers and having the means to fund litigation or be aware of their rights. Third, this negative rights approach is iterative and ad hoc and lacks potential for integrated water policies.

As I have already noted, many of the countries that recognize a positive right to water in their constitutions are countries that nevertheless struggle to equitably and sustainably provide water resources. But this may say less about the viability of such rights than it does about the importance of a strong civil society. Indeed, government incompetence or corruption is often as much a cause of drought as the climate.[38] Strengthening civil society, improving governance institutions, combating corruption through transparency, and protecting civil and political rights are essential for equitable and sustainable water resource management.[39] This creates a difficult chicken-or-egg problem for water policymakers trying to prioritize their efforts. Is water security a function of a free and prosperous society, or is a free and prosperous society a function of water-security?

Perhaps the most obvious objection to a negative rights approach to water policy is that a participation right does not actually require the delivery of sufficient clean water. So long as governments provide due process and avoid authorizing unreasonable or nonbeneficial uses of water, there is no recourse against the government for those disproportionately suffering from water stress. A person may avoid discrimination, deprivation of property without due process, or curtailment of freedom of religion, but still be dying of thirst or cholera. Such a person is, in effect, reading Pushkin without boots on his feet. A negative right in water may maintain and improve control over water resources and hold government actors accountable for discriminatory policies or exclusionary stakeholder processes, but it may still fail to ensure adequate water provision. But when combined with the reforms I have discussed in implementing a positive right to water, a negative rights approach has great potential for addressing the types of discriminatory water policies implemented in many parts of the world.

A negative right in water is more than a strategic decision of selecting a right that is immediately binding and more likely to be enforced as compared to the positive right. It is also more than the cautious approach of using rights rhetoric while avoiding issues of sustainability incidental to many positive rights. A negative right in water would foster participatory and adaptive water governance by encouraging a more inclusive and diverse community engaged in water policy formulation. A negative right in water gives those suffering most from water stress, and most often excluded or discriminated against in water services, the necessary legal leverage to secure a place at the stakeholder table in the development of water policy.

This leverage facilitates a broadly inclusive stakeholder group, with the least advantaged empowered by an enforceable right. Individuals or communities suffering from water stress who may otherwise be marginalized in water policy development use the negative rights approach to enforce a transparent and inclusive process in water policy development and implementation. Such a process builds a "normative community" within which values of equity, inclusivity, and sustainability develop organically.[40] A negative rights approach could be best suited for ensuring diverse and representative stakeholder participation because of the focus of participation rights on equal protection and nondiscrimination. This includes stakeholder participation in tendering concession contracts (meaning governments contracting with private parties to provide public goods, like water utilities), setting water rates, and financing water infrastructure. These rights therefore provide not only the basis for holding the government accountable in discriminatory water cutoffs or rate increases or rate structures but also in discriminatory exclusion from the processes establishing the regulations underlying these actions.

Beyond facilitating transparency to prevent discriminatory policies or acts and creating legal leverage for diverse and inclusive stakeholder participation, a negative rights approach to water policy also facilitates policy experimentation and adaptation. Experimentalism and adaptive management are part of so-called "new governance" methods adapted from the industrial management context.[41] The *Mazibuko* case and Johannesburg are again illustrative. In that positive rights context, the city had a "one-size-fits-all" approach to water quantity (six kiloliters per household per month) in part because the city was not familiar with the household sizes in Phiri. By including a diverse group of voices in water policy development, water policy can adapt to new information and differences between communities, and change as they learn new information from stakeholders.[42] Had the residents of Phiri recognized and enforced a right to be included and participate in water policy development, perhaps the "free basic water" program could have been effectively adapted to that community's unique needs and conditions.

Adaptive management is "a systematic process for continually improving management policies and practices by learning from the outcomes of implemented management strategies."[43] This experimental and adaptive approach requires multiple institutions or jurisdictions implementing different, parallel strategies to achieve the same policy end. These separate institutions or jurisdictions collect data and compare costs, benefits, and outcomes, including evaluating whether success or failure can be reproduced in other institutions or jurisdictions or if success or failure could be attributed to unique local or institutional issues. It is not possible to successfully adapt if some communities' voices are excluded or ignored.

Governments operating under an experimentalist approach to water policy do not come up with a one-size-fits-all, once-and-for-all solution, but instead encourage a participatory and deliberative process adapted to each community and continuously updated as the community changes.[44] There is some evidence that an approach of recognizing and enforcing rights with an eye toward policy experimentation and adaptation, grounded in these theories of new governance, yield positive results in water policy. Commentators have noted the success of the European Union Water Framework Directive in establishing an enforceable right of stakeholders to participate in the development of water policy and that such enforcement has improved access and sustainability, as well as adaptation and awareness of different community needs and conditions.[45] The success of a participatory, localized, and experimental process based on new governance approaches is not unique to the

European Union. An empirical analysis of forty-seven case studies around the world involving a similar approach has demonstrated improvements in sustainable resource management when integrated with an inclusive stakeholder process and adaptive management.[46] This approach may be particularly useful in the example of the Romani people, who face widespread ethnic discrimination in many E.U. countries, and in particular in ways manifested in water services.

A rights-based approach to water policy is not about an expansive interpretation of "rights," but is about participatory governance.[47] Without the legal leverage of rights, discrimination against individuals and communities, whether overtly aggressive or the result of institutionalized and historic bigotry that might not be evident to privileged communities, results not only in poor water provision, but exclusion from the very processes that could improve water services for these communities. Water policy thus is a negative feedback loop, where exclusion from water policy development begets poor water services for marginalized communities, who then lack the water access necessary to effectively engage in water policy development.[48] An enforceable negative right in water would ideally empower disadvantaged groups to influence water policy without requiring unsustainable water provision that fails to account for local conditions. The growing global water crisis is not a crisis of nature or lack of available technology. There is enough water, and the capacity to produce enough clean water, to meet existing and expected global populations.[49] The water crisis is a crisis of governance.[50] Rights to equal protection, the public trust doctrine, and the duty to serve provide a foundation upon which to build a broadly inclusive water community by giving the least advantaged the legal leverage necessary to engage in the stakeholder process at the local level, thereby promoting an adaptive and nuanced water policy.

Water Security and Indigenous Communities

Virtually all of the challenges, and potential legal claims, I have discussed in this chapter apply equally, if not even more so, to indigenous communities. Indeed, the Basarwa example in Botswana is an example of disparate racial impacts in water policy impacting an indigenous group, and the potential benefits of a negative rights approach for indigenous communities to secure access to traditional water resources. Indigenous people are the first human inhabitants of a territory and often confront discrimination through the legacy of invasion and colonization of their traditional lands. Indigenous peoples are often uniquely marginalized in water policy, but also may provide uniquely beneficial perspectives in water policy. I will discuss these challenges and opportunities in four broad categories. First, indigenous groups, by virtue of their generations of experience, often have a familiarity with local water resources that greatly exceeds that of any other colonizing group in that region. Second, while not universally true, indigenous communities frequently have a unique spiritual and cultural connection to their traditional waters. Third, indigenous claims to water resources often raise sovereignty concerns in ways not implicated in other instances of discriminatory water policies. Fourth, indigenous rights to resources are often asserted on a "first-in-time, first-in-right" basis, and indigenous people are first in time.

Regarding the first broad category—the unique and extensive experience indigenous people have with their traditional waters—a helpful illustration can be found by referring back to the Altaian people in the Katun River basin in Siberia I mentioned in the introduction. The Altaians are a Turkic indigenous community who have lived in Siberia for generations. Their traditional religious beliefs prohibit the subjugation of the natural world.[51] Based on these beliefs, the Altaians opposed the construction of a dam on the Katun River within their traditional territory. Part of their strategy in successfully opposing the dam was informing scientists of their approach to characterizing fish species within the river basin based on physical characteristics, and their knowledge of the medicinal properties of certain plants that would have been harmed by the dam's development.[52] This information revealed undiscovered species within the river basin and potentially beneficial resources that were not previously known to scientists without the Altaians' knowledge, gained through generations of familiarity. This type of knowledge is often referred to as "traditional ecological knowledge" meaning a "body of knowledge, practice and belief, evolving by adaptive processes and handed down through generations by cultural transmission, about the relationship of living beings (including humans) with one another and with their environment."[53]

Discrimination against indigenous peoples in the development and implementation of water policy not only violates the types of negative rights to equal protection and nondiscrimination discussed previously but risks excluding essential traditional ecological knowledge that could improve water management. Of course, referencing the Altaians' knowledge in protecting the Katun River basin runs the risk of promoting the myth of the "ecologically noble savage."[54] While indigenous peoples' traditional ecological knowledge may prove invaluable to resource management, they may engage in resource mismanagement like any other community. The indigenous people of Rapa Nui—commonly referred to as Easter Island—engaged in wide-scale deforestation and introduced harmful invasive species that brought about the near collapse of their civilization.[55] Nevertheless, eons of experience managing a resource invariably generates useful knowledge, often embedded in and transmitted by cultural or religious means, which can benefit everyone who shares the resource and will harm all if excluded from management by discriminatory policies.

The second broad category of unique issues confronting indigenous communities in water policy—the cultural or religious significance of water for many of the communities—is evidenced again by the Altaian people. Their religious traditions communicated over generations the community's ecological knowledge related to the river and how it might be effectively managed.[56] The Altaian opposition to dam development in the Katun River basin based on their religious traditions is similar to the Navajo opposition to the use of treated wastewater to make artificial snow on their sacred mountains, also referenced in the introduction to this book.[57] In cases where discriminatory water policies impact religious uses or meaning of water resources for indigenous people, such cases expand the potential negative rights claims beyond claims of equal protection. The vast majority of national constitutions include clauses protecting the free exercise of religion and prohibiting governmental overreach or discrimination in the area of religious expression.[58] This same principle is reflected in international law.[59] Thus, in the same way the Basarwa people could claim water policies violated their right to be free from degrading or inhumane treatment, or the people of Flint could argue that the failure to disclose elevated lead in drinking water violated their right to equal protection under each country's respective constitution, so indigenous communities facing discriminatory water policies that implicate the religious use or meaning of water could claim that such policies violate constitutional protections of freedom of religion or violate human rights protecting religious expression under international law.

These religious rights claims, however, are complicated. Should the sacred nature of the Katun River to the Altaian's preclude the development of a dam, which may improve drought and flood resiliency in the basin and generate renewable hydroelectric energy? Should the sacred nature of the San

Francisco Peaks to the Navajos preclude using recycled water to conserve freshwater and operate ski resorts that provide jobs to local communities, including many Navajo people? The connection between indigenous religious rights claims and their traditional ecological knowledge may seem to weigh in favor of taking these claims very seriously, but religiously-based claims to water resources or management practices risks privelging a minority religious belief over widely beneficial water policies.

Successful religious rights claims by indigenous peoples may establish precedent for other parties with less experience with the resource and less responsible approaches to resource management making religious claims to secure water rights. Imagine someone founding the Holy Mountain Church, with rituals based on snow skiing, asserting a competing religious rights claim to the Navajos in the dispute involving the San Francisco Peaks. But the difference between that kind of claim and religious claims by indigenous peoples is that the religious practices of indigenous peoples have legal relevance precisely because of their status as long-standing, demonstrable tradition. For example, Article 25 of the U.N. Declaration on the Rights of Indigenous Peoples states that indigenous peoples "have the right to maintain and strengthen their distinctive spiritual relationship with their traditionally owned or otherwise occupied and used land, territories, [and] waters."[60] The demonstrable fact that the spiritual relationship with the water is traditional changes the strength of any legal claims to resources based on religious rights.

The traditional and cultural connection indigenous people have with their resources can provide the basis for even broader claims of human rights than those founded on freedom of religion. For example, in 2001, the Inter-American Court for Human Rights (IACHR) held that the American Convention on Human Rights includes the right of indigenous peoples to protect their traditional natural resources. The IACHR held that Nicaragua violated the rights of the indigenous Awas Tingni people by granting a timber concession to a logging company within the tribe's traditional lands without the tribe's consent.[61] Similarly, in 2001, the African Commission on Human and Peoples' Rights found that the contamination of the Ogoni people's water supply by petroleum production operations in the Niger River delta violated the community's rights to health and a clean environment.[62]

The third broad category of issues complicating the intersection of discriminatory water policies and indigenous people is that these claims often implicate issues of sovereignty that are not necessarily involved when other minority groups face discrimination. For example, the doctrine of "beneficial use" governs water rights in most of the western United States. The doctrine use means that a water right is only legally recognized if the water is put to a "beneficial use," typically meaning a statutorily defined use that is accepted as beneficial to society, like agriculture, industrial, domestic, or recreational uses.[63] The Wind River Reservation, encompassing the indigenous Shoshone and Arapahoe people, developed the Wind River Water Code, which provides that religious and in-stream uses of water fall within the definition of "beneficial use," thereby legally protecting water rights based on ceremonial and ecological conservation uses.[64] So in these instances, indigenous legal regimes and doctrines may collide with those of colonizing jurisdictions, so that the claims by indigenous people go beyond discrimination or violations of basic rights and into interference with sovereign authority.[65] The question is not only "What did the government do wrong?" but the more complicated question of "Who is the legitimate government?"

For example, the Pueblo of Isleta, a tribal nation located in the southwestern U.S., sought approval from the U.S. Environmental Protection Agency (EPA) for water quality standards established by the tribe.[66] The standards proposed by the Pueblo were more stringent than the EPA-approved water quality standards established by states neighboring the Pueblo, in part because the Pueblo sought protection for ceremonial water uses.[67] The EPA approved these standards, in an acknowledgment of the tribe's sovereignty.[68] However, upstream states and water users complained that these stringent standards were unreasonable (in part because they were based on religious beliefs, and thus not based on best available science) and placed an undue burden on their water uses.[69] These sorts of interjurisdictional disputes between sovereigns are not in play in other instances of discriminatory water policies. These issues are perhaps most legally salient in the United States or other countries that recognize some form of sovereignty for indigenous peoples. But many countries are, or will be, confronting these issues as indigenous people assert sovereignty claims. For example, European colonizers in Australia claimed dominion over resources on that continent under the doctrine of *terra nullius* (or land belonging to no one). In many instances of colonization, the colonizers would declare *terra nullius*—essentially concluding that the land is vacant and legally owned by no one, despite the presence of indigenous peoples and their obvious occupation and use of the land.[70] In a case called *Mabo v. Queensland*, the High Court of Australia rejected the doctrine of *terra nullius*, and recognized the land rights of certain aboriginal Australians and Torres Strait Islanders.[71]

However, Australia's legal regime struggles with how to confront the legacy of *aqua nullius*, or the idea of "water belonging to no one."[72] There are growing calls for an approach along the lines of the *Mabo* case, with litigation efforts aimed at overturning *aqua nullius* and recognizing the water rights of aboriginal Australians.[73] Part of this effort has included the recognition of aboriginal rights to "cultural flows" in the Murray-Darling River Basin, recognizing and legally protecting the cultural value of water released to the streams for indigenous people within the basin.[74] This has included a commitment from the government to provide $40 million to acquire water entitlements committed to aboriginal Australians for cultural and economic uses.[75]

The colonial legacy of concepts like *aqua nullius* speaks to unique issue of the sovereignty of indigenous peoples. But these legal doctrines also apply in the context of the fourth broad category of unique challenges and opportunities confronting indigenous peoples facing discriminatory water policies—property rights in water based on a "first-in-time, first-in-right" claim. Even if indigenous communities are not legally considered "sovereigns" over water under a given nation's laws, they may nevertheless be water rights owners. Indeed, indigenous peoples may be owners with superior claim to others by virtue of the ancient character of their claims. So much of our lives, explicitly or implicitly, are governed by this simple rule—whoever gets to the resource first has the better claim to all subsequent claimants. We wait in lines at bus stops and box offices based on this principle. We allocate items on the shelves of grocery stores or parking spots in public parking lots based on this principle. And in many jurisdictions, we allocate rights to shared water resources based on this principle.

This seems like a simple and fair way to allocate resources, rights, and interests, and that is likely why it so common, from parking spots and movie tickets to bus seats and water rights. And the claim of "we were here first" is a common foundation for the claim of indigenous peoples to their traditional lands and resources. However, these sorts of claims are often much more complicated than they seem, with complex legal disputes over what "we" and "here" and "first" mean. Often, these disputes resemble an experience I had with my children as we were leaving the movie theater. When getting in the car, as is typical where I'm from, my children understand that the person who first yells "Shotgun!" gets the front passenger seat. As we were leaving the movie theater, my son yelled "Shotgun!" My oldest daughter, however, explained, "You can't just yell 'Shotgun!' It only counts if you yell 'Shotgun!' when you can see the car." So we rounded the corner and spotted the car, and my younger daughter yelled "Shotgun!" My oldest daughter explained, "It doesn't count if you see the car and yell 'Shotgun!' first. You have to see the car, be standing on the same surface as the car, and yell 'Shotgun!' " At which point, my oldest daughter hopped off the concrete curb and onto the asphalt parking lot surface and yelled, "Shotgun!" The other children conceded as if they had been defeated by sound legal reasoning. They shrugged their shoulders as if to say, "Well, that's the law."

A similar phenomenon can occur when indigenous people seek to lay claim to water rights based on the same seemingly simple, "first-in-time, first-in-right" rule. For example, recognition of "aboriginal title" or customary law exists under both Roman and British law and thus has been integrated into the legal systems of many former colonies of both of these empires.[76] Under this principle, indigenous peoples could assert rights to land or resources if their use of the land or resources is (1) ancient (typically meaning predating colonization); (2) reasonable (typically meaning within a scope that would not preclude other reasonable uses); (3) certain (typically meaning having strong evidentiary support); and (4) uniformly observable.[77] Some countries formulate the requirements for establishing aboriginal title slightly differently. For example, Canadian courts have recognized customary law as a potential basis for aboriginal claims to title and rights to land use. To assert such rights, indigenous communities in Canada must demonstrate (1) that their ancestors were members of an organized society; (2) that the organized society occupied the specific territory over which the indigenous community asserts title or right; (3) the occupation was to the exclusion of other organized societies; and (4) the occupation preceded colonization.[78] Canadian law views such claims as establishing a spectrum of interests, with absolute ownership at one end, no claim at all on the other, and in the middle, some limited right of use or occupancy.[79]

Effectively, this law both recognizes and complicates the otherwise simple "first-in-time, first-in-right" principle, just as my oldest daughter did with her younger siblings' claims of "shotgun" rights. Indigenous communities can establish claims to land and resources predating colonization based on their claim to being first in time, but must make complicated and potentially difficult demonstrations to tribunals interpreting colonial laws. How ancient, reasonable, and certain enough must claims be to be successful, and where will "success" be placed on a spectrum of rights? Aboriginal title provides a possible avenue for indigenous communities to seek redress in discriminatory water policies by securing some ownership of traditional waters, but also risks facing discrimination in the interpretation of what, at least on its face, seems like a simple and fair assertion: "We have some superior claim to this water because we used it first."

South Africa provides an example of how these sorts of aboriginal title claims might work. The indigenous people of the Richtersveld region occupied their land for centuries, long before European colonization, until their land was largely turned over to international corporations for diamond mining.[80] Under South Africa's 1994 Restitution of Land Rights Act (RLRA), which aimed to turn back discriminatory land deals made during the apartheid regime, indigenous communities could secure title to traditional lands by demonstrating "exclusive beneficial occupation" for at least ten years prior to annexation by the British Crown in 1847.[81] The Richtersveld community brought suit under the RLRA, claiming title to land and waters in the region. The Land Claims Court of South Africa denied the Richtersveld community's claim, which was appealed to the South African Constitutional Court.[82] While the Constitutional Court upheld the lower court's denial of the Richtersveld community's RLRA claim, it upheld their claim under common law aboriginal title based on the community's own demonstrated indigenous law.[83]

The western United States allocates water rights largely on a "first-in-time, first-in-right" basis for all water right claimants, not just indigenous peoples. This approach—called the doctrine of prior appropriation—provides that earlier water users have superior claim to the quantity they used as compared to all subsequent users. So, for example, imagine a farmer diverted ten cubic meters of water in 1875 to irrigate corn. Another farmer came in 1900, and diverted another ten cubic meters to mine copper. A third came in 1925 and did the same thing to provide water to a town. Each water user has a water right to ten cubic meters each year for that particular use, with a priority date set the date they first used the water. If there is only fifteen cubic meters of water in the river in a given year, then the 1875 farmer gets the full allocation of ten cubic meters, the 1900 miner gets only half of the allocation, and all other users are left high and, quite literally, dry. This is a simplified illustration of a regime that often includes thousands of water users with a variety of uses and quantities stretching over centuries. As with my oldest daughter's version of the "shotgun" rule, and as with the application of aboriginal title, the doctrine of prior appropriation is much more complicated than one might think from this example. If the use is not considered "beneficial" or is otherwise wasteful, the water right is void. If the water user does not use their water right for a certain period of time, they will lose their water right.[84]

Still, one might think that surely, even with these complicating considerations, a "first-in-time, first-in-right" system like the prior appropriation doctrine would privilege indigenous people. And in some ways, at least in theory, it does. In the western United States, where the majority of the fifty-six million acres of Native American tribal land is located, Native American tribes hold significant claims to water rights. [85] When the U.S. government reserves federal public land for any reason, including reservations for Native American tribes, it implicitly reserves water rights.[86] These rights are called *Winters* rights after the 1908 U.S. Supreme Court case *Winters v. United States*.[87] The amount of water reserved to the tribe is the minimum amount of water necessary to meet the primary purpose of the reservation.[88] The "primary purpose" of Indian reservations is to establish a permanent homeland for the tribe.[89] To quantify the minimum amount of water necessary to achieve this purpose, courts have generally used the reservation's practicably irrigable acreage (PIA).[90] Effectively, courts determine how much of the land granted to the tribe can be practicably irrigated (meaning the land has arable soil, and it is cost-effective and technical feasible to irrigate that land), and then bases the amount of water associated with the tribe's *Winters* rights on how much water it would take to efficiently grow crops. In prior appropriation regimes, the priority date for tribal *Winters* rights depends on the use, with some uses having a priority date of "time immemorial," while others have the date of the treaty between the tribe and the U.S. federal government.[91]

This approach seems, at least in comparison to many *aqua nullius* jurisdictions that do not recognize any indigenous water rights, to be reasonably fair. However, it is still rife with problems and potential discriminatory interpretations. Many small tribes do not have large practicably irrigable acreage, and thus would prefer an alternative quantification method that recognizes cultural and spiritual water uses, or the value of the water for ecotourism or other opportunities for economic development.[92] Additionally, tribes must often adjudicate their claims over decades in courts, or else settle their water claims by making difficult trade-offs of trading water rights in exchange for infrastructure development.[93]

While far from perfect, the recognition of *Winters* rights held by tribes, and the relatively early priority date of those rights, allows indigenous communities in these jurisdictions to hold significant leverage in water policy, combat discriminatory water policies on a firm legal basis, and play an important role in effectively intervening in transboundary water disputes between jurisdictions and facilitate resolution of those disputes by selling, leasing, temporarily forgoing, or storing water claimed under their *Winters* rights.[94] Indigenous communities have played a central role in facilitating how the Colorado River is shared between all jurisdictions in the basin by making these kinds of agreements.[95] Additionally, the PIA approach to quantification has obvious limitations for some tribes. However, courts in Arizona engage in a reservation-specific approach to quantifying tribal water rights by considering other factors, like tribal cultural water uses, current and projected populations, and future water use plans.[96] Arizona's quantification method suggests that a more nuanced and adaptive approach can be implemented within the *Winters* rights regime.

A similar approach to recognizing the rights of indigenous communities to water resources could provide protections against discriminatory water polices. The Constitution of Ecuador, for example, recognizes the rights of indigenous communities to "participate in the use, usufruct, administration, and conservation of natural renewable resources" associated with their ancestral lands.[97] Indigenous communities have asserted this right as a means of enhancing tribal political leverage and control over natural resources through water "juntas"—cooperative water use districts formed by indigenous groups in Ecuador to finance and develop water infrastructure.[98] Other Andean countries have taken similar approaches regarding indigenous water juntas.[99] In cases such as these, the recognition of commonly held and legally enforceable indigenous water rights could facilitate improved participation and cooperation with tribal groups in water policy and provide some protection against discriminatory water policies.

And just as such rights provided certain tribes greater leverage in engaging in basin-wide water policy development in the Colorado River Basin, broader recognition of similar indigenous water rights will encourage a more inclusive, and thus less discriminatory, approach to international water law. Some progress has already been made on this front. In 1992, the United Nations Conference on Environment and Development in Rio de Janeiro recognized "Agenda 21," which included the full participation of water-user groups and indigenous peoples in water management decision-making.[100] Tribes with *Winters* rights in the Colorado River Basin, and communities with organized juntas in the Amazon River Basin, have at least some leverage to secure a place at the table when broader, basin-wide decisions are made. Indigenous communities in such transboundary water management regimes will be unlikely to invest in a collaborative manner in a basin-level governance institution if they view such commission as indifferent or hostile to their interests.[101] Indigenous communities should be part of a basin commission that promotes and encourages inclusive and transparent stakeholder participation and a recognition of their rights to traditional waters.[102]

Conclusion

Indigenous communities, of course, are only one group that has often been marginalized or excluded from participation in transboundary water management or faced discrimination in narrower forms of water policy. One potential foundation upon which to build greater recognition of the rights of marginalized communities to water resources is Article 20 of the Berlin Rules, prepared by the International Law Association (ILA) in 2004.[103] The Berlin Rules are not binding international law per se, but the ILA represents a large scholarly nongovernmental organization whose membership includes many leading international law experts and which aims to codify evolving international law.[104] Under Article 20 of the Berlin Rules, nations "shall take all appropriate steps to protect the rights, interests, and special needs of communities and of indigenous peoples or other particularly vulnerable groups likely to be affected by the management of waters, even while developing the waters for the benefit of the entire State or group of States."[105] Communities facing racial or ethnic discrimination can use existing negative rights, such as the right to equal protection or religious freedom, as well as some of the unique legal rights held by indigenous communities, to influence the development of water policy at the international and domestic level in ways that will combat discrimination and ensure equitable water security for all.

5
Water Security and Gender Inequality

Discrimination and inequality manifest themselves in water policy, and can be magnified by water policy, in ways other than in racial or ethnic discrimination. Water insecurity disproportionately impacts women and girls around the world for a host of reasons, some because of discrimination in water policy, but other times because of traditional gender roles surrounding water gathering or sanitation and hygiene.[1] The water shortage crisis facing the Indian city of Chennai in 2019 illustrates the myriad disparate impacts water insecurity has on women and girls.

Chennai is the capital of the Indian state of Tamil Nadu and the sixth-largest city in India, with a population of over 8.5 million people.[2] The city has confronted water variability for centuries, depending on an unpredictable monsoon season to fill reservoirs each year. Climate change has aggravated the water variability challenge in Chennai, with more severe drought and flood cycles. As the city's population has grown, the city has filled in wetlands and converted small-scale rainwater-harvesting systems that provided water to rural communities to centralized reservoirs. These reservoirs provide water to the city, from which a public water system and a variety of private water vendors draw water with limited regulation.[3] Unregulated groundwater pumping has lowered the water table (meaning the depth at which the ground is saturated with water), and wells have dried up. The resulting water crisis has been severe, with tens of thousands of women and girls lining up each day to fill containers of water from a small number of state water trucks.[4] One sixteen-year-old girl standing in line to gather water said, "I carry a bottle with me to school from the water we get from the tanker. I feel bad because it feels like stealing water from my family."[5] Procedures in the labor and delivery wards of Chennai's Government Hospital for Women and Children were delayed as the hospital waited for the water trucks to arrive. A nurse at the hospital said, "Smaller hospitals like ours are not given any importance."[6]

Despite the water insecurity issues impacting the women of Chennai, the city has also been a leader in some ways in promoting water security for women. Chennai planned the installation of 348 "She Toilets" at various locations across the city.[7] These toilets are electronic, fully automated, and include sanitary napkin dispensers and disposal systems.[8] The intention was to provide sanitation facilities for the many women working outdoors all day as vendors, construction workers, and police officers.[9] This effort has been undertaken in response to an acute shortage adequate public toilets for women, as well as inadequate menstrual health products and product disposal in the city.[10]

The challenges confronting Chennai illustrate many of the reasons water insecurity particularly impacts women and girls. The young woman waiting in line in Chennai to bring water to her family demonstrates the impact such responsibilities have on gender inequality in education and the relationship between such inequality and water insecurity. In developing countries where water must be gathered from locations far away from the home, women and girls bear the primary responsibility for water gathering.[11] Every day, women and girls spend an estimated 152 million hours in collecting water for domestic uses.[12] In many sub-Saharan African communities, girls spend between six and eight hours each day gathering water.[13] These responsibilities not only interfere with the ability of women and girls to attend school and seek employment but also expose them to danger.[14] These young women often confront physical and sexual violence while engaged in water-gathering work.[15]

The inadequate water provision for the hospital serving women and children in Chennai and the "She Toilets" effort illustrate other ways water insecurity disproportionately impacts women. Unequal or discriminatory investment in water and sanitation impacts women and girls all over the world even when such failures do not result in long, dangerous hours engaged in water gathering. Lack of education and employment opportunities, as well as negative health impacts, result from inadequate menstrual hygiene products and product disposal.[16] Often, cultural taboos and lack of education regarding hygiene and sanitation lie at the heart of this failure to adequately invest in menstrual health.[17] For example, in some communities in India, menstruation is considered impure, based on beliefs dating back to Vedic times and the mythical slaying of Vritras by Indra, with menstrual flow seen as evidence of women taking part in Indra's guilt for murder.[18] These communities thus place restrictions on girls and women entering kitchens or engaging in certain religious practices during menstruation. Such taboos are not uncommon but instead are present in cultures around the world and across all stages of economic development.[19] It is a nearly universal human impulse: we do not want to talk about what we put down the toilet.

The connection between water, sanitation, and hygiene is so strong that in water policy dialogues, policymakers and scholars frequently refer to the sector as WASH, a collective term that refers to water, sanitation, and hygiene.[20] The relationship between WASH issues and gender inequality, however, are not limited only to the sanitation and hygiene aspects of water security, nor are water access issues and gender inequality limited only to water-collection work in developing countries. Water rights are often connected to property rights, and gender inequality in property ownership impacts the degree to which women can influence water policy and assert control over water resources. In fact, unequal allocation of property rights, and therefore access to water rights, forms a part of the Chennai water crisis, even if not obvious from media reports. In India, as in many other countries, ownership of water, particularly groundwater, is often connected to the ownership of land.[21] Yet, in many parts of India and for a host of reasons, women are underrepresented as landowners.[22] Thus, gender inequality impacts water security for women not only in terms of sanitation, hygiene, and drinking-water provision, but in control of the raw water source itself.

This chapter will discuss three potential broad legal interventions or strategies that can address the disparate impacts of gender inequality in the WASH sector, as well as using water policy as a means of advancing gender equality. First, human rights law can play a unique role in addressing gender inequality in water policy, in ways similar and dissimilar to the role played in racial inequality. Second, reforms in general landownership laws can facilitate greater access to, and control of, water resources by women. Third, improved laws regarding information sharing, data reporting and modeling, and enhanced incentives for stakeholder participation can encourage a more influential role for women in the formulation and implementation of water policy.

Human Rights Approach to Gender Equality in Water Policy

As in the Chennai water crisis, the importance of water security in sub-Saharan Africa was brought to greater international attention with the "Day Zero" water crisis in Cape Town, South Africa in 2018.[23] The "Day Zero" crisis refers to anticipated day in which the water level at the main reservoir in Cape Town, a city of approximately four million residents, reached a point so low that the government would implement mandatory water shutoffs and rationing within the city, to as little as fifty liters (around thirteen gallons) per person per day.[24] Like Chennai, the Cape Town crisis was caused by a combination of poor water policy (inadequate conservation measures and a failure to diversify the city's water supply portfolio) and drought (likely caused, or aggravated, by climate change).[25] To give a sense of how the Day Zero restrictions would have limited Cape Town residents' water use, it's helpful to compare the thirteen-gallon limit to the approximately ninety gallons of water used each day for household uses by the average American.[26]

Cape Town avoided Day Zero through conservation efforts, rapidly bringing new water supplies online, and by the fortunate arrival of desperately needed rain.[27] However, just as in Chennai, the water supply challenges confronting Cape Town leading up to the potential declaration of a "Day Zero" were not borne equally by all residents.[28] Nearly a quarter of Cape Town residents live in informal settlements that rely on communal water taps.[29] Women in these informal settlements faced greater challenges surrounding the potential risks of Day Zero, because they would have to walk further and wait longer for water.[30] The Cape Town crisis, even though widely reported around the globe, is not the only or most severe example of such disproportionate impacts of water insecurity on women in sub-Saharan Africa. Many other nations in sub-Saharan Africa confront water insecurity and its disproportionate impact on women and girls.[31]

The traditional role of women in collecting water over great distances remains fairly common in many parts of sub-Saharan Africa.[32] The process of collecting water is arduous, time-consuming, and at times, dangerous for the young women and girls tasked with this responsibility, and these challenges are only exacerbated when water is scarce.[33] The list of hazards that women and girls face while gathering water is immense, including but not limited to drowning, exhaustion, harassment, and exposure to disease.[34] The time taken to collect water often limits or precludes other educational or employment opportunities for women and girls. If the law could encourage or require tapped and treated water availability closer to the point of use, such laws would contribute immensely to the safety, health, education, and economic security of women.[35]

One possible legal approach is a human rights approach similar to those discussed in previous chapters. As with race, religion, and ethnicity, many national constitutions guarantee a right of equal protection under the law regardless of gender and prohibit government discrimination on the basis of gender.[36] Corollaries exist for such rights under international human rights instruments, like the U.N. Covenant for Civil and Political Rights (the "CP Covenant").[37] As with disparate racial impacts in water policy, lawsuits alleging unequal treatment of women in water policy could encourage governments to invest in tapped and treated water sources closer to the point of use to limit disparate impacts of water gathering on women. Women in Chennai or Cape Town could assert that government policies that resulted in, or contributed to, these water crises disproportionately impacted women, and thus violated guarantees of equal protection enshrined in both the Indian and South African national constitutions, and could assert similar claims in international tribunals under the CP Covenant.[38] However, except perhaps in some rare instances, the law does not require women and girls to bear greater water-gathering responsibilities than men, but such disparate impacts are the result of cultural issues that may not implicate a violation of constitutional duties by the state.

Water conditions and policies in Kenya provide a useful illustration. As in Cape Town , women and girls in many parts of Kenya disproportionately bear the burden of water insecurity.[39] Kenya enacted a new constitution in 2010. A few of the objectives of the new constitution were "to address several contentious issues, including land and environmental governance," as well as to provide more economic and social rights, which included rights to "reasonable standards of sanitation," "clean and safe water in adequate quantities," "education," and "reasonable standards for sanitation."[40] To aid in the enforcement of these water-related rights, the Kenyan government implemented the 2016 Water Act. The goals of this act were "to align the water sector with the Constitution's primary objective" of giving the responsibility of water and sanitation services to the forty-seven counties in Kenya and to "redefine the roles and responsibilities for the management, development, and regulation of water resources and water services" in Kenya.[41]

Kenya's 2010 Constitution also employs gender-neutral pronouns, utilizing the term "every person" rather than men/women or males/females.[42] This neutral terminology should ensure that all Kenyans, regardless of gender, possess the same rights, including those water-related rights already referenced. Furthermore, the 2010 Constitution obligates the Kenyan government to treat international law created by treaty or convention as if it were their own law, and thus incorporates the protections embodied in international legal instruments like the CP Covenant.[43] The constitution specifically states that "any treaty or convention ratified by Kenya shall form part of the law of Kenya under this Constitution" and "the state shall enact and implement legislation to fulfil its international obligations in respect of human rights and fundamental freedoms."[44]

On paper, these legal reforms appear to be moving Kenya in the right direction of advancing gender equality in water policy implementation. Kenyan women could claim that water policies that fail to provide tapped, treated sources close to the point of use or that fail to adequately invest in menstrual hygiene facilities in schools and places of public accommodation, violate both the negative right protecting women against discrimination and unequal treatment, as well as the positive rights to education, sanitation, and clean and sufficient water. However, according to the nongovernmental organization (NGO) Womankind Kenya, many communities continue to follow traditional practices when it comes to the treatment of women in the provision of water, sanitation, and hygiene regardless of these new laws.[45] This is not to suggest that the types of legal reforms made in Kenya are useless, but instead to point out that these reforms, by themselves, are inadequate. There may be other human rights avenues, beyond the types of equal protection claims or positive rights claims I have already discussed, unique to the issue of gender equality in water policy with greater potential than a violation of the right to equal protection.

While water is not specifically referenced in either of the two main international human rights conventions—the CP Covenant and the U.N. Covenant on Economic, Social, and Cultural Rights (the "ESC Covenant")—water is specifically referenced in two other broadly recognized international human rights instruments.[46] The first is the U.N. Convention on the Elimination of All Forms of Discrimination Against Women (CEDAW).[47] Established in December 1979, and entered into force in September 1981, CEDAW acts as an international bill of rights for women, establishing guidelines for its nation parties to recognize and end discrimination against women.[48] CEDAW provides that "States Parties shall take all appropriate measures to eliminate discrimination against women in rural areas . . . and, in particular, shall ensure to such women the right . . . to enjoy adequate living conditions, particularly in relation to housing, sanitation, electricity and water supply."[49] Periodically, a committee of experts expands CEDAW by making general recommendations for issues affecting women to which its parties should pay particular attention.[50] As of today, the CEDAW Committee has made thirty-seven general recommendations, several of which include issues pertinent to women and water, such as the right of girls and women to education (2017); the rights of rural women (2016); women and health (1999); and education and public information programs (1987).[51]

A second international human rights instrument also makes reference to water and is uniquely relevant in the context of gender equality. The Convention on the Rights of the Child (CRC) was first signed in 1989 and provides that state parties "shall take appropriate measures . . . to combat disease and malnutrition, including . . . through the provision of adequate nutritious foods and clean drinking-water."[52] The CRC was the most rapidly ratified human rights treaty in history, and has over 190 ratifying state parties. The Committee on the Rights of the Child, an elected body of independent experts, monitors state parties' compliance through the submission of regular reports and provides guidance and assistance to state parties. The CRC is particularly important in gender equality in water policy because of the role girls play in water gathering and the large role women play in child care around the world.

Although both CEDAW and the CRC are widely recognized as binding international law and are quite comprehensive (indeed, the only two international human rights treaties that even addresses water directly), both treaties lack sufficient mechanisms for enforcement.[53] For example, every nation discussed in this chapter, including India, Kenya, and South Africa, are parties to both CEDAW and the CRC, and yet each can provide an example of limitations and failures in ensuring gender equality in water policy. Additionally, even if more effective enforcement mechanisms could be implemented, many girls and women may lack access to the justice system. In its latest recommendation concerning women and education, the CEDAW Committee referenced the justiciability of the right to an education, citing a suit brought by a Nigerian human rights NGO against Nigeria and its public education system.[54] Although this case recognized that citizens could challenge their nation's failure to provide basic human rights, the court was unable to grant genuine relief.[55] Further, this case was brought by a human rights NGO and not individual citizens, suggesting the challenges individual women may face in enforcing rights without some additional institutional support.[56]

Moreover, neither CEDAW nor the CRC adequately address the critical issue of sanitation and hygiene. The CRC does not mention either sanitation or hygiene directly, nor has the issue been addressed in any of the treaty's optional protocols. In 2017, CEDAW Committee recommendations for the right of women and girls to an education only superficially mention improving sanitation to support female hygiene and overall health in two of the suggestions.[57] Further, the 1999 recommendations for women and health do not even expressly allude to *female* sanitation, and neither of these recommendations includes the words "hygiene" or "menstruation."[58] The 1987 recommendations for education and public information programs fail to advocate for any specific programming related to hygiene or menstruation at all.[59] The 2016 CEDAW Committee recommendations do expressly address menstruation and its related challenges for women who lack access to proper sanitation facilities either at home or at school, but only in relation to "rural women."[60]

Despite their limitations, the admirable advancements made by CEDAW and the CRC in addressing water issues can be built upon to more effectively address gender inequality in water policy. State parties could be required to contribute funds to support educational programming for both governments and citizens that addresses cultural taboos surrounding menstrual hygiene and the role women and girls play in water gathering. Additionally, the United Nations could partner with international development organizations to help nations specifically request funding or other assistance for projects aimed at improving education, infrastructure, and product provision for menstrual health. International banks, such as the World Bank and the African Development Bank, could similarly facilitate greater funding for hygiene and sanitation education in connection with financing larger improvements to water and sanitation infrastructure.[61]

CEDAW and CRC committees could partner with these organizations to provide education materials and oversee monitoring and reporting. Through such partnerships between CRC and CEDAW committees and potential development funders, these treaties could be more effectively tied to necessary education and infrastructure improvements and greater transparency and accountability.[62] CEDAW and CRC committees could also help development organizations and banks to provide preferential funding and financing terms to nations with demonstrated commitments to complying with obligations under these treaties over other nations that have not provided adequate reporting or transparency as required by CEDAW and the CRC. Finally, the CEDAW and CRC committees, in partnership with development agencies and banks, could expand access to courts for women by supporting legal aid organizations providing representation to women in matters related to water and sanitation under applicable international human rights treaties and national constitutional rights.

Empower Women to Participate
in Water Policy and Provision

Given the role women play globally in water provision and the disproportionate burden women bear due to inadequate hygiene and sanitation, it is perhaps unsurprising that the only two international human rights treaties that expressly address water are the two international human rights treaties particularly formulated to protect women and girls. And perhaps that is one of the most important functions these two treaties serve—to state the challenge. As noted in several examples already, the burdens women bear in the WASH sector are often either underappreciated because culturally assumed and taken for granted, or else ignored because culturally taboo. At the very least, CEDAW and the CRC address these issues explicitly. Law, however, can do more to elevate the WASH sector, the role women and girls play in the sector, and the unique challenges they confront in our public policy discourse. We shy away from discussing the things that we flush away, but our water policy dialogue is incomplete if we cannot talk seriously about poop, pee, and periods. Many of these proposed reforms related to CEDAW and the CRC are aimed at using those treaties not as tools of litigation or legal compulsion, but as catalysts for conversations. But such legal catalysts do not need to be limited only to these two remarkable international treaties. A few examples from several countries can illustrate principles upon which legal reforms can build to encourage a healthier dialogue surrounding the role of women in, and the impacts on women from, the WASH sector.

The first promising example comes from Egypt. From January 2003 to December 2004, the Better Life Association for Comprehensive Development (BLACD) implemented a water and sanitation project in the Egyptian village of Nazlet Faragallah, focused on empowering local women and increasing their access to water and sanitation resources.[63] Prior to the project, most of the 1,500 households in the village did not have latrines or access to reliable and clean running water, forcing women to collect and dispose of their family's waste in the nearby canal.[64] Since the canal was contaminated with sewage, women became infected with bilharzia and other diseases when they used the canal for washing the family's clothes and dishes. Although women in Nazlet Faragallah were responsible for providing their families with water, women had limited influence on water-management decisions in the village.[65]

The BLACD project provided two water taps with treated water and one latrine for each of the seven hundred households in the village.[66] The project improved health among village residents and reduced time women and girls spent in water-gathering and waste-disposal responsibilities, which consequently improved attendance in schools by village girls.[67] The project's success was in part the result of integrating local women in the project planning process. Before implementing the project, BLACD enlisted twenty women to act as "health visitors," receiving and then providing training on improved hygiene and sanitation and reporting problems or maintenance issues.[68] Importantly, village men contributed to the project as well and received training on maintenance skills to encourage all members of the community to share in WASH responsibilities.[69] Many of the "health visitors" in Nazlet Faragallah remained involved in their community's WASH systems after the completion of the BLACD project and formed a formally registered community development association, strengthening the leadership role of women in the community as well as improving sustained attention to WASH issues in the village.[70] Laws should require NGOs and development agencies investing in WASH systems to integrate community feedback and invest in community training and leadership development, particularly for women. Such laws would help WASH projects achieve similar sustained success as the project in Nazlet Faragallah.

A second promising example comes from the East African nation of Togo. In 2003, international NGO Plan Togo partnered with the African-based Regional Centre for Cost-Effective Fresh Water and Sanitation (CREPA) to develop a school sanitation and hygiene pilot program in three rural villages in Togo's Est-Mono province: Agan, Ayona and Effufami.[71] Only 10 percent of the population in this region had access to tapped potable water, and only 26 percent of schools in the region had access to water, with only 30 percent of schools having sanitary toilets or latrines.[72] This inadequate access to clean water and sanitation at schools, as well as the lack of household tapped-water sources combined with girls typically tasked to collect water, contributed to low attendance in schools by girls, with girls representing only 43.8 percent of students in this region of Togo prior to the Plan Togo/CREPA project.[73]

The project provided to each school a hand pump for water, a sanitary latrine for girls, a hand-washing pot, a garbage dump, a plastic drinking pot for potable water in each classroom, and nine area-specific educational kits for each school in the identified communities.[74] The project established two committees in each community: the Water Committee to manage money, maintenance, and repair; and the School Health Committee to control equipment and oversee hygiene.[75] The School Health Committee was composed of both female and male teachers and students, and focused on improved hygiene practices and education in school.[76] The rate of girls' attendance in school has increased in the wake of the project's completion.[77] The schools were even able to generate income by selling water to their communities, and the communities followed the schools' example by appointing a sanitation controller, establishing a garbage dump, and repairing old pumps.[78] Of the many lessons the Plan Togo/CREPA project offers those interested in WASH sector development, one is the potential success of prioritizing investment in community schools. One of the challenges in WASH development is that donors and development agencies quite understandably want to advertise and promote project successes. Pictures of new wells and hand pumps, treatment systems, and taps make for more broadly acceptable marketing materials than pictures of latrines and toilets. This may account for why donor and development dollars in the WASH sector often focus on drinking water, when money invested in sanitation and hygiene may make a bigger impact in terms of lives saved or school days attended per dollar spent. A focus on investment in schools may allow donors and development agencies to tout project success with pictures of children in school, and then allow schools to become the epicenter of community WASH improvements, as was the case in many of these communities in Togo.

A focus on WASH investments in community schools can facilitate education and establish reasonable and focused priorities in where to invest sometimes scarce WASH resources. However, such efforts may not amount to enough success if cultural taboos remain an obstacle. For example, the traditional Nepali Hindu practice of Chhaupadi is similar to the cultural taboos already noted in India. Chhaupadi is the practice of banishing menstruating women to outside of the home for the duration of their period due to the belief that during this time women are impure.[79] Despite the fact that in 2005, the Supreme Court of Nepal issued a directive to the Nepalese government to create laws to eliminate Chhaupadi, it has remained a prevalent practice in parts of Western Nepal and has resulted in the deaths of many women.[80] In 2017, the Nepalese legislature passed a law criminalizing the practice, which, however, allowed over a year for a "grace period" for its citizens to adjust to the new law.[81] During this grace period, another young woman died.[82] These deeply embedded cultural practices and taboos surrounding sanitation and hygiene make water management in this sector uniquely challenging, and particularly critical for gender equality.

Our third promising example shows that such taboos need not be insurmountable obstacles to legal reforms aimed at WASH improvements. In Nepal, WaterAid has worked to remove the taboo associated with menstruation, and their Nepal country director, Tripti Rai, has expressed optimism for a project that again focuses on schoolchildren.[83] Rai said, "[S]chool has been a good entry point to help break the silence, because when you talk to students about change, they can go home and talk to their parents."[84] The executive director of the German Toilet Organization (GTO), Thilo Panzerbieter, has affirmed the success of this strategy, encouraging organizations to empower children, because they have not yet fully internalized sanitation taboos.[85] Panzerbieter described one school visit, saying, "[A]fter a very short time we had the children in the room very openly talking about toilets . . . . [T]hey compared what they have at home with what they see in the pictures from other countries. The toilet taboo was swept away and all the adults in the room learnt from the kids."[86] Additionally, starting educational campaigns at the primary-school level will save future time and resources, since kids will not only educate their parents but will educate their own children one day, perpetuating a society well informed about women's WASH-related issues. Educational law reforms that integrate hygiene and sanitation into the basic curriculum at a young age can thus have broad and long-lasting impacts on addressing unequal treatment by women in the WASH sector.

These sorts of educational endeavors, however, do not need to be limited to the classroom. Another nonprofit, the World Toilet Organization (WTO), is working to remove the toilet taboo and to improve the dialogue about how sanitation and proper toilet systems improve people's health and overall quality of life.[87] In 2001, the WTO established "World Toilet Day" (November 19) and the World Toilet Summit, which brings together international NGOs as well as industry leaders to develop strategies for global sanitation issues.[88] In 2013, the U.N. General Assembly declared "World Toilet Day" an official U.N. international observance day and now partners with numerous organizations each year to host events to raise awareness and to encourage global action in the WASH sector.[89] Since 2009, the United Nations and the WTO have used Twitter and Facebook to spread sanitation awareness and continue to use the hashtag #WorldToiletDay to promote and coordinate events around the globe. "World Toilet Day" highlights the effectiveness of social media and online campaigns to raise awareness about global WASH-related challenges. Social media is an easy and effective tool that can make education more accessible and engage young people. The role of law in this particular approach is simple. Promote and protect freedom of expression and establish laws that require investments in internet access for rural populations.

India—which began this chapter as an example of the problems of gender equality in the WASH sector as seen during the Chennai water crisis— provides an example for optimism in achieving greater gender equality in water services as well. CORO, a grassroots organization in India that trains local women to be leaders in their communities, addressed head-on the sanitation taboo and its potential to promote inequality. In Mumbai, men had free access to public urinals, whereas women were charged a fee.[90] CORO worked with their newly trained leaders in Mumbai to create the "Right to Pee" campaign, which advocated for clean, safe, and *free* public urinals for women.[91] In 2016, CORO partnered with U.N. Women India to create the National Convention on Women's Right to Pee, which brought together female activists, female organization leaders, and women in government positions to collaborate and raise awareness for women's sanitation issues, several of which issues are now legally recognized by state authorities.[92]

The challenge with cultural taboos regarding sanitation, and particularly menstrual hygiene, is that law can only do so much. Legal reforms can provide resources and incentives, and in some cases causes of action to support litigation, but these legal tools are blunt instruments when wielded against generations of cultural practices and beliefs. But as education and awareness expands, and the experience of women begins to influence decisions, real cultural change is possible. For nearly fifteen years, single women in the Indian state of Haryana have been telling potential suitors they will not marry anyone who does not have a toilet. The "No Toilet, No Bride" campaign, which was launched by state authorities in 2005, encourages women and their families to demand that all male suitors provide a functioning and sanitary private latrine as a condition of marriage. Private sanitation coverage in Haryana expanded by 21 percent from 2004 to 2008. A government survey reported that 1.42 million toilets were built between 2005 and 2009.[93] The effectiveness of such an approach has obvious limitations and problems, and depends on the scarcity of suitable marriage partners for men in order for women and their families to have meaningful leverage. But the relative success of the program does illustrate that the potential to counter harmful cultural taboos may take time, but legal reforms that encourage dialogue can result in real success in overcoming taboos and improving WASH conditions for women and girls.

Property Rights Approach to Gender Equality in Water Policy

Most of the discussion in this chapter has focused on gender equality in the WASH sector as it relates to either water-gathering work by women or girls, or the disparate impact of inadequate sanitation and hygiene experienced by women in many parts of the world. However, because landownership is often tied to water rights, where men disproportionately own land, women may also have unequal influence on water policy.

Many approaches to allocating water rights are based on landownership. Riparian water rights regimes, common in many parts of the world because of their roots in Roman and British law, provide that owners of land that directly abut a natural watercourse have the right to make reasonable use of the water.[94] Groundwater rights are similarly frequently connected to landownership. Some jurisdictions limit the quantity of groundwater a landowner can withdraw to a "reasonable" amount, sometimes referred to as the "American Rule."[95] Other jurisdictions limit the amount of groundwater a landowner can withdraw based on the size of the overlying land, sometimes called "Correlative Rights."[96] Still other laws grant landowners an absolute right to pump as much groundwater as possible, without regard to impacts on neighbors or the sustainability of the system, also called the "English Rule," though it is used in other parts of the world, including India and the U.S. state of Texas.[97] Even water rights regimes that do not explicitly tie water rights to landownership nevertheless often privilege landowners. For example, in the western United States prior appropriation regime, a water right is perfected by putting the water right to a beneficial use, including frequently an in-stream use, without necessarily requiring landownership.[98] Nevertheless, the location of diversion points and the return flows from water applications on the land form such an integral part to many of these water rights that they represent a major source of controversy in water rights disputes. Indeed, water lawyers often refer to sales of such water rights as "sever and transfer," because the right is severed from the appurtenant land.[99] In regimes where the government simply grants licenses to divert or pump water, landownership is still virtually essential, as the well, ditch, or pipeline must be installed somewhere.

In many of these jurisdictions, water rights are not necessarily even pure property rights in the same way as landownership. Many nations recognize something akin to the public trust doctrine, meaning the state owns the water and holds it in trust for the benefit of all citizens.[100] These water rights are "usufructory"—meaning the state is granting a license to capture a specified quantity of water for a particular purpose.[101] In a way, water in these jurisdictions is managed like wildlife and hunting licenses. In their wild state, animals are owned by the state and protected in trust for the benefit of all. But the state may grant hunting licenses for certain animals for certain times of the year, specifying how many can be caught or killed. A water right, in many instances, is something like a hunting license, and water is not that dissimilar from a wild animal. Water runs across, flies over, and burrows under property lines like a wild animal. If the only people who could get hunting licenses were landowners, and people could only hunt on land they owned, then the non-landowning population would be effectively excluded from asserting control over a resource that is ostensibly held in trust for the benefit of all. Even if hunting licenses were not solely granted to landowners, landowners would still be privileged in this system. The more land you own, the more likely wild animals are on your land, and the cheaper it is for you to hunt them (since you do not have to worry about trespass), and the more rents you can charge to people who want to hunt on your land. The same is true of water rights. Even where water rights are not explicitly tied to landownership, water rights regimes still tend to privilege landowners because they do not have to worry about buying, leasing, or securing easements for pipes, ditches, and wells on their own land, and can charge others for those installations on land they own. This sort of privileging of landownership in water rights allocations unequally burdens women in the WASH sector in nations where women have been, or are, disadvantaged in owning land. For example, in the Upper East Region of Ghana, men typically own land close to the river and can irrigate with dug diversions, whereas women, when they own farmland, typically own land farther from the river and struggle to access labor to dig wells or diversions, and so irrigate by hauling water with buckets or jerrycans.[102]

Women have been disadvantaged in landownership in countries all over the world based on generations of laws relating to dowries, inheritance, banking, and prohibitions against women owning land.[103] This includes everything from British common law fee tail systems that prevented women from inheriting certain lands for generations, made notable by the television series *Downton Abbey* and the novel *Pride and Prejudice*, to more modern limitations. For example, as recently as the handover of Hong Kong from the British to the Chinese in the 1990s, the Joint Declaration governing that handover provided that "a person descended through the male line from a person who was in 1898 a resident of an established village in Hong Kong, the rent shall remain unchanged so long as the property is held by that person or by one of his lawful successors in the male line."[104] In 1999, the Supreme Court of Zimbabwe upheld a lower court decision based on customary law that a woman cannot be the heir to her father's estate when there is a man in the family who is entitled to claim the land.[105] The legal limitations on women owning property have had the consequence of limiting their influence over water, because land rights and water rights are so often connected. In India, women have been denied enforceable irrigation rights because they are often not the formal landowners, and studies have shown similar issues throughout the world.[106] This is true despite the fact that most farmers are women, and most food is produced by women.[107]

Justifications for connecting rights to natural resources (whether water or hunting) to landownership are often based on the tragedy of the commons. The tragedy of the commons refers to the prediction that, when people share a common pool resource, the resource will be depleted by each user acting in their own rational self-interest, unless some collective action is taken or the common pool resource is restructured as private property.[108] Common pool resources are resources that are rivalrous (meaning one user's consumption precludes consumption by another user) but nonexcludable (meaning users have no means of keeping others from making use of the resource). A common example of the tragedy of the commons is grazing land for cattle. The land is nonexcludable—it can't be reasonably fenced in and no individual owns the land. But the grass is rivalrous—every blade of grass my cows eat is a blade of grass your cows cannot eat. If I act in my own self-interest, I will overgraze the land, even if it means destroying the pasture. I will get 100 percent of the benefit of having my own fat cows, but I will share the cost of destroying the grazing land with everyone else. Water is generally a common pool resource. It is difficult to exclude people from large water systems like lakes, rivers, and aquifers. And while water is a renewable resource, consumption of water faster than nature replenishes it still makes the resource effectively rivalrous.

One possible way to avoid the tragedy of the commons would be private property rights—split up the grazing land into fenced-in private lots. That way, if I overconsume my own land, I get 100 percent of the benefit but also 100 percent of the cost. This is a difficult approach to take with water, because water (like wild animals) is a fugitive resource, meaning it runs across both private property boundaries as well as political borders. Another possible answer to the tragedy of the commons is to impose a regulatory regime that says you can only graze on this part of the land with a certain number of cattle for a certain period of time, and then impose penalties for violators. This is effectively the approach with hunting licenses. In either of these approaches, the response to the risk of the tragedy of the commons privileges landowners. The first approach is to simply grant private property rights. And the second approach—though not explicitly connected to landownership—would still privilege landowners because access to the land is still essential to graze cattle. Whether water rights are incidental to owning land rights explicitly, or water rights are government permits which still nevertheless effectively privilege landownership, such water rights regimes often disadvantage women.

However, these two landownership-based methods of avoiding the tragedy of the commons in water policy are not the only means by which to encourage sustainability and equitable sharing of common pool resources. The Nobel Prize–winning economist Elinor Ostrom concluded, based on extensive research on pasture lands in Africa and irrigation systems in Nepal, that local communities often avoid the tragedy of the commons through collective institutional arrangements that do not require privatization or top-down permitting structures.[109] Ostrom's argument mirrors the rationale for regionalist water controls discussed in chapter 1 on climate change and water security. In that chapter, I compared the Earth to a golf ball, a sphere covered in divots with each divot representing a drainage basin. If the water jurisdiction is too small (many jurisdictions within one basin), then these jurisdictions will pollute or dam water and externalize the costs of water management to their neighbors. But if the jurisdiction is too large (many basins within one jurisdiction), then the transaction costs of water management are too high, because there will be too many stakeholders unfamiliar with the unique local conditions of water. Ostrom argues that the tragedy of the commons most often occurs when external groups assert control over the common pool resource to the exclusion or minimization of local control.

Ostrom set forth eight design principles to better manage commons, like water: (1) clearly define the scope of the common pool resource; (2) adapt the management system to local conditions; (3) govern in a way that allows most resource users to participate in the decision-making process; (4) effectively monitor and hold users accountable for norm violations; (5) impose a scale of graduated sanctions imposed on violators; (6) provide accessible dispute resolution mechanisms; (7) promote self-determination within the community; and (8) in the case of large-scale common pool resources, form an organization that allows for multiple layers of governance within the system.[110] What is striking about Ostrom's design principles is the extent to which, if effectively implemented, they would facilitate management of commons in a way that would avoid gender inequality, unlike other landownership-based approaches. These eight principles have at their core, values of inclusivity, self-determination, transparency, and respect for the expertise of users most familiar with the characteristics of the common pool resource.

These are the principles evident in the management of small-scale irrigation cooperatives in Nepal, case studies Ostrom relies on in developing these principles. She compared the productivity, infrastructure condition, and efficiency of small-scale, community-based irrigation systems with larger, top-down systems. Ostrom found that the community-based systems generally outperformed the larger systems, even though the larger systems often had the better materials and technology. She noted that the larger systems were installed with the assumption that farmers would resolve water rights between them, whereas the smaller systems were installed to meet the expectations and understanding of water rights that already existed in the community. This practical approach to the design of management systems is reflected in what is often called "Ostrom's Law," expressed by property law theorist Lee Anne Fennel as "a resource arrangement that works in practice can work in theory."[111] Because women have traditionally performed essential roles of water gathering, and because they represent the largest number of subsistence farmers, their practices and input in management systems should inform how, and whether, any intervention in improved water management is designed.

Women's access to commons, like water, has historically been limited in part because they have been excluded from private property ownership. Unsurprisingly, women have been at the forefront in protecting access to commons in the face of increasing pressures toward privatization, whether in protecting forests, opposing dams, or protesting water privatization.[112] Water development should therefore move cautiously in assuming that privatization or top-down permitting mechanisms are preferable approaches to avoiding the tragedy of the commons because of the risk of exacerbating or perpetuating gender inequality in the WASH sector.

Nevertheless, even bottom-up traditional community water governance designs can result in gender inequality. For example, *qanat*, or *aflaj*, irrigation systems have existed in the Middle East and West Asia for nearly two thousand years. *Qanat* systems rely on gravity to channel water though underground channels to villages for irrigation and domestic uses, and some millennia-old *qanat* systems remain important water supply infrastructure to this day.[113] However, even in some of these communities, women function as the primary water gatherers. To prevent water contamination of these systems, women have to walk long distances up mountainous terrain to collect water.[114] While the community-based approach complying with Ostrom's design principles may seem an ideal way to address gender inequality, existing cultural norms and property laws may make such designs difficult and may nevertheless privilege male-dominated landownership in terms of influencing water policy.

Thus, in some instances, land reform may be another essential feature of legal changes needed to address gender inequality in the WASH sector. Some of these reforms may seem obvious—legalizing ownership of land by women and eliminating inheritance laws that discriminate against women. But land reform is complex and runs into difficult legal and cultural obstacles. In Rwanda, for example, precolonial, colonial, and postcolonial land laws limited the rights of women to inherit or own land.[115] However, in the wake of the Rwandan genocide, women made up a larger majority of the country and larger percentage of the heads of households, land productivity was impacted by years of conflict, and disputes over landownership in the wake of so much death threatened a fragile peace and emphasized the need to build a foundation for the rule of law in Rwanda. In 2006, Rwanda amended its constitution to explicitly affirm its adherence to the principles of CEDAW and passed the Organic Land Law, which provided that "[a]ny person or association with legal personality has the right over the land and to freely exploit it as provided for by this organic law. . . . Any discrimination either based on sex or origin in matters relating to ownership or possession of rights over land is prohibited."[116] The Organic Land Law also formalized land title registration, which protected women against more powerful people or groups taking land or against other relatives making claims to land under previous customary laws. Rwanda also enacted the Abunzi Law, which provided for local dispute resolution committees, of which women must comprise at least

30 percent, to make adjudication of land rights less expensive and more accessible to women.[117] Despite these reforms, resistance to granting inheritance to daughters and the persistence of informal marriages continue to perpetuate gender inequality in landownership in Rwanda, and thus impact the ability of women to control water resources.[118] Similar land reform attempts were made during Operation Barga in the late 1970s—a land reform effort in West Bengal, India. While the law expanded the legal rights of women to own land (and water rights in India are connected to land), the law itself may have resulted in family efforts to draft wills to ensure land was inherited by sons rather than daughters.[119]

Conclusion

Land reform may thus be a necessary, but not sufficient, effort to address gender inequality in water rights. Reform of landownership laws, a focus on community-based water governance regimes, educational efforts to address menstrual hygiene taboos, and a focus on investment in hygiene, sanitation, and tapped and treated water sources close to the point of use may, in combination, facilitate greater gender equality. But overcoming long-standing cultural and legal bases of discrimination can take time and may be a generational endeavor. In my experience, however, an investment that pays relatively quick returns in terms of gender equality is technical training for women in the WASH sector. I have worked for the last three years on a project providing improved water to refugee host communities in Lebanon and Jordan. One of the focuses of this project was to ensure training and job opportunities for women in the WASH sector. Even where cultural or legal norms prevent women from directly owning water resources or accessing adequate sanitation, it is difficult to exclude women from influencing the WASH sector when they are the technical experts in the systems treating drinking water and disposing of wastewater. Thus, an additional reform I would suggest is for development agencies, NGOs, and banks to explicitly connect investments in WASH infrastructure and enterprises with job training and employment for women. Because irrigation and domestic water provision roles are gendered, women's preferences for water technology may be different than men's, so technology training should include an evaluation of whether and how the technology meets women's needs and expectations.

The Chennai water crisis—and similar large urban water challenges like Day Zero in Cape Town—illustrate the myriad ways water insecurity disproportionately impacts women and girls. However, it is more often in rural communities where the day-to-day challenges of water, sanitation, and hygiene impact the ability of women and girls to be healthy and safe and to enjoy education and employment opportunities. I had the opportunity to emphasize this once with my own daughter. We were living in Ecuador, in an area with inadequate water quality from the taps. We purchased treated drinking water from a local vendor in large five-gallon containers. My daughter and I went together one morning to collect the water and bring it to our home. I talked with her about how many young girls her age struggle every day in water gathering, so much that they cannot attend school. As we worked together to bring water home, she asked, "Why don't the men help?" Perhaps, when it comes to addressing the disparate impacts women and girls face in confronting water insecurity, this is the most important question.

6

Water Security and Armed Conflict

Former U.N. Secretary General Kofi Annan warned in 2001 that the wars of the twenty-first century would be fought over water.[1] Yet the relationship between water and war is so complicated as to make such predictions difficult to evaluate. Water has been a direct and indirect cause of violence, and a strategic target in war and terrorism, but is much more commonly a catalyst for cooperation and peace.[2] As climate change increases water variability throughout the world, it does not take much imagination to assume that the destabilizing effects of stronger drought and flood cycles could result in violence. Indeed, dystopian novels and films like *Water World, Dune, Mad Max,* and *The Water Knife* have depicted a future rife with violent conflict over scarce water.[3] The "water war" narrative, whether in fiction, media reporting, or research, is understandably compelling and serves to emphasize the critical importance of water policy. Nevertheless, that narrative is not wholly accurate and is somewhat sensationalistic given that violence over water is rare, particularly when compared to instances of peaceful water sharing. Still, while water is far more often a bulwark of peace and stability, this should not be taken to mean that water is not ever, or that it never will be, the cause or target of violence.

Many of the major modern international conflicts around the world have some relationship to water.[4] Dam development on the Indus River has aggravated tensions in the Kashmir region disputed between India and Pakistan, with the cry of some being "Water must flow, or blood will flow."[5] Nevertheless, despite having fought three full-scale wars since 1974, India and Pakistan have been able to negotiate the Indus Water Treaty and implement many of its provisions, even as bullets were flying. The Six-Day War of 1967 between Israel and its neighboring states was sparked in part when Israel attacked Syrian diversions on the Yarmouk River, based on a claim that such diversion constituted a violation of Israeli water rights.[6] Yet in many respects, the Joint Water Committee between Israel, Jordan, and Palestine has been one of the relative successes of peace negotiations in the region. Tensions over shared water resources are not merely regional but have reverberations as refugees flee areas of conflict or water insecurity, which may result in rising concerns of nationalism and anti-immigrant conflicts.[7] And tensions over shared water resources that ultimately result in violence are not limited to the international context, but happen at the local level.[8] Of course, few if any of these conflicts are wholly, or even largely, water-based, but water insecurity functions as a "threat multiplier" aggravating other security concerns.[9] Additionally, and as has already been noted, water is much more frequently the locus of cooperation than conflict.[10] It is perhaps unsurprising that humanity's earliest civilizations grew around rivers in deserts, because that environment encouraged cooperation, specialization, and administration to develop a critical scarce resource.[11]

This chapter examines water as the target or weapon in armed conflict, as the direct and indirect cause or aggravator of violent conflicts, and how water instead often mitigates conflicts and encourages peaceful collaboration in otherwise fraught relationships.

Water as a Weapon or Target in Violent Conflict

Water has been both threat and protector throughout human history. While water has more frequently been a locus of human cooperation, with early civilizations rising along the banks of desert rivers, water has also been both weapon and target in violent conflict throughout history. Strategic contamination of water supplies has been used in warfare for millennia, from Solon of Athens poisoning the water supply of the besieged Cirrhaeans in 600 BCE, to the Scottish King Macbeth contaminating the Danes' water supply in the eleventh century.[12] The threat of such acts is serious enough that the provisions of the Geneva Convention address the protection of water security during times of conflict, and make an attack against or the destruction of essential civilian water infrastructure a war crime.[13] Today Solon of Athens and Macbeth of Scotland might well be war criminals.

But the legal consequences of acts of war targeting, or weaponizing, water are often very complicated. The conflict in Libya illustrates this difficulty. In 1983, Libyan leader Muammar Gaddafi initiated a massive water development project, tapping into the enormous Nubian Sandstone Aquifer System (NSAS) underlying parts of Libya, Egypt, Chad, and Sudan to create the "Great Man-Made River" (GMMR) as an engineering marvel to improve water supplies in arid Libya. During the 2011 Libyan revolution against

Gaddafi, there were reports that Gaddafi's forces had sabotaged water-supply facilities, attacked water-supply personnel working with the transition Libyan government, and maintained control over strategic water-supply locations.[14] Assuming the reports were true, Gaddafi's forces appear to have violated prohibitions against attacking drinking-water installations indispensable to the civilian population under Article 54 of Protocol I and Article 14 of Protocol II to the Geneva Convention. Libya acceded to both protocols in 1978. Gaddafi forces could therefore be held as war criminals for their actions relating to attacks on water installations.[15]

However, NATO airstrikes supporting anti-Gaddafi rebels may also have targeted GMMR installations where Gaddafi forces had hidden military assets along a pipeline for the GMMR.[16] Most NATO countries have acceded to or ratified the Geneva Convention protocols. According to reports, the NATO attacks occurred at storage sites for unused pipeline and thus arguably were not to water installations "indispensable to the civilian population." Protocol I has exceptions to the prohibition on attacks of water installations, including when those installations provide only for sustaining military forces (as opposed to civilian populations). Nevertheless, attacks on water installations are strictly prohibited under Protocol I if the attack would leave a civilian population without adequate food or water, leaving to starvation or mass migration. But the legality of such attacks and the practical application of the Geneva Convention Protocols are difficult when military assets are integrated with critical civilian water infrastructure, or when both sides of the conflict may have violated the same legal protections for water.

The Israeli-Palestinian conflict has long included a major water dispute component. The first reported attack by the Palestinian National Liberation Movement (Al-Fatah) was on Israeli water infrastructure in 1965.[17] Palestinians attacked and vandalized pipes providing water to the Israeli settlement of Yitzhar in 2001.[18] At around the same time, Israel destroyed water cisterns and blocked water deliveries in Palestinian territories.[19] Human Rights Watch reported that Israel destroyed dozens of wells, water-distribution pipes, and two major sewage treatment plants in Gaza with bombing in 2014, which have led to accusations that Israel targeted such infrastructure in violation of the Geneva Convention.[20] Importantly, targeting civilian water supplies and infrastructure would not only violate the laws of war under the Geneva Convention but could also violate an international human right to water to the extent such right exists and is enforceable.

Not just water infrastructure can be targeted or weaponized in war. Water in the sky poses other risks. Cloud seeding presents a security challenge that may be more legally complex and speculative. Cloud seeding involves the dispersal of condensation nuclei (usually silver iodide or frozen carbon dioxide) into the atmosphere to induce precipitation.[21] The viability of cloud seeding as a water-supply augmentation method depends upon a multitude of factors, but studies show that it can be effective under certain circumstances. Between 1967 and 1972, the U.S. military deployed cloud seeding as a weapon in Vietnam, in Operation Popeye, to flood areas and roads used or occupied by enemy forces. The controversy surrounding Operation Popeye eventually led to the International Convention on the Prohibition of Military or Any Other Hostile Use of Environmental Modification Techniques of 1977 (ENMOD).[22] The convention demonstrates fears that cloud seeding would cause damage and death from induced flooding and that water augmentation technology, like water infrastructure, can be a means of either enhancing or threatening water security.

Water's role in conflict is not always as concrete as flooding, but is sometimes more symbolic. Water often has deep cultural meaning, as a symbol of nationhood or sovereignty. Its possession, protection, and development can represent legitimacy, and because of that it is a frequent locus of conflict. In *The Prince*, Niccoló Machiavelli wrote that "[n]othing makes a prince so well esteemed as undertaking great enterprises." Taking a national symbol like a river and bridling it with a "greater enterprise" is a powerful means of asserting and maintaining political power. History is rife with regimes seeking legitimacy through great enterprises in water development, including Gaddafi's Great Man-Made River. The North Crimean Canal once provided 85 percent of Crimea's water supply but was cut off by the quick development of a dam by the Ukraine following the annexation of Crimea by Russia.[23] Control of the canal has thus become a strategic military and political target, while the elimination of supply has caused a major water crisis in the region.[24] Whoever controls water claims a veneer of political legitimacy by imprinting the regime's power on a national symbol. But such symbols are tempting targets in violent conflict.

Nowhere is this more evident than the battle between Kurds, Iraqis, and ISIS to control the Mosul Dam in Iraq. The dam is the largest in Iraq, providing electricity and drinking water to the 1.7 million residents of the city of Mosul.[25] It was originally named the Saddam Hussein Dam and was intended as a monument to his regime and its strength.[26] The national anthem of Iraq during Saddam Hussein's Ba'athist regime was "The Land of the Two Rivers," with the repeated refrain of "Blessed be the land of the Euphrates, a homeland of glorious determination and tolerance."[27] Reining in a national symbol with an imposing piece of infrastructure was the quintessential Machiavellian "great enterprise." But this makes the dam strategically significant, as both a security threat and symbol of the shifting balance of power in the region. The Mosul Dam is the largest dam in Iraq. In August 2014, the Islamic State took control of this strategically vital asset, with Kurdish and Iraqi forces retaking control after several months, with assistance from U.S. airstrikes. When a river that symbolizes national identity is controlled by infrastructure aimed at granting political legitimacy, water and waterworks can become strategic targets in war. Economies of scale may require the development of large water infrastructure, but such infrastructure may also be unnecessary or redundant vanity projects aimed at propping up a regime and can present serious vulnerabilities in armed conflict. Development banks and international aid agencies can encourage diversification of water supply portfolios and prioritization of maintenance and conservation over unnecessary "great enterprises" to avoid making water infrastructure a contentious political symbol.

The Indus River holds some similar lessons regarding water and its development as a national or political symbol, and the risks of such symbols in violent conflicts. Some of humanity's oldest civilizations arose on the banks of the Indus River, and it has held special significance not only as a source of water and energy but also as a symbol of sovereignty and identity for nations and communities in the region.[28] India's first prime minister, Jawaharlal Nehru, called dams on the Indus the "temples of the new India."[29] With the end of British rule in the Indian subcontinent in 1947 and the partition of Pakistan and India, conflict resulted over the disputed Kashmir region, through which the Indus flows.[30] The strategic importance of the river and its role in national identity remains as strong as ever, with Indian Prime Minister Narendra Modi committed to a $90 billion river-linking project.[31] While it remains to be seen if this investment is further evidence of the risks of Machiavellian "great enterprises" in water development, the Indus example does show how such infrastructure development may not only be a strategic and symbolic target in armed conflict but also a potential weapon.

On August 19, 2019, Pakistan accused India of waging "fifth-generation warfare" by making an unexpected release of water from its dams into the Sutlej River, resulting in flooding and damage inside of Pakistan, and has threatened to no longer share excess water after a suicide bomb attack by a Pakistan-based Kashmiri militant group killed forty Indian police officers.[32] Muzammil Hussain, the chairman of the Pakistani Water and Power Development Authority, said of India's actions: "They try to isolate diplomatically, they try to strangulate economically, they're trying to strangulate our water resources—and water automatically will have an impact on your economy, your agriculture, and your irrigation."[33] In this instance, the additional investments on India's tributaries to the Indus may not be merely "great enterprises" with strategic and political significance like the GMMR, North Crimean Canal, or Mosul Dam, but potential water weapons like cloud seeding in Operation Popeye or the contaminated water supplies of Macbeth or Solon of Athens.

One possible approach to protect water from being either a weapon or a target is also a potential vulnerability. Integrating water infrastructure with digital communication—smart water systems—can alert water managers to contamination or sabotage at an early enough stage to allow for intervention. These smart water systems would include smart gates for irrigation and dam operations, smart meters for water consumption, and smart appliances for adjusting to water supply and costs. The integration of water infrastructure with smart technology could not only improve water efficiencies and thus water security but also protect water from being a target or weapon in armed conflict. But such smart technology also makes water infrastructure vulnerable to cyberattacks. Hostile states or organizations could use the connectedness of smart water systems to damage critical infrastructure, to hold water supplies hostage, or as a weapon by opening flood gates or sabotaging water treatment systems. Information generated from smart systems would be a prime espionage target regarding the numbers and behavior of populations located in cities, factories, and military bases. One possible legal intervention to address the security risks surrounding smart water systems, while still encouraging their use, is the establishment of a global water fund to finance cybersecurity measures in developing countries.

Water as a Cause or Aggravator of Violent Conflict

Water is not only a vulnerability as a weapon or target in violent conflict but also can be the cause or aggravating factor in such conflicts. Rare, or even perhaps even unheard of, is a war fought between two nations solely, or even largely, over shared water resources. The only potentially pure "water war" in history is perhaps the conflict between the Mesopotamian city-states of Umma and Lagash over four thousand years ago.[34] Still, "the absence of war does not mean the absence of conflict."[35] Most serious international conflicts in history that are multifaceted, and water conflict is at times a very real aggravating factor in violent conflicts and sometimes the means through which nations assert a broader claim to sovereignty underlying the conflict. Water disputes have unquestionably featured prominently in conflicts between Israel and its Arab nation neighbors, but these conflicts are so multifaceted that isolating water issues from other sources of conflict is nearly impossible. Disputes over the Jordan River Basin still provide a useful case study to consider the role of water in war. The Jordan River Basin is a useful case study because, in such an arid region, actual disputes over water are real and serious, but also because it is a region where sovereignty and cultural identity can be even more contentious than resource disputes, and water can become a sort of token through which parties argue, and sometimes fight violently, to assert deeper and broader claims underlying conflict.

The Jordan River is formed by the convergence of several tributaries, including the Banias in Syria and the Hatzbani in Lebanon, and the Yarmouk, which originates in Syria and flows through Jordan, in its lower reaches before it drains into the Dead Sea. Varying degrees of conflict and cooperation had persisted between the co-riparian nations in the Jordan River Basin for decades.[36] However, tensions over transboundary water resources escalated in the wake of the 1948 Arab-Israeli War. Israel began development of what was then known as the Jordan Valley Unified Water Plan (JVUWP) in 1953, and which would develop into part of the Israeli National Water Carrier (NWC).[37] The NWC was an ambitious plan to integrate and develop water supplies throughout Israel as one of the highest priorities of the nascent state. While Israel proceeded with the JVUWP, Syria filed complaints with the Secretary-General and Security Council of the United Nations in 1953, accusing Israel of violating the 1949 armistice agreement between the two nations, which created a demilitarized zone. These complaints were based in part on concerns that the diversion plan was an attempt by Israel to occupy the demilitarized zone, that it would expand Israel's capacity to absorb new immigrants, and that the project would undermine Arab efforts to address Palestinian sovereignty.[38]

Under pressure from the United States, Israel suspended development of the JVUWP to focus on a diversion of water from the Sea of Galilee to the

Negev Desert through the NWC, which was ultimately completed in 1964.[39] Meanwhile, U.S. Special Envoy Eric Johnston promoted a regional plan for developing and distributing water between the nations sharing the Jordan River Basin.[40] The "Johnston Plan" became a "memorandum of understanding" between the nations, but never materialized into a formal, binding treaty.[41] Israel and Syria continued to take hardline stances regarding their rights to the waters of the Jordan and its tributaries.[42] The Arab League considered a preventive technical response, meaning a preemptive diversion of water, or military mobilization to prevent Israel's diversion. But there were sharp divisions between members of the Arab League about the preferred course of action and whether to focus efforts solely to address water supplies or a unified Arab effort in opposition to Israel and in support for Palestinians. Ultimately, with pressure coming from Egyptian President Gamal Abdel Nasser, the Arab League focused on the preemptive technical response. Syria began diversion from the Banias in 1964 and Lebanon began diversions of water from the Hatzbani in March 1965, in quantities roughly in accordance with the Johnston Plan. Israel stated that it would regard such diversions as an infringement upon its sovereignty, and there were sporadic attacks on Syrian diversion operations by Israeli forces beginning in 1964. Syrians also fired on Israeli construction operations, and tensions quickly escalated, including air strikes by Israel against Syria in November 1964 and a skirmish over Israeli water development in the demilitarized zone in March 1965.[43]

Syria renewed diversion efforts in 1966. Israel launched an air attack on Syrian diversion operations on July 14, 1966, resulted in the deaths of several Syrian soldiers, workers, and civilians.[44] This was the final Israeli Defense Force attack on Syrian before the beginning of the Six-Day War in June 1967. While the Six-Day War is a complicated conflict involving, among other issues, control of the Straits of Tiran, there is little question that the violence over water between Israel and Syria contributed to the atmosphere of tension leading up to the war. But the violent conflict over shared water resources from 1964 through 1966 could not be accurately described as solely about water either. While Israel viewed Syrian water diversions as a violation of its sovereignty, it had others reasons for attacking Syria, including Syrian support of the Palestinian Fatah organization and evidence of Syrian involvement in land-mine installations and sabotage in Israel that resulted in Israeli casualties.[45] But this is partly why the Jordan River Basin is an important example of water conflict. Water typically cannot be easily disentangled from other sources of conflict. While the conflict in the 1960s in the Jordan River

Basin cannot be accurately characterized as a pure "water war," it would be equally inaccurate to suggest that the violent conflict had little to do with water. The nations in the Jordan River Basin saw a shared, scarce resource and knew its strategic importance. But they also saw control over water resources as evidence of national sovereignty and security.[46]

Despite the violence that rose around sharing the Jordan River in the 1960s, the history of the Jordan River is largely one of peaceful, if not necessarily harmonious, cooperation. Indeed, cooperation and conflict are not mutually exclusive, and the politics of most shared river basins include some degree of both conditions.[47] Despite the conflict over the Jordan River, the Israeli-Palestinian Joint Water Committee, created in 1995 by the Oslo Accords, and the Israeli-Jordanian Joint Water Committee, created by the 1994 peace treaty between the two countries, remain functioning, albeit imperfect, institutions for transboundary water cooperation in a region with few examples of comparable successes.[48] The Indus River Basin is also a good example of this seemingly incoherent cohabitation of cooperation and conflict over transboundary water sharing between nations at war.

While the conflict between India and Pakistan over Kashmir is complex and serious, including four major wars and many other instances of violence, the two countries signed the Indus Water Treaty in 1960.[49] The "Goldilocks governance" concept discussed in chapter 1—attempting to govern water at the river basin level collaboratively—would have been the ideal, with principles of international law like reasonable and equitable use and avoiding significant harm to neighbors controlling the relationship over the river. But the intractability and brutality of the Kashmir conflict made such an arrangement impossible. As such, the Indus Water Treaty instead effectively "cut the baby in half" by assigning absolute rights to three tributaries to each country with no requirement for cooperative management.[50] This has been hailed as an example of how hostile states can reach peaceful agreements even in the midst of war.[51] However, the deal is frequently criticized by both nations.[52] The renewed investment by India in infrastructure development in the basin, as well as climate change impacts on glaciers at the head of the Indus, impact downstream flows to Pakistan-controlled parts of Kashmir even though tributary rights are absolute and allocated equally between the countries.[53] Even though the Indus Water Treaty granted absolute rights to tributaries, India's development on its tributaries does have impacts to flows into Pakistan-controlled parts of Kashmir. Some protestors in those areas have adopted the refrain: "Water will flow, or blood will flow."[54] As such, while the Indus Water

Treaty is perhaps rightfully lauded as an example of warring nations finding some common ground, it is also a potential example of how quickly common ground can shift under foot.

The conflict over, or involving, water in the Indus and Jordan basins is perhaps not terribly surprising. These two regions have been embroiled in conflicts for generations. But water's potential to aggravate disputes to the point of violence is evident in other, perhaps less obvious, contexts. In the Colorado River Basin in North America, interstate water disputes nearly resulted in a twentieth-century U.S. civil war.[55] The Colorado River Basin includes seven states and two countries in an arid region with a growing population and large agricultural sector, and the Colorado River forms part of the boundaries between Arizona, California, and Nevada.[56] The states sharing the Colorado River had agreed to a compact in 1922 regarding its allocation, but Arizona refused to agree to the compact. California, ignoring Arizona's opposition, proceeded with the development of the Parker Dam on the Colorado River. In 1935, Arizona Governor Benjamin Baker Moeur had spies embedded in the dam's construction crew, reporting on California progress.[57] When his spies alerted him that California operations had crossed into Arizona territory, Moeur sent the National Guard to halt construction.[58] Harold L. Ickes, the U.S. secretary of the interior at the time, intervened to delay dam construction in exchange for Moeur agreeing to recall troops.[59] Four years previous to the Parker Dam conflict, the states of Texas and Oklahoma had a dispute over the Red River, which formed the border between the two states. This dispute resulted in Texas ordering rangers to defend bridges and the governor of Oklahoma declaring martial law to secure the state's control over the river.[60] The intensity of these interstate water conflicts in the 1930s led officials within Germany's Third Reich to speculate that such disputes demonstrated national disunity that would preclude the United States from entering World War II.[61]

These domestic water conflicts illustrate that the potential for violence over water is not limited to wars between nations. Violent water conflicts arise at the national level. Indeed, subnational, interstate conflict like that between Arizona and California is one of the major challenges in the Indus River Basin, with Indian states disputing water allocations between them.[62] And conflicts between subnational communities and individuals are perhaps the most common form of violence over water. For example, in 2012 in Kenya, conflict between cattlemen and farmers has resulted in several instances of violence, and even murder. Upstream irrigation diversion on the Ewaso Kedong River impacted downstream water supplies for cattle and related communities, resulting in violent clashes between farmers and cattlemen, and between those parties and police.[63] Similar violent clashes have occurred over the waters of Lake Turkana, between the Kenyan Turkana and the Ethiopian Daasanach, resulting in the deaths of at least twenty-four people.[64] A man was charged with murder in Australia in 2007 over a dispute regarding water restrictions.[65] The Los Angeles Aqueduct was subjected to repeated bombings to prevent diversions from the Owens Valley.[66] Sporadic violence has resulted from water shortages in Chennai, India, including an arrest of one person who stabbed a neighbor over a water dispute.[67] And as I mentioned in chapter 3, the violence that broke out in response to the privatization of Cochabamba's water system in 2000 resulted in the deaths on both the side of protestors and of police.[68]

The role of water stress in violent conflict is sometimes indirect but still important. The rise of ISIS in Syria or the Taliban in Afghanistan coincided with historic droughts in those countries, which arguably contributed to conditions ripe for instability and radicalization.[69] Drought in those basins result in crop failure and rising food prices, which drive migration, urbanization, and poverty, which create a fertile atmosphere for conflict.[70] Water has a similar indirect role in the conflict in Yemen. Just as in Afghanistan and Syria, water is not the primary driver, but its role in the conflict is perhaps underappreciated. Yemen is the most water-insecure country in the world. Prior to the conflict involving Houthi rebels, Yemen's population was largely rural and coastal, and its economy largely based on water-efficient farming. However, more recently, Yemen's farming operations shifted to more water-intensive cash crops and its population has shifted to larger urban centers. These cultural and agricultural changes have coincided with increased drought and have included violence that specifically focused on water in areas such as Taizz and Abyan, but have the broader effect of aggravating conflict and instability in a country that would likely be embroiled in war even with less serious water challenges.[71]

Despite the severity of these conflicts, the Joint Commissions continue to function in the Jordan River Basin; Pakistan and India have agreed to the Indus Water Treaty; Texas and Oklahoma resolved a water dispute in 2011 peacefully through the U.S. Supreme Court; and the states sharing the Colorado River Basin recently agreed to a Drought Contingency Plan under which all states would share in water shortages in the basin. The work of Aaron Wolf has provided a strong response to overheated concerns of water wars, as his research has demonstrated that there are far more instances of states cooperating over shared waters than fighting over them.[72]

However, risks of violence related to water at the local level, like that seen in Kenya, India, Bolivia, Australia, and the United States, may continue or even worsen with more intense droughts due to climate change, as would the kind of instability and risks of radicalization seen in the Euphrates and Kabul river basins. And while "water wars" have been largely avoided so far in tense regions like the Jordan River Basin and the Indus River Basin, that is no guarantee that such will always be the case, particularly as drought conditions worsen with climate change. Why, in the face of so many reasons to perpetuate or escalate conflict, have water disputes most often been resolved peacefully or managed cooperatively? And what can be done to promote this pattern into an uncertain future?

Water as a Catalyst for Peace and Cooperation

I have addressed some possible reforms to promote peace and cooperation and avoid conflict over water. Careful investment in smart water systems, combined with effective cybersecurity, can promote water security while avoiding creating new water system vulnerabilities. International development banks and agencies can encourage such investments, as well as promoting diversified water portfolios and appropriate prioritization of water infrastructure and maintenance over Machiavellian "great enterprises" whose symbolic and strategic importance invites attack. Compliance with international laws like the Geneva Convention prohibition on targeting civilian water supplies and infrastructure, the ENMOD prohibitions on using climate engineering as a weapon, and respect for an international human right to water would also limit the impacts of war on water security.

Still, this leaves open the questions of why water is more often a source of cooperation than conflict, and how we can preserve that legacy in a world of changing water supplies and demands. I'll focus my attempt to answer these questions first on international conflict between shared waters. Perhaps the better way to understand transboundary water relations are not in terms of conflict or cooperation, as if one is always bad and the other always good and they cannot coexist, but instead in terms of water interaction.[73] International water law largely accepts this reality of water interaction that includes some degree of both healthy conflict and cooperation. By healthy conflict, I mean a nation using peaceful means of dispute resolution to encourage account-ability and transparency in shared water management. International water law takes many different forms, as I've already discussed in the different approaches in the Indus and Jordan river basins. But the general approach is reflected in the U.N. Convention on the Law of the Non-Navigational Uses of International Watercourses (the "Watercourse Convention").[74] The Watercourse Convention was adopted by the United Nations in 1997 and entered into force in 2014.[75]

The Watercourse Convention reflects the consensus approach to transboundary water allocation in four broad principles. First, all states have the right to the reasonable and equitable utilization of waters within their ter-ritory. Second, states must avoid causing significant harm to their co-riparian nations in their use of shared waters, or else pay for the harms they cause. Third, co-riparian states must cooperate in good faith, provide adequate no-tice, and share information regarding their use of transboundary waters.[76] Fourth, dispute resolution mechanisms should facilitate peaceful resolution of any conflict over the shared watercourse.[77] In implementing these prin-ciples, co-riparian states are to give "special regard" to the "requirements of vital human needs," thus effectively including a human right component into the sharing of international watercourses.[78] Furthermore, the Watercourse Convention effectively integrates the concerns of the Geneva Convention, providing that international watercourses and related installations should "enjoy the protection accorded by the principles and rules of international law applicable in international and non-international armed conflict."[79] These principles demonstrate the capacity to both encourage cooperation but address inevitable conflict in international water interactions and the recognition of the reality that conflict and cooperation must frequently co-exist in international river basins.

Additionally, the Watercourse Convention explicitly references the for-mation of interjurisdictional commissions to jointly manage the shared resource.[80] This approach mirrors what I prescribed for the "Goldilocks gov-ernance challenge" in chapter 1. To the extent possible, river basins should be managed as a unit, and such interjurisdictional commissions can approx-imate such unified management. However, many countries, particularly in basins that have experienced armed conflict, will be reluctant to cede any degree of sovereignty of a critical strategic resource to their neighbors. In such circumstances, how can basin-level management be achieved? One possibility is for international law to impose a fiduciary obligation upon interjurisdictional commissions to manage the shared resource for the benefit of all member states.[81] In many basins, there is concern that a "hydrohegemon" (a co-riparian state with disproportionate economic, political, and or military power) will dominate any international commission.[82] But a fiduciary obligation would provide other member states with a possible cause of action against the river basin commission were it to be co-opted by the hydro-hegemon.

Still, such a fiduciary obligation may be difficult to enforce even if it existed. And the principles of the Watercourse Convention, while in force and widely recognized, are not universal. Many international river basins have their own treaty regimes which are starkly different from the principles of the Watercourse Convention, including the Indus Water Treaty. Additionally, the applicability of the Watercourse Convention to some international groundwater resources, including the Nubian Sandstone Aquifer System in northern Africa, is uncertain, as the Watercourse Convention applies to watercourses that are a "system of surface waters and groundwaters constituting by virtue of their physical relationship a unitary whole and normally flowing into a common terminus."[83] War and regime change have occurred in other countries overlying the NSAS besides Libya, including Egypt and Sudan, without any clearly applicable principles of governing international law. The law governing transboundary aquifers like the NSAS is underdeveloped compared to the law governing transboundary rivers like the Euphrates or Indus, and Libya remains the only country to develop the NSAS to any significant extent. However, there is an effort to develop a regional strategy for using and protecting the NSAS, including a current monitoring and data-sharing initiative involving all four overlying nations.[84] It is difficult to predict what impact any regime changes (should they prove durable) would have on relations in the region as they relate to the NSAS. But some governing principles for sharing the NSAS would provide some means for peaceful cooperation and dispute resolution between the nations sharing the NSAS. These principles could be derived from the Watercourse Convention, the International Law Commission's Draft Article on the Law of Transboundary Aquifers, or the treaty principles embodied in the Guarani Aquifer Treaty (between Argentina, Brazil, Paraguay, and Uruguay) or the al-Disi Aquifer Treaty (between Jordan and Saudi Arabia).[85]

Respect for the rule of law, in general, may be another explanation for why violent conflict over water is rare at both the international and domestic level. Most international river basins are governed by treaties, and most of those treaties integrate the principles of the Watercourse Convention.[86] Where disputes have arisen, most are resolved by adhering to dispute resolution principles of the treaty or governing international law, and in some instances, international tribunals have been called upon to decide upon water disputes. International water disputes—including between Argentina and Uruguay, Chile and Bolivia, Costa Rica and Nicaragua, Benin and Niger, Botswana and Namibia, and Hungary and Slovakia—have been peacefully overseen by international tribunals.[87]

And at the local and domestic level, law continues to facilitate peaceful settlements or resolution of water disputes. Take my home state of Arizona in the southwestern United States as an example. Arizona lies within an arid region, has a growing population and a large agricultural base, encompasses twenty-one Native American tribal reservations, and shares a hotly contested transboundary river—the Colorado River—with two neighboring states and one neighboring country. And yet violence over water is rare if not unheard of in Arizona. Part of the explanation for this is that Arizona has repeatedly treated disputes over water rights—what water lawyers call "paper water"—as serious challenges requiring reforms, which have helped Arizona largely avoid disputes over "wet water." Disputes in the early twentieth century between farmers in the Salt River Basin led to building the Salt River Project—a series of dams and conveyances built by the U.S. federal government and financed by farmers in the basin pledging their land as collateral. In the middle of the twentieth century, the disputes between Arizona and California over the Colorado River resulted in the U.S. Supreme Court's decision in *Arizona v. California*, and a compromise under which Arizona agreed to be the junior water appropriator on the river in exchange for California's support in securing federal funds to build the Central Arizona Project, which brings a portion of Arizona's Colorado River allocation to central Arizona, where most of the population of the state resides. In the late twentieth century, disputes over groundwater rights between the city of Tucson, copper-mining operations, and pecan farmers resulted in the enactment of the Arizona Groundwater Management Act. That act constituted a grand compromise, under which farmers and miners would agree to quantify their water rights and limit new appropriations, but cities would agree not to approve new subdivisions if they could not establish that there was enough water to provide for the new development.[88] When jurisdictions respond to legal disputes as opportunities for water policy reforms, such reforms may prevent more intense conflicts over actual water scarcity.

Still, even effective international and domestic laws cannot fully explain why water wars have largely been avoided, even in basins with frequent conflicts. The NSAS has no meaningful legal structure yet, but the nations sharing it have never come into conflict over the resource, even though these nations have dealt with war and instability and even though NSAS infrastructure has been the target of war. The Euphrates River and Nile River basins have only minimal transboundary governance structures and are basins in arid regions that have frequently seen war. Yet no wars have ever been fought between nations over sharing these rivers. The Indus Water Treaty is a rough division of rights to tributaries and not a cooperative treaty like the Watercourse Convention. The Joint Water Committees between the co-riparians to the Jordan River bear little resemblance to the governance structure of the Watercourse Convention. And yet, even though there has been some water-based conflict in these two basins, there has not been a true "water war."

One possible reason why water wars have been avoided, even in instances where water laws and governance institutions are relatively weak or under-developed, has simply been the role of international trade. Many countries in arid regions have been able to import virtual water and avoid scarcity. Tony Allan argues that has mitigated water scarcity and allowed governments to construct an image of domestic water security despite depending on virtual water imports.[89] Claudia Sadoff and David Grey have pointed out the role of "shared benefits" in discouraging water conflicts.[90] The concept of "shared benefits" comes from welfare economics, and this concept means that water is a valuable scarce commodity with multiple possible alternative uses, with the highest and best use often dictated by geography.[91] The 1961 Columbia River Treaty between the United States and Canada is a good example of how shared benefits work to mitigate or avoid water conflict. In that treaty, Canada as the upstream riparian had the best potential to develop hydroelectric energy and flood control, and the United States as the downstream riparian had the best potential for agriculture.[92] So rather than each jurisdiction trying to inefficiently develop the fully panoply of water uses, each developed its portion of the river according to its geographic advantage, and then traded the benefits of that development with each other.[93] A similar shared benefits approach works in the Colorado River Basin. Mexico agrees to share in water shortages in the basin, even though Mexico's water rights are quantified by treaty, and in exchange the United States stores some of Mexico's water in U.S. reservoirs.[94] The concept of shared benefits is taking root in other parts of the world facing potential conflict over water stress, including the Nile River Basin.[95] Shared benefits may even play a role in limiting water conflict at the domestic level. The Colorado River Basin again provides a good example. Arizona has the appropriate hydrogeology to take water from the river and recharge aquifers. The Arizona Water Banking Authority takes advantage of Arizona's geographic strength by allowing other basin states, California and Nevada, to bank a portion of their annual water allocation underground. In this way, in years of shortage, Arizona forgoes some portion of its water from the river for its co-riparian states while then using the water those neighbors stored underground.[96]

Another possible reason we see few international water wars is the mutual involvement of water science experts (hydrologists, engineers, etc.) who are "expected to rise above political maneuvering as they work for the greater good of ecological and economic sustainability."[97] The frequent involvement of technical and scientific experts increases the likelihood of cooperation because they tend to share a professional lexicon and methodology that helps to overcome cultural or political differences. In this context, it is helpful to consider the conditions surrounding the rare instances of heightened international water conflict in formulating policy interventions to promote water security. The likelihood of water conflict increases when water governance institutions cannot adapt to either political changes in the basin (meaning new or shifting power dynamics) or physical changes in the basin (meaning both changes in supply and demand, as well as new infrastructure, like a dam).[98] Anders Jägerskog's research using regime theory suggests that scientific experts play a critical role in water negotiations and that their role reduced uncertainty for decision makers and legitimizes political decisions.[99] Still, he notes that expert advice can still be politicized, or ignored for political reasons, noting that experts have encouraged Palestinians to focus on the international legal principles of equitable utilization rather than securing quantified water rights, but "that advice does not fit the sanctioned discourse."[100] As such, measures that encourage greater institutional competency in the water field, and in particular in water negotiations and dispute resolution, should promote the pattern of greater water cooperation.[101] But experts will also increase the capacity of water governance institutions to adapt to changing conditions. I will discuss adaptive water management further in coming chapters. Additionally, in disputes involving scarce resources, proposals to either conserve the resource or augment the resource are important suggestions for avoiding or resolving conflict, and I will discuss conservation and augmentation measures in coming chapters as well.

Based on these observations, water cooperation is the normal dominant condition in most international basins and can continue to be so because of responsible international trade, institutional competency in water management and dispute resolution, respect for the rule of law, increased adaptive capacity of water governance institutions, and appropriate prioritization of water infrastructure development and cybersecurity. Several water policy scholars suggested measures for addressing international water conflict that are similar to those already mentioned that would also benefit local water conflict, including (1) experienced neutral experts to facilitate negotiations; (2) support and patience for a long-term process; (3) leadership from the riparian stakeholders; (4) strengthening water governance institutions and the rule of law; and (5) balancing closed-door, high-level meetings with inclusive stakeholder processes.[102] In asking why cooperation and not conflict is the norm in water interactions, these same water policy scholars responded, "Because water is so important, nations cannot afford to fight over it. Instead, water fuels greater interdependence. By coming together to jointly manage their shared water resources, countries can build trust and prevent conflict."[103]

But do these explanations and prescriptions for the norm of cooperation in international water interactions also work in the context of national or local water interactions? A quote attributed to Mark Twain is often cited in western U.S. water circles: "Whisky is for drinking, and water is for fighting over." In his book *Water Is for Fighting Over: And Other Myths about Water in the West*, John Fleck does for Western water what Aaron Wolf and Peter Gleick have done for international water—demonstrate that water cooperation is common in part because conflict is counterproductive and water users know it.[104] While the history of western U.S. water policy has some examples of heightened water tensions (like the conflict over the Colorado River in the 1930s, or the bombing of the Los Angeles Aqueduct), the normal condition has been far more collaborative and peaceful. Fleck points out the importance of conservation, adaptation, and institutional competency as well stakeholder participation and informal conversations and management approaches like those studied by Elinor Ostrom serve to avoid and mitigate conflict.[105]

Conclusion

Many of the dynamics that influence transboundary water disputes at the international level impact such disputes at the national or domestic level.

This includes the potential influence of hydro-hegemons. For example, in the Delaware River Basin, shared by the states of New York, Pennsylvania, New Jersey, and Delaware, there is a transboundary river commission called the Delaware River Basin Commission (DRBC).[106] The DRBC issued a moratorium on the use of water within the basin for hydraulic fracturing to produce natural gas.[107] The state of Pennsylvania petitioned the DRBC to lift the moratorium to allow fracking operations in the basin. To prevent this, the state of New York—the largest, wealthiest, and most politically influential state in the basin—sued the DRBC. In response, the DRBC left the moratorium in place.[108] The fracking issue and its governance by the DRBC illustrate that even domestic water disputes include power asymmetries and political agendas, sometimes as complex and fraught as those that exist in international water disputes. Addressing these asymmetries may require similar reforms, including a fiduciary obligation on transboundary governance institutions that would allow member states with less power, like Pennsylvania in the DRBC example, to sue the institution for breaching its fiduciary duty if it manages the shared resource in a way that unduly benefits the hydro-hegemon. One way to reduce the role of the hydro-hegemon in these disputes—whether international or domestic—is to emphasize the role of institutional competency and neutral technical expertise.

In addition to these suggestions, I offer a word of caution about the role of technical experts in water disputes, as important as they are, and the importance of giving a voice to all stakeholders in the basin, whether international or local. I was once involved in a water dispute between an irrigation district providing water to local farmers and a Native American tribe. The irrigation district's diversions and dams had interrupted flow on the river, so that very little water was reaching the tribe in the stream. The irrigation district proposed settlement for the dispute, which would include building a pipeline to provide a large quantity of treated water to the tribe. When I discussed the proposal with the tribal leaders and attorneys, they stated, "We don't want their water. We want our water." They went on to explain to me that the river was sacred to them. In my mind, I thought, "Water is fungible—one water molecule is the same as the next. And if what is meant by 'sacred' is that water is very important economically, aesthetically, and culturally, then this was something the tribe has in common with the irrigation district." It took time, education, and a healthy dose of humility for me to better understand the tribe's position. Water conflict does not always occur because of scarcity or military strategy. Sometimes it is the meaning of water and how it represents sovereignty, nationhood, or cultural identity that lie at the heart of a water dispute. Indeed, a "water dispute" is often not really about water, but water is instead the means through which parties engage in a deeper argument about independence, or dignity, or political or cultural differences. Technical and legal expertise are critical in avoiding and resolving water disputes and preserving the norm of peaceful water interactions, but cultural sensitivity and education regarding the meaning of water are equally important in achieving and preserving water security.

7

Water Security and Mass Migration

Many of the major conflicts discussed in the previous chapter have related refugee crises, as people flee violence and instability. For example, the conflict (and related drought conditions) in the Euphrates River Basin, including the rise of ISIS and the Syrian Civil War, has displaced nearly seven million people, including more than half of all Syrians.[1] But water plays a role in mass migration beyond refugees fleeing violence. For example, on March 14, 2019, Tropical Cyclone Idai struck the coast of Mozambique, displacing nearly one hundred fifty thousand people practically overnight.[2] Drought, like flood, also drives migration. Climate change increases the frequency and intensity of El Niño events, weather patterns driven by anomalous warming of the Pacific Ocean.[3] El Niño years impact precipitation patterns in Central America, which have contributed to one of the region's worst droughts, with 3.5 million in need of humanitarian assistance, thousands of dead cattle, and the failure of up to 75 percent of corn and bean crops in Honduras, Guatemala, and El Salvador from 2018 to 2019.[4] Since 1970, northern migration from Central America has increased twenty-eight-fold, from 118,000 to nearly 3.3 million each year.[5] Over four million people have fled Venezuela in response to the recent economic and political crisis during President Nicolas Maduro's regime.[6] During that time, twenty million people (two-thirds of all Venezuelans) suffered from water shortages or water cutoffs, with increases in infectious diseases and other public health effects.[7]

Of course, just like violent conflict, migration often defies simple explanations like drought or flood. People move for myriad reasons. For example, in 2018, the International Organization for Migration conducted a survey of Salvadoran migrants and found that 52 percent cited economic opportunity as their reasons for migration, 18 percent cited violence and insecurity, 2 percent cited family reunification, and 28 percent cited a combination of these reasons.[8] Many migrants and refugees say they are seeking peace or prosperity, but peace and prosperity are functions of water security. But this is also a "chicken or the egg" problem—water security is also a function of peace and prosperity. But just as in the case of armed conflict, water plays an important and often underappreciated role in human migration. The World Bank estimates that there will be 140 million climate refugees by 2050, with a third of these forced to move by sudden weather events (like floods or forest fires), and the remaining displaced over time by rising sea levels and desertification and drought.[9] The world faces an unprecedented refugee and migrant crisis, as millions flee famine, poverty, persecution, and violence in Syria, Iraq, Myanmar, Central America, Venezuela, and other places. These most recent refugees and migrants add to the millions of displaced people all over the world and the millions more seeking economic opportunities in a different country or moving from rural communities to cities. Still, while the movement of these people can appear, on the surface, as a response to political or economic conditions, these migrations can also be understood by considering an ancient explanation. People are doing what they have done for thousands of years—they are moving to find water.[10]

Water-based migrations are not simply matters of fleeing water insecurity but also of following the promise of water security. The earliest migration of humans from Africa 120,000 years ago was along a humid corridor following available water.[11] Human migrations continued to be driven by water, whether pastoral communities following rain or sedentary communities fleeing disruptive climate changes like drought.[12] If we examine the movement of immigrants and refugees in recent decades, we will see a mass migration away from water insecure regions and toward water secure regions.[13] Even the westward expansion of the United States of America can be at least partially attributed to the law of prior appropriation, promising superior priority in water rights to those first immigrants who migrated west.[14] While these people move for a variety of reasons, including from conflict and poverty, many of these reasons have a nexus with water security and the opportunities it affords. The challenge of mass migration will grow more pronounced with the effects of climate change, as water insecurity is likely to be aggravated in the regions from which migrants leave, and water stress placed on areas absorbing migrants due to increased demand. This water stress will be seen in increased desertification, more serious drought and flood cycles, and rising sea levels not only flooding coastal communities but also causing saline intrusion of freshwater aquifers, thus limiting groundwater supplies to coastal urban communities (the largest and fastest-growing communities in the world).[15]

Discussing migration in the context of water security is complicated, not simply because it is difficult to know how much water insecurity factored into the decisions of individual migrants to move. It is also complicated because oftentimes migrants flee water insecurity, only to find it again in another form where they settle. For example, in one of the most obvious instances of a connection between mass migration and drought, many migrants from Oklahoma (so-called Okies) fled the Dust Bowl of the 1930s, during a period of severe drought, crop failure, and dust storms in the Great Plains of the United States that coincided with the Great Depression.[16] Many of these Okies settled in informal camps in California and worked in agriculture in a region facing its own water challenges.[17] Additionally, many Okies settled in camps alongside the Los Angeles River, which at the time was a wild and highly variable river, with banks so overgrown they featured as the setting for old Tarzan movies.[18] Many Okies died in catastrophic flooding alongside the Los Angeles River, including on New Year's Day 1934, a tragedy immortalized in the Woody Guthrie song, "The New Year's Flood."[19] Thus many Okies, like many migrants and refugees, fled one form of water insecurity, only to fall victim to another form in their new home.

Perhaps the best response to the challenge of increasing refugee and migration challenges is not to build walls but to invest in global water security, both to help people stay where they are and to help those who migrate. This chapter focuses on three broad categories of such investments and evaluates them for their potential to address water security as a driver of mass migration. The first is the construction of large dams, which have the potential to promote greater drought and flood resiliency but also often displace communities or impact downstream regions. Thus, dams are a both a potential aggravating and mitigating factor to migration challenges. The second possible investment is in the protection and promotion of environmental flows and improved watershed management. These investments may seem to have little to do with migration, but watershed management may help protect forests to limit migration due to deforestation, and environmental flows may help mitigate the challenges of rising sea levels displacing communities. The third possible investment is support for refugee host communities. As refugees settle in new areas, they often place strains on water resources in regions already struggling with water insecurity, and this can create tension between refugees and their hosts. Greater support for these refugee host communities will both promote water security and reduce the risks of water-related conflict.

Dam Development and Mass Migration

If at least some of drivers of mass migration are drought and flood, then a potential solution is the construction of more dams. Large dams can manage river flows, absorbing and holding flood waters to protect downstream communities while storing water for times of drought. But dams destroy ecosystems, displace communities, and as I have already discussed, present tempting national security targets and political symbols. The construction of the Ilusu Dam on the Euphrates will result in the submersion of the historic city of Hasankeyf in Turkey and has already proven a target of attack by the Kurdistan Workers' Party and a source of tension between Turkey and Iraq, its downstream co-riparian on the Euphrates.[20] I have already discussed the human health impacts of the Diama Dam in Senegal and its role in increasing the instances of water-related and water-based diseases.[21] The Aswan Dam on the Nile in Egypt submerged priceless archeological sites.[22] But in each of these instances, the dams provided important water storage, flood mitigation, and renewable energy to the surrounding communities. Dams illustrated that, when it comes to water management, "we can never do merely one thing."[23] Whatever resource management approach we take, there will always be both costs and benefits, both risks and potential rewards. The development of the Tennessee Valley Authority (TVA)—a series of large dams and reservoirs built during the early part of the twentieth century in the southeastern United States—expanded access to electricity, made access to safe drinking water and sanitation universal in the region, wiped out malaria, and nearly eliminated the risks of deadly flooding.[24] But the TVA also gave rise to some of the most controversial and consequential lawsuits involving endangered species in the history of the United States due to its impacts on the environment.[25]

One of the most controversial dam projects, and one of the best illustrations of Hardin's Law in the context of human migration, is the Three Gorges Dam on the Yangtze River in China, the largest hydroelectric project on Earth. Like many large dams, it fits the description of the Machiavellian "great enterprises," as much a political symbol as critical infrastructure. Mao Tse Tung wrote a poem, entitled "Swimming," anticipating the dam and its cultural meaning:

> Walls of stone will stand upstream to the west
> To hold back Wushan's clouds and rain

Till a smooth lake rises in the narrow gorges.
The mountain goddess, if she is still there,
Will marvel at a world so changed.[26]

The dam would come to represent the power of the People's Republic of China, to remake its geography, to harness its natural resource, and to symbolize the power of a regime to bridle a force as powerful as the Yangtze. The Three Gorges Dam had been discussed, both as a political and technical opportunity, since before the rise of the Communist Party of China.[27] But the symbolic meaning and political influence of dams as "greater enterprises" does not mean that they cannot also be critical water infrastructure. The dam cost nearly $24 billion, but increased energy capacity to 22,500 megawatts, based on renewable and low-greenhouse-gas-emitting energy (at least relative to fossil fuel power generation). Power from the project is distributed across nine provinces and three cities, providing energy to tens of millions of people. The Three Gorges Dam reduces coal consumption in the region by thirty-one million tons per year, avoiding one hundred million tons of greenhouse gas emissions annually, according to the National Development and Reform Commission of China. Increased barge traffic, made possible by the dam, has reduced the need for trucking in the region and further lowered greenhouse gas emissions.[28]

Despite these benefits, there are many costs associated with such a project. While the dam generates an enormous amount of renewable energy, it was expected to provide 10 percent of China's power demands. But just as low-flow showers often don't conserve water because people just take longer showers, increased demand for power in China has meant that the Three Gorges Dam only provides about 2 percent of China's total power demands.[29] The dam prevents critical sediment transport downstream.[30] The dam has had huge environmental and ecological impacts, including contributing to the functional extinction of the baiji river dolphin.[31]

The dam's impact on migration is similarly complex, with both serious costs and benefits. Improved energy security, combined with potential air-quality benefits, may limit the need for migration from areas served by the project. But likely the most important impact the dam has had in terms of limiting migration is its improvement of flood management in the basin. The project has flood storage capacity of twenty-two cubic kilometers, with the potential to limit the impact of even enormous flood events. For example, in 1954, a flood on the Yangtze killed over 33,000 people and displaced over

18 million people. In 1998, four years into the construction of the project, a flood of similar size occurred in the same region, displacing 2.3 million people and killing 1,526. Since its completion in 2012, and despite increased flooding risk in the basin by the increasing frequency and intensity of El Niño years caused by climate change, no flood-related deaths were recorded, and damage to farms and flood-related relocations were limited.[32] Despite the dam's capacity to limit flood-related relocations, the project itself has permanently displaced over a million people who formerly lived and farmed along its banks.[33] The flooding of the gorges caused by the project submerged 13 cities, 140 towns, and over 1,000 small villages.[34] And the human cost of such relocations cannot be measured simply in numbers. There is an enormous cultural cost. The Three Gorges Dam project has submerged more than two thousand known archeological sites, with some structures dismantled and moved, and others looted or lost.[35]

The example of the Three Gorges Dam demonstrates why those seeking to reduce the impact of water insecurity on human migration should cautiously evaluate the role of large dams. Displacement by dam development occurs all over the world, from the Bui Dam in Ghana, to Indonesia and the Saguling Dam, to the Sudan and the Merowe Dam.[36] People displaced by large dam projects share some similarities with other migrants and refugees, but are different for three reasons. First, resettlement for the relocatees is often planned by the government, typically meaning they receive more support than other forced migrations. However, dam relocation raises legal issues surrounding the exercise of eminent domain to take private property and the adequacy of compensation for such takings. Second, unlike many migrants and refugees, dam relocatees settle internally, and the location to which they are moved may be driven by the policy or political aims of the current regime. Third, unlike many other migrants, dam relocatees have no hope of ever returning to their homes.[37] These differences require reforms to water policy that more effectively integrate the concerns of dam relocatees into decisions regarding dam financing, siting, and construction.

The challenge for many countries facing water insecurity now is that they deal with more dynamic, less predictable hydrologies because of climate change and are more aware of the social, economic, and environmental costs of large dams than were countries that invested in large dams during the era of the industrial paradigm discussed in chapter 1.[38] David Grey and Claudia Sadoff discussed the challenge of evaluating investments in water infrastructure in water-insecure countries, noting that bad water investments are not necessarily better than no water investments.[39] However, they also note that making no water investments because policymakers are paralyzed by fear of trade-offs is certainly worse than making good water investments, "which follow a thorough examination of all options: actions and inactions; water conservation and water development; natural and man-made infrastructure at all scales; alternative technologies, incentives, and institutions; capacity building and so forth."[40]

Individual countries facing water insecurity, and indeed the entire world, cannot afford to dismiss outright investments in large dams as a possible means of addressing water-based mass migration. There will certainly be many instances where the costs and risks of large dam development outweigh the potential benefits, including in simple of terms of protecting people from forced migration. A dam might displace more people than it protects. However, some policy reforms could facilitate the type of broad considera-tion of options proposed by Grey and Sadoff. I have already mentioned a few of these reforms. In chapter 2, I discussed the use of water footprints in lieu of carbon footprints as a metric for sustainability. While not entirely carbon neutral, hydroelectric energy is a much lower carbon-emitting energy source than fossil fuel combustion, and thus a carbon footprint would suggest large dam development as a means of both mitigating climate change (by reducing greenhouse gas emissions) and adapting to climate change (by enhancing both drought and flood resilience). However, a water footprint might better integrate the environmental costs of large dam development better than a carbon footprint, by demonstrating loss of water to evapotranspiration in new reservoirs, impacts to downstream communities and ecosystems, and loss of reservoir storage and generating capacity over time.

In chapter 3, I propose the use of public health assessments for dam projects to evaluate how they might impact disease-vector habitats and their interaction with human communities. A dam project may create more hab-itat for disease vectors and bring them closer to humans. Focusing on shared benefits, with the examples of the Columbia River and Colorado River basins discussed in chapter 6, demonstrate reforms for improved dam management in transboundary water governance institutions. These institutions could also implement the fiduciary duties to member states I proposed in chapter 2 as a means of ensuring that hydro-hegemons do not co-opt decisions re-garding dam development on transboundary waters. Additionally, the human rights approach I have discussed in this book has an important role to play in providing leverage to marginalized communities to promote responsible water development, facilitating local stakeholder engagement in decision-making regarding dams, or opposing dam projects that would prejudice their interests.

In this chapter, however, I'd like to suggest an idea that is at once novel and based on very old legal approaches to dam development to facilitate evaluation of dam investments with an eye to impacts on migration. In the early years of hydropower, when dams were used largely to power grist mills to grind wheat into flower, dam development would flood areas and displace farmers. In England and many British colonies that inherited its common law, landowners flooded by dam development could sue the dam owner, claiming the flood constituted a nuisance or a trespass. The problem was that such lawsuits could prevent dam development when many farmers wanted to have access to grist mills for their crops. To address the challenge of compensating property owners flooded by dams without stifling needed dam development, legislatures in these areas enacted Mill Acts, which preempted common law trespass and nuisance claims. These statutes gave a remedy to the flooded party, with an annual payment to the affected owner based on a jury's ruling that accounted for the benefit the dam gave to the flooded party, if any. Thus, a grist-mill owner could build a dam that would flood property owned by neighbors without their permission, and then compensate those neighbors under a lawsuit brought pursuant to a Mill Act. The rationale behind these statutes was that in farming and timber areas, it was beneficial to all to encourage the development of dams, and one way to encourage development was to limit liability.[41]

When a dam, carefully considered, is in the best interests of the residents of a region to promote water security and address mass migration, but some residents bear an inequitable burden associated with dam development because they will be displaced, then a similar approach could be taken as was used in the case of Mill Acts. To do this, legal reforms would first recognize a vested right held by riparian residents abutting watercourses, whether in domestic laws as between citizens or by treaty or under the concept of equitable apportionment of the international waters under the Watercourse Convention in the context of disputes over dam development on international rivers.[42] The calculation of damages could be based on the market value of the impacts to land and the value of the water lost to any downstream communities. This calculation would also integrate some contingent valuation of the loss of certain ecosystem services, with the amount of damages offset by any benefits to the landowners or nations arising because of the dam. Compensation could be made by either direct payments, royalty payments to landowners based on resource development and sales, or by ownership interest in the dam enterprise. These payments cannot fully compensate people for the loss of their way of life and certainly cannot fully compensate for impacts to ecosystems or cultural resources. But when the lives and homes saved by enhanced water security outweigh the costs imposed on displaced people, such legal reforms could facilitate responsible and necessary dam development in some areas.

Environmental Flows and Mass Migration

Perhaps nothing is more disruptive to the preservation of environmental flows in rivers than a large dam. Indeed, once a large dam is installed, much of the downstream flows are no longer "natural" but instead released based on human decisions. It is thus somewhat paradoxical that another measure to address water-based mass migration besides dam development is the protection and promotion of environmental flows, which in some instances may require dam removal. Of course, dams can be operated in ways that mimic a more natural hydrologic cycle in the river and to maintain a minimum flow to preserve aquatic and riparian ecosystem health. And such operation may be important not only for environmental purposes but as a mechanism for addressing water-based mass migration. The ecological and cultural value of preserving environmental flows is obvious. However, the role environmental flows play in addressing water-based mass migrations is less obvious, though no less important.

One major challenge in water law and policy, as I discussed in chapter 2 regarding public health, is the silo effect in water institutions and expertise. This is true of silos that separate public health officials from environmental officials and agricultural officials and of silos that separate national security officials from water resource officials. But it is also true within the field of water resource management itself. Often, those focused on water quality in rivers and lakes operate in different silos from those working on water treatment and distribution. And even within water law, often lawyers working in environmental protection do not interact enough with lawyers working in water rights or land use. One of the most frustrating areas where silos should be torn down are those silos that separate freshwater and saltwater systems. And one of the most important ways in which laws and policies of both freshwater and saltwater interact is how they can influence mass migration.

For example, Indonesia is planning on moving its capital from Jakarta to the underdeveloped areas of Balikpapan and Samarinda in Borneo, largely due to water issues.[43] Climate change has resulted in rising ocean levels, largely due to melting of polar ice and the expansion of warming ocean water.[44] Rising sea levels threaten to displace millions of people in coastal communities, including the loss of entire small island nations and submersion of large coastal cities, which constitute the largest and fastest growing populations on Earth.[45] The migration of people fleeing rising seas in coastal cities and small island nations will be compounded by those in coastal areas fleeing stronger and more frequent extreme weather events.[46] Indonesia is one of the world's most populous countries, with more than ten million people living in Jakarta, and is also an archipelago nation with many small islands.[47] Rising sea levels are slowly swallowing and destabilizing the capital city, so Indonesia is now looking to move its capital to a more stable part of the country. This will have significant consequences for mass migration as millions move to follow the economic and political power, as it shifts from one sinking city to the new capital.

Indonesia's decision to move its capital is emblematic of two other issues associated with environmental flows and water-based mass migration besides those driven by rising seas. First, Jakarta is not being inundated only because of rising sea levels. It is also sinking because of overpumping groundwater.[48] Many coastal cities depend on groundwater as river deltas generally have higher salt concentrations than inland surface water bodies. But as coastal city populations grow, more and more groundwater is pumped from coastal freshwater aquifers, which threatens the cities' water supplies while at the same time resulting in ground subsidence. As freshwater is pumped and sea levels rise, saline intrusion into coastal aquifers means that these water supplies are not only unsustainably pumped but are also becoming contaminated by salt.[49] Cities will be thirsting for freshwater with saltwater up to their knees. Second, Indonesia's decision to move its new capital to Borneo threatens further deforestation of the endangered jungle ecosystems of that island. Deforestation is another water-related reason driving mass migration. Loss of forest habitat, often driven by agricultural practices, displaces not only flora and fauna but also forest peoples, while at the same time aggravating erosion's impact on the water supplies of downstream communities.[50] While there may be several ways in which environmental flows impact human migration, I will focus on the two aspects evidenced in the Indonesian example: forestry management and protection of coastal aquifers.

The relationship between forests and water is one that is well established.[51] Indeed, the phrase "watershed management" refers to the integrated management of land, water, and biota and is frequently synonymous with forestry management.[52] Watershed management is a possible avenue for enhancing environmental flows, and such an approach could garner a strong consensus from the public and water policymakers in supporting investments and legal reforms. Improved forest management protects snowpack from melting too fast and limits water losses from evaporation.[53] Additionally, without effective watershed management, wildfires may expose forest snowpack to greater evaporation losses.[54] Decades of research throughout forests in the western United States have documented the potential for improved forest management to enhance water supplies.[55]

In this chapter, watershed management is the improved maintenance of forests for the purpose of protecting and enhancing water supplies, including in particular the removal of scrub brush, immature trees, and invasive species from the upland reaches of the basin.[56] Watershed management has many potential benefits. First, removal of some vegetation, particularly invasive species or scrub brush, may enhance forest health by allowing other trees to fully mature.[57] Second, vegetation removal may result in decreased risks of wildfire.[58] Third, the resulting improved forest health and decrease in wildfires would limit erosion and runoff to rivers, thereby improving water quality and wildlife habitat.[59] Fourth, preservation of forest health protects the water cycle in general, by limiting overabstraction associated with agriculture that replaces forests, sources of transpiration that drive global precipitation patterns, and preserving essential microbes that serve as condensation nuclei in the formation of clouds and rain.[60] Fifth, responsible and sustainable thinning of forests may increase flows to the river by removing plants that would otherwise have taken up that water, and thus increase environmental flows.[61] Those environmental flows would help replenish coastal freshwater aquifers and provide some pushback against rising sea level and saline intrusion. Sixth, protection of forests will allow forest communities to remain rather than flee deforestation and thus potentially exacerbate the strain on coastal cities' water supplies.[62]

The potential benefits and broad support for watershed management can be illustrated by the ongoing implementation of the Four Forest Restoration Initiative (4FRI) in Arizona.[63] This endeavor is the largest watershed management project in the United States. It aims to improve water supplies in Arizona by rehabilitating the large ponderosa pine forests in the upper reaches of the Verde River Basin.[64] The 4FRI project began in 2011, incorporating four national forests at the headwaters of the river that provides a substantial portion of the water supply to several large cities.[65] The project is a partnership between the U.S. Forest Service, state and tribal land management agencies, local governments, nongovernmental conservation organizations, and water and energy utilities.[66] It plans to rehabilitate 2.4 million acres of forest land, including forest thinning, invasive species removal, prescribed preventative forest burns, and incorporation of a twenty-year adaptive management plan.[67] Many of the parties promoting and engaging in the 4FRI are also parties to the Gila River General Stream Adjudication, a decades-long water rights dispute in Arizona involving virtually every water right holder in the southern two-thirds of the state. Litigants in the General Stream Adjudication support the 4FRI in part because of its potential to increase water supplies in the hope that helps alleviate water disputes.[68]

Ecuador has another similar cooperative approach to watershed management, with municipalities, utilities, and environmental conservation organizations working together to protect upland forests in the Paute River Basin.[69] Unlike Arizona, which has a typical property rights–based approach to water allocation with a prior appropriation water rights regime, Ecuador's constitution guarantees a human right to water to all, grants rights to nature itself, and constitutionally codifies the indigenous concept of *Sumak Kawsay*, an aim to secure the dignified "good life" to all citizens.[70] The FONAPA water fund was created in 2008 as a partnership between ETAPA, the municipal water utility for the city of Cuenca, the Nature Conservancy (which also works on the 4FRI), the University of Cuenca, and several energy companies. As with the 4FRI, the aim is to protect upland forest areas, in part by investing in watershed management in several national parks. Unlike the 4FRI, the focus is largely aimed at protecting ecosystems and preserving downstream water quality, rather than the additional water augmentation goal in Arizona.

Despite the potential benefits from watershed management programs like the 4FRI and FONAPA, such vegetation removal projects can negatively impact wildlife habitat if done unsustainably, resulting in reduced shade cover, fewer nesting areas, and increased access by grazing livestock to fragile river banks.[71] Additionally, these projects involve removing scrub brush, immature trees, and invasive species for improved forest health, and the line between sustainable and responsible removal of scrub brush and immature trees and unsustainable deforestation is not always obvious. Additionally, these projects can be expensive and may lack long-term commitment from funding partners or reliable returns on investments, partly because much of the removed vegetation has a narrow trunk diameter unsuitable for timber.[72] Burning removed vegetation for energy or using removed vegetation for paper production are also possibilities, but such industries can result in pollution from energy production emissions and paper manufacturing.[73] Despite these risks, improved forestry management will help forest communities in both Ecuador and Arizona remain in their homes without having to move in response to deforestation or wildfires, and will enhance and preserve water supplies in two places absorbing thousands of refugees—Arizona with migrants from Central America and Ecuador with migrants from Venezuela.

Arizona's water laws prevent those investing in forestry management from claiming any rights to the water that might be generated from such efforts, and environmental laws impose certain permitting costs and liability concerns, including conducting environmental impact assessments, habitat conservation plans for endangered species, and permits for any pollutant to water sources from forestry work. One possible reform that could facilitate watershed projects like this is to adopt "Good Samaritan Permits." These permits would authorize projects deemed to have a net ecological benefit and would shield those implementing the project from environmental liability so long as they complied with permit conditions.[74] Additionally, Arizona could benefit from following the course set by FONAPA in Ecuador, which implemented the project as a trust, under which the project partners would manage the forests with a fiduciary obligation to those depending on the forests. The state of Washington has a water trust that bears some similarities to FONAPA, in which water rights could be placed in trust for the preservation of environmental flows and protection of salmon fisheries.[75] Arizona could take a similar approach as Ecuador and Washington, creating a water trust that would allow watershed projects to place water and forest resources in trust, or for conservation organizations to purchase water and place it in trust, for the purpose of protecting environmental flows. Ecuador, on the other hand, could follow some of the approach in the 4FRI by focusing on greater involvement of indigenous communities in FONAPA.[76]

Additionally, Ecuador has one of the more progressive approaches in water management in the world, in which the river itself has recognized legal rights and legal personhood.[77] This has become a cutting-edge approach to water governance, with rivers in New Zealand, India, and Colombia also gaining legal personhood and efforts made in litigation to recognize the rights of the Colorado River in the United States.[78] This approach remains somewhat experimental but could be a mechanism for ensuring the maintenance of environmental flows. However, this approach could also be problematic. For one, it arguably assumes rivers are vulnerable like people or communities, needing rights and laws to protect them from exploitation by more powerful interests. But the river is not vulnerable, as compared to any community. The river is ancient and powerful and will flow long after even the most powerful regimes have fallen and been forgotten. This "river as legal people" approach suggests that communities have a responsibility to recognize rivers' rights as if they are a persecuted minority, rather than the more accurate characterization, which is that the river is so powerful that we protect it not for the river's sake, but for our own. The river does not need us. We need the river. And law may function better by recognizing that reality rather than the fiction that rivers are people with rights. Furthermore, the river cannot assert its rights like a person, and thus who asserts the river's rights may simply end up as a political question, with the most powerful being the ones who presume to speak for the river. A better approach to protecting environmental flows may be a more straightforward application of the public trust doctrine. I discuss the public trust doctrine in chapter 3, and this doctrine places responsibility on the state to manage resources like rivers for the benefit of all citizens, with a fiduciary obligation upon which those harmed by a lack of environmental flows could sue to protect those flows.[79]

Watershed management has many goals, from preserving forests, to preventing wildfires, to limiting water pollution, to augmenting water supplies. But one potential consequence of watershed management is that it will contribute to the preservation of environmental flows in rivers. And environmental flows may be one of the most important ways of combating saline intrusion into coastal aquifers and limiting overpumping in coastal aquifers. When rivers are allowed to flow to the ocean, they both push back against rising sea levels and sea water intrusion—some of the main drivers of water-based mass migration—and recharge aquifers to limit the impacts of overpumping coastal aquifers.[80] Effectively, environmental flows could address the primary reasons of why Indonesia is looking to move its capital from Jakarta, and watershed management would address some of the challenges of moving the capital to Borneo. The challenge of overpumping groundwater and saline intrusion into coastal aquifers, combined with flooding from rising sea levels, is not limited to the case of Borneo. This same combination of factors impacting mass migration is occurring in many cities, including Dhaka, Guangzhou, Ho Chi Minh City, Hong King, Manila, Melbourne, Miami, Rotterdam, and Venice.[81] Of course, the challenge of rising sea levels is enormous, and minor rivers flows cannot hold back that threat. As such, greater support will be necessary for communities absorbing residents inevitably displaced by the combination of rising sea levels, saline intrusion in freshwater aquifers, and depletion of coastal aquifers.

Supporting Water Security in Refugee Host Communities

Improved planning and operation of large dams and better protection of environmental flows are policies aimed at preventing or mitigating mass migrations driven in part by water insecurity. But with climate change increasing water variability, and increasing the risks of drought and flood, some water-based migration may be inevitable. Thus, policy measures should aim to help migrants and refugees as they relocate. Of course, good water policy in general will facilitate security in regions currently suffering due to mass migrations, whether from losing or absorbing migrants. I have discussed many possible policy reforms that may help in this book. Additionally, humanitarian aid to support refugees fleeing violence or natural disasters is essential. However, in this chapter, I want to focus on an intervention that is sometimes underemphasized. Humanitarian support for refugees and migrants is important, and policy interventions to promote water security could limit migration, but greater focus is needed to support refugee host communities. All over the world, communities that are already facing water insecurity are also hosting thousands of refugees, straining not only limited water resources but also the hospitality of the host community. When humanitarian aid is extended to refugees but not to the host community, resentment can build and fester into conflict, including conflict over water resources.

The refugee crisis that has resulted from the Syrian civil war presents unique water challenges for communities hosting refugees and is a good example of how even small interventions in water management can improve conditions for both refugees and hosts.[82] The ongoing civil war in Syria has resulted in the most serious refugee crisis since World War II.[83] The two countries that have borne the greatest burden of absorbing Syrian refugees are two of Syria's neighbors—Jordan and Lebanon.[84] As of early 2017, over one million Syrian refugees reside in Lebanon and over six hundred thousand in Jordan.[85] One in every four people in Lebanon is a Syrian refugee, and one in every eight people in Jordan is a Syrian refugee.[86] While U.N. refugee camps in Jordan absorb a certain number of Syrians fleeing conflict, there are no such formal refugee camps in Lebanon, and most Syrian refugees in both countries do not settle in camps but in cities and towns among Jordanians and Lebanese citizens.[87]

This influx of refugees places an enormous strain on host communities in Lebanon and Jordan and, in some instances, has resulted in tensions between refugees and their hosts.[88] Both countries were already struggling with economic challenges, with annual GDP growth dropping from 8.5 percent to 1.4 percent in Lebanon and from 5.5 percent to 2.7 percent in Jordan between 2009 and 2012.[89] Most Syrian refugees in Jordan have settled in the country's most densely populated governorates—Amman, Irbid, and Zarqa—where 57 percent of Jordanians already live below the poverty line.[90] In Lebanon, 60 percent of Syrian refugees have settled in the north or in the Beka'a Valley—the two poorest regions in Lebanon.[91]

Perhaps even more significant than this general economic strain, the refugee crisis imposes an enormous strain on an already difficult water management situation in both Lebanon and Jordan.[92] Both Lebanon and Jordan fall below the water poverty line.[93] In Jordan, Syrian refugees have increased total water consumption by 5.5 percent since 2012, a significant increase over such a short time and in such an arid country.[94] In Lebanon, groundwater pumping in some regions has increased due to the influx of refugees to the point of drying up wells, resulting in many Syrian refugees in Lebanon living on less than two gallons of clean water each day.[95] The presence of Syrian refugees and the strain their presence places on already limited water resources have caused tensions between refugees and host communities in both Lebanon and Jordan.[96]

In Shatila, a refugee host community in Lebanon, overpumping and deepening of wells has resulted in withdrawals of highly brackish groundwater that is not potable.[97] In Jordan, refugee host communities are similarly facing challenges with strains on available water resources, resulting in attempts to rely on groundwater with high salinity levels.[98] If these brackish groundwater sources could be cost-effectively treated to potable standards, they may be the key to injecting a sufficient supply of clean water to alleviate tensions between Syrian refugees and their host communities in Lebanon and Jordan.

Since 2016, I have been the Principal Investigator in a project exploring the potential for water development to mitigate water-related tension in refugee host communities in Jordan and Lebanon. The U.S. Agency for International Development (USAID) granted $1.94 million to an international partnership between Arizona State University, Zero Mass Water, GreenCo, H2O for Humanity, Mercy Corps in Jordan, and the René Moawad Foundation in Lebanon to address water security issues in the Middle East and North Africa. The project is called "A Holistic Water Solution for Underserved and Refugee Host Communities in Lebanon and Jordan" (the Project).[99] The views and information expressed in this book are solely my own and do not necessarily reflect the views of USAID, the U.S. government, Arizona State University, or the other partners to the Project.

The Project is holistic in the sense that it attempts to address the four primary aims of water policy: quality, quantity, sustainability, and security. The Project addresses water quality by adapting the successful business model and technology used by H2O for Humanity (HFH) in serving tens of thousands of people in India in the context of refugee host communities in Lebanon and Jordan.[100] HFH implemented reverse osmosis water treatment kiosks in communities where entrepreneurs treat brackish groundwater sources and sell drinking-quality water in businesses that are sustainable, with charges as low as 0.2 cents per liter.[101]

On the quantity aspect of this holistic approach, Zero Mass Water (ZMW) has developed a solar-powered unit that can generate drinking water from water vapor in the air.[102] This technology allows for augmented water supplies at the household level, relying on renewable, low-cost energy. On the sustainability aspect of water policy, Arizona State University has connected HFH's technology to solar power that allows the water-treatment system to operate independent of the electrical grid and to modulate between on-and-off-grid power, thus making the system both more reliable and resilient in power outages and more sustainable in relying on a renewable energy source.[103] The concept of sustainability is not just environmental sustainability but also the financial sustainability of the project. Each kiosk is either integrated within the existing water utility network of the host community or implemented as an independent business, providing training and employment opportunities while establishing a sustainable business model with water charges below market rates.[104] The water security aspect of the project is achieved with GreenCo's Pak Flat technology, which is a food-grade plastic collapsible water-storage tank that allows each kiosk to store water in cases of system failure, drought, or other emergencies.[105]

Cutting-edge sustainable treatment, augmentation, and storage technologies can take the project only so far. In-country partners—Mercy Corps in Jordan and the René Moawad Foundation in Lebanon—provide community-level guidance to ensure access, training, site-selection, and remote monitoring of system integrity and water quality.[106] The partnership established in this project and the support of USAID aim to avoid or mitigate water disputes between refugee host communities and Syrian refugees by providing affordable and sustainable augmented water supplies in the communities, as well as employment opportunities, community engagement in water resource development, and applied research in water treatment, water supply augmentation and storage, and water governance.

The project initially proposed providing improved drinking-water supplies to 36,500 people in eighteen refugee host communities in Lebanon and Jordan in two years for under $2 million. After two years, the project is now providing improved drinking water to over 185,000 people in twenty-nine communities in these two countries, on time and on budget. The Project's success has required adaptation of the technology, with larger treatment systems in some locations and aeration systems to address unique contaminants of concern in other locations. The systems provide sustainable, affordable water to these communities, as well as employment opportunities for 135 people, mostly women. Support for refugee host communities has reduced tensions between hosts and refugees over shared water resources, and the Project is looking to scale up and expand to support other refugee host communities around the world.

To support water security projects for refugees and their hosts, international aid agencies should establish a global water fund for water projects that support migrants, refugees, displaced people, and their hosts, while improving water infrastructure and management to limit such displacements. The global water fund would oversee maintenance of safeguards to ensure public accountability, stakeholder participation, sustainable water development, and affordable water pricing. It could help fund education and entrepreneurial training to ensure that these water projects are financially viable enterprises that include job training and expansion of employment opportunities.

A global water fund would also direct investments to protect water infrastructure, both domestically and internationally, from attack, including improved cybersecurity. Improved technology and training, including firewalls and stronger passwords, could yield enormous security benefits for water infrastructure, particularly as projects that support refugees and their hosts, like the Holistic Water Solutions Project in Jordan and Lebanon, increasingly integrate smart technologies and automation. The global water fund could also support dispute resolution forums for funded projects to limit water conflict. Furthermore, these funds could provide support across the WASH sector, including investments in hygiene and sanitation. In 1943, Abraham Maslow wrote of a hierarchy of needs, with the primary motivation of humans to first meet their physiological needs by securing access to food and water.[107] Efforts to address the global challenges of mass migration should focus on investment in the base of Maslow's hierarchy (water and food), with a particular focus on agricultural resiliency to simultaneously address both food and water security.[108] The future success of projects like the Holistic Water Solutions Project will depend on their ability to secure necessary investments, to prove sustainable and scalable and also to integrate hygiene, sanitation, and agricultural water uses.

A global water fund could have long-lasting domestic benefits as well for nations making such investments. The current immigration crisis impacts developed countries all over the world. A desire for peace and stability abroad may mean more investments in water than in weapons. And nations desiring to address the strain of increasing immigrant and refugee challenges may do better to invest in the water security of their neighbors than in walls along their borders.

Conclusion

Former president of the Soviet Union and Nobel Peace Prize laureate Mikhail Gorbachev said, "Water, like religion and ideology, has the power to move millions of people. Since the very birth of civilization, people have moved to settle close to water. People move when there is too little of it. People move when there is too much of it. People journey down it. People write and sing and dance and dream about it. People fight over it. And all people, everywhere and every day, need it."[109] Gorbachev's words speak not only to the power of water to literally move people but of its power to move them emotionally, spiritually, and culturally. Sometimes, both the literal and figurative power of water to move us intersect in ways that are instructive.

Woody Guthrie sang of the power of water to move people in his music about the effects of the Dust Bowl on Okies.[110] The Los Angeles River, the scene of the tragic New Year's flood of which Guthrie sang and the setting for the wild jungles of Tarzan movies, is now encased in concrete as a flood channel. Instead of Tarzan's jungle, the Los Angeles River is now iconic as the gritty roadway in the race scene of *Grease* or the chase scene in *Terminator 2: Judgment Day*. To spare future communities the same fate as the Okies, the river was tamed by concrete and the ecosystem altered, with enormous environmental impacts.[111] New communities, many of them immigrant communities, have settled along the banks of the river for generations.[112] But there is now an effort in Los Angeles, involving renowned architect Frank Gehry, to restore or reimagine the Los Angeles River as a permanent surface water feature, groundwater-recharge facility, and public amenity.[113] This redevelopment could include taking land along the banks of the river settled by immigrant communities and displacing the communities to create a flowing river. The history of the Los Angeles River thus epitomizes the complexities of water and migration—people flee drought to settle along a river, only to suffer from floods, to be replaced by immigrants who settle along a river plagued with environmental problems caused partially by efforts to avoid floods, only to be displaced by redevelopment aimed at addressing the environmental problems. We are often so quick to forget the not-too-distant past in an effort to address an imminent problem. John Steinbeck, whose novels, like Guthrie's music, spoke to the plight of the Okies, wrote: "And it never failed that during the dry years the people forgot about the rich years, and during the wet years they lost all memory of the dry years. It was always that way."[114] Perhaps the place to begin addressing mass migration driven, in part, by water insecurity is to remember that we are all moved by water.

8
Water Security and Technological Innovation

Just as water drove early innovations in governance, as complex civilizations rose around the Nile and the Indus and in Mesopotamia, so water drove early technological innovation. As I said in the introduction to this book, the desert is the great incubator of human ingenuity, both in political and technological ideas. The *shaduf* was an early form of lift irrigation, using a bag and rope attached to a wooden beam and counterbalance, and in use during the times of Sargon of Akkad, approximately 2300 BCE. The *qanat* or *aflaj* system I mention in chapter 5, using tunnels to move underground water from mountains to fields, was developed over three thousand years ago in ancient Persia. Many of these ancient *qanat* systems remain an important, functioning water supply for communities to this day. In the early Bronze Age, around 2500 BCE, sophisticated sewage systems had been developed by the Harappa culture of the Indus River Basin.[1] The ability of humans to use collective learning to overcome challenges of water security is an integral part of our collective history and a reason for optimism in the future. It is hard, perhaps, to read this book and not feel discouraged or overwhelmed by the challenges of water insecurity. But our history of creative collaboration gives me hope that we can solve these problems.

Despite growing populations, increasing consumption, and climate change, the world's water future can be bright. However, a bright water future depends on cooperation, investment, adaptation, and the right priorities. In conversations about water, often the first impulse I notice in many people, including water experts, is to assume that water conservation should be our first and highest priority. I disagree. Water conservation is essential, to be sure. But I believe there is a higher priority. The first priority is to understand our water. This requires technological innovation. Improved water models and better and more accurate reporting of water data are essential to inform all policy choices, including how, and how much, to conserve water. This includes integration of smart meters on wells, water-treatment systems, head gates, and homes to improve our understanding of how and where water is being used. Greater computing power is needed to improve water-system models based on this and other data. The challenge with investing in advanced technology to improve our understanding of our water is the same as the challenge for any other new technology. New technologies frequently require new or reformed laws, which then confront social and political challenges. For example, a law that requires mandatory installations of smart meters on wells, irrigation gates, and homes would generate beneficial information to improve water management. But efforts to implement laws mandating metering are often met with opposition. Such measures are often perceived as invasions of privacy, or perhaps the beginning of an effort to gather information to curtail water supplies in rural communities or otherwise regulate water uses.

I have seen this kind of opposition firsthand in many parts of the world. One possible solution, however, is to integrate both the policy and technology innovations. Take, for example, the technologies used in the Holistic Water Solutions Project to improve water supplies for the refugee host communities in Jordan and Lebanon discussed in the previous chapter. Our project, and local water management in general, would have often benefited enormously from more information regarding the location, depth, and use of wells in the region. In many towns, family members living abroad would send money home to drill a well. The well would be drilled with no government permission or oversight. Some communities were concerned about integrating these wells, some of which had been drilled illegally, with smart technology that would subject them to government sanctions and regulation. One possible solution is to trade technologies—provide the improved water treatment and augmentation technology in exchange for the smart meters, with illegally drilled wells grandfathered in without penalty as long as they agree to mandatory metering. To be frank, many communities remain skeptical of subjecting their water supplies to new technologies and related new regulations, even when such a trade of technologies and increased exchange of water information improves water services.

The first priority of water policy—understanding the water supply—is like all other water policy priorities. It will often drive and benefit from technological innovation. But that innovation will create new legal, social, and political challenges that will require corresponding governance innovations. This chapter deals with the challenges facing the next three likely priorities in water policy: conservation, augmentation, and discovery/exploration.

After understanding our water better, the next priority is to conserve water. Technological advances can promote water efficiency, but these technologies can face difficult and antiquated legal obstacles. Indeed, perhaps the greatest problem with water policy is that we frequently have nineteenth-century laws, twentieth-century infrastructure, and twenty-first-century populations and climate.[2] Policy reforms should aim at bringing laws and infrastructure into the twenty-first century by carefully considering the available state of the art of water conservation technology and adapting laws and infrastructure to promote and advance that technology.

After that, if necessary and practicable, water supplies may be augmented. Technologies aimed at conserving, augmenting, or even re-sourcing water supplies will require related innovations in water policy. In some instances, the Machiavellian "great enterprises" approach to water policy is evidenced in water-augmentation projects, such as large dams and other large-scale water infrastructure projects. For example, in the 1960s, U.S. President John F. Kennedy and other elected officials promoted the North American Water and Power Alliance, which would have involved both integration and large-scale transfers between U.S. and Canadian water and energy systems.[3] It was around this same time that President Kennedy said, "[I]f we could ever competitively, at a cheap rate, get fresh water from salt water, it would be in the long-range interests of humanity [and] would really dwarf any other scientific accomplishments."[4] The political motivation to invest in water augmentation was soon dwarfed in Kennedy's mind by another scientific priority and "great enterprise" with immense water implications, when the Soviet Union launched Yuri Gagarin into space.

The final priority in water policy is water driving discovery, and most particularly, space exploration. As I discussed in the previous chapter, the human species has always moved with water. And if there is any impulse as common as our drive to innovate and migrate alongside water, it is our collective will to discover, to explore new frontiers. But exploring new frontiers has nearly always required solving water problems. Indeed, some of the earliest known experiments in turning seawater into fresh-water (desalination) were conducted onboard ancient ocean-faring ships.[5] Our next frontier is space and interplanetary travel, a journey that will challenge our ability to innovate around water in ways we cannot imagine, as we leave the comfort of our blue planet for the hostile desert among the stars.

Innovations in Water Conservation

The first priority of water policy should be to understand our water supply as best we can in order to inform our other policy choices. The second priority should be to better conserve, protect, and store our water supply. But even this second priority comes with an important initial question. To what end are we protecting and conserving our water? Conservation, by itself, is neither a good nor bad thing. If we conserve water by reducing agricultural uses, but in doing so threaten our food security or affordability, such conservation may not have resulted in real progress. If we replace computer data centers (which use massive amounts of water to cool servers) with less water-intensive golf courses (which employ fewer people), has the conservation been worth the effort?[6] And in some instances, much of the low-hanging fruit of water conservation has been picked and additional efforts to conserve water will require significant investments and technological innovations. Better water information, and a better understanding of our water policy aims, will inform how we make such investments and innovations.

Israel has become a world leader in investments in cutting-edge water conservation technology.[7] As described by author Seth Siegel, despite its challenging hydrology, or perhaps because of it, Israel has invested in advanced water technologies to achieve water security. Israel has pioneered major advances in drip irrigation, or micro-irrigation, which drips small amounts of water directly at plant roots, rather than the inefficient method of flood irrigation used in many parts of the world. This approach can conserve as much as 75 percent of the water used in some instances with minimal loss of productivity and quality. The technology also improves water quality because there is far less agricultural runoff, meaning less pollution from fertilizers and pesticides.[8] Technology can go even further than drip irrigation. New pipe material comprised of biosynthetic membranes could respond to the presence of growth hormones in the soil, emitted by plant roots. These pipes or tubes would release water only when they detect those chemicals. Effectively, it would mean the irrigation system would only provide water to the crops when the crops ask for it. Such an approach would have similar, but perhaps even more dramatic, benefits as those that have come from drip irrigation. This is particularly true as agriculture is the largest driver of water use in the world, accounting for approximately 70 percent of all of human water consumption globally.[9] Investments in efficient irrigation thus may have the greatest returns in terms of water conservation.

In addition to agricultural inefficiencies, another major issue for water conservation is water loss—meaning leaking pipes. Water lost to leaking pipes amounts to as much as 30 percent of distributed water in Western Europe, and around 50 percent in Egypt. But in Israel, water lost to leaks is less than 10 percent.[10] Israel invests in technology that integrates water-distribution systems with digital information, including "smart pigs." Smart pigs are machines that move through water pipes, removing scaling within the pipe while simultaneously using lasers to detect leaks. They are called "pigs" because of the squealing sound they make as they move through the pipes. These machines can help reduce water lost to leaks by quickly identifying leaks and prioritizing their repair before they result in major water losses or cutoffs, or even sinkholes damaging other infrastructure.[11] Improved efficiency in appliances and fixtures can also conserve water. Dual-flush toilets use only small amounts of water to flush urine. Switching from a conventional flush toilet to a dual-flush, low-flow toilet saves 1.28 gallons per flush, with annual water savings for the average household in the United States of 27,000 gallons.[12] Dual-flush toilets are the only toilets available in Israel.[13] Another way Israel has been so successful is in developing and implementing water recycling technologies, treating and reusing as much as 95 percent of its wastewater.[14]

The potential for these technologies raises the question of why the whole world does not simply follow the Israeli model for achieving water security. The effectiveness of drip irrigation depends on the type of crop and the soil. Shifting from one form of irrigation to another is expensive, particularly when major investments have been made in rigid infrastructure. Some of these technologies are in their infancy and either not yet ready for widespread adoption or else very expensive. Water recycling requires the construction of expensive treatment and distribution systems. Shifting to more water-efficient household fixtures can be expensive for individuals and families, and requiring that shift could thus confront political opposition. Furthermore, Israel has a unique sociolegal environmental that has allowed for these kinds of investments, including the presence of a National Water Carrier, a coastline where a large portion of its population lives, a strong historical and cultural commitment to a water ethos, and a relatively small country within which to move water.[15]

But the unique sociolegal environment of other countries may present unique obstacles to implementing innovative technologies to conserve water. For example, many communities are reluctant to embrace recycled water.

Recall from the introduction to this book that the Navajo Nation opposed on religious grounds the use of recycled water on the San Francisco Peaks to improve skiing conditions. But social opposition is also particularly strong for direct potable water reuse, meaning treating wastewater for distribution as drinking water. Many jurisdictions prohibit direct potable reuse based largely on that social opposition.[16] But all water is recycled water, and every drop of water we drink was urine at some point in time. Social opposition to improved water technology can be addressed through greater investment in public education on water. But policy reforms aimed at public awareness and education may be insufficient.

In many parts of the western United States, where the law of prior appropriation controls the allocation of many interests in water, the law proves to be a major obstacle to implementing water efficient technologies. In these states, water rights are subject to forfeiture, meaning that if water users do not use their water for a defined statutory period, they will lose their water right.[17] For example, in Arizona, a holder of a surface-water right under prior appropriation will lose that right if the water is not put to beneficial use for five years.[18] A farmer in Arizona could invest in switching from flood irrigation to drip irrigation and potentially increase productivity while cutting water use by half. But under the law of forfeiture, that farmer has little incentive to make that investment because they will lose half of their water right if they do not use it. Of course, the farmer could sell half of the water right and thus avoid forfeiture while monetizing the water savings. But there are significant obstacles to selling water rights in a prior appropriation regime. When a party sells water rights, it often involves changing the diversion point (meaning the location from which water is taken from the stream, like a ditch or pump), which can impact other rights on the stream. For example, a downstream user might have relied on runoff from that farmer's crops to keep the river flowing, and the sale moved the water diversion further downstream of that user. Or else the party that bought the water right moved the diversion upstream, and that diversion would deprive downstream users of necessary pressure and flow, also called "hydraulic head," needed to push the water down to their diversion points. These water users have the right to oppose the sale of the water right and can prevent it if they can demonstrate that such a sale will prejudice their vested right. Thus, high transaction costs combined with laws like forfeiture often preclude capturing potential gains in efficiencies from water conservation technologies.[19]

One possible solution to this problem is to expand the water trust idea I introduced in the previous chapter related to preserving environmental flows to address water-based mass migration. As I noted, both Ecuador and the state of Washington have implemented something akin to a water trust. The general legal concept of a trust is that property can be placed in the care of one person (the trustee) for the benefit of another (the beneficiary), with the trustee having a fiduciary obligation to only use the property to the beneficiary's advantage. In a prior appropriation state, this concept could be adapted to facilitate water transfers and encourage investments in water conservation. Where water users conserve water, they can put that conserved portion of their water right into the trust. So long as that portion of their right is in trust, it is shielded from forfeiture, meaning that the water right holders would not lose their water rights simply because it was not used. The state would maintain the trust, with water in the trust maintaining in-stream flows. The trust could also serve as a clearinghouse for water transfers. Those interested in purchasing water rights could go to the trust and purchase or lease a portion of the water in trust. Those leases or purchases could be made under expedited conditions with limited interference from other water users. This would create an incentive for water users to put water in trust, both to shield water rights from forfeiture and to lower transaction costs associated with water rights conveyances.[20]

Domestic water rights regimes are not the only water laws that may discourage investment in water conservation technology. Many water law disputes involve complaints by downstream riparians against upstream neighbors. Indeed, one common refrain in talking about water law is: "It's better to be upstream with a shovel than downstream with a water right." Hydrology, it seems, privileges the upstream riparian. However, there are instances when downstream riparians assert themselves in ways that can impact the upstream riparian. One way is the concept of "foreclosure of future use," examined and explored extensively by water law expert Salman Salman.[21] There are instances in international hydro-politics in which the hydro-hegemon is the downstream riparian. For example, Egypt is the downstream riparian on the Nile, but has historically been the most powerful riparian nation in the basin. In the case of the Nile, Egypt would assert that it had reasonably and equitably made use of the entirety of the Nile, thus foreclosing any future uses by upstream riparians. This is, in some sense, a "first-in-time, first-in-right" approach to water rights allocations at the international level.[22] Professor Stephen McCaffrey phrased the question as follows: "If a downstream State continued to develop its water resources to the point that it foreclosed otherwise reasonable future uses of the watercourse by an upstream State, could this constitute the causing of 'significant harm' to the upstream State? And, does the downstream State have any procedural obligation toward the upstream State regarding new projects it plans?"[23] The downstream riparian may thus attempt to secure rights to the maximum quantity of water as quickly as possible and thereby foreclose future uses. Such an approach would discourage the use of water conservation technology in downstream riparians. It is for this reason that both Professor Salman and Professor McCaffrey have noted that such uses could constitute "significant harm" by downstream riparians to their upstream neighbors, giving rise to damages under the Watercourse Convention.[24]

Israel, of course, is a downstream hydro-hegemon in the Jordan River Basin. The benefits of its hydro-hegemony, combined with the exigencies of its hydrology and politics, the ethos of a hydro-culture, and the centralized management of the National Water Carrier have allowed Israel to lead in many ways in the development of water conservation technology. But these advantages do not exist for all jurisdictions facing water scarcity challenges. The decentralized, property rights–based approach of some regimes makes it difficult to create effective incentives to invest in water conservation. But perhaps market forces could be deployed in these environments to effectively encourage innovation in water conservation technology and investment. In countries like Australia, India, and the United States, where individuals or corporations can own water rights or shares in river basins, those interests could be used to allow water users to access credit to invest in water conservation. For example, a farmer looking to invest in converting from flood irrigation to drip irrigation could approach a bank and secure a loan for that investment with the saved water as collateral. A similar approach could be taken with companies investing in fixing leaking pipes, where the water savings would be the security for loans to finance smart pigs and leak repairs. Perhaps even more ambitious, farmers or reservoir managers could seek to implement "floatovoltaics." Floatovoltaics is the use of photovoltaic solar panels to cover canals or reservoirs. In this way, the panels limit evaporation losses while at the same time generating energy. Such an investment is expensive, but those interested in making that investment may be able to secure lines of credit if they are able to use the water savings as collateral. In any event, innovative water-conservation technologies, like many of those development and implemented in Israel, require equally innovative policy reforms to facilitate their deployment, but these reforms have to be adapted to the legal and social environment.

Innovations in Water Augmentation

Ideally, the first two priorities of water policy—understanding water supply and protecting and conserving water supply—would result in water security and would be advanced with both technological and policy innovations. However, there may be some instances where these priorities are insufficient and water supplies need to be technologically augmented. Water augmentation technologies always have costs, and often significant ones, that limit their effectiveness and advisability. I have already addressed one way in which water supplies could be augmented in discussing watershed management in the previous chapter. Removal of scrub brush, immature trees, and invasive species in upland forests could increase water supplies downstream. However, as I noted, there are environmental risks and costs, including the risk of deforestation.[25]

I have referenced another approach to water augmentation in chapter 6, in discussing the use of cloud seeding as a weapon.[26] As global temperatures rise, clouds may become an increasingly important source of water into which countries, corporations, and individuals attempt to tap. For every 1°C rise in the atmosphere's temperature, the water-holding capacity of the atmosphere increases by 7 percent.[27] As such, rising ambient temperatures due to global warming will increase the amount of water held in the air, and one way to access that water is through cloud seeding.[28] There are various cloud-seeding methods.[29] Condensation nuclei, or "seeds," are usually charged particles with significant surface area, like silver iodide or frozen carbon dioxide, and dispersed by airplanes or cannons.[30] Precipitation can begin within thirty minutes of seeding and can range broadly, as far as one hundred miles downwind of the seeding site.[31] The viability of cloud seeding depends on a number of factors, but studies show that seeding can be effective and induces, depending on operational parameters, an additional 5–25 percent precipitation from clouds.[32] The state of Wyoming in the United State conducted a study on cloud seeding from 2008 to 2014, which indicated a 5–15 percent increase in precipitation.[33]

But just as with watershed management, cloud seeding has risks and uncertainties. The image of aircraft blazing through the sky spraying chemicals and cannons booming as they fire at the clouds understandably raises concerns. Cloud seeding raises sufficient concerns regarding flooding risks that it was outlawed as a tactical weapon after its use in the Vietnam conflict under the ENMOD treaty, as I noted in chapter 6.[34] The same concerns that gave rise to ENMOD would make cloud seeding a complex legal issue at the domestic level, with difficult cases involving lawsuits for damages caused by flooding against cloud-seeding operations, where judges and juries would have to decide on issues of causation and liability allocation. While some studies suggest cloud seeding can work, it would be difficult to prove that those operations were the sole cause of any particular flood event. Just as watershed management raises environmental concerns of deforestation, cloud seeding raises concerns of bioaccumulation of silver iodide in the environment.[35]

However, these are not the only legal issues confronting these types of water augmentation approaches. Under prior appropriation regimes, the law distinguishes between developed water and salvaged water in allocating water rights.[36] Developed water is new water imported into a catchment that was not previously part of the basin—like seawater desalination or water imported by tanker or pipeline. Salvaged water, on the other hand, is water that is part of the basin but not accessible, but is made usable by human intervention, like water in deep fossil aquifers or water embedded in vegetation like forests. Developed water is owned by the party that developed it, and the rights to that water are independent of the prior appropriation system. So, if I pay to desalinate seawater, or to re-source water into the basin by tanker, pipeline, or watercourse, that water is mine. Salvaged water, on the other hand, remains part of the prior appropriation regime, and the party that invests in water salvage has no special or superior claim to the water.[37] For example, in *Southeastern Colorado Water Conservancy District v. Shelton Farms*, a party that removed invasive species from the banks of a stream claimed superior rights to the water liberated by that effort.[38] The court held that such water was salvaged water and subject to prior appropriation and the party that invested efforts to remove invasive species had no legal claim to the augmented water.[39]

The distinction between developed and salvaged water is both highly relevant, and potentially highly problematic, for water-augmentation projects in general. Water generated from seawater desalination is almost certainly developed water, whereas water generated from desalinating brackish groundwater or saline-contaminated surface water is likely salvaged water.[40] This distinction may encourage seawater desalination over treating pollution, but may also limit investment in developing brackish groundwater.[41] Water supplies generated from forestry management, like the 4FRI project referenced in the previous chapter, will almost certainly be treated the same as the water augmented in the *Shelton Farms* case, and thus will be considered salvaged water.[42] This means that the work invested in forestry management will not result in any water rights advantage for those parties investing in projects like the 4FRI. The legal status of water liberated by cloud seeding, whether developed or salvaged, is unknown. If it is salvaged water, then there is little incentive, from a water rights perspective, to invest in cloud seeding, for better or worse. If it is developed water, then the challenge would be how to quantify the water that belongs to the cloud-seeding project, a difficult if not impossible task. But it is these exact kinds of legal characterizations that can either encourage or discourage water-augmentation projects, with all their attendant risks and benefits.

The risks and benefits of cloud seeding remain somewhat speculative, as it is a relatively recent approach to water-augmentation technology. Desalination, as I noted at the beginning of this chapter, is very old. Indeed, Aristotle is one of the first known scientists to have experimented with desalination.[43] Desalination has always held an understandable fascination for anyone interested in solving water insecurity. While the Earth is a water-rich planet, 97 percent of the planet's water is saltwater, with 2.7 percent of the remaining freshwater virtually inaccessible in ice caps or fossil aquifers.[44] Being able to cost-effectively tap into and distribute that 97 percent supply for freshwater uses would utterly transform the world. However, historically, desalination on a large scale has only made sense for countries that are very energy-rich and very water-poor, like Saudi Arabia.[45] This is because desalination has always been an energy-intensive enterprise.

There are two broad categories of desalination technologies. Thermal distillation involves heating saltwater to create water vapor, which then condenses and is collected on a cool surface with relatively low salinity levels.[46] Membrane treatment requires a pressure or electrically charged gradient to move water or salt ions through a membrane, thereby separating water from salt.[47] Both approaches are energy-intensive, and both create a brine waste. As with cloud seeding or watershed management, desalination carries environmental risks, including greenhouse gas emission from energy consumption, treatment and disposal of waste (that often include membrane cleaners and other chemicals), and ecological impacts from seawater intake to thermal contamination of aquatic or marine ecosystems where the waste is discharged.[48] And just as with those other approaches to water augmentation, desalination presents its own unique legal challenges beyond those related to environmental contamination.

One understandable response to such legal concerns is to disregard them because desalination will never be widely used because of its attendant energy costs. However, since 2005, over ten thousand large-scale desalination plants have been put into operation, including in the United States, Australia, Spain, Japan, Iran, China, Israel, India, Italy, and Mexico.[49] The technology has made enormous advances in efficiency in recent years, from the $9 per cubic meter of water produced in the desalination plants of the Arabian Gulf in the 1950s to 63 cents per cubic meter in the desalination plant constructed in Israel in 2003.[50] There are many reasons for these improvements. First, many of the recently developed desalination plants have been co-located with energy-generating plants and wastewater-disposal plants, thus lowering energy and waste disposal costs. Second, many of these newer facilities have integrated desalination with photovoltaic solar panels, further lowering energy costs. Third, some of these facilities use a pressure recycling system, which allows the plant to recycle pressure from the waste stream back to the production stream, thereby cutting energy costs.[51] The desalination plant on the mouth of the Llobregat River in Barcelona, Spain, takes advantage of these three approaches and operates at around 2.5 kWh/m^3, compared to the 25 kWh/m^3 of the typical desalination plant of the 1980s.[52]

I have already discussed one way in which desalination has been used to attempt to mitigate water stress. The kiosks used to treat water supplies in refugee host communities in Lebanon and Jordan mentioned in the previous chapter are effectively small-scale membrane desalination plants. These kiosks allow treatment of brackish groundwater, which increases water supplies in areas placed under stressed by growing refugee populations. Those kiosks, combined with the Zero Mass Water systems that condense atmospheric vapor to produce drinking water, allow for small-scale water augmentation that addresses intracommunity water stress. A similar approach could help address water stress between communities in other parts of the world. For example, the Navajo and Hopi people have been engaged in a long-standing dispute over water rights in the Little Colorado River Basin. These are indigenous tribes, with the Hopi land located entirely within the Navajo land.[53] There have been many efforts over the years to negotiate a settlement between these two tribes regarding water rights. One possible approach would be to use small-scale desalination of the abundant brackish groundwater beneath the land of both tribes. Many of the Hopi and Navajo communities are small and remote, meaning there are not necessarily economies of scale for large water treatment and distribution systems. Thus, small-scale water treatment could augment supplies in these communities at relatively low costs and perhaps facilitate a settlement to the disputes over shared waters.

The promise of desalination, based on these recent advances in the technology, mean that it has the potential to either aggravate or mitigate water disputes. For example, disputes over the Colorado River between states and countries have persisted for decades, as discussed throughout this book. In the 1944 Rivers Treaty, the United States agreed to ensure 1.5 million acre-feet of Colorado River water crossed into Mexico each year.[54] However, that treaty said nothing about the quality of the water that would cross the border. In the 1970s, salinity levels at the headwaters of the Colorado were less than fifty parts per million (ppm), but because of agricultural runoff, the Colorado River crossed the Mexican border at a toxic 1,200 ppm.[55] This had devastating impacts on farmers in northern Mexico, and Mexico protested that this violated the 1944 Rivers Treaty. Because this was during the OPEC oil embargo of 1973, and the United States was depending on oil imports from Mexico, the United States enacted the Colorado River Basin Salinity Control Act, which authorized the construction of a desalination plant in Yuma, Arizona, to desalinate the Colorado River before it entered into Mexico.[56] The plant proved far too expensive to operate consistently. Instead, the United States, in an effort to comply with its treaty obligations, diverted agricultural runoff away from the river and toward the Cienega de la Santa Clara wetlands. This meant that a large amount of contaminated agricultural runoff was diverted to protected wetlands to protect the quality of Mexico's Colorado River allocation. However, ceasing this diversion would likely mean that the wetlands would dry up and would exacerbate the environmental and economic problems associated with operating the desalination plant in Yuma.

The countries of the Jordan River Basin face a different challenge related to desalination. In the 1994 Peace Treaty between Israel and Jordan, Israel agreed to use desalination to treat certain saline springs in the basin to produce potable water for Jordan.[57] Until it completes this treatment, Israel is obligated under the treaty to ensure an allocation of water from the Jordan River to offset the quantity from the saline springs. So far, Israel has not engaged in desalination on behalf of Jordan.[58] Israel, as the basin's hydro-hegemon, has the resources to engage in desalination and has the coastline and coastal population to make desalination a reasonable economic choice. On the other hand, Jordan has a comparatively small coastline and a largely inland population center and faces greater water stress than Israel. This raises a difficult question in international water law and hydro-diplomacy: What is the obligation of a riparian hydro-hegemon that can economically develop desalination toward co-riparians that cannot? Should the hydro-hegemon forgo allocations from the shared river because it can afford to rely on desalination? The principles of the Watercourse Convention require that riparian states make "equitable and reasonable utilization" of the shared river and expressly considers the "availability of alternatives" in evaluating such equity and reasonableness.[59] However, placing such an obligation on desalinating states could discourage investments in improving and expanding desalination technology.[60]

Israel and Jordan have discussed an ambitious approach to transboundary desalination. It is called the Red Sea–Dead Sea Project. While the specifics have been discussed and debated for years, the rough plan would include a desalination plant in Jordan on the Gulf of Aqaba, providing water to Israel, with Israel providing Jordan with water from the Jordan River. The desalination plant would generate a brine-reject stream that would be pumped to the top of the mountains and then descend to refill the Dead Sea, which has been gradually drying up due to climactic forces and water use in the basin.[61] Interestingly, a similar approach could be considered in the Colorado River Basin, which faces similar issues. The United States could support a desalination plant in Mexico or California, with the desalinating jurisdiction forgoing allocations from the shared river for the benefit of its co-riparians. The brine-reject stream could then be used to refill the Salton Sea, an inland saltwater body that has dried up and caused both environmental and economic challenges for the nearby community in much the same way as the drying up of the Dead Sea. In each of these basins, desalination has proven both a source of contention and the promise of cooperation.

The double-sided sword of water-augmentation technology evidenced in desalination is also true for another augmentation approach—bulk water transfers. Bulk water transfers are the export of large amounts of water by tanker or pipeline across basins, typically from a water-rich region to a water-poor region. In some instances, this involves new technologies, including ships towing large bags of water through the ocean.[62] For example, Singapore has historically relied on bulk water imports via pipeline from

Malaysia.[63] In an effort to wean itself from dependency on a neighboring country, however, Singapore has made progress toward achieving independence in its water supply from Malaysia under its NEWater program.[64] Singapore plans to rely entirely on recycled water and desalination and no longer depend on Malaysian water imports.[65] Effectively, Singapore prefers the energy-intensive but independently sustainable development of its own water resources rather than depending on raw water imports from a neighboring state.[66]

Bulk water transport raises difficult legal questions. For example, water in rivers, aquifers, and lakes is subject to water allocations laws, like prior appropriation, riparian rights, or the Watercourse Convention. Virtual water— water embedded in goods like food—is an article of commerce and regulated as such both internationally and domestically. But bulk water does not fit comfortably in either of those categories and thus operates under a cloud of legal uncertainty.[67] Canada provides a particularly useful example of repeated efforts to develop water export programs, and the obstacles facing such development and implementation.[68] A Canadian company called the Nova Group obtained a permit to export six hundred million liters of water from Lake Superior via tanker to Asian buyers in 1998.[69] But public opposition based on the national security and environmental risks resulted in the permit being revoked.[70] Another deal between a Canadian company, called Snowcap, and a California company, called Sunbelt, involving a bulk water transport met with similar opposition and resulted in a rescinded permit and litigation.[71] However, not all Canadian bulk water exports have been large projects that were ultimately not implemented due to public opposition.[72] Smaller water transfers occur frequently between Canadian and U.S. border communities, typically without any national-level oversight. These include continuing water-transfer relationships between Surrey, British Columbia, and Blaine, Washington, and LaSalle, Ontario, and Detroit, Michigan.[73] One legal reform associated with bulk water transport is to distinguish between small-scale, localized, intrabasin transfers like these, and other larger projects with greater environmental and economic consequences.

Larger transfers of bulk water illustrate one of the unique challenges of regulating water. Water is strange, in that when it is embedded in lettuce or wine and shipped away from the basin, the conveyance is typically applauded as an example of free trade. But if that same quantity of water is simply loaded onto a tanker or sent off by pipeline, the conveyance meets with public opposition. One possible legal reform that would at least limit confusion would be to treat bulk water transports as the transfer of goods under international trade and investment law.[74] There is no reason to treat water embedded in goods differently than raw water. Under international trade law, governments typically cannot discriminate in exporting goods, which suggests that calling water a "good" could result in trade law being used to justify its export. However, international trade law does allow limits on exports of goods in cases of critical shortage or to preserve environmental or human health, which would certainly apply in instances of unsustainable bulk water exports. Ultimately, bulk water exports are likely to be uncommon, simply because water is so heavy that the energy costs associated with moving large amounts of water over a long distance are prohibitive when compared with other options.[75]

As with other examples of water augmentation technology, bulk water transports have the potential to both aggravate and mitigate water conflict. Turkey provides water from a reservoir on the Euphrates River in bulk to northern Cyprus via an undersea pipeline.[76] This project has been controversial, as it introduces helpful water supplies to Cyprus, but has increased tensions between Turkish Northern Cypriots and Greek Southern Cypriots, as well as between Turkey and its co-riparians on the Euphrates River.[77]

Bulk water transports can have implications for domestic water policy.[78] In both the domestic and international context, bottled water constitutes a bulk water transfer.[79] The growing market for bottled water creates stronger incentives to move water in bulk between basins.[80] Besides bottled water, piped and diverted bulk water transports occur at the domestic level. For example, the Imperial Canal in California diverts water away from the Colorado River for use outside of the basin, effectively creating a bulk water export out of the Colorado River Basin.[81] Interstate water rivalries were sparked when Texas contemplated a project that would involve exporting water from neighboring Oklahoma.[82] And despite the typical high costs, just as with desalination, improved technology may result in bulk water transfers being more common someday.[83] Desalination in San Diego could cost as much as $5 per cubic meter of water, whereas transport of water from Alaska, via towed oceangoing bag technology, could be as low as $2 per cubic meter.[84] As is often the case with other water augmentation technological innovations, old legal regimes will need to adapt to new technologies.[85]

One question regarding any approach to technologically augmenting water supplies is whether or not such efforts will aggravate or mitigate water conflict. In the case of water disputes between refugees and their host communities, or between neighboring tribes with small, remote communities like the Navajo and Hopi, investments in increasing water supplies may ease tensions. This is perhaps because the parties to the water dispute are relatively similarly situated. However, where a hydro-hegemon with significantly more resources than its neighbor engages in augmentation, the technology could aggravate existing inequities and thus heighten tensions. This could be the case in both the Jordan and Colorado river basins, where hydro-hegemons have, and are considering more, desalination projects. However, perhaps where an environmental concern exists that multiple co-riparians share with the hydro-hegemon and which cannot be effectively addressed without collaborative efforts—like the Salton Sea or Dead Sea issues—augmentation efforts could serve as a catalyst for cooperation. In any event, aims to mitigate or avoid water disputes solely through a "grow the pie" strategy should proceed cautiously and prioritize improved water monitoring, modeling, and water conservation before augmentation. Take it from a father of a large family—sometimes a bigger pie just means a bigger argument.

Water and Space Exploration

As I have noted throughout this book, and particularly in the preceding chapter, the promise of water has compelled human movement and discovery throughout history. But when we stare into the sky from the security of our small, blue, wet planet, we stare into the depths of an unimaginable desert and the most challenging water frontier. But with NASA's recent discovery of liquid water on the desert planet Mars, perhaps there is a future for humanity on another planet if we can harness extraterrestrial water. But who will, or should, have the legal right to that extraterrestrial water? Perhaps the answer lies in a nineteenth-century U.S. innovation in water law designed to encourage the innovations and entrepreneurialism necessary to explore and colonize another vast desert—the American West.[86]

In the nineteenth century, the United States acquired enormous tracts of undeveloped desert land. American leaders, under the rallying cry of Manifest Destiny, created policies to promote settlements in that arid region. Key among those policies was a new approach to allocating water rights—the law of prior appropriation. As discussed, prior appropriation is a first-in-time, first-in-right regime. It is, in many ways, an intuitive approach to allocating resources. We rely on it all the time without thinking about it—in deciding who gets a parking spot or the last loaf of bread at the store. It lies at the very heart of much of the advocacy for the rights of indigenous people. Why, then, should it not govern who owns the water in space? Under prior appropriation law, the first person to capture a quantity of water and put it to beneficial use has superior rights to that quantity of water over all other subsequent users. This regime created a strong incentive for industrious people to run as fast as they could into the desert. After all, what better prize to the winner of a race in the desert than the most valuable resource one can possess in the desert?

The problem with this approach is that it has created challenges with managing water in the western United States. Early farmers and miners were able to secure water rights that were superior to those of subsequent cities and towns, and to quantities of water that might not be sustainable as populations and climate change. The prior appropriation regime functioned very well to encourage an orderly and entrepreneurial settlement of the arid West, but it struggles to provide an adaptive foundation for responding to modern water challenges. Recall the example of my children calling "shotgun" to get first-in-time rights to sit in the front seat of the car from chapter 4. What seems like a very simple rule—whoever gets there first—has many complicating exceptions and prerequisites. Often proving who was there first is difficult, because the evidence is old and poorly preserved. The first use must be beneficial, and not wasteful. Filing to provide notice of that use has certain formalities that typically must be followed. Furthermore, there are sometimes difficult questions about what it means to be "first-in-time." For example, a farmer begins digging a ditch to divert water to irrigate crops in Arizona on November 30, 1941. Shortly after the attack on Pearl Harbor on December 2, 1941, the farmer is drafted into the military and spends five years in combat overseas. During those five years, several of the farmer's neighbors begin and complete diversions and irrigate their crops. When the farmer returns after five years of war, and completes his diversion and irrigates his crop, is his priority date the date he first started digging the ditch in 1941, or the date he actually put the water to use in 1946? The farmer's priority date "relates back" to his original effort to divert so long as he was "diligent." But these rules leave water right holders arguing over the meaning of words like "beneficial" and "diligent." Sometimes the effort to simply line up water right holders in order of priority date takes court proceedings that can last decades. And even when those proceedings are finalized, the highest priority water rights, secured over a century earlier, may not reflect the highest priority of water uses for the community as it exists now.[87] The challenge for constructing a water rights regime in space is to capture the benefits of prior appropriation while avoiding its pitfalls.

There are few laws governing resource rights in space. The Outer Space Treaty of 1967 bans weapons of mass destruction in Earth's orbit or on the moon, and the Space Liability Convention of 1972 allocates liability between nations for objects that fall out of Earth's orbit. The Registration Convention of 1974 creates a registry of objects launched into Earth's orbit, and established the U.N. Office for Outer Space Affairs. But none of these treaties addressed rights to extraterrestrial resources. In 1979, the Moon Treaty stated that all states have equal rights to conduct research on extraterrestrial bodies and banned claims of sovereignty over those bodies, or any claim of ownership by any person or organization.[88] In 2015, however, the United States enacted the Spurring Private Aerospace Competitiveness and Entrepreneurship (SPACE) Act, under which U.S. citizens are permitted to "engage in the commercial exploration and exploitation of 'space resources,'" which would expressly include water.[89] Rights to these resources would be based on a "first-in-time, first-in-right" approach, similar to prior appropriation. How this legislation can be reconciled with U.S. treaty obligations under the Moon Treaty of 1979 remains to be seen.

But perhaps the approach of the SPACE Act is a good way to encourage broad investment in space exploration and development, and other countries should follow the example of the United States. Thinking about water rights in space is valuable for three reasons. First, missions to develop Martian natural resources may be a lucrative business in the future, and this may extend to mining (including water mining) on asteroids. Mars has potentially valuable mineral resources, including copper, zinc, gold, and the kinds of rare minerals used in lasers, microelectronics, and batteries. Second, someday interplanetary colonization may be possible, or even essential, for the survival of mankind. Third, considering a prior appropriation regime in space may help us better understand what we did right, and what we did wrong, in establishing the prior appropriation regime in the western United States and how to think about the changes to water law that may be necessary to adjust to a changing climate.

Securing these benefits of prior appropriation and developing extraterrestrial resources, without incurring the costs that the western United States now pays under a similar water rights regime, will require safeguards. If the international community knew that the first nation (or company) to capture a quantity of Martian water and put it to beneficial use had superior rights to all subsequent users, it could spur the types of technological innovations needed for interplanetary exploration and colonization, with attendant benefits to life on Earth. Human curiosity and the impulse to explore have already motivated some private efforts to engage in space exploration, including by Amazon CEO Jeff Bezos and Tesla founder Elon Musk.[90] But sustainable investment in the development of Mars will likely require stronger incentives. Under a prior appropriation water rights regime, those who succeed in a venture to Mars, and put Martian water to a beneficial use, would have superior rights to any subsequent users. Imagine having the highest priority water rights on a planet with enormous mineral wealth. That's a very strong incentive to win the race to Mars. But prior appropriation requires water users to remain "diligent" in order for their rights to retain priority, and they must continue to use their water or risk forfeiture. This would encourage long-term planning and investment for multiple missions to Mars, and even permanent colonization.

Of course, a Martian prior appropriation water rights regime would require a change in international law, which currently forbids any nation from claiming extraterrestrial resources. The change would have to be something along the lines of the SPACE Act. While a prior appropriation system creates strong incentives for an exciting new space race, it has potentially serious problems. We need look no further than the challenges in the western United States in responding to ongoing drought conditions. A farmer with water rights dating to 1875 may use inefficient irrigation methods and grow low-value crops. But that farmer may still insist on his rights, leaving junior right holders high and dry, even if those junior uses are for homes, schools, and hospitals. Additionally, because of the law of forfeiture, the farmer has very few incentives to invest in innovation or conservation. Prior appropriation rights in extraterrestrial water could lead to the first Martian mission and mining of Martian resources, but that mining operation could have superior water rights to future scientific explorations or human colonies.

Perhaps the biggest challenge to a prior appropriation regime on Mars is that there is no existing government to say what uses are "beneficial" or when water has been wasted or forfeited, or to resolve water rights disputes. Even in the highly competitive and contentious world of water rights in the western United States, state governments hold water resources in trust for the benefit of their citizens, and prior appropriation rights are only the right to use a state-sanctioned amount of water for a state-approved beneficial use. States, along with the federal government, regulate water quality as well, both to protect human water uses and ecosystems that depend on the water. But on Mars, there is no state to act as that trustee to preserve water quality and prioritize water uses and no humans or ecosystems to protect.

Four measures could help the world create the incentives of the prior appropriation regime, while avoiding the mistakes in implementation that continue to plague Western water policy in the United States. First, the United Nations could be designated as the trustee of extraterrestrial water for purposes of determining beneficial use, with the International Court of Justice adjudicating water rights disputes. Second, water rights owned, but not used, by states or companies could be held temporarily in trust by the United Nations for research purposes and shielded from forfeiture, similar to the trust concept I discussed earlier in this chapter and in the previous chapter. Third, if colonization creates a demand for domestic water, and water rights holders will not sell or lease the water, the United Nations could condemn a limited percentage of water rights by paying rights holders the fair market value of those rights, or else those companies can lease or sell water rights to colonizers. Fourth, the United Nations could issue permits for water use that impose best management practices to encourage sustainable management and avoid contamination. These measures could spur an international interplanetary Manifest Destiny, while still protecting Mars from invading earthlings and the invading earthlings from themselves.

Like our earliest ancestors who moved from Africa along corridors of water, or pastoral communities following the rains, or nineteenth-century settlers in the western United States chasing the promise of prior appropriation, we may look to the stars as the next great water migration and follow water to our next frontier. These reforms could help move us toward that frontier. But even with a cautious approach to encouraging space exploration, a prior appropriation regime in space has other risks. The settlers who won the race to water in the western United States imposed their culture, their laws, and their priorities on that arid land. Unlike in the western United States, however, there are no indigenous communities on Mars. But a prior appropriation system in space would mean that the first explorers on Mars would, like settlers in the American West, plant the seeds of law and culture. If it is a race, then there is no guarantee that the first seed of law and culture will come from the U.N. Universal Declaration of Human Rights, but might instead come from the Amazon employee handbook. Those seeds of law and culture will grow and evolve into a Martian society. And if a great interplanetary conflict arises after generations of Martian settlement, we may look back to water law as the reason Martians are so different from earthlings.

Conclusion

As the father of four children and a water law and policy scholar, I spend both my professional and home life thinking about how to allocate scarce resources between competing users. Fatherhood has taught me some lessons that I believe could influence how we think about technological innovation in water policy. As my children sit around the table for a meal, I may open a big bag of chips for them to share. Or else (just to show I also feed them healthy food), I'll cut up a watermelon and put a bowl of cubed watermelon in the middle of the table. There will then be inevitable disputes, as the children accuse one another of taking more than their fair share, and even deeper disputes about what "fair share" even means.

But I have learned that if I place slices of watermelon still on the rind, I will often avoid the conflict. The same is true if I give each child an individually wrapped bag of chips. The reason, I suppose, that this approach generates less conflict is that consumption is in discrete packages, and the consumption of the package generates concrete evidence—a watermelon rind or an empty chip bag on the plate. Each child knows how much the others have consumed. This phenomenon works in other meal settings. When I sit at a table with friends for dinner, and we share a plate of chicken wings or shrimp, I change my behavior if the chicken wings have bones, or if the shrimp have tails. Because my consumption is conspicuous—the evidence of each chicken wing and shrimp sits on the plate—I am more careful about consuming no more than my fair share. Property theorist and law professor Lee Anne Fennell's book *Slices and Lumps* delves into these ideas across a range of behaviors or realms of regulation that are particularly relevant to water policy.[91]

Perhaps there is something to learn in these parenting experiences about how and where to deploy water technology. Cass Sunstein and Richard Thaler wrote about the psychology and behavioral economics of "nudges."[92] The idea behind nudges is that command-and-control regulation may not be necessary, or cost-efficient, if small interventions can alter behavior, such as putting fruit at eye level in the store, and candy on the bottom or top shelf. Similar nudges, facilitated by technological innovation, may make more expensive innovations like desalination unnecessary. For example, if there were something like the chip bag or watermelon rind for water consumption that was conspicuous to other users, we might change our water-consumption behaviors. At the household level, this could mean a light or other signal showing water consumption compared to your neighbors. At the irrigation district or municipal level, there could be similar public information disclosure allowing comparisons that might nudge communities toward more efficient water uses. These technological innovations are not necessarily directly aimed at either conservation or augmentation but at the first priority of water policy: better understanding. And better understanding will result in better decisions. One of the most exciting innovations I have seen in recent years related to improving our understanding of water are smart hand pumps. This technology mounts an accelerometer on a typical hand pump for a well, which can transmit data related to times and frequency of use remotely to cell phones, allowing greater information about which wells are working and how often they are used. Such technology could even provide information about how far the pump handle is moved, perhaps indicating whether men, women, or children are the ones operating the well.[93]

In addition to understanding how evidence of consumption influences sharing, Fennell explores the myriad ways that property is or can be configured in large lumps or small slices, and how that configuration impacts law and lives. For example, Fennell discusses lumpy conceptions of property in the context of conservation. In doing so, she cites Mary Ellen Hannibal, who observed: "For more than one hundred years, conservation has functioned by drawing a boundary around a special area and limiting human impacts there. . . . But science today tells us this approach is failing. Nature doesn't work without connection."[94] Perhaps the idea of basin-level governance is making a similar mistake. Consider the technologies discussed in this chapter, including desalination, cloud seeding, and bulk water transports. What do many of these technologies have in common? They have impacts outside of the basin. Desertification and deforestation in one region can impact precipitation in a distant region, trade in virtual water moves water around the world, and global warming increases the frequency and intensity of El Niño/Southern Oscillation (ENSO) years (abnormal weather conditions due to warming in the Pacific Ocean), with water-supply implications around the world. Perhaps basin-level governance is thinking in unnecessarily small slices, and water governance should be lumped together in larger geographic, or even global, governance regimes. This suggestion runs counter to the basin-level governance prescriptions I suggest throughout this book. But I raise this suggestion here as an example of caution with any of my, or others', proposed water governance reforms. Global water governance would have enormous transaction costs, with many decision makers distant from the unique local conditions of many water sources. But it could also address many of the ways that water moves between basins that would be excluded from more local regimes. Any reforms we implement will have costs, risks, and benefits. As such, we must be willing to re-evaluate our assumptions and change as we learn.

Conclusion

Achieving Water Security

It is hard to overstate the importance of embracing a water security paradigm. Drought led to the disappearance of many civilizations along the Silk Road in China, in ancient Mesoamerica, and in the ancient Middle East.[1] For each one of these once-vibrant civilizations, something about their water supply changed, and they were incapable or unwilling to change with it. Change, with its attendant promise and peril, is ultimately what water security is all about. Two related ideas about change and water are reflected in a statement made by Bruce Lee regarding his theory of martial arts:

> Be formless, shapeless, like water. Now, you put water into a cup, it becomes the cup. You put water into a bottle, it becomes the bottle. You put water in a teapot, it becomes the teapot. Now, water can flow or it can crash. Be water, my friend.[2]

The two ideas contained in Lee's theory of martial arts represent the core related ideas of water security.[3] First, water flows and crashes, destroys and creates, and is both problem and solution. Second, laws, policies, and institutions involved in water governance must adapt to dynamic water conditions, including changes in supply, demand, quality, and technology.[4] These laws, policies, and institutions should not seek to manage a "normal" natural system but recognize that these systems both flow and crash—they are creative and destructive. Water policy should depend upon data, models, and assumptions regarding water extremes—droughts, floods, epidemics, and water conflicts, the very subjects of the water security paradigm.[5] Laws and policies should seek to manage those extremes, rather than some illusion of the "normal" status of water quality and quantity. Perhaps the most important contribution of the climate change paradigm, and one that must inform the water security paradigm, is that there is no normal in natural resources. The natural world changes, new technologies evolve, populations grow, and consumption patterns alter according to economic conditions, and laws must be able to adapt to manage extreme conditions.

The Aral Sea in Central Asia provides an illustrative example of the importance of adaptation.[6] The Aral Sea is shared between Kazakhstan and Uzbekistan and is fed by two large international rivers. The Amu Darya River is shared by Tajikistan, Kyrgyzstan, Afghanistan, Uzbekistan, and Turkmenistan. The Syr Darya River is shared between Kyrgyzstan, Uzbekistan, Tajikistan, and Kazakhstan. Large diversions and dam projects on these major tributaries, combined with climate change, have resulted in enormous impacts to the Aral Sea, with the maximum water level having declined by more than twenty-six meters and the surface area having decreased by 88 percent. Much of the international law that has governed how water in this basin is allocated between co-riparians is set forth in the 1992 Almaty Agreement, which is based on historic water uses and quantities established when these nations were part of the Soviet Union. While the information and allocations made in the Almaty Agreement became obsolete in a changing world, the transboundary governance institution created by the agreement— the Interstate Commission for Water Coordination (ICWC)—will be essential in adapting to an altered basin. The ICWC positively reviewed a new draft agreement for sharing the basin in 2014 and has largely worked to find compromises and flexibility within the strictures of its mandate.

My home region of the Colorado River Basin also provides an example of the move toward more adaptive water management. The Colorado River is shared between upper-basin jurisdictions (Colorado, Wyoming, Utah, and New Mexico) and lower-basin jurisdictions (Arizona, California, Nevada, and Mexico). Allocations within the basin are based on acre-feet. An acre-foot is 325,851 gallons, or 1,233.5 cubic meters, so these amounts represent enormous quantities of water. The Colorado River Compact allocates 7.5 million acre-feet per year to the upper-basin states and 7.5 million acre-feet per year to the lower-basin states.[7] The 1944 Rivers Treaty allocates 1.5 million acre-feet per year to Mexico.[8] The basin loses approximately 1.5 million acre-feet each year to evapotranspiration. That adds up to a projected 18 million acre-feet that the law assumes is available in the river system each year. But tree ring analysis demonstrates that the river more typically contains around 13 million acre-feet per year.[9] This "structural deficit" exists because the information relied on making allocations was based on data from flood years in the early twentieth century. Many of the controversies surrounding sharing this river have perpetuated because early allocations were based on bad information and were made in rigid, volumetric guarantees.[10]

The upper-basin states allocate their 7.5 million acre-feet based on a percentage of available stream flow, thereby accounting automatically for the structural deficit and adapting to the changing conditions of the river.[11] The lower basin, on the other hand, allocates raw water amounts to each state and is thus in a perpetual state of renegotiation over temporary measures to respond to shortage. However, just as the ICWC showed in the Aral Sea Basin, so institutions in the Colorado River Basin are proving to be potentially more adaptive than the laws that created them. The Minute negotiations between the United States and Mexico's International Boundary and Water Commission (IBWC) have produced shortage-sharing agreements (which include, among other measures, voluntary reductions in water use by farms and cities) and collaborative storage and infrastructure development projects despite the seemingly rigid allocations made in the 1944 Rivers Treaty. Additionally, the lower-basin states agreed to a "Drought Contingency Plan" in 2019 that would require shortage sharing across the basin under certain circumstances and efforts to keep water in reservoirs. The examples of the Aral Sea and Colorado River suggest that even when laws appear inflexible on their surface, the institutions that implement those laws can find flexibility if the water situation becomes stressed enough to make such flexibility sufficiently critical and politically palatable.

Laws must therefore integrate an adaptive management approach. Claudia Paul-Wostl defines adaptive management as "a systematic process for continually improving management policies and practices by learning from the outcomes of implemented management strategies."[12] Because our ability to predict future events is limited, governance institutions must periodically evaluate and adapt decisions, laws, and policies to respond to new information or changing circumstances.[13] Adaptive management has become a central feature of water policy, as policymakers must respond to changing supplies, demands, and technologies.[14] Sustainable development is thus not just a matter of maintaining and improving human life but of maintaining and improving human life under changing conditions. As such, water law and policy must "do development differently" through adaptive management.[15]

Adaptive management is important because no paradigm in any policy field is perfect, and the water security paradigm is no exception.[16] Early in this book I recommended basing the scope of the jurisdiction of water governance institutions on catchments. And yet, in the previous chapter, I noted technologies like desalination and cloud seeding that have significant impacts beyond the catchment and may require institutions with a broader scope. Perhaps a shift to water footprints as the primary metric for evaluating environmental stewardship will prove ineffective in discouraging greenhouse gas emissions. Water security, as I have discussed it in this book, can appear to be an anthropocentric way of thinking about natural resources and may need to be expanded to include more consideration of ecosystem health and biodiversity. Additionally, the water security paradigm cannot expect to improve policy if it attempts to draw a line between saltwater and freshwater. The water security paradigm must effectively integrate marine resources. Finally, perhaps the most significant criticism of the water security paradigm is whether or not water-based rhetoric resonates in ways that motivate action and improvements. Whatever limits or deficiencies of the reforms I have proposed under the water security paradigm, they will be revealed through implementation, evaluation, reconsideration, and adaptation. In concluding, I want to emphasize the importance of adaptation and how adaptive management can be promoted in the water security paradigm.

Principles of Adaptive Management

Much of natural resource law and policy has begun shifting toward a more experimental and adaptive approach.[17] This approach relies less on a stationary conception of ecosystems and the idea of "conservation" of some suggested "normal" natural state, and focuses instead on human institutions changing alongside nature.[18] While a thorough review and critique of the broad literature is not my aim here, it is helpful to provide some overview of the basic principles. Adaptive management is a process that "promotes flexible decision making that can be adjusted in the face of uncertainties as outcomes from management actions and other events become better understood. . . . It is not a 'trial by error' process, but rather emphasized learning while doing."[19] This requires both more accurate monitoring and modeling and the flexibility in sociolegal institutions to respond to that new and better data.[20] For purposes of water allocations, this means laws that establish water rights or allocate water would be subject to regular re-evaluation and recalibration based on new information.[21]

In the context of natural resource management, adaptation is typically referred to as a positive attribute whenever it exists in the law.[22] Adaptive capacity is the degree of flexibility within a legal system to respond to change without requiring fundamental alterations to legal doctrines and governance structures.[23] If laws and institutions are too rigid, they will be unable to integrate new information and respond to changed conditions and are thus vulnerable to wholesale transformation, which will either come at great cost or over a long period of time. But if laws and institutions can be adapted too easily, they will prove unpredictable and unreliable and may discourage investment due to uncertainty.[24] The adaptive capacity of the law is something like a tree, designed to have different degrees of flexibility at different levels.

The roots of the tree represent the sociocultural norms and traditions that feed into the law. At this level, society typically places a premium on the preservation and transmission of culture and values. Just as roots draw nutrients to nourish the entire tree, so fundamental cultural values permeate all layers of law and policy. As such, these values, like tree roots, have little adaptive capacity. The cultural values, norms, and traditions change slowly and organically, or else require enormous, high-cost disruption to spur rapid change. Such changes are so large that they do not constitute adaptation but transformation—effectively uprooting the tree and planting a new seed.[25]

The trunk of the tree represents foundational legal principles—the national constitution, or perhaps fundamental approaches to law, such as British common law or Napoleonic civil law. Just as a tree trunk has limited flexibility, so also do foundational legal principles have limited adaptive capacity, with a high premium placed on legitimacy. It is easier to amend a constitution or overturn long-standing legal precedent than to alter a society's values or traditions, just as a tree trunk will bend to some degree, but the roots run deep and hold fast. Nevertheless, a thick trunk is rigid, and too much flexibility at this level risks the perceived legitimacy of the entire system. To cut the tree is a high-cost and high-risk endeavor, justified only by extremely significant disruptions.[26]

Tree branches are designed to be highly flexible and help the tree weather storms. At this level, the law is designed to be fairly adaptive, changing without either very high costs or major disruptions, but still prioritizing predictability and competence. This level would include statutes that establish regulatory frameworks that can be expected to govern for years, with some changes implemented by government agencies and some through legislative amendments as politics shift. The leaves of the tree provide energy, but are designed to fall and be regularly replaced. This level would include administrative regulations, industry standards, contractual arrangements, or community efforts. At this level, the law aims to address problems quickly and energetically, but is also thus less reliable and predictable. The costs of adaptation are extremely low, and change is the rule rather than the exception. Reformers can make the fastest and lowest cost interventions at this level, but such interventions may prove ephemeral. [27]

Promoting water security requires efforts at all of these levels, with the attendant costs and benefits characteristic of each level. Long-term investments in education, stakeholder participation, and promoting a strong water ethic will have enormous benefits at the root level but will require patience with long-held traditions and values. Human and constitutional rights at the trunk level can be an effective means of promoting water security, but constitutional protections of property rights and democratic processes may delay or prevent, for better or for worse, some potential reforms. Efforts to create or change legislation at the branch level, such as water trusts to protect environmental flows or Health Impact Assessments to integrate disease-vector evaluations into water infrastructure development, can improve policy but require sustained political efforts. At the leaf level, small regulations that encourage use of water-efficient technologies or nudge water conservation efforts by showing and comparing evidence of consumption, can make incremental and meaningful progress toward water security. For those seeking to promote water security, the challenge is finding the "sway in the tree," where adaptive capacity already exists and can be deployed at relatively low cost. There are two relatively common principles of water law that may provide enough low-cost flexibility to prove effective means of promoting water security: water markets and the public trust doctrine.

The Public Trust Doctrine and Adaptive Water Management

As discussed in previous chapters, the public trust doctrine means that the state owns certain resources, which are held in trust with the state having the fiduciary duty to manage the resource for the benefit of all citizens.[28] Although far from universal, and interpreted and implemented in various ways and to varying degrees of effectiveness, the public trust doctrine forms part of the water laws of several countries, including India, Kenya, Brazil, Ecuador, Canada, and the United States, among many others.[29] Because the public trust doctrine places a fiduciary obligation on the state to ensure water management decisions are broadly beneficial, that doctrine can form the basis for adapting water management to changing water conditions.[30]

The public trust doctrine has provided the basis for such adaptations. For example, in the state of Arizona, courts relied on the public trust doctrine in holding that restrictions on groundwater pumping did not constitute an unlawful exercise of eminent domain and that certain legislative grants of title over river ownership to private parties constituted a violation of the public trust doctrine.[31] In Kenya, the High Court stated that the "essence of the public trust [doctrine] is that the [S]tate, as trustee, is under a fiduciary duty to deal with trust property, being the common natural resources, in a manner that is in the interests of the general public." The court further stated that "the water table and the river courses affected are held in trust by the present generation for the future generations."[32] In the Kenyan formulation, the public trust doctrine can encourage intergenerational equity by providing the basis for litigation against unsustainable water polices.[33] Similarly, in 2005, the Canadian Supreme Court explained that if the government can sue "as guardian of the public interest, to claim against a party causing damage to that public interest, then it would seem in another case, a beneficiary of the public interest ought to be able to claim against the government for a failure to properly protect the public interest . . . [because a] right gives a corresponding duty."[34] Where the public trust doctrine provides a citizen cause of action, the doctrine creates a degree of public oversight of water management decisions to encourage adaptation.

The public trust doctrine thus may provide some degree of "sway" in the tree—flexibility already built into some countries' legal structures governing water.[35] A version of the public trust doctrine in institutions governing international river basins could provide similar flexibility. As discussed in previous chapters, transboundary governance institutions could have a fiduciary obligation to manage the shared resource to the benefit of all co-riparians, which might provide some check on the power of hydro-hegemons while providing oversight to encourage adaption at the international level. Treaties would impose this duty on the transboundary governance institution and create a dispute-resolution mechanism whereby member states could enforce that duty if breached.[36] The IBWC, while not expressly adopting this sort of approach to an international public trust doctrine, has nevertheless demonstrated a reasonable degree of adaptive capacity at the international transboundary level in successfully implementing regular treaty amendments, or "Minutes," that allow for adaptive shortage sharing arrangements.[37]

While the public trust doctrine has proven a useful tool in encouraging adaptive management in water policy in some instances, it remains a controversial, and fairly limited, basis upon which to reform laws governing natural resources, particularly when those laws protect private property rights.[38] Where the public trust doctrine would be used as a means for interfering with private property rights in water without compensation, the benefits of flexibility come at the cost of disrupting vested expectations, and the sway in the branches of the public trust doctrine conflicts with the designed rigidity of property law and constitutional rights. Furthermore, the conception of an international corollary of the public trust doctrine, and the implementation of such a concept in international basins, is novel and sure to face legitimate concerns about how such a doctrine would interact with national sovereignty over natural resources. In many instances, these controversies and concerns will raise the cost of relying on the public trust doctrine as a source of flexibility and require those promoting adaptive water governance to find that capacity elsewhere.

Water Markets and Adaptive Water Governance

Another potential source of flexibility in water law to promote adaptive management is the use of water markets. Efficient water markets can allow for reallocations of water to address changing conditions without interfering with vested property rights. However, efficient markets require, among many things: (1) clearly assigned property rights; (2) limited information and power asymmetries; (3) limited externalities; and (4) low transaction costs.[39] But water seems, by its very nature, to defy the characteristics of efficient markets. Because it flows, flies, and sinks, it almost inevitably carries with it externalities, and the limits of its ownership are difficult to define. Because it is of interest to virtually everyone for a myriad of reasons and its management is highly technical, water transactions nearly always include relatively high transaction costs and information and power asymmetries. And where water rights are privately held—in riparian or prior appropriation regimes, for example—the law struggles to clearly define those rights.

Furthermore, market-based approaches to the reallocation of water can face opposition if viewed as the unregulated commodification of water.[40] Water, as a political, religious, and cultural symbol, as a resource with unique aesthetic values, and as the subject of human rights protection, defies, in the minds of many, any effort at commodification. The costs of even reasonably efficient water markets are often high, and the consequences felt by those not directly engaged in the market. The notorious example of the water transfer from the Owens Valley to Los Angeles, which formed part of the plot of the movie *Chinatown*, illustrates these risks. Developers and civic leaders in Los Angeles knew that water supplies could limit the city's growth, so they pursued supplies from the upland Owens Valley, which could provide water to Los Angeles through an aqueduct. The sale of water rights to these developers for the ultimate benefit of Los Angeles has been heavily criticized as corrupt. The Owens Valley is frequently cited as a warning of thirsty, unscrupulous urbanites seeking to claim rural water supplies. However, most of the farmers in the Owens Valley received respectably fair value for the water rights they sold, at least based on the market for agricultural lands and water rights at the time. The people who ultimately paid the highest price for these transactions were not the farmers who sold land and water rights but instead the other people and businesses of the Owens Valley who depended on the presence and vitality of the agricultural economy to maintain their communities and enterprises. Thus, even a "fair" water market may leave many people and communities behind.[41]

Despite these risks and limitations, water markets have been successfully implemented in some circumstances to address, and have even been instigated in response to, major environmental change.[42] As a tool to facilitate adaptive management, water markets have four characteristics: (1) an established limit on use, like a cap in a cap-and-trade system; (2) use that is authorized by an initial allocation of property rights; (3) a mechanism for the transfer of those property rights that integrates incentives for conservation and ecological protection; and (4) regulatory oversight, including monitoring.[43] Rather than a concern about commodification, advocates of water markets contend that it is the very failure to truly value water that results in environmental degradation and unsustainable resource exploitation and that markets can more effectively assign water its true value.[44] Water markets address this concern by allowing diffuse, localized knowledge and information to be integrated into management decisions through market transactions, and because the price signal inherent in a market-based approach encourages efficiency and investment in conservation techniques and technology.[45]

Australia's approach to water management in the Murray-Darling Basin is the paradigmatic example of an adaptive, market-based approach. Australia's early water allocation regimes were similar to other property rights–based approaches of former British colonies, which shifted over time to an approach characterized by administrative licensing. Severe drought in the 1990s

forced reconsideration of national water policies and resulted in the creation of transferable shares and allocations in available water supplies within
individual basins, which included limits on appropriations and minimum
environmental flow requirements. This market functions both at the individual level and as a management tool for transboundary water allocations
in a federal, interstate system. The Murray-Darling Basin water market has
evolved as national and state politics shift and in response to other drought
conditions.[46]

The Murray-Darling Basin has become synonymous with the promise
and pitfalls of water markets. It has become a model of water management to
which many jurisdictions, including South Africa and Chile, have looked for
lessons.[47] According to Cameron Holley and Darren Sinclair, the Murray-
Darling Basin market-based approach has several signature achievements,
including greater flexibility in responding to droughts, and thus can introduce greater adaptive capacity into water law and policy. However, Holley
and Sinclair also note the limits of the market-based approach, including
failures in accurate accounting and effective regulation, particularly in the
context of groundwater.[48]

Arizona has also relied on markets as a management tool, and particularly in the context of groundwater. In the 1970s, a legal dispute arose over
lowered water tables and groundwater pumping between farmers, mining
operations, and the city of Tucson. In response to this dispute, the state legislature enacted the Arizona Groundwater Management Act (AZGMA)
in 1980. The AZGMA functioned as something of a compromise between
rural mining and agricultural interests on the one hand and growing urban
centers on the other. Groundwater rights were frozen and quantified, and
grandfathered into a new management structure within legislatively designated "Active Management Areas" where groundwater overdraft was at its
worst. In exchange for these limits on groundwater pumping, cities inside
Active Management Areas would not allow the sale of subdivided land unless developers could prove the availability of one hundred years of water
supplies to support the growth. The goal for most Active Management Areas
was "safe yield" (meaning groundwater would be recharged at least as fast as
it is pumped) by 2025. This policy has resulted in a strong market for groundwater recharge credits. Facilities will take renewable water supplies, including treated wastewater, and artificially recharge aquifers in exchange for
credits, which can be sold within Active Management Areas to developers
looking to prove compliance with AZGMA. Additionally, there is a similarly

strong market for extinguishment credits, whereby grandfathered ground-water right holders will extinguish their rights in exchange for a credit, which can be similarly sold within the Active Management Area.[49]

As with water markets in Australia, the AZGMA has demonstrated many successes, including rebounding water tables, more efficient agriculture, and more incentives for water storage and conservation. However, no Active Management Area has yet achieved safe yield. Additionally, the AZGMA, like the Murray-Darling Basin markets, faces very real limitations. Most significantly, Active Management Areas in Arizona depend on renewable surface water sources—especially the Colorado River—as the main source of water for artificial groundwater recharge. Yet, as noted in this chapter, there is a structural deficit in the Colorado River that is worsened by climate change and has required careful and regular renegotiation between riparians on how to share limited supplies and avoid shortage. Arizona exempted certain de minimis wells from the AZGMA, but these wells have proliferated and limited the ability to achieve safe yield. Ongoing legal disputes over water rights in Arizona also prevent water rights from being clearly assigned and impede efficient water markets.[50]

Water supplies are changing. Pollution and sea-level rise are altering water quality, and climate change is making precipitation patterns more extreme and less predictable. Populations are growing and developing, placing greater demands on those changing supplies. Water law and policy must adapt to these changes. That adaptation can come with immediate tinkering where flexibility already exists, whether through the public trust doctrine, water markets, or other more easily implemented regulatory interventions or incentives for conservation and efficiency. Such efforts, like leaves on a tree, can energize water policy, but may not be sufficient to respond to the magnitude of our water challenges and the impact of water change. Major disruptive events may spur greater and faster adaptations and innovations, but at great cost. But water does not lend itself well to crisis management—infrastructure and attitudes take time to build and change.

Conclusion

Bruce Lee's "be water" philosophy of martial arts, applied in the context of water policy, is about awareness and adaptation. By awareness, I mean respecting water's power to both flow and crash, to create and destroy. The 2030

Agenda for Sustainable Development, adopted by all members of the United Nations in 2015, lays out fundamental global challenges and proposed solutions. Included in that Agenda are seventeen Sustainable Development Goals (SDGs). These SDGs include such aims as the elimination of poverty and hunger, racial and gender equality, clean water and sanitation, affordable clean energy, innovation, addressing climate change, and advancing peace and justice.[51] My hope is that this book has helped emphasize the role water plays as both the flow and the crash in each of these goals. Just as water is the foundation of life, so it is a foundational problem and foundational solution to much of life's problems. Water insecurity is an important, and often underappreciated, driver of conflict and inequality, poverty and disease, war and instability. Water security is an essential, and often underestimated, driver of equality, health, peace, and prosperity.

Bruce Lee's philosophy in the water context, though, is not just about awareness of the importance of water security. It is also an admonition to mimic water's adaptive capacity in how we manage such a dynamic resource. Adapting water policy in the face of climate change is inevitable. The admonition to "be water" in the water policy context is as much a prediction as a prescription. Water will inevitably adapt to the container it is placed in, and water policy will inevitably adapt to changing water supplies. The question is not whether water policy will adapt, but when and at what cost.

There is another characteristic of water besides its adaptive capacity that we should emulate in our approach to water governance. It is perhaps the most important characteristic of water that we should adopt if we are to achieve global water security. When I was growing up, I had a favorite song I learned in church. I have sung this song on a boat on the Amazon River, on the banks of the Jordan River, and looking down on the Colorado River from the rim of the Grand Canyon. The song is entitled, "'Give,' Said the Little Stream."

> "Give," said the little stream,
> "Give, oh, give! Give, oh, give!"
> "Give," said the little stream,
> As it hurried down the hill.
> "I'm small, I know, but wherever I go
> The grass grows greener still."
> Singing, singing all the day
> "Give away! Oh, give away!"

> Singing, singing all the day
> "Give, oh, give away!"[52]

Water is generous. It renews, enlivens, beautifies, and cleanses. Water gives. If we are to achieve water security, we must be water. We must be generous—generous with our time, our means, and our compassion. We want to give like the stream, but we often feel overwhelmed when we think about how small we are as individuals in the face of so many problems. When we feel overwhelmed, when we feel small in the face of our desire to give, I suggest we begin at the beginning. The Qur'an says that God "made every living thing of water"—it is the starting point for all life and is a good place to start solving life's problems.[53] The subject of our generosity should be water. When we see poverty, inequality, violence, and fear, we should give like the little stream and just add water.

Notes

Introduction—Understanding Water Security

1. Tilman Sauer, *Einstein's Unified Field Theory Program*, in THE CAMBRIDGE COMPANION TO EINSTEIN 281 (M. Janssen & C. Lehner eds., 2014).
2. F. DAVID PEAT, SUPERSTRINGS AND THE SEARCH FOR THE THEORY OF EVERYTHING (1989).
3. ARISTOTLE, THE METAPHYSICS (John H. McMahon trans., Dover Publications, 2007).
4. C.W. Churchman, *Free for All*, 14 MGMT. SCI. B141–B142 (1967); H.W. Rittel & M.M. Weber, *Dilemmas in a General Theory of Planning*, 4 POL'Y SCI. 155–69 (1973).
5. David Grey & Claudia W. Sadoff, *Sink or Swim? Water Security for Growth and Development*, 9 WATER POL'Y 545 (2007).
6. M. Fitzmaurice, *The Human Right to Water*, 18 FORDHAM ENVTL. L. REV. 537, 539 (2007).
7. Amy Liu, *Desalination Is No Panacea, But Holds Potential as Water Shortage Solution*, 22 J. YOUNG INVESTIGATORS (Sept. 2008), https://www.jyi.org/2008-september/2017/11/5/desalination-is-no-panacea-but-holds-potential-as-water-shortage-solution.
8. J.A. Allan, *Virtual Water—The Water, Food, and Trade Nexus: Useful Concept or Misleading Metaphor?*, 28 WATER INT'L 4 (2003).
9. For a broad examination of the intersection of religious rights and water law, *see* Rhett B. Larson, *Holy Water and Human Rights: Religious Rights Claims to Water Resources by Indigenous Peoples*, 2 ARIZ. J. ENVTL. L. & POL'Y 81 (2011).
10. 553 F.3d 1058 (9th Cir. 2008).
11. 553 F.3d at 1097.
12. Louise Erdrich, *Holy Rage: Lessons from Standing Rock*, THE NEW YORKER, Dec. 22, 2016, https://www.newyorker.com/news/news-desk/holy-rage-lessons-from-standing-rock.
13. Robinson Meyer, *The Last-Ditch Attempt to Stop the Dakota Access Pipeline*, ATLANTIC, Feb. 10, 2017, https://www.theatlantic.com/science/archive/2017/02/the-dakota-access-pipelines-final-stand/516225/.
14. S. Farooq & Z. Asari, *Wastewater Reuse in Muslim Countries: An Islamic Perspective*, 7 ENVTL. MGMT. 119 (1983).
15. B. Gopal, *Holy Ganga and the Mighty Amazon*, 16 AMAZONIANA 337 (2001).
16. KELLY D. ALLEY, ON THE BANKS OF THE GANGA: WHEN WASTEWATER MEETS A SACRED RIVER 20–25 (2002).
17. Priyam Das & Kenneth R. Tamminga, *The Ganges and the GAP: An Assessment of Efforts to Clean a Sacred River*, 4 SUSTAINABILITY 1647–68 (2012).

18. Alon Gelbman, *Border Tourism in Israel: Conflict, Fear and Hope*, 10 Tourism Geographies 193–213 (2008).

19. Larson, *supra* note 9, at 81.

20. Adam Smith, The Wealth of Nations (Penguin Classics, 1982) (1776).

21. Plato, Euthydemus (Gregory A. McBrayer & Mary P. Nichols trans., Focus Publishing, 2011).

22. Farhana Sultana, *Water Justice: Why It Matters and How to Achieve It*, 43 Water Int'l 483 (2018).

23. Raul Pacheco-Vega, *(Re)theorizing the Politics of Bottled Water: Water Insecurity in the Context of Weak Regulatory Regimes*, 11 Water 658 (2019).

24. Joseph W. Dellapenna, *International Law's Lessons for the Law of the Lakes*, 40 U. Mich. J.L. Reform 747, 763–64 (2007).

25. John Rawls, A Theory of Justice (1971).

26. Isaiah Berlin, *Two Concepts of Liberty, in* Four Essays on Liberty 118 (1969).

27. *See generally* J. Häusermann, A Human Rights Approach to Development (1998); *see also* Tarah Melish, *Maximum Feasible Participation of the Poor: New Governance, New Accountability, and a 21st Century War on the Sources of Poverty*,13 Yale Hum. Rts. & Dev. L.J. 1 (2010).

28. Justin Rheingold, *Sultana Discusses Intersection of Water, Gender, Citizenship*, Tufts Daily, Mar. 12, 2014, https://tuftsdaily.com/archives/2014/03/12/sultana-discusses-intersection-of-water-gender-citizenship/.

29. Aaron Wolf, *Criteria for Equitable Allocations: The Heart of International Water Conflict*, 23 Nat. Resources F. 1, 3 (1999).

30. Allan, *supra* note 8, at 4 (2003); *see also* J.A. Allan, *Virtual Water—Part of an Invisible Synergy that Ameliorates Water Scarcity, in* Water Crisis: Myth or Reality, at ch. 8 (Peter Rogers et al. eds., 2006) (virtual water is water embedded in commodities like food, energy, and clothing).

31. Peter Gleick, Pac. Inst., Dirty Water: Estimated Deaths from Water-Related Diseases 2000–2020 (2002), http://pacinst.org/reports/water_related_deaths/water_related_deaths_report.pdf.

Chapter 1—Water Security and Climate Change

1. Much of what follows in this chapter is based on my article, "Water Security," which provides an overview of the comparison of the benefits of the water security paradigm versus the climate change paradigm. *See* Rhett B. Larson, *Water Security*, 112 Nw. L. Rev. 139 (2017).

2. *See generally* Intergovernmental Panel on Climate Change: The Scientific Basis (J.T. Houghton et al. eds., 2001).

3. Jody Freeman & Andrew Guzman, *Climate Change and U.S. Interests*, 109 Colum. L. Rev. 1531 (2009).

4. Robin Kundis Craig, *The Social and Cultural Aspects of Climate Change Winners*, 97 Minn. L. Rev. 1416, 1427 (2013).

5. *See, e.g.*, Carol E. Lee & William Mauldin, *U.S., China Agree on Implementing Paris Climate-Change Pact*, WALL ST. J., Sept. 3, 2016, https://www.wsj.com/articles/u-s-china-agree-on-implementing-paris-climate-change-pact-1472896645.

6. J.B. Ruhl, *The Political Economy of Climate Change Winners*, 97 MINN. L. REV. 206, 220 (2012).

7. Ben Wolfgang, *Republican Attorneys General Eager to Dismantle Obama Climate Change Agenda Under Donald Trump*, WASH. TIMES, Dec. 26, 2016, https://www.washingtontimes.com/news/2016/dec/26/republican-attorneys-general-eager-to-dismantle-ob/.

8. Lisa Viscidi & Nate Graham, *Brazil Was a Global Leader on Climate Change. Now It's a Threat*, FOREIGN POL'Y (Jan. 4, 2019, 3:14 PM), https://foreignpolicy.com/2019/01/04/brazil-was-a-global-leader-on-climate-change-now-its-a-threat/; Damien Cave, *It Was Supposed to Be Australia's Climate Change Election. What Happened?*, N.Y. TIMES, May 19, 2019, https://www.nytimes.com/2019/05/19/world/australia/election-climate-change.html.

9. *See* Patricia Wouters et al., *Water Security, Hydrosolidarity, and International Law: A River Runs Through It . . .*, 19 Y.B. INT'L ENVTL. L. 97, 98 n.6 (2009) (quoting Professor John Beddington, U.K. Government Chief Scientist, who refers to the water stress caused by economic development, population growth, and climate change as the "perfect storm" for a global energy and food crisis).

10. *See, e.g.*, Richard J. Lazarus, *Super Wicked Problems and Climate Change: Restraining the Present to Liberate the Future*, 94 CORNELL L. REV. 1153, 1159–60 (2009).

11. Sarah Tran, *Expediting Innovation*, 36 HARV. ENVTL. L. REV. 123, 154–55 (2012).

12. *See generally* JONG S. JUN, PUBLIC ADMINISTRATION, ch. 4, 68–90 (1986). For a general discussion of how public policy and scientific paradigms shift, and a review of the literature related to that broader debate, *see* Terence Ball, *Is There Progress in Political Science?*, *in* IDIOMS OF INQUIRY: CRITIQUE AND RENEWAL IN POLITICAL SCIENCE (Terence Ball ed., 1987).

13. *See generally* THOMAS KUHN, THE STRUCTURE OF SCIENTIFIC REVOLUTIONS (1970).

14. *See generally* Jay M. Feinman, *The Jurisprudence of Classification*, 41 STAN. L. REV. 661 (1989) (providing a history of the approach to "paradigmatic" classification theory in the law).

15. Jeremy Allouche, *The Multi-Level Governance of Water and State Building Processes: A Longue Durée Perspective*, *in* THE POLITICS OF WATER: A SURVEY 45 (Kai Wegerich & Jeroen Warner eds., 2010).

16. *See, e.g.*, GREEN PARADIGMS AND THE LAW (Nicole Rogers ed., 1998).

17. *See generally* Sheila Foster, *Justice from the Ground Up: Distributive Inequities, Grassroots Resistance, and the Transformative Politics of the Environmental Justice Movement*, 86 CAL. L. REV. 775 (1998).

18. RACHEL CARSON, SILENT SPRING (1962); *see also* Shannon M. Roesler, *The Nature of the Environmental Right to Know*, 39 ECOLOGY L.Q. 989 (2012); Timur Kuran & Cass R. Sunstein, *Availability Cascades and Risk Regulation*, 51 STAN. L. REV. 683, 691–99 (1999).

19. Alice Kaswan, *Greening the Grid and Climate Justice*, 39 ENVTL. L. 1143, 1158–59 (2009).

20. *See generally* Daniel Bodansky, *A Tale of Two Architectures: The Once and Future U.N. Climate Change Regime*, 43 ARIZ. ST. L.J. 697 (2011).

21. *See, e.g.*, Jason Scott Johnston, *Desperately Seeking Numbers: Global Warming, Species Loss, and the Use and Abuse of Quantification in Climate Change Policy Analysis*, 155 U. PA. L. REV. 1901 (2007) (noting that climate change is the great natural resource debate of this generation).

22. *See, e.g.*, Kenneth W. Abbott, *Strengthening the Transnational Regime Complex for Climate Change*, 3 TRANSNATIONAL ENVTL. L. 57 (2014) (examining private governance responses to climate change).

23. Reuven S. Avi-Yonah & David M. Uhlmann, *Combating Global Climate Change: Why a Carbon Tax Is a Better Response to Global Warming than Cap and Trade*, 28 STAN. ENVTL. L.J. 3 (2009); Robert L. Glicksman & Richard E. Levy, *A Collective Action Perspective on Ceiling Preemption by Federal Environmental Regulation: The Case of Global Climate Change*, 102 NW. U. L. REV. 579 (2008).

24. *See, e.g.*, Jody Freeman, *The Obama Administration's National Auto Policy: Lessons from the "Car Deal,"* 35 HARV. ENVTL. L. REV. 343 (2011).

25. Hari Osofsky, *Diagonal Federalism and Climate Change: Implications for the Obama Administration*, 62 ALA. L. REV. 237 (2011).

26. *See, e.g.*, Lyle Scruggs & Salil Benegal, *Declining Public Concern About Climate Change: Can We Blame the Great Recession?*, 22 GLOBAL ENVTL. CHANGE 505 (2012).

27. Stephen Burns, *Environmental Policy and Politics: Trends in Public Debate*, 23 NAT. RESOURCES & ENV'T 8 (2008) ("Climate change has come to dominate the public discourage on the environment unlike any other issue today."); Hope M. Babcock, *Assuming Personal Responsibility for Improving the Environment: Moving Toward a New Environmental Norm*, 33 HARV. ENVTL. L. REV. 117, 169 (2009) (noting the dominance of climate change in public discourse on the environment).

28. Karl S. Coplan, *Climate Change, Political Truth, and the Marketplace of Ideas*, 2012 UTAH L. REV. 545, 553 (2012).

29. Michele Betsill, *Environmental NGOs Meet the Sovereign State: The Kyoto Protocol Negotiations on Global Climate Change*, 13 COLO. J. INT'L ENVTL. L. & POL'Y 49, 57 (2002).

30. Cinnamon P. Carlarne, *Rethinking a Failing Framework: Adaptation and Institutional Rebirth for the Global Climate Change Regime*, 25 GEO. INT'L ENVTL. L. REV. 1, 26 (2012).

31. Alice Kaswan, *Greening the Grid and Climate Justice*, 39 ENVTL. L. 1143, 1159 (2009).

32. DEBIKA SHOME & SABINE MARX, The Psychology of Climate Change Communication: A Guide for Scientists, Journalists, Educators, Political Aides, and the Interested Public 10 (Andria Cimino ed., 2009), http://guide.cred.columbia.edu/pdfs/CREDguide_full-res.pdf.

33. Aaron M. McCright & Riley E. Dunlap, *The Politicization of Climate Change and Polarization in the American Public's Views of Global Warming, 2001–2010*, 52 SOC. Q. 155 (2011).

34. Eric Biber, *Climate Change and Backlash*, 17 N.Y.U. ENVTL. L.J. 1295, 1354 (2009).

35. Gary E. Marchant & Karen Bradshaw, *The Short-Term Temptations and Long-Term Risks of Environmental Catastrophism*, 56 JURIMETRICS 345 (2016).

36. Kevin M. Stack & Michael P. Vandenbergh, *The One Percent Problem*, 111 COLUM. L. REV. 1385 (2011); Victor B. Flatt & Heather Payne, *Not One Without the Other: The Challenge of Integrating U.S. Environment, Energy, Climate, and Economic Policy*, 44 ENVT'L L. 1079, 1085 (2014).

37. Alejandro E. Camacho, *Adapting Governance to Climate Change: Managing Uncertainty through a Learning Infrastructure*, 59 EMORY L.J. 1, 62 (2009).

38. Wouters et al., *supra* note 9, at 98 (2008) (discussing how population growth, urbanization, climate change, and the current lack of financial resources, "could lead to what Professor John Beddington, the U.K. Government Chief Scientist, refers to as a 'perfect storm' of food, energy, and water shortages"); *see also* Christine McGourty, *Global Crisis to Strike by 2030*, BBC NEWS, Mar. 19, 2009, http://news.bbc.co.uk/1/hi/uk/7951838.stm (containing additional commentary by Professor Beddington on the "perfect storm").

39. Scott K. Miller, *Undamming Glen Canyon: Lunacy, Rationality, or Prophecy?*, 19 STAN. ENVTL. L.J. 121, 156 (2000).

40. John B. Weldon, Jr. & Lisa M. McKnight, *Future Indian Water Settlements in Arizona: The Race to the Bottom of the Waterhole?*, 49 ARIZ. L. REV. 441 (2007) (discussing CAP's role in tribal water settlements).

41. Chuck DeVore, *The EPA's All Pain, No Gain Plan to Nationalize the Electric Grid*, FORBES, Mar. 23, 2016, https://www.forbes.com/sites/chuckdevore/2016/03/23/the-epas-all-pain-no-gain-plan-to-nationalize-the-electric-grid/#59bfe2162813; Beth Kleiman, *The Water-Energy Nexus Dimensions of the Central Arizona Project System Use Agreement*, CENT. ARIZ. WATER CONSERVATION DIST. (Sept. 14, 2016), http://www.cap-az.com/documents/education/2016-Kleiman.pdf.

42. Abrahm Lustgarten, *End of the Miracle Machines: Inside the Power Plant Fueling America's Drought*, PROPUBLICA, June 16, 2015, https://projects.propublica.org/killing-the-colorado/story/navajo-generating-station-colorado-river-drought.

43. *See* Michael Burger et al., *Legal Pathways to Reducing Greenhouse Gas Emissions Under Section 115 of the Clean Air Act*, 28 GEO. ENVT'L L. REV. 359, 382 (2016).

44. Coral Davenport, *Nations Approve Landmark Climate Accord in Paris*, N.Y. TIMES, Dec. 12, 2015, https://www.nytimes.com/2015/12/13/world/europe/climate-change-accord-paris.html.

45. WORLD WATER COUNCIL, E-CONFERENCE SYNTHESIS: VIRTUAL WATER TRADE—CONSCIOUS CHOICES 3 (2004), https://waterfootprint.org/media/downloads/virtual_water_final_synthesis.pdf.

46. *See* Bandana Kaur Malik, *Like Water for Energy, and Energy for Water*, ENVTL. & ENERGY STUDY INST. (Aug. 1, 2009), https://www.eesi.org/articles/view/like-water-for-energy-and-energy-for-water.

47. *See, e.g.*, Prevention of Significant Deterioration and Title V Greenhouse Gas Tailoring Rule, 75 Fed. Reg. 31,514, 31,516 (June 3, 2010) (codified in various sections at 40 C.F.R. pts. 51, 52, 70, and 71).

48. Hilary Hylton, *Why the U.S. Fracking Industry Worries About the Weather in India*, TIME, July 17, 2012, http://world.time.com/2012/07/17/why-the-u-s-fracking-industry-worries-about-the-weather-in-india/.

49. N. Liberman & Y. Trope, *The Role of Feasibility and Desirability Considerations in Near and Distant Future Decisions: A Test of Temporal Construal Theory*, 75 J. PERSONALITY & SOC. PSYCHOL. 75 (1998).

50. A. Leiserowitz, *Communicating the Risks of Global Warming: American Risk Perceptions, Affective Images, and Interpretive Communities, in* CREATING A CLIMATE FOR CHANGE: COMMUNICATING CLIMATE CHANGE AND FACILITATING SOCIAL CHANGE 44–63 (S.C. Moser & L. Dilling eds., 2007).

51. JAMES SCOTT, SEEING LIKE A STATE: HOW CERTAIN SCHEMES TO IMPROVE THE HUMAN CONDITIONS HAVE FAILED (1998).

52. Friedrich Hayek, *The Use of Knowledge in Society*, 35 AM. ECON. REV. 519 (1945).

53. *See* ROBERT D. COOTER, THE STRATEGIC CONSTITUTION 105–07 (2000).

54. A. Dan Tarlock, *The Potential Role of Local Governments in Watershed Management*, 20 PACE ENVTL. L. REV. 149, 153 (2002) (describing the watershed as "the 'right' organizing unit for integrated land and water resource management").

55. *See, e.g.*, Village of Euclid v. Ambler Realty Co., 272 U.S. 367, 387 (1926). For a general discussion of the role of transaction costs on intergovernmental cooperation and federalism, *see* Robert D. Cooter & Neil S. Siegel, *Collective Action Federalism: A General Theory of Article I, Section 8*, 63 STAN. L. REV. 115 (2010).

56. *See* Daniel C. Esty, *Revitalizing Environmental Federalism*, 95 MICH. L. REV. 570, 614–15 (1996). For a general discussion of the role of externalities on intergovernmental cooperation and federalism, *see* Charles Fried, *Federalism—Why Should We Care?*, 6 HARV. J.L. & PUB. POL'Y 1 (1982).

57. J.B. Ruhl & Harold J. Ruhl, Jr., *The Arrow of the Law in Modern Administrative States: Using Complexity Theory to Reveal the Diminishing Returns and Increasing Risks the Burgeoning of Law Poses to Society*, 30 U.C. DAVIS L. REV. 405, n.159 (1997).

58. David A. Dana & Hannah J. Wiseman, *A Market Approach to Regulating the Energy Revolution: Assurance Bonds, Insurance, and the Certain and Uncertain Risks of Hydraulic Fracturing*, 99 IOWA L. REV. 1523, 1527 (2014).

59. Shi-Ling Hsu, *A Game-Theoretic Model of International Climate Change Negotiations*, 19 N.Y.U. ENVTL. L.J. 14, 24 (2011).

60. *See* Michael Fakhri, *Images of the Arab World and the Middle East—Debates About Development and Regional Integration*, 28 WIS. INT'L L.J. 391, 394 (2010).

61. COOTER, *supra* note 53, at 105–07.

62. *See generally* JOHN WESLEY POWELL, THE EXPLORATION OF THE COLORADO RIVER AND ITS CANYONS (1961) (1895); JOHN WESLEY POWELL, REPORT ON THE LANDS OF THE ARID REGION OF THE UNITED STATES, WITH A MORE DETAILED ACCOUNT OF THE LANDS OF UTAH (1983) (1879); SEEING THINGS WHOLE: THE ESSENTIAL JOHN WESLEY POWELL (William deBuys ed., 2001); DONALD WORSTER, A RIVER RUNNING WEST: THE LIFE OF JOHN WESLEY POWELL (2001).

63. Powell's arguments have been reiterated in recent legal scholarship. *See, e.g.*, Craig Anthony Arnold, *Adaptive Watershed Planning and Climate Change*, 5 ENVTL. &

ENERGY L. & POL'Y 417, 420 (2010) ("[W]ater resources should be managed at ecosystem scales, or at watershed scales, as watersheds are the ecological systems of water."); A. Dan Tarlock, *The Potential Role of Local Governments in Watershed Management*, 20 PACE ENVTL. L. REV. 149, 153 (2002) (describing the watershed as "the 'right' organizing unit for integrated land and water resource management").

64. ROBERT ELLICKSON, ORDER WITHOUT LAW: HOW NEIGHBORS SETTLE DISPUTES (1991).

65. Margaret A. Palmer et al., *Climate Change and the World's River Basins: Anticipating Management Options*, 6 FRONTIERS ECOLOGY & ENV'T 81 (2008).

Chapter 2—Water Security and Public Health

1. Much of this chapter is based on my article, Rhett B. Larson, *Law in the Time of Cholera*, 92 NOTRE DAME L. REV. 1271 (2017).

2. No, not that Jon Snow. GEORGE R.R. MARTIN, A GAME OF THRONES (1996). *This* John Snow. PETER VINTEN-JOHANSEN ET AL., CHOLERA, CHLOROFORM, AND THE SCIENCE OF MEDICINE: A LIFE OF JOHN SNOW (2003). *See generally* Rita R. Colwell, *Global Climate and Infectious Disease: The Cholera Paradigm*, 274 SCI. 2025, 2026 (1996) (discussing the impact of John Snow's work on subsequent scientific endeavors, including modeling of global climate change).

3. JOHN SNOW, ON THE MODE OF COMMUNICATION OF CHOLERA 3–5 (London, John Churchill 2d ed. 1855).

4. *Id.; see also* Mervyn Susser & Ezra Susser, *Choosing a Future for Epidemiology: I. Eras and Paradigms*, 86 AM. J. PUB. HEALTH 668, 669 (1996).

5. SNOW, *supra* note 3, at 118; *see also* Nigel Paneth, *Assessing the Contributions of John Snow to Epidemiology: 150 Years After Removal of the Broad Street Pump Handle*, 15 EPIDEMIOLOGY 514, 515–16 (2004).

6. SNOW, *supra* note 3, at 76; *see also* SANDRA HEMPEL, THE STRANGE CASE OF THE BROAD STREET PUMP: JOHN SNOW AND THE MYSTERY OF CHOLERA 163 (2007).

7. SNOW, *supra* note 3, at 64.

8. *Id.; see also* Lewis C. Vollmar, Jr., *The Effect of Epidemics on the Development of English Law from the Black Death Through the Industrial Revolution*, 15 J. LEGAL MED. 385, 416–17 (1994).

9. SNOW, *supra* note 3, at 64.

10. *Id.* at 75–77; *see also* HEMPEL, *supra* note 6, at 174.

11. *See* HEMPEL, *supra* note 6, at 174.

12. *Id.* at 182.

13. *Id.* at 178–85.

14. *Id.* A handleless water pump remains on Broadwick Street in Soho as a memorial to John Snow. Kari S. McLeod, *Our Sense of Snow: The Myth of John Snow in Medical Geography*, 50 SOC. SCI. & MED. 923, 932 (2000).

15. Charles D. Larson, *Historical Development of the National Primary Drinking Water Regulations*, *in* SAFE DRINKING WATER ACT: AMENDMENTS, REGULATIONS AND STANDARDS 3, 4–5 (Edward J. Calabrese et al. eds., 1990).

16. VINTEN-JOHANSEN ET AL., *supra* note 2, at 7.

17. *Id.*

18. *See, e.g.*, Kim Shayo Buchanan, *When Is HIV a Crime? Sexuality, Gender and Consent*, 99 MINN. L. REV. 1231 (2015) (discussing the role of epidemiology in evaluating the potential for criminal prosecution of persons intentionally spreading HIV).

19. Enrico Bertuzzo et al., *On the Probability of Extinction of the Haiti Cholera Epidemic*, 30 STOCHASTIC ENVTL. RES. & RISK ASSESSMENT 2043, 2043 (2016).

20. Guy R. Knudsen, *Cholera in Haiti: A Perfect Storm of Scientific and Legal Uncertainty*, 29 NAT. RES. & ENV'T 14, 15–16 (2014).

21. *Id.*

22. Patricia Hurtado, *UN Claims Immunity from Haiti Post-Quake Cholera Lawsuit*, BLOOMBERG, Oct. 23, 2014, http://www.bloomberg.com/news/articles/2014-10-23/un-claimsimmunity-from-haiti-cholera-lawsuit.

23. *Id.*

24. R.R. Frerichs et al., *Nepalese Origin of Cholera Epidemic in Haiti*, 18 CLINICAL MICROBIOLOGY & INFECTION E158 (2012).

25. *See generally* Brian Concannon, Jr. & Beatrice Lindstrom, *Cheaper, Better, Longer-Lasting: A Rights-Based Approach to Disaster Response in Haiti*, 25 EMORY INT'L L. REV. 1145 (2011).

26. Lawrence O. Gostin et al., *The Law and the Public's. Health: A Study of Infectious Disease Law in the United States*, 99 COLUM. L. REV. 59, 64, 70 (1999).

27. Malgosia Fitzmaurice, *The Human Right to Water*, 18 FORDHAM ENVTL. L. REV. 537, 538 (2007).

28. Reed Johnson et al., *Spreading Virus Adds to Brazil's Woes*, WALL ST. J. , Dec. 22, 2015, http://www.wsj.com/articles/spreadingvirus-adds-to-brazils-woes-1450830661; *see also* Shasta Darlington, *Brazil Warns Against Pregnancy Due to Spreading Virus*, CNN, Dec. 24, 2015, http://www.cnn.com/2015/12/23/health/brazil-zika-pregnancy-warning/.

29. Kate Lyons, Yemen's cholera outbreak now the worst in history as millionth case looms, GUARDIAN, Oct. 12, 2017, https://www.theguardian.com/global-development/2017/oct/12/yemen-cholera-outbreak-worst-in-history-1-million-cases-by-end-of-year.

30. Matt Ford, *A Legionnaires' Disease Outbreak in Flint*, ATLANTIC, Jan. 13, 2016, http://www.theatlantic.com/politics/archive/2016/01/flint-michigan-water-crisis/424062/.

31. *See generally* Lisa Heinzerling, *Climate Change, Human Health, and the Post-Cautionary Principle*, 96 GEO. L.J. 445 (2008).

32. *See, e.g.*, Janet C. Neuman, *Drought Proofing Water Law*, 7 U. DENV. WATER L. REV. 92 (2003).

33. Rhett B. Larson, *Interstitial Federalism*, 62 UCLA L. REV. 908 (2015) [hereinafter Larson, *Interstitial Federalism*]; Rhett B. Larson, *The New Right in Water*, 70 WASH. & LEE L. REV. 2181 (2013) [hereinafter Larson, *The New Right in Water*].

34. *See, e.g.*, Anthony DeLaPaz, Note, *Leed Locally: How Local Governments Can Effectively Mandate Green Building Standards*, 2013 U. ILL. L. REV. 1211, 1212–13.

35. Rhett B. Larson, *Orphaned Pollution*, 45 ARIZ. ST. L.J. 991 (2013).

36. *See, e.g.*, Nat'l Cotton Council of Am. v. EPA, 553 F.3d 927 (6th Cir. 2009) (holding that pesticide applications require a Clean Water Act permit, which has implications for dispersal of pesticides to address insect-carried diseases); Larson, *The New Right in Water, supra* note 33, at 2234.

37. *See, e.g.*, John H. Minan & Tracy M. Frech, *Pesticides as "Pollutants" Under the Clean Water Act*, 47 San Diego L. Rev. 109, 135–37 (2010).

38. Erin K. MacDonald, Comment, *Playing by the Rules: The World Bank's Failure to Adhere to Policy in the Funding of Large-Scale Hydropower Projects*, 31 Envtl. L. 1011, 1018 (2001).

39. Timothy M. Straub & Darrell P. Chandler, *Towards a Unified System for Detecting Waterborne Pathogens*, 53 J. Microbiological Methods 185 (2003), and David J. Bradley, *Water Supplies: The Consequences of Change, in* Human Rights in Health 81 (G.E.W. Wolstenholme & Katherine Elliott eds., 1974).

40. *See* Kaci Hickox, *Caught Between Civil Liberties and Public Safety Fears: Personal Reflections from a Healthcare Provider Treating Ebola*, 11 J. Health & Biomedical L. 9, 17 (2015).

41. *See* Richard O. Zerbe, Jr., *An Integration of Equity and Efficiency*, 73 Wash. L. Rev. 349 (1998).

42. Elizabeth Cooper, *Social Risk and the Transformation of Public Health Law: Lessons from the Plague Years*, 86 Iowa L. Rev. 869 (2001).

43. Mary Jane Angelo & Jon Morris, *Maintaining a Healthy Water Supply While Growing a Healthy Food Supply: Legal Tools for Cleaning Up Agricultural Water Pollution*, 62 U. Kan. L. Rev. 1003, 1033 (2014).

44. *See, e.g.*, Amy Hardberger, *Life, Liberty, and the Pursuit of Water: Evaluating Water as a Human Right and the Duties and Obligations It Creates*, 4 Nw. U. J. Int'l Hum. Rts. 331 (2005) (discussing the role of the human right to access water in improving human health); Sharmila L. Murthy, *The Human Right(s) to Water and Sanitation: History, Meaning, and the Controversy Over-Privatization*, 31 Berkeley J. Int'l L. 89, 99–100 (2013) (discussing the impacts for human health associated with an effective human right to sanitation).

45. *See, e.g.*, Robin Kundis Craig, *Removing the "Cloak of a Standing Inquiry": Pollution Regulation, Public Health, and Private Risk in the Injury-in-Fact Analysis*, 29 Cardozo L. Rev. 164 (2007); *see also* Steven Johnson, The Ghost Map: The Story of London's Most Terrifying Epidemic—And How It Changed Science, Cities, and the Modern World 30–44, 103–05 (2006).

46. Gilbert F. White et al., Drawers of Water: Domestic Water Use in East Africa (1972); *see also* J. Bartram & R. Carr, *An Introduction to Emerging Waterborne Zoonoses and General Control Principles, in* Waterborne Zoonoses: Identification, Causes, and Control 17, 18 (J.A. Cotruvo et al. eds., 2004) [hereinafter Waterborne Zoonoses].

47. *Id.; see also* D.D. Mara & R.G.A. Feachem, *Water—And Excreta-Related Diseases: Unitary Environmental Classification*, 125 J. Envtl. Engineering 334 (1999).

48. White et al., *supra* note 46.

49. *Id.; see also* C.L. Moe, *What Are the Criteria for Determining Whether a Disease Is Zoonotic and Water Related?, in* WATERBORNE ZOONOSES, *supra* note 46, at 27.

50. Moe, *supra* note 49, at 31–32.

51. *Id.*

52. Christine L. Moe, *Waterborne Transmission of Infectious Agents, in* MANUAL OF ENVIRONMENTAL MICROBIOLOGY 222, 222–48 (Christon J. Hurst et al. eds., 3d ed. 2007).

53. *Id.*

54. *See, e.g.,* Thomas Clasen et al., *Microbiological Effectiveness and Cost of Disinfecting Water by Boiling in Semi-Urban India,* 79 AM. J. TROPICAL MED. HYGIENE 407 (2008); J.V. Pinfold, *Faecal Contamination of Water and Fingertip-Rinses as a Method for Evaluating the Effect of Low-Cost Water Supply and Sanitation Activities on Faeco-Oral Disease Transmission II: A Hygiene Intervention Study in Rural North-East Thailand,* 105 EPIDEMIOLOGY & INFECTION 377 (1990); Mark A. Shannon et al., *Science and Technology for Water Purification in the Coming Decades,* 452 NATURE 301 (2008).

55. *See generally* Jose Martines et al., *Diarrheal Diseases, in* DISEASE CONTROL PRIORITIES IN DEVELOPING COUNTRIES 91, 91–99 (Dean T. Jamison et al. eds., 1993); *see also* Itzchak Kornfeld, *A Global Water Apartheid: From Revelation to Resolution,* 43 VAND. J. TRANSNATIONAL L. 701, 708–09 (2010).

56. Kornfeld, *supra* note 55, at 708. The 1.6 million children who die annually from waterborne diseases is five times the number of deaths annually from HIV/AIDS. *Id.*

57. William L. Andreen, *Environmental Law and International Assistance: The Challenge of Strengthening Environmental Law in the Developing World,* 25 COLUM. J. ENVTL. L. 17, 18–19 (2000).

58. Ida Ngueng Feze et al., *The Regulation of Novel Water Quality Assessment Biotechnologies: Is Canada Ready to Ride the Next Wave?,* 26 J. ENVTL. L. & PRAC. 201, 206–07 (2014).

59. *Id.; see also* Jeffrey P. Davis, *The Massive Waterborne Outbreak of Cryptosporidium Infections, Milwaukee, Wisconsin, 1993, in* OUTBREAK INVESTIGATIONS AROUND THE WORLD: CASE STUDIES IN INFECTIOUS DISEASE FIELD EPIDEMIOLOGY 197, 219, 223 (Mark S. Dworkin ed., 2010).

60. *See supra* note 49 at 27–36; *see also* Panagiotis Karanis et al., *Waterborne Transmission of Protozoan Parasites: A Worldwide Review of Outbreaks and Lessons Learnt,* 5 J. WATER & HEALTH 1, 2 (2007).

61. STEVE E. HRUDEY & ELIZABETH J. HRUDEY, ENSURING SAFE DRINKING WATER: LEARNING FROM FRONTLINE EXPERIENCE WITH CONTAMINATION 11–21 (2014).

62. Mara & Feachem, *supra* note 47, at 334; *see also* Moe, *supra* note 49, at 31–32.

63. Moe, *supra* note 52, at 226.

64. Minnie M. Mathan & V.I. Mathan, *Ultrastructural Pathology of the Rectal Mucosa in* Shigella *Dysentery,* 123 AM. J. PATHOLOGY 25 (1986). Dysentery is the inflammation of the intestine resulting in diarrhea with blood and is a symptom of both bacterial infections (like shigella) and amoebic infections (like that of Entamoeba histolytica). *Id.* at 37.

65. Thomas M. Lietman et al., *Clinically Active Trachoma Versus Actual Chlamydial Infection*, 172 MED. J. AUSTL. 93 (2000).

66. Larry G. Arlian et al., *Resistance and Immune Response in Scabies-Infested Hosts Immunized with* Dermatophagoides *Mites*, 52 AM. J. TROPICAL MED. & HYGIENE 539 (1995).

67. WHITE ET AL., *supra* note 46; *see* JOHN THOMPSON ET AL., INT'L INST. FOR ECON. DEV., DRAWERS OF WATER II: 30 YEARS OF CHANGE IN DOMESTIC WATER USE & ENVIRONMENTAL HEALTH IN EAST AFRICA (2002), http://pubs.iied.org/pdfs/9049IIED.pdf.

68. *Id.* at 38.

69. *Id.* at 75; *see also* Peter H. Gleick, *Basic Water Requirements for Human Activities: Meeting Basic Needs*, 21 WATER INT'L 83 (1996).

70. *See generally* James G. Hodge, Jr. et al., *Global Emergency Legal Responses to the 2014 Ebola Outbreak*, 42 J.L. MED. & ETHICS 595, 597 (2014).

71. Hickox, *supra* note 40, at 17.

72. Ed Pilkington, *Haitians Launch New Lawsuit Against UN over Thousands of Cholera Deaths*, GUARDIAN, Mar. 11, 2014, https://www.theguardian.com/world/2014/mar/11/ haiti-cholera-un-deaths-lawsuit.

73. David A. Walton & Louise C. Ivers, *Responding to Cholera in Post-Earthquake Haiti*, 364 NEW ENGLAND J. MED. 3, 4 (2011).

74. Concannon & Lindstrom, *supra* note 25, at 1167–68.

75. Kashmira A. Date et al., *Considerations for Oral Cholera Vaccine Use During Outbreak After Earthquake in Haiti, 2010–2011*, 17 EMERGING INFECTIOUS DISEASES 2105 (2011).

76. WHITE ET AL., *supra* note 46; *see also* Mara & Feachem, *supra* note 47, at 334–35.

77. *See* WHITE ET AL., *supra* note 46.

78. *See* WHITE ET AL., *supra* note 46.

79. *See* WHITE ET AL., *supra* note 46.

80. Chris Greenaway, *Dracunculiasis (Guinea Worm Disease)*, 170 CAN. MED. ASS'N J. 495 (2004).

81. Edward J. Pearce & Andrew S. MacDonald, *The Immunobiology of Schistosomiasis*, 2 NATURE REVS. IMMUNOLOGY 499 (2002).

82. Allen W. Cheever, *Schistosomiasis: Infection Versus Disease and Hypersensitivity versus Immunity*, 142 AM. J. PATHOLOGY 699 (1993).

83. *Id.*

84. *Id.; see also* Bruno Gryseels et al., *Human Schistosomiasis*, 368 LANCET 1106, 1113 (2006).

85. John O. Gyapong et al., *Integration of Control of Neglected Tropical Diseases into HealthCare Systems: Challenges and Opportunities*, 375 LANCET 160 (2010).

86. WHITE ET AL., *supra* note 46; *see also* Mara & Feachem, *supra* note 47, at 334.

87. WHITE ET AL., *supra* note 46.

88. WHITE ET AL., *supra* note 46; *see also* Stuart Batterman et al., *Sustainable Control of Water-Related Infectious Diseases: A Review and Proposal for Interdisciplinary Health-Based Systems Research*, 117 ENVTL. HEALTH PERSP. 1023 (2009).

89. WHITE ET AL., *supra* note 46.

90. WHITE ET AL., *supra* note 46; *see also* Gerry F. Killeen et al., *Habitat Targeting for Controlling Aquatic Stages of Malaria Vectors in Africa*, 74 AM. J. TROPICAL MED. HYGIENE 517 (2006).

91. William R. Brieger, *Pile Sorts as a Means of Improving the Quality of Survey Data: Malaria Illness Symptoms*, 9 HEALTH EDUC. RES. 257 (1994).

92. Dirk M. Elston, *Life-Threatening Stings, Bites, Infestations, and Parasitic Diseases*, 23 CLINICS IN DERMATOLOGY 164, 167–68 (2005).

93. *See, e.g.*, Davidson H. Hamer et al., *Improved Diagnostic Testing and Malaria Treatment Practices in Zambia*, 297 J. AM. MED. ASSOC. 2227 (2007); Zvi Shimoni et al., *Treatment of West Nile Virus Encephalitis with Intravenous Immunoglobulin*, 7 EMERGING INFECTIOUS DISEASES 759 (2001).

94. Duane J. Gubler, *Resurgent Vector-Borne Diseases as a Global Health Problem*, 4 EMERGING INFECTIOUS DISEASES 442 (1998); Atul A. Khasnis & Mary D. Nettleman, *Global Warming and Infectious Disease*, 36 ARCHIVES MED. RES. 689 (2005).

95. WORLD HEALTH ORG., WORLD MALARIA REPORT 2014, at 32.

96. Edward B. Hayes & Duane J. Gubler, *West Nile Virus: Epidemiology and Clinical Features of an Emerging Epidemic in the United States*, 57 ANN. REV. MED. 181 (2006); Sean B. Hecht, *Climate Change and the Transformation of Risk: Insurance Matters*, 55 UCLA L. REV. 1559, 1575–76 (2008).

97. David P. Fidler, *Return of the Fourth Horseman: Emerging Infectious Diseases and International Law*, 81 MINN. L. REV. 771, 802–03 (1997); Douglas E. Norris, *Mosquito-Borne Diseases as a Consequence of Land Use Change*, 1 ECOHEALTH 19 (2004).

98. William E. Cox, *Evolution of the Safe Drinking Water Act: A Search for Effective Quality Assurance Strategies and Workable Concepts of Federalism*, 21 WM. & MARY ENVTL. L. & POL'Y REV. 69, 111–12 (1997); Judith Kimerling, *International Standards in Ecuador's Amazon Oil Fields: The Privatization of Environmental Law*, 26 COLUM. J. ENVTL. L. 289, 371 n.229 (2001).

99. *See, e.g.*, Paul W. Morenberg, Comment, *Environmental Fraud by Government Contractors: A New Application of the False Claims Act*, 22 B.C. ENVTL. AFF. L. REV. 623, 666 n.381 (1995); *see also* Lee R. Okster, *Smithfield Foods: A Case for Federal Action*, 23 WM. & MARY ENVTL. L. & POL'Y REV. 381 (1999).

100. Knudsen, *supra* note 20, at 15–16.

101. *Id.; see also* Rosa Freedman, *UN Immunity or Impunity? A Human Rights Based Challenge*, 25 EUR. J. INT'L L. 239, 240 (2014).

102. Freedman, *supra* note 101, at 39–41; *see also* Allen R. Prunty & Mark E. Solomons, *The Federal Black Lung Program: Its Evolution and Current Issues*, 91 W.VA. L. REV. 665, 683–84 (1989).

103. Johnson et al., *supra* note 28; *see also* Darlington, *supra* note 28.

104. Edward B. Hayes, *Zika Virus Outside Africa*, 15 EMERGING INFECTIOUS DISEASE 1347, 1347 (2009).

105. Darlington, *supra* note 28.

106. *Id.*; Johnson et al., *supra* note 28.

107. Darlington, *supra* note 28; Johnson et al., *supra* note 28.

108. Darlington, *supra* note 28; Johnson et al., *supra* note 28; *see also* Madeline A. Lancaster et al., *Cerebral Organoids Model Human Brain Development and Microcephaly*, 501 NATURE 373, 373 (2013).

109. Johnson et al., *supra* note 28.

110. *Id.*

111. *Id.*

112. CDC, *Chikungunya Virus: Geographic Distribution* (May 12, 2016), https://www.cdc.gov/chikungunya/geo/.

113. CDC, *Chikungunya Virus: 2016 Provisional Data for the United States* (Nov. 22, 2016), https://www.cdc.gov/chikungunya/geo/united-states-2016.html.

114. Hannah Rappleye et al., *Bad Decisions, Broken Promises: A Timeline of the Flint Water Crisis*, NBC NEWS, Jan. 19, 2016, http://www.nbcnews.com/news/us-news/bad-decisionsbroken-promises-timeline-flint-water-crisis-n499641.

115. Suzannah Gonzales, *Legionnaires' Spike in Michigan County Dealing with Water Crisis*, REUTERS, Jan. 13, 2016, http://www.reuters.com/article/us-michigan-water-idUSKCN0 UR23120160113.

116. Stephen Rodrick, *Who Poisoned Flint, Michigan?*, ROLLING STONE, Jan. 22, 2016, http://www.rollingstone.com/politics/news/who-poisoned-flint-michigan-20160122.

117. 42 U.S.C. § 300f(1)(A) (2012); H.R. REP. No. 93-1185 1 (1974); 1 WORLD HEALTH ORG., GUIDELINES FOR DRINKING-WATER QUALITY 1 (3rd ed. 2004).

118. *See id.*; Keith S. Porter, *Fixing Our Drinking Water: From Field and Forest to Faucet*, 23 PACE ENVTL. L. REV. 389, 403 (2006).

119. *See* Larson, *The New Right in Water, supra* note 33, at 2234.

120. Guanghui Hua & David A. Reckhow, *Comparison of Disinfection Byproduct Formation from Chlorine and Alternative Disinfectants*, 41 WATER RES. 1667, 1667 (2007).

121. *Id.*

122. Nicholas John Ashbolt, *Risk Analysis of Drinking Water Microbial Contamination Versus Disinfection By-Products (DBPs)*, 198 TOXICOLOGY 255 (2004); *see also* Larson, *The New Right in Water, supra* note 33, at 2234.

123. Larson, *The New Right in Water, supra* note 33, at 2234.

124. *Id.*

125. *Id.* The World Health Organization has cautioned against universal, one-size-fits-all quality standards, noting that "[i]t must be emphasized that the guideline values recommended [by the WHO] are not mandatory limits. In order to define such limits, it is necessary to consider the guideline values in the context of local or national environmental, social, economic, and cultural conditions." Ashok Gadgil, *Drinking Water in Developing Countries*, 23 ANN. REV. ENERGY & ENV'T 253, 255 (1998) (internal quotation marks omitted) (quoting 2 WORLD HEALTH ORG., GUIDELINES FOR DRINKING-WATER Quality § 1.1 (2d ed. 1996)). To the extent a positive human right to water is framed as a requirement for water of "equal" quality across the globe, such a requirement could pose risks to public health.

126. *See, e.g.*, Gabriel Eckstein, *Drugs on Tap: Managing Pharmaceuticals in Our Nation's Waters*, 23 N.Y.U. ENVTL. L.J. 37 (2015); Noah Sachs, *Blocked Pathways: Potential*

Legal Responses to Endocrine Disrupting Chemicals, 24 COLUM. J. ENVTL. L. 289, 309 (1999).

127. Adam Babich, *Too Much Science in Environmental Law,* 28 COLUM. J. ENVTL. L. 119, 167 (2003); Michael Carney, *European Drinking Water Standards,* 83 J. AM. WATER WORKS ASS'N 48 (1991); David L. Markell, *The Role of Local Governments in Environmental Regulation: Shoring Up Our Federal System,* 44 SYRACUSE L. REV. 885, 891 n.14 (1993) (citing ENVTL. PROT. AGENCY, EPA 230-R-93-007, LOCAL GOVERNMENT IMPLEMENTATION OF ENVIRONMENTAL MANDATES: FIVE CASE STUDIES, Final Report 11–14 (1993)).

128. Cox, *supra* note 98, at 154; *see also* Rena I. Steinzor, *Unfunded Environmental Mandates and the "New (New) Federalism": Devolution, Revolution, or Reform?,* 81 MINN. L. REV. 97, 208–09 (1996).

129. Cox, *supra* note 98, at 153; *see also* Paul Westerhoff et al., *Fate of Endocrine-Disruptor, Pharmaceutical, and Personal Care Product Chemicals During Simulated Drinking Water Treatment Processes,* 39 ENVTL. SCI. & TECH. 6649 (2005).

130. Long Term 2 Enhanced Surface Water Treatment Rule, 68 Fed. Reg. 47,640, 47,665 (proposed Aug. 11, 2003) (to be codified at 40 C.F.R. pt. 141, 142); AM. WATER WORKS ASS'N, DISTRIBUTION SYSTEM REGULATION 17 (2013), http://www.awwa. org/Portals/0/files/ publications/documents/samples/20428-4e_excerpt.pdf (noting that the new rule permits small systems to perform initial E. coli monitoring to determine if cryptosporidium monitoring is necessary).

131. J. Alan Roberson, *From Common Cup to Cryptosporidium: A Regulatory Evolution,* 98 AM. WATER WORKS ASS'N 198, 204 (2006).

132. Michael F. Craun et al., *Waterborne Outbreaks Reported in the United States,* 4 J. WATER & HEALTH 19 (2006).

133. *See* Eckstein, *supra* note 126; *see also* Sachs, *supra* note 126.

134. 42 U.S.C. § 300i-2(a)(1) (2012). *See generally* Steven D. Shermer, *The Drinking Water Security and Safety Amendments of 2002: Is America's Drinking Water Infrastructure Safer Four Years Later?,* 24 UCLA J. ENVTL. L. & POL'Y 355 (2006).

135. 42 U.S.C. § 300f(15).

136. 42 U.S.C. § 300i-2(a)(1).

137. Larson, *The New Right in Water, supra* note 33, at 2221–22.

138. WHITE ET AL., *supra* note 46; *see also* Mara & Feachem, *supra* note 47, at 334.

139. David Bradley, *Institutional Capacity to Monitor the Interactions of Agricultural and Health Change, in* AGRICULTURE, ENVIRONMENT, AND HEALTH: SUSTAINABLE DEVELOPMENT IN THE 21ST CENTURY 308, 327 (Vernon W. Ruttan ed., 1994).

140. *See, e.g.,* Michael C. Blumm, *Public Choice Theory and the Public Lands: Why "Multiple Use" Failed,* 18 HARV. ENVTL. L. REV. 405, 410 n.37 (1994); Margaret J. Vick, *The Senegal River Basin: A Retrospective and Prospective Look at the Legal Regime,* 46 NAT. RESOURCES J. 211, 223 (2006).

141. David Grey & Claudia W. Sadoff, *Sink or Swim? Water Security for Growth and Development,* 9 WATER POL'Y 545 (2007).

142. *See, e.g.,* Richard Briffault, *The Most Popular Tool: Tax Increment Financing and the Political Economy of Local Government,* 77 U. CHI. L. REV. 65, 68 (2010); Craig, *supra*

note 45, at 910–11; Thomas M. Kerr, *Supplying Water Infrastructure to Developing Countries Via Private Sector Project Financing*, 8 Geo. Int'l Envtl. L. Rev. 91, 92–95 (1995).

143. *See generally* Jonathan A. Patz et al., *Unhealthy Landscapes: Policy Recommendations on Land Use Change and Infectious Disease Emergence*, 112 Envtl. Health Persp. 1092, 1092 (2004) (prescribing certain reforms in land use planning to prevent infectious disease outbreaks associated with agricultural development, deforestation, and population increases and shifts); *see also* Itzchak E. Kornfeld, *Adiós to Paradise: The Yacyretá Dam and the Destruction of Environmental and Human Rights*, 7 Fla. A&M U. L. Rev. 181, 206–07 (2012).

144. William Jobin, Dams and Disease: Ecological Design and Health Impacts of Large Dams, Canals and Irrigation Systems 21 (1999); *see also* Patricia L. Farnese, *Searching for Wildlife: A Critique of Canada's Regulatory Response to Emerging Zoonotic Diseases*, 39 Queen's L.J. 471, 477–78 (2014).

145. Farnese, *supra* note 144, at 477–78.

146. Vick, *supra* note 140, at 215–18.

147. *Id.* at 216; *see also* S. Sow et al., *Water-Related Disease Patterns Before and After the Construction of the Diama Dam in Northern Senegal*, 96 Annals of Tropical Med. & Parasitology 575 (2002).

148. African Dev. Bank Grp., Senegal/Mali/Mauritania Diama Dam Project: Project Performance Evaluation Report (PPER) 1–8 (1988), http://www.afdb.org/fileadmin/uploads/afdb/Documents/Evaluation-Reports-_Shared-With-OPEV_/06004235-EN-MULTINATIONALDIAMA-DAM-PROJECT.pdf; David G. LeMarquand, International Development of the Senegal River, 15 Water Int'l 223, 225 (1990).

149. Andre DeGeorges & B.K. Reilly, Dams and Large Scale Irrigation on the Senegal River: Impacts on Man and the Environment 4 (2006), http://hdr.undp.org/sites/default/files/degeorges_andre.pdf.

150. *Id.* at 10

151. *See* Jennifer Keiser et al., *Effect of Irrigation and Large Dams on the Burden of Malaria on a Global and Regional Scale*, 72 Am. J. Tropical Med. & Hygiene 392, 394 (2005).

152. *Id.* at 401; DeGeorges & Reilly., *supra* note 149, at 18; V.R. Southgate, *Schistosomiasis in the Senegal River Basin: Before and After the Construction of the Dams at Diuma, Senegal and Manantali, Mali and Future Prospects*, 71 J. Helminthology 125, 128 (1997). *But see* Sow et al., *supra* note 147, at 579–83.

153. *See* Keiser et al., *supra* note 151, at 398.

154. *See* M. Picquet et al., *The Epidemiology of Human Schistosomiasis in the Senegal River Basin*, 90 Transactions Royal Soc'y Tropical Med. & Hygiene 340, 340–41 (1996).

155. William Reisen et al., *West Nile Virus in California*, 10 Emerging Infectious Diseases 1369, 1369 (2004).

156. Reed D. Benson, *Deflating the Deference Myth: National Interests vs. State Authority Under Federal Laws Affecting Water Use*, 2006 Utah L. Rev. 241, 251.

157. Paula K. Smith, *Coercion and Groundwater Management: Three Case Studies and a "Market" Approach*, 16 ENVTL. L. 797, 862–69 (1986).

158. Chris Avery et al., *Good Intentions, Unintended Consequences: The Central Arizona Groundwater Replenishment District*, 49 ARIZ. L. REV. 339, 347–48 (2007).

159. *See, e.g.*, Keith H. Hirokawa, *Property as Capture and Care*, 74 ALB. L. REV. 175, 230 (2010); Larson, *The New Right in Water, supra* note 33, at 2187.

160. Erik B. Bluemel, *The Implications of Formulating a Human Right to Water*, 31 ECOLOGY L.Q. 957, 983–85 (2004); Ramin Pejan, Note, *The Right to Water: The Road to Justiciability*, 36 GEO. WASH. INT'L L. REV. 1181, 1188 (2004).

161. *See* Michael Burger, *Bi-Polar and Polycentric Approaches to Human Rights and the Environment*, 28 COLUM. J. ENVTL. L. 371, 381 (2003); Hari M. Osofsky, *Learning from Environmental Justice: A New Model for International Environmental Rights*, 24 STAN. ENVTL. L.J. 71, 129–30 (2005).

162. *See* Sumudu Atapattu, *The Right to a Healthy Life or the Right to Die Polluted?: The Emergence of a Human Right to a Healthy Environment Under International Law*, 16 TUL. ENVTL. L.J. 65, 90–91 (2002); Linda A. Malone & Scott Pasternack, *Exercising Environmental Human Rights and Remedies in the United Nations System*, 27 WM. & MARY ENVTL. L. & POL'Y REV. 365 (2003).

163. *See, e.g.*, Troyen A. Brennan, *Environmental Torts*, 46 VAND. L. REV. 1, 6 n.16 (1993); Wendy E. Wagner, *Commons Ignorance: The Failure of Environmental Law to Produce Needed Information on Health and the Environment*, 53 DUKE L.J. 1619, 1742 n.439 (2004).

164. Avi Brisman, *Double Whammy: Collateral Consequences of Conviction and Imprisonment for Sustainable Communities and the Environment*, 28 WM. & MARY ENVTL. L. & POL'Y REV. 423

165. (2004) (quoting BETH E. LACHMAN, LINKING SUSTAINABLE COMMUNITY ACTIVITIES TO POLLUTION PREVENTION: A SOURCEBOOK 6–7 (1997)); James Gathii & Keith H. Hirokawa, *Curtailing Ecosystem Exportation: Ecosystem Services as a Basis to Reconsider Export-Driven Agriculture in Economies Highly Dependent on Agricultural Exports*, 30 VA. ENVTL. L.J. 1, 16–17 (2012).

166. Patricia Ross McCubbin, *The Risk in Technology-Based Standards*, 16 DUKE ENVTL. L. & POL'Y F. 1, 4–5 (2005); Lynn A. Stout, *Strict Scrutiny and Social Choice: An Economic Inquiry into Fundamental Rights and Suspect Classifications*, 80 GEO. L.J. 1787, 1797 (1992). 266 Nat'l Cotton Council v. EPA, 553 F.3d 927 (6th Cir. 2009).

167. *Id.* at 929.

168. *Id.* at 930–31; *see also* League of Wilderness Defs./Blue Mountains Biodiversity Project v. Forsgren, 309 F.3d 1181 (9th Cir. 2002); Headwaters, Inc. v. Talent Irrigation Dist., 243 F.3d 526 (9th Cir. 2001).

169. Kevin J. Beaton, *Clean Water Act Permitting Requirements for Pesticide Applications in Idaho*, 52 ADVOCATE 15, 16 (2009).

170. *See* Nat'l Cotton Council, 553 F.3d at 930.

171. *Id.* at 934–35; *see also* 40 C.F.R. § 122.3(h) (2009).

172. *Nat'l Cotton Council*, 553 F.3d at 940.

173. *See id.* at 937–38.

174. Final National Pollutant Discharge Elimination System (NPDES) Pesticide General Permit for Point Source Discharges from the Application of Pesticides, 76 FED. REG. 68,750 (Nov. 7, 2011).

175. *See generally* Steven G. Davison, *General Permits Under Section 404 of the Clean Water Act*, PACE ENVTL. L. REV. 35 (2009).

176. Richard E. Levy & Robert L. Glicksman, *Agency-Specific Precedents*, 89 TEX. L. REV. 499, 511 (2011).

177. Joshua A.T. Fairfield & Erik Luna, *Digital Innocence*, 99 CORNELL L. REV. 981, 1016 n.224 (2014); Levy & Glicksman, *supra* note 176, at 511.

178. *See* Francesca Bignami, *European Versus American Liberty: A Comparative Privacy Analysis of Antiterrorism Data Mining*, 48 B.C.L. REV. 609, 622–23 (2007); Fairfield & Luna, *supra* note 177, at 1016 n.224.

179. Levy & Glicksman, *supra* note 176, at 512.

180. *Id.* at 513.

181. *See, e.g.*, Francesca Bignami, *Transgovernmental Networks vs. Democracy: The Case of the European Information Privacy Network*, 26 MICH. J. INT'L L. 807, 812 (2005). Larson, *Interstitial Federalism, supra* note 33, at 911.

182. *See generally* James W. Moeller, *Legal Issues Associated with Safe Drinking Water in Washington, D.C.*, 31 WM. & MARY ENVTL. L. & POL'Y REV. 661 (2007).

183. 42 U.S.C. § 300g-2(a) (2012).

184. *See, e.g., id.* § 300g-4(e); 40 C.F.R. § 142.10 (2015).

185. Inessa Abayev, Note, *Hydraulic Fracturing Wastewater: Making the Case for Treating the Environmentally Condemned*, 24 FORDHAM ENVTL. L. REV. 275, 297 (2013).

186. Larson, *Interstitial Federalism, supra* note 33, at 911.

187. Larson, *The New Right in Water, supra* note 33, at 2243.

188. *See, e.g.*, Henry J. Friendly, Book Review, 49 HARV. L. REV. 163, 165 (1935) (reviewing I.L. SHARFMAN, THE INTERSTATE COMMERCE COMMISSION (1935)); *see also* Emily Rogers & Jasmine Grant, *Water Utilities*, 45 TEX. ENVTL. L.J. 419, 419–21 (2015).

189. *See* National Environmental Policy Act, 42 U.S.C. § 4321 (2012) (note there is no explicit requirement to address disease vectors under NEPA; United Nations Convention on Environmental Impact Assessment in a Transboundary Context, 30 I.L.M. 800 (Feb. 25, 1991) [hereinafter Espoo Convention]; (note there is no explicit requirement to address disease vectors in environmental impact assessments conducted under the Espoo Treaty); Alice M. Noble-Allgire, *Transfrontier Environmental Damage*, 84 AM. SOC'Y INT'L L. PROC. 12, 25 (1990) (reporting the remarks of Ken Murphy and Nicholas A. Robinson, noting that disease-vector issues may be considered in environmental impact assessments).

190. *See, e.g.*, EUROPEAN CTR. FOR HEALTH POLICY, HEALTH IMPACT ASSESSMENT: MAIN CONCEPTS AND SUGGESTED APPROACH, GOTHENBURG CONSENSUS PAPER (1999), http://www.apho.org.uk/resource/item.aspx?RID=44163; Andrew L. Dannenberg et al., *Growing the Field of Health Impact Assessment in the United States: An Agenda for Research and Practice*, 96 AM. J. PUB. HEALTH 262 (2006).

191. *See* Bradley C. Karkkainen, *Whither NEPA?*, 12 N.Y.U. ENVTL. L.J. 333, 339–43 (2004); Veronika Tomoszkova, *Implementation of the EU Directive on Environmental*

Impact Assessment in the Czech Republic: How Long Can the Wolf Be Tricked?, 6 WASH. & LEE J. ENERGY, CLIMATE & ENV'T 451, 495 (2015).

192. *See, e.g.*, Michael LeVine et al., *What About BOEM? The Need to Reform the Regulations Governing Offshore Oil and Gas Planning and Leasing*, 31 ALASKA L. REV. 231, 245 n.74 (2014).

193. Jody Freeman & Jim Rossi, *Agency Coordination in Shared Regulatory Space*, 125 HARV. L. REV. 1131, 1164 n.155 (2012); Mason Baker, Note, *What Does It Mean to Comply with NEPA?: An Investigation into Whether NEPA Should Have Procedural or Substantive Force*, 31 UTAH ENVTL. L. REV. 241, 246–47 (2011).

194. *See generally* Sudhir Anand & Kara Hanson, *Disability-Adjusted Life Years: A Critical Review*, 16 J. HEALTH ECON. 685 (1997).

195. I. Glenn Cohen, *Rationing Legal Services*, 5 J. LEGAL ANALYSIS 221, 287 (2013).

196. *See* Anand & Hanson, *supra* note 194, at 699.

197. *See, e.g.*, ARIZ. REV. STAT. ANN. § 45-153 (2016); Norman K. Johnson & Charles T. DuMars, *A Survey of the Evolution of Western Water Law in Response to Changing Economic and Public Interest Demands*, 29 NAT. RESOURCES J. 347, 357–58 (1989); Jesse Reiblich & Christine A. Klein, *Climate Change and Water Transfers*, 41 PEPP. L. REV. 439, 458 nn.139–40 (2014).

198. Johnson & DuMars, *supra* note 197, at 358.

199. *See, e.g.*, Fitzmaurice, *supra* note 27; Neil A.F. Popovic, *In Pursuit of Environmental Human Rights: Commentary on the Draft Declaration of Principles on Human Rights and the Environment*, 27 COLUM. HUM. RTS. L. REV. 487 (1996).

200. Larson, *The New Right in Water*, *supra* note 33, at 2209; *see also* Daniel Bodansky, *Introduction: Climate Change and Human Rights: Unpacking the Issues*, 38 GA. J. INT'L & COMP. L. 511, 514 (2010); Larson, *The New Right in Water*, *supra* note 33, at 2209–13.

201. *See, e.g.*, Larson, *The New Right in Water*, *supra* note 33, at 2205 n.127; *see also* Barton H. Thompson, Jr., *Water as a Public Commodity*, 95 MARQ. L. REV. 17, 33 (2011).

202. U.N. Econ. & Soc. Council, Comm. on Econ., Soc. & Cultural Rights, Substantive Issues Arising in the Implementation of the International Covenant on Economic, Social and Cultural Rights: General Comment No. 15, The Right to Water, U.N. Doc. E/C.12/2002/11 (Jan. 20, 2003).

203. *See* G.A. Res. 64/292, ¶¶ 5, 8, The Human Right to Water and Sanitation, U.N. Doc. A/RES/64/292 (July 28, 2010) [hereinafter 2010 U.N. Resolution] (acknowledging that access to drinking water is an integral component of expanding human rights); Lori Beail-Farkas, *The Human Right to Water and Sanitation: Context, Contours, and Enforcement Prospects*, 30 WIS. INT'L L.J. 761 (2013); Gonzalo Aguilar Cavallo, *The Human Right to Water and Sanitation: From Political Commitments to Customary Rule?*, 3 PACE INT'L L. REV. ONLINE COMPANION 136 (2012).

204. *See, e.g.*, Nicholas John Ashbolt, *Microbial Contamination of Drinking Water and Disease Outcomes in Developing Regions*, 198 TOXICOLOGY 229, 233–35 (2004).

205. G.A. Res. 55/2, ¶ 19, United Nations Millennium Declaration (Sept. 18, 2000).

206. UNITED NATIONS CHILDREN'S FUND & WORLD HEALTH ORG., PROGRESS ON DRINKING WATER AND SANITATION: 2012 UPDATE 18–25 (2012), http://www.

unicef.org/french/ media/files/JMPreport2012.pdf; David J. Bradley & Jamie K. Bartram, *Domestic Water and Sanitation as Water Security: Monitoring, Concepts and Strategy*, 371 PHIL. TRANSACTIONS OF THE ROYAL SOC'Y 1, 6 (2013). *See generally* Grey & Sadoff, *supra* note 141.

207. *See, e.g.*, Larson, *The New Right in Water*, *supra* note 33 (discussing the distinction between a provision right to water and a participation right to water).

208. *Id.* at 2243.

209. *See id.* at 2220–36.

210. *See id.* at 2237–40, 2260–66.

211. Skylar Marshall, *California Declares a Human Right to Water*, U. DENV. WATER L. REV. (June 10, 2013), http://duwaterlawreview.com/ca-human-right-to-water/.

212. CAL. WATER CODE § 106.3(a) (West 2016). *See generally* INT'L HUMAN RIGHTS LAW CLINIC, U.C. BERKELEY, THE HUMAN RIGHT TO WATER BILL IN CALIFORNIA: AN IMPLEMENTATION FRAMEWORK FOR STATE AGENCIES (2013), http://www.law. berkeley.edu/files/Water_Report_2013_Interactive_FINAL.pdf.

213. CAL. WATER CODE § 106.3(b).

214. *See* Larson, *The New Right in Water*, *supra* note 33, at 2193; *see also* ISAIAH BERLIN, *Two Concepts of Liberty*, *in* FOUR ESSAYS ON LIBERTY 118, 124 (1969) ("First things come first: there are situations, as a nineteenth-century Russian radical writer declared, in which boots are superior to the works of Shakespeare; individual freedom is not everyone's primary need.").

Chapter 3—Water Security and Human Rights

1. Much of what follows is this chapter is based on two of my articles. *See* Rhett B. Larson, *The New Right in Water*, 70 WASH. & LEE L. REV. 2181 (2013); Rhett B. Larson, *Adapting Human Rights*, 26 DUKE ENVTL. L. & POL'Y FORUM 1 (2016); *see also* Andrew Magaziner, *The Trickle Down Effect: The Phiri Water Rights Application and Evaluating, Understanding, and Enforcing the South African Constitutional Right to Water*, 33 N.C. INT'L L. & COM. REG. 509 (2008).

2. S. AFR. CONST. 1996 ch. 2, § 27.

3. Mazibuko v. City of Johannesburg, 2010 BCLR 239 (S. Afr. CC), http://www.saflii. org/za/cases/ZACC/2009/28.pdf [hereinafter *Mazibuko*].

4. *Id.*

5. *Id.* at 15–22.

6. *Id.*

7. *Id.* at 14.

8. *Id.* at 17.

9. *Id.* at 66–67.

10. United Nations General Assembly, The Human Right To Water and Sanitation, Sixty-fourth Session, Agenda Item 48, Res. A/64/L.63/Rev.1 (July 28, 2010), http://www. un.org/News/Press/docs/2010/ga10967.doc.htm [hereinafter 2010 U.N. Resolution].

11. *Id.*

12. Barton H. Thompson, *Water as a Public Commodity*, 95 MARQ. L. REV. 17, 33 (2011).

13. 2010 U.N. Resolution, *supra* note 10 (abstaining countries at the time of introduction included Australia, Botswana, Canada, Denmark, Ethiopia, Greece, Israel, Japan, Kenya, Sweden, Turkey, the United Kingdom, and the United States).

14. ISAIAH BERLIN, *Two Concepts of Liberty*, *in* FOUR ESSAYS ON LIBERTY, 118–72 (1969).

15. RONALD DWORKIN, TAKING RIGHTS SERIOUSLY 269 (1977)

16. United Nations, International Covenant on Civil and Political Rights, G.A. Res. 2200, 21 U.N. GAOR Supp. 52, U.N. Doc. A/6316 (1967) [hereinafter CP Covenant].

17. *See generally* Kenneth Roth, *Defending Economic, Social and Cultural Rights: Practical Issues Faced by an International Human Rights Organization*, 26 HUMAN RTS. Q. 63–73 (2004); *see also* Michael Blumm & Rachel Guthrie, *Internationalizing the Public Trust Doctrine: Natural Law and Constitutional and Statutory Approaches to Fulfilling the Saxion Vision*, 45 U.C. DAVIS L. REV. 741, 789–90 (2012).

18. United Nations (1967), International Covenant on Economic, Social and Cultural Rights, G.A. Res. 2200, 21 U.N. GAOR Supp. 49, U.N. Doc. A/6316 [hereinafter ESC Covenant].

19. *See, e.g.,* Frank B. Cross, *The Error of Positive Rights*, 48 UCLA L. REV. 857 (2001).

20. *See generally,* M. Fitzmaurice, *The Human Right to Water*, 18 FORDHAM ENVTL. L. REV. 537, 539 (2007); Anna Russell, *International Organizations and Human Rights: Realizing, Resisting or Repackaging the Right to Water*, 9 J. HUM. RTS. 1 (2010); Stephen McCaffrey, *A Human Right to Water: Domestic and International Implications*, 5 GEO. INT'L ENVTL. L. REV. 1, 7 (1992); Peter Gleick, *The Human Right to Water*, 1 WATER POL'Y 487–503 (1999).

21. United Nations Economic and Social Council, Subcommittee on the Promotion and Protection of Human Rights (2003). Substantive Issues Arising in the Implementation of the International Covenant on Economic, Social, and Cultural Rights: General Comment No. 15 (2002), U.N. Doc. E/C.12/2002/11 (Jan. 20, 2003) [hereinafter General Comment 15].

22. *See* United Nations, Report on the Right to Water and Sanitation, http://www.righttowater.info/progress-so-far/national-legislation-on-the-right-to-water/#MOZ; *see also* CONSTITUTION OF KENYA, art. 65; CONSTITUTION OF INDONESIA, art. 5; CONSTITUTION OF ECUADOR, art. 23.

23. CONSTITUTION OF INDIA, art. 21.

24. *A.P. Pollution Control Board II v. Prof. M.V. Naidu and Others*, Civil Appeal Nos. 368–73 (1999).

25. Erick Bluemel, *The Implications of Formulating a Human Right to Water*, 31 ECOLOGY L.Q. 957, 981 (2004).

26. LAURENCE H. TRIBE, AMERICAN CONSTITUTIONAL LAW (2d ed. 1988), at 1336.

27. *See, e.g.,* Camille Pannu, *Drinking Water and Exclusion: A Case Study from California's Central Valley*, 100 CAL. L. REV. 223, 268 (2012); JAMES WINPENNY, WORLD PANEL ON FINANCING WATER INFRASTRUCTURE, FINANCING WATER FOR ALL (2003), at 1 [hereinafter Camdessus Report, after Michel Camdessus, former managing director of the IMF, who chaired the panel].

28. *See generally* John Briscoe, *The Changing Face of Water Infrastructure Financing in Developing Countries*, 15 INT. J. WATER RESOURCE DEV. 301 (1999).

29. *See generally* E. Jimenez, *Human and Physical Infrastructure: Public Investment and Pricing Policies in Developing Countries*, 3 HANDBOOK OF DEVELOPMENT ECONOMICS 2773 (1995).

30. Robert Glennon, *Water Scarcity, Marketing, and Privatization*, 83 TEX. L. REV. 1873 (2005).

31. *See generally* JAMES WINPENNY, MANAGING WATER AS AN ECONOMIC RESOURCE (1994).

32. *See* Camdessus Report, *supra* note 27.

33. *See generally* OSCAR OLIVERA & TOM LEWIS, COCHABAMBA! WATER WAR IN BOLIVIA (2004).

34. Simon Marvin, *An Emerging Logic of Urban Water Management, Cochabamba, Bolivia*, 36 J. URBAN STUD. 341–57 (1999).

35. K. Komives, *Designing Pro-Poor Water and Sewer Concessions: Early Lessons from Bolivia* (World Bank, Working Paper No. 2243, 1990), http://papers.ssrn.com/sol3/papers.cfm?abstract_id=629179.

36. Thomas Perreault, *State Restructuring and the Scale of Politics of Rural Water Governance in Bolivia*, 37 ENV'T & PLAN. 263–84 (2005); *see also* Andrew Nickson & Claudia Vargas, *The Limitations of Water Regulation: The Failure of Cochabamba Concession in Bolivia*, 21 BULL. LATIN AM. RES. 99–120 (2002).

37. Olivera & Lewis, *supra* note 33.

38. Juan Forero, *Bolivia Regrets IMF Experiment*, N.Y. TIMES, Dec. 14, 2005, https://www.nytimes.com/2005/12/14/business/worldbusiness/bolivia-regrets-imf-experiment.html; *see also* MICHAEL ROUSE, INSTITUTIONAL GOVERNANCE AND REGULATION OF WATER SERVICES: THE ESSENTIAL ELEMENTS (2007).

39. Thompson, *supra* note 12, at 38.

40. Jennifer Davis, *Private-Sector Participation in Water and Sanitation*, 30 ANN. REV. ENVTL. & RESOURCES 145, 153–56 (2005).

41. David R. Boyd, *No Taps, No Toilets: First Nations and the Constitutional Right to Water in Canada*, 57 MCGILL L.J. 81, 122 (2011).

42. *See* ROUSE, *supra* note 38.

43. Simon Caney, *Climate Change, Human Rights and Moral Thresholds*, in HUMAN RIGHTS AND CLIMATE CHANGE (Stephen Humphreys ed., 2010), 69–90.

44. General Comment 15, *supra* note 21.

45. Jessica Budds, *Are the Debates on Water Privatization Missing the Point? Experiences from Africa, Asia and Latin America*, 15 ENV'T & URBANIZATION 87–114 (2003).

46. Bluemel, *supra* note 25, at 968; *see also* COCHABAMBA DECLARATION, Dec. 8, 2000, http://www.nadir.org/nadir/initiative/agp/free/imf/bolivia/cochabamba.htm#declaration [hereinafter Cochabamba Declaration].

47. *See generally* Joseph Sax, *The Public Trust Doctrine in Natural Resource Law: Effective Judicial Intervention*, 68 MICH. L. REV. 471 (1970); *see also* Ved Nanda & William Ris, *The Public Trust Doctrine: A Viable Approach to International Environmental Protection*, 5 ECOLOGY L.Q. 291 (1976).

48. Thompson, *supra* note 12, at 17.

49. Michael C. Blumm & Rachel D. Guthrie, *Internationalizing the Public Trust Doctrine: Natural Law and Constitutional and Statutory Approaches to Fulfilling the Saxion Vision*, 45 U.C. DAVIS L. REV. 741 (2012).

50. Cochabamba Declaration, *supra* note 46.

51. MAUDE BARLOW, BLUE COVENANT: THE GLOBAL WATER CRISIS AND THE COMING BATTLE FOR THE RIGHT TO WATER, 58–62, 91–101 (2007).

52. JAMES SALZMAN, DRINKING WATER: A HISTORY (2013).

53. Chibli Mallat, *The Quest for Water Use Principles in Water, in* WATER IN THE MIDDLE EAST: LEGAL, POLITICAL, AND COMMERCIAL IMPLICATIONS (C. Mallat & J.A. Allan eds., 1995), 127–37.

54. Ali Ahmad, *Islamic Water Law as a Comparative Model for Maintaining Water Quality*, 5 J. ISLAMIC L. & CULTURE 159 (2000).

55. Jackson Morill & Jose Simas, *Comparative Analysis of Water Laws in MNA Countries, in* WATER IN THE ARAB WORLD (N.V. Jagannathan et al. eds., 2009), 285–334.

56. Joseph Dellapenna, *The Evolution of Riparianism in the United States*, 53 MARQ. L. REV. 61 (2011).

57. JOSEPH SAX & ROBERT ABRAMS, LEGAL CONTROL OF WATER RESOURCES (1986).

58. Frank Trelease, *Coordination of Riparian and Appropriative Rights to the Use of Water*, 33 TEX. L. REV. 23 (1955).

59. *See, e.g.,* Conference Report, *Implementing the Human Right to Water in the West*, 48 WILLAMETTE L. REV. 1 (2011) [hereinafter Willamette Conference Report]; Craig Anthony Arnold, *Water Privatization Trends in the United States: Human Rights, National Security, and Public Stewardship*, 33 WM. & MARY ENVTL. L. & POL'Y REV. 785, 818 (2009).

60. *See* UNITED NATIONS, REPORT ON THE RIGHT TO WATER AND SANITATION, http://www.righttowater.info/progress-so-far/national-legislation-on-the-right-to-water/#MOZ.

61. CONSTITUTION OF KENYA, art. 65.

62. CONSTITUTION OF INDONESIA, art. 5.

63. CONSTITUTION OF ECUADOR, art. 23.

64. *See* CONSTITUTION OF UGANDA; *see also* CONSTITUTION OF ZAMBIA.

65. *See, e.g.,* Monique Passelec-Ross & Karen Buss, *Water Stewardship in the Lower Athabasca River: Is the Alberta Government Paying Attention to Aboriginal Rights to Water*, 23 J. ENVTL. L. & PRAC. 69, 70 (2011).

66. CONSTITUTION OF INDIA, art. 21; *see also* Chameli Singh v. State of Uttar Pradesh, A.I.R. 1996 S.C. 1051 (India).

67. *See, e.g.,* Farooque v. Bangladesh (Radioactive Milk Powder), (1996) WP 92/1996 S.C. P20 (Nepal); *see also* Shala Zia v. WAPDA, PLD 1994 S.C. 693 (1994) (Pakistan).

68. McCaffrey, *supra* note 20, at 7.

69. United Nations (1948), Declaration of Human Rights, G.A. Res. 217, U.N. Doc. A/64.

70. McCaffrey, *supra* note 20, at 7–8.

71. UNHRC Resolution A/HRC/15/L.14 (Sept. 30, 2010). As noted earlier, the 2010 U.N. Resolution is similarly based on a right to water implied within the positive rights

set forth in the ESC Covenant, *see* ESC Covenant, *supra* note 18; *see also* General Comment 15, *supra* note 21; 2010 UN Resolution, *supra* note 10.

72. General Comment 15, *supra* note 21.

73. ESC Covenant, *supra* note 18, at art. 2(1).

74. *Mazibuko, supra* note 3, at 19–20, citing Article 2(1) of the ESC Covenant.

75. *Id.* at 25.

76. Cross, *supra* note 19, at 876–77.

77. *Mazibuko, supra* note 3, at 28.

78. *Id.* at 30.

79. Eric A. Posner, *Climate Change and International Human Rights Litigation: A Critical Appraisal*, 155 U. PA. L. REV. 1925, 1934 (2007).

80. Joseph Dellepenna, *Climate Disruption, the Washington Consensus, and Water Law Reform*, 81 TEMP. L. REV. 383 (2008).

81. CHRISTOPHER E. SMITH, COURTS AND THE POOR 5 (1991).

82. JAVAID REHMAN, INTERNATIONAL HUMAN RIGHTS LAW (2d ed. 2010).

83. ESC Covenant, *supra* note 18, at art. 11; *see also* General Comment 15, *supra* note 21.

84. CP Covenant, *supra* note 16, at art. 2(1); *see also* Optional Protocol to the International Covenant on Civil and Political Rights, G.A. Res. 2200 (XXI), U.N. GAOR, 21st Sess., Supp. No. 16, U.N. Doc. A/6316 (Dec. 16, 1966).

85. S. JOSEPH ET AL., THE INTERNATIONAL COVENANT ON CIVIL AND POLITICAL RIGHTS: CASES, MATERIALS, AND COMMENTARY 163 (2d ed. 2004); *see also* Optional Protocol to the International Covenant on Economic, Social, and Cultural Rights, U.N. Doc. A/RES/63/117 (Dec. 10, 2008).

86. ADAM SMITH, THE WEALTH OF NATIONS 132 (Prometheus Books 1965) (1776). For a discussion surrounding Adam Smith's famous diamond-water paradox, *see* W.M. Hanemann, *The Economic Conception of Water*, *in* WATER CRISIS: MYTH OF REALITY ch. 4 (Marcelino Botin ed., 2004).

87. MAUDE BARLOW & TONY CLARKE, BLUE GOLD: THE FIGHT TO STOP THE CORPORATE THEFT OF THE WORLD'S WATER (2002).

88. Asit K. Biswas, *Water as a Human Right in the MENA Region: Challenges and Opportunities*, 23 INT'L J. WATER RESOURCES DEV. 209, 215 (2007).

89. Stephen McCaffrey & Kate Neville, *Small Capacity and Big Responsibilities: Financial and Legal Implications of a Human Right to Water for Developing Countries*, 21 GEO. INT'L ENVTL. L. REV. 670, 681–86 (2009); Asit K. Biswas, *Water as a Human Right in the MENA Region: Challenges and Opportunities*, *in* WATER AS A HUMAN RIGHT FOR THE MIDDLE EAST AND NORTH AFRICA 1, 7 (Asit Biswas et al., eds., 2008).

90. Jeffry S. Wade, *Privatization and the Future of Water Services*, 20 FLA. J. INT'L L. 179, 195–96 (2008).

91. The United Nations adopted in 2000 its "Millennium Development Goals" (MDGs), which included the goal of "reduc[ing] by half the proportion of people without sustainable access to safe drinking water 2015." United Nations Millennium Declaration, G.A. Res. 55/2, Para. 19, U.N. Doc. A/RES/55/2 (Sept. 8, 2000).

92. James Salzman, *Thirst: A Short History of Drinking Water*, 18 YALE J.L. & HUMAN. 94 (2006).

93. Camdessus Report, *supra* note 27, at 1.

94. Thomas M. Kerr, *Supplying Water Infrastructure to Developing Countries via Private Sector Project Financing*, 8 GEO. INT'L ENVTL. L. REV. 91, 94–95; Camdessus Report, *supra* note 27, at 1–5.

95. Meera Mehta et al., *Financing the Millennium Development Goals for Water and Sanitation: What Will It Take?*, 21 WATER RESOURCES DEV. 239–52 (2005).

96. *See, e.g.*, Amy Hardberger, *Life, Liberty, and the Pursuit of Water: Evaluating Water as a Human Right and the Duties and Obligations it Creates*, 4 Nw. J. INT'L HUM. RTS. 331, 349 (2005); *see also* MAUDE BARLOW, BLUE COVENANT: THE GLOBAL WATER CRISIS AND THE COMING BATTLE FOR THE RIGHT TO WATER (2009).

97. Hubert H.G. Savenije & Pieter van der Zaag, *Water as an Economic Good and Demand Management*, 27 WATER INT'L 98–104 (2002).

98. Peter Rogers et al., *Water Is an Economic Good: How to Use Prices to Promote Equity, Efficiency, and Sustainability*, 4 WATER POL'Y 1–17 (2002).

99. Shelley Ross Saxer, *The Fluid Nature of Property Rights in Water*, 21 DUKE ENVTL. L. & POL'Y 49 (2010).

100. ROUSE, *supra* note 38, at 16, 47.

101. ARTHUR MCINTOSH, ASIA WATER SUPPLIES: REACHING THE URBAN POOR (2003).

102. *See, e.g.*, Jennifer Naegele, *What Is Wrong with Full-Fledged Water Privatization?*, 6 J.L. & SOC. CHALLENGES, 99, 107 (2004).

103. Andre de Moor & Cees van Beers, *The Perversity of Government Subsidies for Energy and Water*, *in* GREENING THE BUDGET: BUDGETARY POLICIES FOR ENVIRONMENTAL IMPROVEMENT 36–40 (J. Peter Clinch ed., 2002).

104. ROUSE, *supra* note 38, at 40.

105. *Id.*

106. *Id.* at 37–39.

107. Darwin C. Hall, *Public Choice in Water Rate Design*, *in* THE POLITICAL ECONOMY OF WATER PRICING REFORMS 189–211 (Ariel Dinar ed., 2000).

108. Thomas W. Hazlett, *Private Monopoly and the Public Interest: An Economic Analysis of the Cable Television Franchise*, 134 U. PA. L. REV. 1335 (1986).

109. David B. Spence & Robert Prentice, *The Transformation of the American Energy Markets and the Problem of Market Power*, 53 B.C. L. REV. 131 (2007).

110. *See generally* NORMAL MYERS & JENNIFER KENT, PERVERSE SUBSIDIES: HOW TAX DOLLARS CAN UNDERCUT THE ENVIRONMENT AND THE ECONOMY (2001); *see also* Robert Glennon, *Water Scarcity, Marketing, and Privatization*, 83 TEX. L. REV. 1873, 1882–84 (2005).

111. *Id.*

112. Violeta Petrova, *At the Frontiers of the Rush for Blue Gold: Water Privatization and the Human Right to Water*, 31 BROOK. J. INT'L L. 577 (2006).

113. McCaffrey and Neville, *supra* note 89, at 700–02.

114. *Id.*; *see also* Alexandra Depolito Dunn & Erin Derrington, *Investment in Water and Wastewater Infrastructure: An Environmental Justice Challenge, A Governance Solution*, 24 NAT. RESOURCES & ENV'T 3 (2010).

115. McCaffrey and Neville, *supra* note 89, at 700–701.

116. Camdessus Report, *supra* note 27, at 18.

117. Petrova, *supra* note 112, at 587–588.

118. NORMAN MYER & JENNIFER KENT, PERVERSE SUBSIDIES: HOW TAX DOLLARS CAN UNDERCUT THE ENVIRONMENT AND THE ECONOMY (2001).

119. Jennifer Hoffpauir, *The Environmental Impact of Commodity Subsidies: NEPA and the Farm Bill*, 20 FORDHAM ENVTL. L. REV. 233 (2009).

120. David L. Feldman & Helen Ingram, *Multiple Ways of Knowing Water Resources: Enhancing the Status of Water Ethics*, 7 SANTA CLARA J. INT'L L. 1, 7 (2009).

121. *Id.* at 38; *see also* T.C. DOUGHERTY & A.W. HALL, ENVIRONMENTAL IMPACT ASSESSMENT OF IRRIGATION AND DRAINAGE PROJECTS (1995).

122. *See generally* Sharad Jain et al., *Freshwater and Its Management in India*, 2 INT. J. RIVER BASIN MGMT. 259–70 (2004).

123. Cross, *supra* note 19, at 879.

124. David A. Skeel, Jr., *When Should Bankruptcy Be an Option (For People, Places, or Things)?*, 55 WM. & MARY L. REV. 2217, 2220 (2014).

125. Matthew Dolan, *Detroit's Water Cutoffs Spark Protests*, WALL ST. J., July 18, 2014.

126. *Id.*

127. Alisa Priddle & Matt Helms, *Bankruptcy Judge Tells Detroit to Address Water Shutoffs*, USA TODAY, July 16, 2014.

128. Alana Semuels, *Thousands Go Without Water as Detroit Cuts Service for Nonpayment*, L.A. TIMES, June 28, 2014.

129. Kate Galbraith, *Ireland Sets Water Fees, Angering Thousands*, N.Y. TIMES, Nov. 12, 2014.

130. *See generally* J. HÄUSERMANN, A HUMAN RIGHTS APPROACH TO DEVELOPMENT (1998).

131. *See generally* Jeffrey W. Stempel, *Two Cheers for Specialization*, 61 BROOK. L. REV. 67 (1995).

132. *Id.* at 69.

133. *See, e.g.*, Bryan T. Camp, *The Failure of Adversarial Process in the Administrative State*, 84 IND. L.J. 57, 125–26 (2009) (discussing the U.S. Tax Court's specialized procedures and its relative institutional competence); Arti K. Rai, *Intellectual Property Rights in Biotechnology: Addressing New Technology*, 34 WAKE FOREST L. REV. 827, 843 (1999) (noting the institutional competence of the Court of Federal Claims in adjudicating intellectual property rights); Richard B. Saphire & Michael E. Solimine, *Shoring Up Article III: Legislative Court Doctrine in the Post CFTC v. Schor Era*, 68 B.U. L. REV. 85, 100 (1988) (noting the flexibility and specializing of bankruptcy courts); John J. Gibbons, *The Quality of the Judges Is What Counts in the End*, 61 BROOK. L. REV. 45, 46 (1995) (noting the role of specializing in the Delaware Court of Chancery).

134. Robert M. Chesney, *Disaggregating Deference: The Judicial Power and Executive Treaty Interpretation*, 92 IOWA L. REV. 1723, 1763 (2007).

135. *Mazibuko, supra* note 3; *see also* Chevron, U.S.A., Inc. v. NRDC, 467 U.S. 837 (1984).

136. Eric Berger, *Individual Rights, Judicial Deference, and Administrative Law Norms in Constitutional Decision Making*, 91 B.U. L. REV. 2029, 2032 (2011).

137. *See generally* Margaret G. Farrell, *Coping with Scientific Evidence: The Use of Special Masters*, 43 EMORY L.J. 927, 950 (1994); *see also* Anne-Marie C. Carstens, *Lurking in the Shadows of Judicial Process: Special Masters in the Supreme Court's Original Jurisdiction Cases*, 86 MINN. L. REV. 625 (2002).

138. Tom I. Romero, *Uncertain Waters and Contested Lands: Excavating the Layers of Colorado's Legal Past*, 73 U. COLO. L. REV. 521, 540 (2002).

139. *Id.* at 547–49.

140. David M. Getches, Foreword to P. ANDREW JONES & TOM CECH, COLORADO WATER LAW FOR NON-LAWYERS, at x (2009).

141. Charles W. Howe, *Reconciling Water Law and Economic Efficiency in Colorado Water Administration*, 16 U. DENV. WATER L. REV. 37, 39–40 (2013).

142. ROUSE, *supra* note 38, at 45–47.

143. ROUSE, *supra* note 38 at 64–66; *see also* Sharmila L. Murthy, *The Human Right to Water and Sanitation: History, Meaning and the Controversy over Privatization*, 3 BERKELEY J. INT'L L. 89, 134 (2013).

144. Robert Glennon, *Water Scarcity, Marketing, and Privatization*, 83 TEX. L. REV. 1873, 1883–84 (2005).

145. Jessica Budds & Gordon McGranahan, *Are the Debates on Water Privatization Missing the Point? Experiences from Africa, Asia, and Latin America*, 15 ENV'T & URBANIZATION 87, 109 (2003) (discussing the water voucher system in Chile).

146. ROUSE, *supra* note 38, at 209–12.

147. *Id.* at 210–11.

148. *Id.*

149. Murthy, *supra* note 143, at 134.

150. Rhett B. Larson, *Reconciling Energy and Food Security*, 48 U. RICHMOND L. REV. 929, 950 (2014).

151. Murthy, *supra* note 143, at 2226–27.

152. *Id.*

153. Elizabeth Burleson, *Emerging Law Addressing Climate Change and Water*, 5 ENVTL. & ENERGY L. & POL'Y J. 489, 496–99 (2010).

154. ROUSE, *supra* note 38, at 36–37.

155. *Id.* at 47–49.

156. *Id.* at 207.

157. *Id.*

158. *Id.*

159. John Ziegler, *The Dangers of Municipal Concession Contracts: A New Vehicle to Improve Accountability and Transparency*, 40 PUB. CONT. L.J. 571, 581 (2011).

160. Courtney Hostetler, *Going from Bad to Good: Combating Corporate Corruption on World Bank–Funded Infrastructure Projects*, 14 YALE HUM. RTS. & DEV. L.J. 231, 271 (2011).

161. ROUSE, *supra* note 38, at 207.

162. Okezie Chukwumerije, *Peer Review and the Promotion of Good Governance in Africa*, 32 N.C. J. INT'L L. & COM. REG. 49, 95 (2006).

163. Rhett B. Larson, *The New Right in Water*, 70 WASH. & LEE L. REV. 2181, 2229–2230 (2013).

164. *See* McCaffrey & Neville, *supra* note 89, at 700.

Chapter 4—Water Security and Racial Discrimination

1. E.G. Stets et al., *Increasing Chloride in Rivers of the Coterminous U.S. and Linkages to Potential Corrosivity and Lead Action Level Exceedances in Drinking Water*, 613 SCI. TOTAL ENV'T 1498 (2018).

2. Steve Almasy & Laura Ly, *Flint Water Crisis: Report Says "Systemic Racism" Played a Role*, CNN, Feb. 18, 2017, https://www.cnn.com/2017/02/18/politics/flint-water-report-systemic-racism/index.html.

3. *Id.*

4. William Taylor Potter et al., *Crumbling Pipes, Tainted Water Plague Black Communities*, NEWS 21, Apr. 14, 2017 (part of "Troubled Waters" series).

5. *See, e.g.*, Hannah Gordon Leker & Jacqueline MacDonald Gibson, *Relationship Between Race and Community Water and Sewer Service in North Carolina, USA*, 13 PLoS ONE 1–19 (2018); Raoul S. Liévanos, *Sociospatial Dimensions of Water Injustices: The Distribution of Surface Water Toxic Releases in California's Bay-Delta*, 60 SOC. PERSP. 575 (2016); Inga T. Winkler & Catherine Coleman Flowers, *"America's Dirty Secret": The Human Right to Sanitation in Alabama's Black Bets*, 49 COL. HUM. RTS. L. REV. 181 (2017).

6. Daria Rothmayr, *Lessons from Mazibuko: Persistent Inequality and the Commons*, 3 CONST. CT. REV. 317 (2010).

7. Mazibuko v. City of Johannesburg, 2010 BCLR 239 (S. Afr. CC), http://www.saflii.org/za/cases/ZACC/2009/28.pdf [hereinafter *Mazibuko*].

8. Rothmayr, *supra* note 6.

9. RICHARD FILČÁK, LIVING BEYOND THE PALE: ENVIRONMENTAL JUSTICE AND THE ROMA COMMUNITY (2012).

10. Martha F. Davis & Natasha Ryan, *Inconvenient Human Rights: Access to Water and Sanitation in Sweden's Informal Roma Settlements* (NW U. Sch. of Law Research Paper No. 272-2016, Apr. 2016), https://ssrn.com/abstract=2814707.

11. Rhett B. Larson, *Holy Water and Human Rights: Religious Rights Claims to Water Resources by Indigenous Peoples*, 2 ARIZ. J. ENVTL. L. & POL'Y 81 (2011).

12. *Id.*; Navajo Nation v. U.S. Forest Service, 535 F.3d 1058 (2008).

13. Felicia Fonseca, *Trial Under Way for Long-Running Northern Arizona Water Case*, ASSOCIATED PRESS, Oct. 11, 2018, https://157-dot-apnews-int.appspot.com/f720 33218d9b43cf99e281ea8a3b4a81; Aaron T. Wolf, *"Hydrostrategic" Territory in the Jordan River Basin: Water, War, and Arab-Israeli Peace Negotiations, in* WATER IN THE MIDDLE EAST: A GEOGRAPHY OF PEACE (Hussein Amery & Aaron Wolf eds., 2000), 63–120.

14. Matsipane Mosetlhanyane v. Attorney General, Civ. App. No. CACLB-074-10, ¶ 20 (Ct. App. Jan. 27, 2011) (Botswana), at 4–7, http://www.escr-net.org/sites/default/files/bushmen-water-appeal-judgment-jan-2011.pdf.

15. *Id.*

16. *Id.* at 7–8.

17. *Id.* at 4.

18. *Id.* at 12–14.

19. *Id.* at 19–20; citing Botswana Const. § 7(1).

20. *Id.* at 20.

21. *Id.* at 24.

22. *Id.* at 15–16.

23. Anja Seibert-Fohr, *The Rise of Equality in International Law and Its Pitfalls: Learning from Comparative Constitution Law*, 35 BROOK. J. INT'L L. 1 (2010).

24. Human Rights Comm., Third Periodic Rep. of States Parties Due in 2007—Israel, U.N. Doc., CCPR/C/ISR/3 (Nov. 21, 2008); *see also* George S. McGraw, *Defining and Defending the Right to Water and Its Minimum Core: Legal Construction and the Role of National Jurisprudence*, 8 LOY. U. CHI. INT'L L. REV. 127, 147 (2011).

25. Similar claims based on civil rights guaranteeing equal protection and religious freedom could also be asserted under the CP Covenant. See International Covenant on Civil and Political Rights, G.A. Res. 2200 (XXI), U.N. GAOR, 21st Sess., Supp. No. 52, U.N. Doc. A/RES/2200(XXI) (hereinafter, the "CP Covenant"), at 50–60, art. 2(1), art. 14 (equal protection), art. 18 (religion); *see also* Optional Protocol to the International Covenant on Civil and Political Rights, 999 U.N.T.S. 302 (Dec. 16, 1966). S. JOSEPH ET AL., THE INTERNATIONAL COVENANT ON CIVIL AND POLITICAL RIGHTS: CASES, MATERIALS, AND COMMENTARY (2d ed. 2004), 163; *see also* Optional Protocol to the International Covenant on Economic, Social, and Cultural Rights, U.N. Doc. A/RES/63/117 (Dec. 10, 2008).

26. Nevertheless, under Part III, Article 7 of the CP Covenant, "[n]o one shall be subjected to torture or to cruel, inhuman or degrading treatment or punishment." CP Covenant, *supra* note 25, at Part III, Art. 7. A claim similar to that asserted by the Basarwa community could be asserted in an international tribunal.

27. Jim Rossi, *The Common Law "Duty to Serve" and Protection of Consumers in an Age of Competitive Retail Public Utility Restructuring*, 51 VAND. L. REV. 1244, 1244–48 (1998).

28. *Id.*

29. Joseph Sax, *The Public Trust Doctrine in Natural Resource Law: Effective Judicial Intervention*, 68 MICH. L. REV. 471 (1970); *see also* MARK DOWIE, IN LAW WE TRUST (2005), at 18–20.

30. Michael Blumm & Rachel Guthrie, *Internationalizing the Public Trust Doctrine: Natural Law and Constitutional and Statutory Approaches to Fulfilling the Saxion Vision*, 45 U.C. DAVIS L. REV. 741, 789–90 (2012) (the public trust doctrine is a recognized legal doctrine in many countries, including India, Pakistan, the Philippines, Uganda, Kenya, Nigeria, South Africa, Brazil, Ecuador, and Canada).

31. William D. Araiza, *The Public Trust Doctrine as an Interpretive Canon*, 45 U.C. DAVIS L. REV. 693 (2012); Barton H. Thompson, *Water as a Public Commodity*, 95 MARQ. L. REV. 17, 35 (2011); Edith Brown Weiss, *Intergenerational Equity: A Legal Framework for Global Environmental Change*, *in* ENVIRONMENTAL CHANGE AND INTERNATIONAL LAW 395 (E.B. Weiss ed., 1992).

32. John D. Echeverria, *The Public Trust Doctrine as a Background Principle Defense in Takings Litigation*, 45 U.C. DAVIS L. REV. 931 (2012).

33. § 3(1) of National Water Act 36 of 1998, 6 JRSA 1-417 (2001) (S.Afr.). *See also* Robyn Stein, *Water Law in a Democratic South Africa: A Country Case Study Examining the Introduction of a Public Rights System*, 83 TEX. L. REV. 2167 (2005). National Environmental Management Act 107 of 1998 § 2(4)(o) (S. Afr.).

34. CONSTITUTION OF THE REPUBLIC OF SOUTH AFRICA, ch. 2, § 9.

35. Sandra Fullerton Joireman, *Inherited Legal Systems and Effective Rule of Law: Africa and the Colonial Legacy*, 39 J. MOD. AFR. STUD. 571 (2001).

36. Blumm & Guthrie, *supra* note 30.

37. *Id.*

38. *See, e.g.*, Janelle Plummer, *Water and Corruption: A Destructive Partnership*, *in* GLOBAL CORRUPTION REPORT 2008, http://www.wasser-in-buergerhand.de/untersuchungen/Transpar_Int_2008_1_Introducing_water_and_corruption.pdf; *see also* Muhammad Sohail & Sue Cavill, *Water for the Poor: Corruption in Water Supply and Sanitation*, *in* GLOBAL CORRUPTION REPORT 2008, http://www.wasser-in-buergerhand.de/untersuchungen/Transpar_Int_2008_3_Water_and_sanitation.pdf; Nejat Anbarci et al., *The Ill Effects of Public Sector Corruption in the Water and Sanitation Sector*, 85 LAND ECON. 363 (2009).

39. *See generally* Emmanuelle Auriol & Aymeric Blanc, *Capture and Corruption in Public Utilities: The Cases of Water and Electricity in Sub-Saharan Africa*, 17 UTIL. POL'Y 203 (2009).

40. Kenneth Abbott & Duncan Snidal, *Pathways to International Cooperation*, *in* THE IMPACT OF INTERNATIONAL LAW ON INTERNATIONAL COOPERATION: THEORETICAL PERSPECTIVES (Eyal Benvenisti & Moshe Hirsch eds., 2004), 50–65.

41. Alana Klein, *Judging as Nudging: New Governance Approaches for the Enforcement of Constitutional Social and Economic Rights*, 39 COLUM. HUM. RTS. L. REV. 351, 393–94 (2008); *see also* Jody Freeman, *Collaborative Governance in the Administrative State*, 45 UCLA L. REV. 1 (1997).

42. *Id.* at 394; Michael Dorf & Charles Sabel, *A Constitution of Democratic Experimentalism*, 98 COLUM. L. REV. 267 (1998); *see also* Orly Lobel, *The Renew Deal: The Fall of Regulation and the Rise of Governance in Contemporary Legal Thought*, 89 MINN. L. REV. 342 (2004).

43. Claudia Paul-Wostl, *Transitions Towards Adaptive Management of Water Facing Climate and Global Change*, 21 WATER RESOURCE MGMT. 49, 51 (2007). Adaptive management is "a decision process that promotes flexible decision making that can be adjusted in the face of uncertainties as outcomes from management actions and other events become better understood. . . . It is not a 'trial by error' process, but rather emphasizes learning while doing." Dept. of the Interior (USDOI), Adaptive

Management Technical Guide 4 (2009), http://www.doi.gov.initiatives/Adaptive Management/TechGuide.pdf.

44. Klein, *supra* note 41, at 396.

45. Joanne Scott & Susan Sturm, *Courts as Catalysts: Re-Thinking the Judicial Role in New Governance*, 13 COLUM. J. EUR. L. 565, 580–82 (2007).

46. *See, e.g.*, Jens Newig & Oliver Fritsch, *Environmental Governance: Participatory, Multi-Level—And Effective?*, 19 ENVTL. POL. GOV. 197–214 (2009); for an illustration of the challenges of implementing a participatory, localized approach to water management, *see* Andreas Neef, *Lost in Translation: The Participatory Imperative and Local Water Governance in North Thailand and Southwest Germany*, 1 WATER ALTERNATIVES 89–110 (2008).

47. Stephen McCaffrey & Kate Neville, *Small Capacity and Big Responsibilities: Financial and Legal Implications of a Human Right to Water for Developing Countries*, 21 GEO. INT'L ENVTL. L. REV. 670 (2009).

48. "Water stress" means a per capita supply of 1,700 cubic meters per year or less. *See* Malgosia Fitzmaurice, *The Human Right to Water*, 18 FORDHAM ENVTL. L. REV. 537, 538 (2007).

49. Deborah Zabarenko, *River Basins Could Double Food Production*, REUTERS, Sept. 26, 2011, http://www.reuters.com/article/2011/09/27/us-rivers-food-idUSTRE78Q0BZ 20110927.

50. A. Mukherji, *Is Intensive Use of Groundwater a Solution to the World's Water Crisis?*, in WATER CRISIS: MYTH OR REALITY? 181 (P. Rogers et al. eds., 2006).

51. Kheryn Klubnikin et al., *The Sacred and the Scientific: Traditional Ecological Knowledge in Siberian River Conservation*, 10 ECOLOGICAL APPLICATIONS 1296, 1300 (2000).

52. *Id.* at 1300–02.

53. FIKRET BERKES, SACRED ECOLOGY: TRADITIONAL ECOLOGICAL KNOWLEDGE AND RESOURCE MANAGEMENT 8 (1999).

54. Kent H. Redford & Allyn Maclean Stearman, *Forest-Dwelling Native Amazonians and the Conservation of Biodiversity: Interests in Common or in Collision?*, 7 CONSERVATION BIOLOGY 248, 254 (1993).

55. JARED DIAMOND, COLLAPSE: HOW SOCIETIES CHOOSE TO FAIL OR SUCCEED, at ch. 2 (2005).

56. Klubnikin et al., *supra* note 51.

57. Rhett B. Larson, *Holy Water and Human Rights: Indigenous Peoples' Religious-Rights Claims to Water Resources*, 2 ARIZ. J. ENVTL. L. & POL'Y 81–91 (2011).

58. Jonathan Fox & Deborah Flores, *Religions, Constitutions, and the State: A Cross-National Study*, 71 J. POL. 1499 (2009).

59. CP Covenant, *supra* note 25.

60. G.A. Res. 61/295, Declaration on the Rights of Indigenous Peoples (Sept. 7, 2007).

61. C. Grossman & S. Anaya, "The Case of the *Awas Tingni v. Nicaragua*: A New Step in the International Law of Indigenous Peoples," 19 ARIZ. J. INT. & COMP. L. 1; *see also* Case of the Mayagna (Sumo) Awas Tingni Community v. Nicaragua, 2001 Inter-Am. Ct. H.R. (ser. C) No. 79 (Aug. 31, 2001), http:www.corteidh.or.cr/docs/casos/articulos/seriec_79_ing.pdf.

62. Fons Coomans, *The* Ogoni *Case Before the African Commission on Human and Peoples' Rights*, 52 INT. & COMP. L. Q. 749 (2003); African Commission on Human and Peoples' Rights Decision, Ctr. For Econ. And Soc. Rights (2002), http://cesr.org/downloads/AfricanCommissionDecision.pdf.

63. *See, e.g.*, Lawrence v. Clark County, 254 P.3d 606, 611 (2011); *see also* Stephen F. Williams, *The Requirement of Beneficial Use as a Cause of Waste in Water Resource Development*, 23 NAT. RESOURCE J. 7 (1983).

64. Cathleen Flanagan & Melinda Laituri, *Local Cultural Knowledge and Water Resource Management: The Wind River Indian Reservation*, 33 ENVTL. MGMT. 262, 270 (2004).

65. *See, e.g.*, Geringer v. Runyan, 235 P.3d 867, 870 (2010); *see also* R. Lambeth Townsend, *Cancellation of Water Rights in Texas: Use It or Lose It*, 17 ST. MARY'S L.J. 1217 (1986).

66. Rebecca Tsosie, *Tribal Environmental Policy in an Era of Self-Determination: The Role of Ethics, Economics, and Traditional Ecological Knowledge*, 21 VT. L. REV. 225, 234–35 (1996); *see also* City of Albuquerque v. Browner, 865 F. Supp. 733 (D.N.M. 1993).

67. *Id.*

68. *Id.*

69. *Id.*

70. Merete Borch, *Rethinking the Origins of Terra Nullius*, 32 AUSTRALIAN HIST. STUD. 222 (2001).

71. Mabo v. Queensland [No. 2] (1992) 175 CLR 1 (Austl.).

72. Virginia Marshall, *Deconstructing Aqua Nullius: Reclaiming Aboriginal Water Rights and Communal Identity in Australia*, 8 INDIGENOUS L. BULL. 9 (2016).

73. Lorena Allam, *Ending "Aqua Nullius": Calls for Laws to Protect Indigenous Water Rights*, GUARDIAN, June 28, 2018.

74. *Id.*

75. *Id.*

76. Jérémie Gilbert, *Historical Indigenous Peoples' Land Claims: A Comparative and International Approach to the Common Law Doctrine of Indigenous Title*, 56 INT'L & COMP. L.Q. 583 (2007).

77. Yvette Trahan, The Richtersveld Community and Others v. Alexkor Ltd.: *Declaration of a "Right in Land" Through a "Customary Law Interest" Sets Stage for Introduction of Aboriginal Title into South African Legal System*, 12 TUL. J. INT'L & COMP. L. 565, 566 (2004).

78. Id. at 571–72.

79. Id.

80. Trahan, *supra* note 77, at 565.

81. *Id.*; *see also* Restitution of Land Rights Act 22 of 1994 § 1(xi) (S. Afr.).

82. *Id.*

83. *Id.* at 556.

84. Rhett Larson & Kelly Kennedy, *Bankrupt Rivers*, 49 U.C. DAVIS L. REV. 1335 (2016).

85. ECON. RESEARCH SERV., U.S. DEP'T OF AGRIC., MAJOR USES OF LAND IN THE UNITED STATES 35 (2002).

86. Arizona v. California, 373 U.S. 546, 601 (1963); Winters v. United States, 207 U.S. 564 (1908).

87. *Winters*, 207 U.S. 564.

88. Cappaert v. United States, 426 U.S. 128, 141 (1976); *see also* United States v. New Mexico, 438 U.S. 696, 718 (1978).

89. *Winters*, 207 U.S. at 576–77.

90. *Arizona*, 373 U.S. at 595–601. Included in calculating the PIA is total acreage, arability of the land, and engineering and economic feasibility. *In re* Gen. Adjudication of All Rights to Use Water in Big Horn River Sys., 753 P.2d 76, 101 (Wyo. 1988), *aff'd*, Wyoming v. United States, 492 U.S. 406 (1989).

91. United States v. Adair, 723 F.2d 1394, 1414 (9th Cir. 1983).

92. Rhett B. Larson, *Inter-State Lessons for International Water Law*, 2.3 BRILL RES. PERSP. ON INT'L WATER L. 1–82 (2017).

93. Larson & Kennedy, *supra* note 84.

94. *Arizona*, 373 U.S. 546 (1963).

95. Elizabeth Whitman, *Gila River Indian Community Approves Major Deal to Provide Water to CAP*, PHOENIX NEW TIMES (Dec. 5, 2018).

96. *In re* the Gen. Adjudication of All Rights to Use Water in the Gila River Sys. & Source, 35 P.3d 68, 78–80 (Ariz. 2001).

97. CONSTITUTION OF THE REPUBLIC OF ECUADOR, art. 57(6) (2008).

98. *See generally* Rutgerd Boelens et al., *Indigenous Water Rights in the Andes: Struggles Over Resources and Legitimacy*, 20 J. WATER L. 268 (2009).

99. *Id.*

100. U.N. Conference on Environment and Development, *Agenda 21*, U.N. Doc. A/CONF.151/26 (Vol. II) (June 3–14, 1992).

101. Erin Ryan, *Negotiating Federalism*, 52 B.C. L. REV. 1, 130 (2011); *see also* Matthew J. Parlow, *Civic Republicanism, Public Choice Theory, and Neighborhood Councils: A New Model for Civic Engagement*, 79 U. COLO. L. REV. 137–84 (2008).

102. Jeffrey T. Matson, *Inter-state Water Compact Version 3.0: Missouri River Basin Compact Drafters Should Consider an Inter-Sovereign Approach to Accommodate Federal and Tribal Interests in Water Resources*, 88 NOTRE DAME L. REV. 97–138 (2012).

103. International Law Association, Final Report of the Water Resources Law Committee, in Report of the Seventy-First Conference of the International Law Association (2004) [hereinafter Berlin Rules], https://www.unece.org/fileadmin/DAM/env/water/meetings/legal_board/2010/annexes_groundwater_paper/Annex_IV_Berlin_Rules_on_Water_Resources_ILA.pdf.

104. Salman Salman, *The Helsinki Rules, the UN Watercourses Convention and the Berlin Rules: Perspectives on International Law*, 23 WATER RESOURCES DEV. 625–40 (2007).

105. Berlin Rules, *supra* note 103, at art. 20.

Chapter 5—Water Security and Gender Inequality

1. Inga T. Winkler et al., *Treasuring What We Measure and Measuring What We Treasure: Post-2015 Monitoring for the Promotion of Equality in the Water, Sanitation, and Hygiene Sector*, 32 WIS. INT'L L.J. 547 (2014).

2. Nityanand Jayaraman, *Why India's Chennai Has Run Out of Water*, BBC, July 2, 2019.

3. *Id.*
4. Divya Karthikeyan & Swati Gupta, *"I'm Scared for My Daughter": Life in India's First City That's Almost Out of Water*, CNN, June 22, 2019.
5. *Id.*
6. *Id.*
7. Divya Chandrababu, *With She-Toilets, Chennai Shows the Way in Sanitation*, TIMES OF INDIA, June 15, 2014.
8. *Id.*
9. *Id.*
10. *Id.*
11. World Health Organization & the United Nations Children's Fund [UNICEF], *Progress on Sanitation and Drinking Water*, at 34 (2010), http://www.wssinfo.org/fileadmin/user_upload/resources/1278061137-JMP_report_2010_en.pdf.
12. *Water Facts: Women*, WATER.ORG, http://water.org/water-crisis/water-facts/women/.
13. David Hemson, *"The Toughest of Chores": Policy and Practice in Children Collecting Water in South Africa*, 5 POL'Y FUTURES IN EDUC. 315 (2007).
14. Naila Kabeer, *Gender Equality and Women's Empowerment: A Critical Analysis of the Third Millennium Development Goal*, 13 GENDER & DEVEL. 13, 20–24 (2010).
15. Winkler et al., *supra* note 1; *see also* Human Rights Council, Independent Expert on the Issue of Human Rights Obligations Related to Access to Safe Drinking Water and Sanitation, Addendum: Mission to Egypt, U.N. Doc. A/HRC/15/31/Add.3, at 22 (July 5, 2010) (by Catarina de Albuquerque).
16. Sarah House et al., *Menstrual Hygiene Matters: A Resource for Improving Hygiene Around the World*, 21 REPROD. HEALTH MATTERS 257 (2013).
17. *See, e.g.*, Emily Wilson et al., *Dismantling Menstrual Taboos to Overcome Gender Inequality*, 2 LANCET: CHILD & ADOLESCENT HEALTH 379 (2018).
18. Suneela Garg & Tanu Anand, *Menstruation Related Myths in India: Strategies for Combating It*, 4 J. FAM. MED. & PRIMARY CARE 184 (2015).
19. *See, e.g.*, Marni Sommer & Murat Sahin, *Overcoming the Taboo: Advancing the Global Agenda for Menstrual Hygiene Management for Schoolgirls*, 103 AM. J. PUB. HEALTH 1556 (2013); Marni Sommer et al., *A Comparison of the Menstruation and Education Experiences of Girls in Tanzania, Ghana, Cambodia, & Ethiopia*, 45 COMPARE: J. COMP. & INT'L EDUC. 589 (2014).
20. *See, e.g.*, Ricard Giné Garriga & Agustí Pérez Foguet, *Unravelling the Linkages Between Water, Sanitation, Hygiene and Rural Poverty: The WASH Poverty Index*, 27 WATER RESOURCES MGMT. 1501 (2013).
21. Phillippe Cullet & Sujith Koonan, *Water Law and Policy in India*, in WATER LAW IN INDIA: AN INTRODUCTION TO LEGAL INSTRUMENTS (2018), 3–21. .
22. *See, e.g.*, Nitya Rao, "GOOD WOMEN DO NOT INHERIT LAND": POLITICS OF LAND AND GENDER IN INDIA (2017); Reena Patel, HINDU WOMEN'S PROPERTY RIGHTS IN RURAL INDIA (2018); Sonia Bhalotra et al., *Property Rights and Gender Bias: Evidence from Land Reform in West Bengal*, 11 AM. ECON. J.: APPLIED ECON. 205 (2019).
23. Amal Ahmed, *The People of Cape Town Are Running Out of Water—And They're Not Alone*, POPULAR SCI., Mar. 18, 2018, https://www.popsci.com/water-crisis-cape-town-world (last visited May 2, 2018).

24. *Id.*; Craig Welch, *Why Cape Town Is Running Out of Water, and Who's Next*, NAT'L GEOGRAPHIC, Mar. 5, 2018, https://news.nationalgeographic.com/2018/02/cape-town-running-out-of-water-drought-taps-shutoff-other-cities/ (last visited May 2, 2018).

25. Welch, *supra* note 24.

26. *How Much Water Does the Average Person Use at Home Per Day*, U.S. GEOLOGICAL SURVEY, https://water.usgs.gov/edu/qa-home-percapita.html (last visited Sept. 2, 2019).

27. Krista Mahr, *How Cape Town Was Saved from Running Out of Water*, GUARDIAN, May 4, 2018.

28. Bram Janseen, *"Day Zero": What Cape Town's Water Crisis Says About Inequality*, USA TODAY, Feb. 3, 2018.

29. *Id.*

30. *Id.*; *see also* Alexandra E. Petri, *Without Water, the Women of Cape Town Are Redefining "Self Care,"* GLAMOUR, Mar. 7, 2018.

31. Robert Kibet, *Consecutive Droughts Spell Disaster and Hunger for Kenya in 2018*, IRIN NEWS, Jan. 10, 2018, https://www.irinnews.org/feature/2018/01/10/consecutive-droughts-spell-disaster-and-hunger-kenya-2018 (last visited May 2, 2018).

32. Vicky Hallet, *Millions of Women Take a Long Walk with a 40-Pound Water Can*, NPR (July 9, 2016, 9:20 AM), https://www.npr.org/sections/goatsandsoda/2016/07/07/484793736/millions-of-women-take-a-long-walk-with-a-40-pound-water-can (last visited May 2, 2018).

33. U.N. Dep't of Econ. & Soc. Aff., Gender and Water: International Decade for Action "Water for Life" 2005–2015 (Oct. 23, 2014), http://www.un.org/waterforlifedecade/gender.shtml.

34. *Id.*

35. Marcia M. Brewster et al., *A Gender Perspective on Water Resources and Sanitation*, in WAGADU VOLUME 3: WATER AND WOMEN IN PAST, PRESENT AND FUTURE (Zdeňka Kalnická ed., 2007), 1–19.

36. Amy Raub et al., *Protections of Equal Rights Across Sexual Orientation and Gender Identity: An Analysis of 193 National Constitutions*, 28 YALE J.L. & FEMINISM 149 (2016).

37. G.A. Res. 2200, United Nations, International Covenant on Civil and Political Rights (Dec. 16, 1966) [hereinafter CP Covenant].

38. CONSTITUTION OF THE REPUBLIC OF SOUTH AFRICA, ch. 2, art. 9; CONSTITUTION OF INDIA, part III, art. 14.

39. Jay P. Graham et al., *An Analysis of Water Collection Labor Among Women and Children in 24 Sub-Saharan African Countries*, 11 PLOS ONE 1–14 (2015); Camille Morgan et al., *Water, Sanitation, and Hygiene in Schools: Status and Implications of Low Coverage in Ethiopia, Kenya, Mozambique, Rwanda, Uganda, and Zambia*, 220 INT'L J. HYGIENE & ENVTL. HEALTH 950 (2017).

40. CONSTITUTION OF KENYA (2010) § 43(1)(b), (d), (f).

41. WORLD BANK GROUP, UNDERSTANDING THE KENYA 2016 WATER ACT (2016), https://www.2030wrg.org/wp-content/uploads/2016/12/Understanding-the-Kenyan-Water-Act-2016.pdf.

42. CONSTITUTION OF KENYA (2010).

43. *Id.*

44. *Id.* at art. 21(4). This characteristic is not unique to the Kenyan Constitution, and similar provisions can be found in the South African and Ugandan Constitutions. CONSTITUTION OF THE REPUBLIC OF SOUTH AFRICA, Oct. 11, 1996, § 14(231) (1–5); CONSTITUTION OF THE REPUBLIC OF UGANDA, 1995, § 19(287)(a), (b).

45. Tina Hlimi, *Kenyan Constitution and Gender Equality: Issues of Implementation*, LEGAL AID KENYA (Mar. 31, 2013), https://legalaidkenya.com/2013/05/31/kenyan-constitution-and-gender-equality-issues-of-implementation.

46. G.A. Res. 2200, International Covenant on Economic, Social and Cultural Rights [hereinafter ESC Covenant] (Dec. 16, 1966).

47. The Convention on the Elimination of All Forms of Discrimination against Women, Dec. 18, 1979, https://www.ohchr.org/en/professionalinterest/pages/cedaw.aspx.

48. *Id.*

49. *Id.* at art. 14.

50. Comm. on the Elimination of All Forms of Discrimination Against Women, *General Recommendations*, http://www.ohchr.org/EN/HRBodies/CEDAW/Pages/Recommendations.aspx (last visited May 5, 2018).

51. *Id.*

52. Convention on the Rights of the Child, art. 24, Nov. 20, 1989, https://www.ohchr.org/en/professionalinterest/pages/crc.aspx.

53. The Convention on the Elimination of All Forms of Discrimination against Women, *supra* note 47, ch. IV, https://treaties.un.org/Pages/ViewDetails.aspx?src=TREATY&mtdsg_no= IV-8&chapter=4&lang=en#21.

54. Comm. on the Elimination of All Forms of Discrimination Against Women, *General Recommendation No. 36 on the Right of Girls and Women to Education* (2017), http://docstore.ohchr.org/SelfServices/FilesHandler.ashx?enc=6QkG1d%2fPPRiCAqhKb7yhsldCrOlUTvLRFDjh6%2fx1pWDgG%2fSFCLpV5OLQVxCscp3MZM6j7xfSLU3eour%2bfQfEzg63VJG4W%2b869aQ22uce%2bSyQK7vFFa%2fuGduuqn-FzK7%2bn; *see also* SERAP v. Nigeria, judgment, Court of Justice of the Economic Community of West African States (suit No. ECW/CCJ/APP/12/07; judgment No. ECW/CCJ/JUD/07/10 (30 November 2010)).

55. *Id.*

56. *Id.*

57. *Id.*

58. Comm. on the Elimination of All Forms of Discrimination Against Women, *General Recommendation No. 24: Article 12 of the Convention (Women and Health)* (1999), http://tbinternet.ohchr.org/Treaties/CEDAW/Shared%20Documents/1_Global/INT_CEDAW_GEC_4738_E.pdf.

59. Comm. on the Elimination of All Forms of Discrimination Against Women, *General Recommendation No. 3: Education and Public Information Campaigns* (1987), https://tbinternet.ohchr.org/Treaties/CEDAW/Shared%20Documents/1_Global/INT_CEDAW_GEC_5825_E.pdf.

60. Comm. on the Elimination of All Forms of Discrimination Against Women, State Party Obligations to Respect, Protect and Fulfil the Rights of Rural Women (2016), http://docstore.ohchr.org/SelfServices/FilesHandler.ashx?enc=6QkG1d%2fPPRi CAqhKb7yhsldCrOlUTvLRFDjh6%2fx1pWB6lCUVZF6giuQZbHO4%2fX%2b4 Db%2bKev44QYdiHl9FsT1evybcMuaSbhtRSEgF9LzC%2bftEbBrdWL2QQi2xD xGAzgBP.

61. *Financing Water and Sanitation in Developing Countries: The Contribution of External Aid*, OECD, 7 (June 2013), http://www.oecd.org/dac/stats/Brochure_water_2013.pdf (last visited May 2, 2018).

62. *Id.*

63. *Id.*

64. *Id.*

65. *Id.*

66. *Id.* at 11

67. *Id.*

68. *Id.*

69. *Id.*

70. *Id.*

71. *Id.* at 34.

72. *Id.* at 35.

73. *Id.* at 34.

74. *Id.*

75. *Id.* at 35–36.

76. *Id.* at 35–36.

77. *Id.* at 38–39.

78. *Id.* at 37.

79. SHANTI KADARIYA & ARJA R. ARO, CHHAUPADI PRACTICE IN NEPAL—ANALYSIS OF ETHICAL ASPECTS, MEDICOLEGAL AND BIOETHICS 54–55 (2015), https://www. researchgate.net/publication/282447220_Chhaupadi_practice_in_Nepal_-_ analysis_of_ethical_aspects.

80. *Id.*

81. Bhadra Sharma & Jeffrey Gettleman, *In Rural Nepal, Menstruation Taboo Claims Another Victim*, N.Y. TIMES, Jan. 10, 2018, https://www.nytimes.com/2018/01/10/ world/asia/nepal-woman-menstruation.html.

82. *Id.*

83. Sophie Cousins, *How Sanitation and Hygiene Strategies Can Promote Women's Rights*, DEVEX, Nov. 19, 2015, https://www.devex.com/news/how-sanitation-and- hygiene-strategies-can-promote-women-s-rights-87315.

84. *Id.*

85. Karl Mathiesen, *Reading, Writing and Sanitation: How Kids Are Key to Ending Toilet Taboos*, GUARDIAN, Nov. 19, 2015, https://www.theguardian.com/global- development-professionals-network/2015/nov/19/reading-writing-and- sanitation-how-kids-are-key-to-ending-toilet-taboos.

86. *Id.*

87. *WTO: Our Story*, WORLD TOILET ORG., http://worldtoilet.org/our-story/ (last visited May 5, 2018).

88. WORLD TOILET ORGANIZATION, http://worldtoilet.org/what-we-do/wts2017/#themes (last visited May 5, 2018).

89. *World Toilet Day*, U.N. WATER, http://www.worldtoiletday.info/2017/ (last visited May 5, 2018).

90. Abigail Constantino, *World Toilet Day Sheds Light on Poo Taboo*, WTOP, Nov. 18, 2017, https://wtop.com/health-fitness/2017/11/world-toilet-day-sheds-light-poo-taboo/slide/1/.

91. CORO, REGIONAL CAMPAIGN IN MUMBAI: RIGHT TO PEE (Sept. 16, 2016), http://www.coroindia.org/about/project/regional-campaign-in-mumbai-right-to-pee.

92. *Id.*

93. Yaniv Stopnitzky, *No Toilet, No Bride? Intrahousehold Bargaining in Male-Skewed Marriage Markets in India*, 127 J. DEV. ECON. 269 (2017); Joanne Lu, *Women in Northern India Said "No Toilet, No Bride," and It Worked*, HUMANOSPHERE, May 18, 2017, available at http://www.humanosphere.org/global-health/2017/05/women-northern-india-said-no-toilet-no-bride-worked/.

94. Joseph W. Dellapenna, *The Evolution of Riparianism in the United States*, 95 MARQ. L. REV. 53 (2011); Roscoe Pound, *The Theory of Judicial Decision*, 36 HARV. L. REV. 641 (1923).

95. Joseph W. Dellapenna, *A Primer on Groundwater Law*, 49 IDAHO L. REV. 265 (2013).

96. *Id.*

97. *Id.*

98. Rhett Larson & Kelly Kennedy, *Bankrupt Rivers*, 49 U.C. DAVIS L. REV. 1335 (2016).

99. A. Dan Tarlock, *Reconnecting Property Rights to Watersheds*, 25 WM. & MARY ENVTL. L. & POL'Y REV. 69 (2000).

100. Joseph L. Sax, *The Public Trust Doctrine in Natural Resource Law: Effective Judicial Intervention*, 68 MICH. L. REV. 471 (1970); Michael C. Blumm & Rachel D. Guthrie, *Internationalizing the Public Trust Doctrine: Natural Law and Constitutional and Statutory Approaches to Fulfilling the Saxion Vision*, 45 U.C. DAVIS L. REV. 741 (2012).

101. Rhett B. Larson, *Interstitial Federalism*, 62 UCLA L. REV. 908 (2015).

102. Elizabeth Bryan & Hagar El Didi, *Considering Gender in Irrigation: Technology Adoption for Women Farmers*, CHICAGO COUNCIL ON GLOBAL AFF. (Mar. 13, 2019), https://www.thechicagocouncil.org/blog/global-food-thought/guest-commentary-considering-gender-irrigation-technology-adoption-women.

103. *See, e.g.*, Aparna Polavarapu, *Procuring Meaningful Land Rights for Women of Rwanda*, 14 YALE HUM. RTS. & DEV. J. 105 (2011); David M. Bigge & Amélie von Briesen, *Conflict in Zimbabwean Courts: Women's Rights and Indigenous Self-Determination in Magaya v. Magaya*, 13 HARV. HUM. RTS. J. 289 (2000); Elisabeth Wickeri, *"Land Is Life, Land Is Power": Landlessness, Exclusion, and Deprivation in Nepal*, 34 FORDHAM INT'L L.J. 930 (2011).

104. I, December 18, 1984, U.K.-China, 1985 Gr. Brit. T.S. No. 26 (cmd. 9534), 23 I.L.M. 1366 (Annex III).

105. Magaya v. Magaya, 3 L.R.C. 35, 40 (Sup. Ct. Zimbabwe, 1999).

106. Isha Ray, *Women, Water, and Development*, 32 ANN. REV. ENVTL. RESOURCES 421 (2007).

107. *Id.*

108. Garrett Hardin, *The Tragedy of the Commons*, 162 SCI. 1243 (1968).

109. Elinor Ostrom, *Coping with Tragedies of the Commons*, 2 ANN. REV. POL. SCI. 493 (1999).

110. ELINOR OSTROM, GOVERNING THE COMMONS: THE EVOLUTION OF INSTITUTIONS FOR COLLECTIVE ACTION (1990).

111. Lee Anne Fennell, *Ostrom's Law: Property Rights in the Commons*, 5 INT'L J. COMMONS 9–27 (2011).

112. Silvia Federici, *Feminism and the Politics of the Commons*, *in* USES OF WORLDWIND, MOVEMENT, MOVEMENTS, AND CONTEMPORARY RADICAL CURRENTS IN THE UNITED STATES (Craig Huges et al. eds., 2010), 225–40.

113. Grace Remmington, *Transforming Tradition: The Aflaj and the Changing Role of Traditional Knowledge Systems for Collective Water Management*, 151 J. ARID ENV'TS 134 (2018); Homayoun Motiee et al., *Assessment of the Contributions of Traditional Qanats in Sustainable Water Resources Management*, 22 INT'L J. WATER RESOURCES DEV. 575 (2006).

114. *Id.*; *see also* T. Mazjoub, *Water Laws and Customary Water Arrangements*, *in* 2010 REPORT OF THE ARAB FORUM FOR ENVIRONMENT AND DEVELOPMENT (2010), 137–52.

115. Aparna Polavarapu, *Procuring Meaningful Land Rights for the Women of Rwanda*, 14 YALE HUM. RTS. & DEV. L.J. 101, 105 (2011).

116. CONSTITUTION OF THE REPUBLIC OF RWANDA, art. 26; Organic Law No. 08/2005 of 14/07/2005 Determining the Use and Management of Land in Rwanda, art. 5.

117. Organic Law No. 31/2006 of 14/08/2006 on Organisation, Jurisdiction, Competence and Functioning of the Mediation Committee, arts. 1–4.

118. Aparna Polavarapu, *Procuring Meaningful Land Rights for the Women of Rwanda*, 14 YALE HUM. RTS. & DEV. L.J. 105 (2011).

119. Sonia Bhalotra et al., *Property Rights and Gender Bias: Evidence from Land Reform in West Bengal*, 11 AM. ECON. J.: APPLIED ECON. 205–37 (2019).

Chapter 6—Water Security and Armed Conflict

1. Alexander Carius et al., *Water, Conflict, and Cooperation*, 10 POLICY BRIEF: THE UNITED NATIONS AND ENVIRONMENTAL SECURITY 60 (2004).

2. JEROME DELLI PRISCOLI & AARON T. WOLF, MANAGING AND TRANSFORMING WATER CONFLICTS (2005).

3. PAOLO BACIGALUPI, THE WATER KNIFE (2015); FRANK HERBERT, DUNE (1965).

4. Rhett B. Larson, *Water Security*, 112 NW. L. REV. 139 (2017).

5. Neal A. Kemkar, *Environmental Peacemaking: Ending Conflict Between India and Pakistan on the Siachen Glacier Through the Creation of a Transboundary Peace*

Park, 25 STAN. ENVTL. L.J. 67, 75 (2006); Sonaullah Phapho, *Unquenchable Thirst*, ECONOMIST, Nov. 19, 2011.

6. Donald Neff, *Israel-Syria: Conflict at the Jordan River, 1949–1967*, 23 J. PALESTINE STUD. 26 (1994).

7. Craig (Tony) Arnold, *Fourth-Generation Environmental Law: Integrationist and Multimodal*, 35 WM. & MARY ENVTL. L. & POL'Y REV. 771, 818 (2011); John Wendle, *Syria's Climate Refugees*, 315 SCIENTIFIC AM. 50, 51–55 (2016).

8. Kevin Mwanza, *Deadly Ranch Invasions Shows Land-Use Conflicts in Kenya—Experts*, REUTERS, Nov. 28, 2018.

9. U.S. DEP'T OF DEFENSE, QUADRENNIAL DEFENSE REVIEW (2014), http://archive.defense.gov/pubs/2014_Quadrennial_Defense_Review.pdf.

10. Aaron T. Wolf, *Shared Waters: Conflict and Cooperation*, 32 ANN. REV. ENVTL. RESOURCES 241–69 (2007).

11. Itzchak Kornfeld, *Mesopotamia: A History of Water and Law*, in THE EVOLUTION OF THE LAW AND POLITICS OF WATER (Joseph W. Dellapenna & Joyeeta Gupta eds., 2008), 21–36; LUDWIK A. TECLAFF, THE RIVER BASIN IN HISTORY AND LAW (1967).

12. Peter H. Gleick, *Water and Terrorism*, 8 WATER POL'Y 481 (2006).

13. Geneva Convention Relative to the Treatment of Prisoners of War (Oct. 21, 1950), 75 U.N.T.S. 135; International Armed Conflicts (Protocol I) (June 8, 1977), 1125 U.N.T.S. 3; Protocol Additional to the Geneva Conventions of 12 August 1949, and Relating to the Protection of Victims of Non-International Armed Conflicts (Protocol II), 1125 U.N.T.S. 609 (June 8, 1977).

14. Rhett Larson, *Libya and Water as a Weapon*, INT'L WATER LAW PROJECT (Aug. 15, 2011), https://www.internationalwaterlaw.org/blog/2011/09/15/libya-and-water-as-a-weapon/.

15. *Id.*

16. Simba Russeau, *Libya: Water Emerges as a Hidden Weapon*, GUARDIAN, May 27, 2011.

17. WATER IN THE MIDDLE EAST: CONFLICT OR COOPERATION? (Thomas Naff & Ruth Matson eds., 1984); Peter Gleick, *Water and Terrorism*, 8 WATER POL'Y 481 (2006).

18. *Id.*

19. *Id.*

20. *World Report 2015: Israel/Palestine*, HUMAN RIGHTS WATCH, https://www.hrw.org/world-report/2015/country-chapters/israel/palestine; Erika Weinthal & Jeannie Sowers, *Targeting Infrastructure and Livelihoods in the West Bank and Gaza*, 95 INT'L AFF. 319 (2019).

21. Rhett B. Larson, *Augmented Water Law*, 48 TEX. TECH L. REV. 757 (2016).

22. James R. Fleming, *The Climate Engineers*, 31 WILSON Q. 46 (2007); Noah Byron Bennheim, *History of Climate Engineering*, 1 WILEY INTERDISCIPLINARY REVIEWS: CLIMATE CHANGE 891 (2010).

23. Mansur Mirovalev, *Dam Leaves Crimea Population in Chronic Water Shortage*, AL JAZEERA, Jan. 4, 2017.

24. *Id.*

25. Rhett B. Larson, *War and Water*, THE HUFFINGTON POST, Dec. 7, 2014.

26. JOSEPH SASSOON, SADDAM HUSSEIN'S BA'TH PARTY (2012).

27. ERNEST MAIN, IRAQ FROM MANDATE TO INDEPENDENCE (2019).

28. SUNIL AMRITH, UNRULY WATERS: HOW RAINS, RIVERS, COASTS, AND SEAS HAVE SHAPED ASIA'S HISTORY (2018).

29. *Id.*

30. DANIEL HAINES, RIVERS DIVIDED: INDUS BASIN WATERS IN THE MAKING OF INDIA AND PAKISTAN (2016).

31. Keith Johnson, *Are India and Pakistan on the Verge of a Water War?*, FOREIGN POL'Y (Feb. 25, 2019, 3:00 PM), https://foreignpolicy.com/2019/02/25/are-india-and-pakistan-on-the-verge-of-a-water-war-pulwama-kasmir-ravi-indus/.

32. Mehr Nadeem et al., *Pakistan, India Spar Over Using Water as a Weapon in Kashmir Dispute*, REUTERS, Aug. 19, 2019.

33. *Id.*

34. Haleh Hatami & Peter H. Gleick, *Conflicts Over Water in the Myths, Legends, and Ancient History of the Middle East*, 36 ENV'T: SCI. & POL'Y FOR SUSTAINABLE DEV. 10–11 (2010).

35. Mark Zeitoun & Joeroen Warner, *Hydro-Hegemony—A Framework for Analysis of Transboundary Water Conflicts*, 8 WATER POL'Y 435 (2006).

36. MIRIAM LOWI, WATER AND POWER: THE POLITICS OF A SCARCE RESOURCE IN THE JORDAN RIVER BASIN (1995).

37. Moshe Shemesh, *Prelude to the Six-Day War: The Arab-Israeli Struggle Over Water Resources*, 9 ISRAEL STUD. 1–45 (2004).

38. *Id.*

39. Aaron Wolf, *Water for Peace in the Jordan River Watershed*, 33 NAT. RESOURCES J. 797 (1993).

40. *Id.*

41. Shemesh, *supra* note 37.

42. *Id.*

43. *Id.; see also* Wolf, SHARED WATERS (2007), *supra* note 10.

44. *Id.*

45. *Id.*

46. JEFFREY K. SOSLAND, COOPERATING RIVALS: THE RIPARIAN POLITICS OF THE JORDAN RIVER BASIN (2007).

47. Mark Zeitoun & Naho Mirumachi, *Transboundary Water Interaction I: Reconsidering Conflict and Cooperation*, 8 INT'L ENVTL. AGREEMENTS 297 (2008).

48. ANDERS JÄGERSKOG, WHY STATES COOPERATE OVER SHARED WATER: THE WATER NEGOTIATIONS IN THE JORDAN RIVER BASIN, http://www.columbia.edu/~tmd2118/situstudio/why_cooperation.pdf.

49. IJAZ HUSSAIN, POLITICAL AND LEGAL DIMENSIONS OF THE INDUS WATER TREATY (2017).

50. *Id.*

51. Opangmeren Jamir, *Understanding India-Pakistan Water Politics Since the Signing of the Indus Water Treaty*, 18 WATER POL'Y 1070 (2016).

52. *Id.*

53. *Id.*

54. *Unquenchable Thirst*, ECONOMIST, Nov. 19, 2011, https://www.economist.com/briefing/2011/11/19/unquenchable-thirst.

55. Rhett B. Larson, *Interstitial Federalism*, 62 UCLA L. REV. 908 (2015).

56. *Id.*

57. MARC REISNER, CADILLAC DESERT: THE AMERICAN WEST AND ITS DISAPPEARING WATER 256–60 (1993).

58. Jon Kyl & Ryan A Smith, *Foreword: Water Law and Policy Conference*, 49 ARIZ. L. REV. 209–10 (2007).

59. A. Dan Tarlock, *Safeguarding International River Ecosystems in Times of Scarcity*, 3 U. DENVER WATER L. REV. 231 (2000); JACK L. AUGUST, JR., THE VISION IN THE DESERT: CARL HAYDEN AND HYDROPOLITICS IN THE AMERICAN SOUTHWEST 146–48 (1999).

60. Jerry B. Lincecum, *Red River Bridge War*, *in* FOLKLORE IN MOTION: TEXAS TRAVEL LORE 25–32 (Kenneth L. Untiedt ed., 2007).

61. BILL CANNON, TEXAS: LAND OF LEGEND AND LORE 39 (2004).

62. Nina Singh, *Inter-State Water Sharing in India: From Conflict to Cooperation*, *in* SPATIAL DIVERSITY AND DYNAMICS IN RESOURCES AND URBAN DEVELOPMENT (2015), 415–27.

63. Protus Onyango, *Kenya's Water Wars Kill Scores*, INTER PRESS SERVICE (Sept. 11, 2012), http://www.ipsnews.net/2012/09/kenyas-water-wars-kill-scores/.

64. Codi Kozacek, *Water Conflict: Violence Erupts Along Ethiopia-Kenya Water-Stressed Border*, CIRCLE OF BLUE (June 21, 2011), https://www.circleofblue.org/2011/world/water-conflict-violence-erupts-along-ethiopias-and-kenyas-water-stressed-border/.

65. Barbara McMahon, *Man Charged with Killing Neighbor for Watering His Lawn*, GUARDIAN, Nov. 1, 2007, https://www.theguardian.com/world/2007/nov/01/australia.barbaramcmahon.

66. WILLIAM KAHRL, WATER AND POWER: THE CONFLICT OVER LOS ANGELES' WATER SUPPLY IN THE OWENS VALLEY (1983).

67. Alan Neuhauser, *Hundreds of Protesters Arrested in India After Water Runs Dry*, U.S. NEWS & WORLD REP., June 20, 2019, https://www.usnews.com/news/world-report/articles/2019-06-20/hundreds-of-protesters-arrested-in-india-after-water-runs-dry.

68. OSCAR OLIVERA & TOM LEWIS, COCHABAMBA! WATER WAR IN BOLIVIA (2004).

69. Stanley McChrystal, *The Politics of Water Security in the Kabul River Basin*, ATLANTIC MONTHLY, Nov. 10, 2011; Samantha Wilson, *Climate Change and the Rise of Terrorism in Northeastern Syria*, 15 ESSAI 127 (2017).

70. Justin Worland, *Why Climate Change and Terrorism Are Connected*, TIME, Nov. 15, 2015.

71. Margaret Suter, *Running Out of Water: Conflict and Water Scarcity in Yemen and Syria*, ATLANTIC COUNCIL, Sept. 12, 2017.

72. Aaron T. Wolf, *Transboundary Freshwater Dispute Database* ORE. ST. U. (2004), https://transboundarywaters.science.oregonstate.edu/content/transboundary-freshwater-dispute-database; Aaron T. Wolf, *Shared Waters: Conflict and Cooperation*, 32 ANN. REV. ENVTL. RESOURCES 241 (2007).

73. Mark Zeitoun & Najo Mirumachi, *Transboundary Water Interaction I: Reconsidering Conflict and Cooperation*, 8 INT'L ENVTL. AGREEMENTS 297 (2008).

74. Convention on the Law of the Non-Navigational Uses of International Watercourses, May 21, 1997, 36 I.L.M. 703 [hereinafter Watercourse Convention].

75. For an overview and commentary on the Watercourse Convention, *see* THE UN WATERCOURSE CONVENTION IN FORCE: STRENGTHENING INTERNATIONAL LAW FOR TRANSBOUNDARY WATER MANAGEMENT (Flavia Rocha Loures & Alistair Rieu-Clarke eds., 2013); Jason Rudall et al., THE UN CONVENTION ON THE LAW OF THE NON-NAVIGATIONAL USES OF INTERNATIONAL WATERCOURSES: A COMMENTARY (2018).

76. Watercourse Convention, arts. 5–9.

77. Watercourse Convention, art. 33.

78. Watercourse Convention, art. 10.

79. Watercourse Convention, art. 29.

80. Watercourse Convention, art. 8.

81. Larson, *Interstitial Federalism* (2015), *supra* note 55.

82. Mark Zeitoun & Joeroen Warner, *Hydro-Hegemony—A Framework for Analysis of Transboundary Water Conflicts*, 8 WATER POL'Y 435 (2006).

83. Watercourse Convention, art. 2; *see also* GABRIEL ECKSTEIN, THE INTERNATIONAL LAW OF TRANSBOUNDARY GROUNDWATER RESOURCES (2017).

84. Gabriel E. Eckstein, *Managing Buried Treasure Across Frontiers: The International Law of Transboundary Aquifers*, 36 WATER INT'L 573 (2011).

85. Eckstein, THE INTERNATIONAL LAW OF TRANSBOUNDARY GROUNDWATER RESOURCES (2007), *supra* note 83.

86. Joyeeta Gupta, *The Watercourses Convention, Hydro-Hegemony and Transboundary Water Issues*, 51 INT'L SPECTATOR 118 (2016); Salman Salman, *The United Nations Watercourses Convention Ten Years Later: Why Has Its Entry into Force Proven Difficult*, 32 WATER INT'L 1–15 (2007).

87. Gabriel Eckstein, *International Court of Justice—International Water Law Cases*, INT'L WATER LAW PROJECT, https://www.internationalwaterlaw.org/cases/icj.html.

88. Rhett Larson & Brian Payne, *Unclouding Arizona's Water Future*, 49 ARIZ. ST. L.J. 465 (2017).

89. J.A. Allan, *Hydro-Peace in the Middle East: Why No Water Wars?: A Case Study of the Jordan River Basin*, 22 SAIS REV. 255 (2002).

90. Claudia Sadoff & David Grey, *Beyond the River: The Benefits of Cooperation on International Rivers*, 4 WATER POL'Y 389 (2002).

91. A. Dan Tarlock & Patricia Wouters, *Are Shared Benefits of International Waters an Equitable Apportionment?*, 18 COLO. J. INT'L ENVTL. L. 523 (2007).

92. Treaty Between Canada and the United States of America Relating to Cooperative Development of the Water Resources of the Columbia River Basin, January 17, 1961, 542 U.N.T.S. 244 (1964).

93. Rhett B. Larson, *Inter-State Water Law in the United States of America: What Lessons for International Water Law?*, 2.3 BRILL RES. PERSP. ON INT'L WATER L. 1–82 (2017).

94. *Id.*

95. UNESCO, From Potential Conflict to Co-Operation Potential: Promoting Water as a Catalyst for Peace Through Capacity Building, Research, and Technical Assistance. Paris, France. A Contribution of UNESCO's International Hydrological Programme to the World Water Assessment Programme—2nd Phase (2004); Mark Zeitoun & Naho Mirumachi, Transboundary Water Interaction I: Reconsidering Conflict and Cooperation, 8 INT'L ENVTL. AGREEMENTS 297 (2008).

96. Larson, Inter-State Water Law in the United States of America (2017), supra note 93.

97. David Brooks & Julie Trottier, Confronting Water in an Israeli-Palestinian Peace Agreement, 382 J. HYDROLOGY 103–14 (2010).

98. Aaron T. Wolf, A Long Term View of Water and International Security, 142 J. CONTEMPORARY WATER RES. & EDUC. 67–75 (2009).

99. JÄGERSKOG, supra note 48.

100. Id.

101. Larson, Inter-State Water Law in the United States of America (2017), supra note 93.

102. Aaron T. Wolf et al., Water Can Be a Pathway to Peace, Not War, 1 NAVIGATING PEACE (July 2006), https://www.wilsoncenter.org/sites/default/files/Navigating PeaceIssue1.pdf.

103. Id.

104. JOHN FLECK, WATER IS FOR FIGHTING OVER: AND OTHER MYTHS ABOUT WATER IN THE WEST (2016).

105. Id.

106. Delaware River Basin Compact, Pub. L. No. 87-328, 75 Stat. 688 (1961).

107. Robin Kundis Craig, Hydraulic Fracturing (Fracking), Federalism, and the Water-Energy Nexus, 49 IDAHO L. REV. 241, 251–52 (2013).

108. Larson, Interstitial Federalism (2015), supra note 55.

Chapter 7—Water Security and Mass Migration

1. U.N. High Comm'n on Refugees, Syrian Refugee Crisis, UNHCR, https://www.unrefugees.org/emergencies/syria/ (last visited Aug. 24, 2019).

2. John Podesta, The Climate Crisis, Migration, and Refugees, BROOKINGS INST., July 25, 2019.

3. Rhett B. Larson, Global Climate Change and the Reallocation of Water, in THE OXFORD RESEARCH ENCYCLOPEDIA OF ENVIRONMENTAL SCIENCE (David McQueen ed., 2019), 1–34.

4. Oliver-Leighton Barrett, Central America: Climate, Drought, Migration and the Border, CTR. FOR CLIMATE & SEC., Apr. 17, 2019.

5. Steven A. Camarota & Karen Zeigler, Central American Immigrant Population Increased Nearly 28-Fold Since 1970, CTR. FOR IMMIGRATION STUD., Nov. 1, 2018.

6. Nicholas Casey & Jenny Carolina González, A Staggering Exodus: Millions of Venezuelans Are Leaving the Country, On Foot, N.Y. TIMES, Feb. 20, 2019.

7. Arelis R. Hernández & Mariana Zuñiga, "Why Are You Crying, Mami?" In Venezuela, the Search for Water Is a Daily Struggle, WASH. POST, Apr. 4, 2019.

8. U.S. Congressional Research Service, *Central American Migration: Root Causes and U.S. Policy*, FED'N OF AM. SCIENTISTS (June 13, 2019), https://fas.org/sgp/crs/row/IF11151.pdf.

9. *Id.*; Kanta Kumari Rigaud et al., *Groundswell: Preparing for Internal Climate Migration*, WORLD BANK, https://openknowledge.worldbank.org/handle/10986/29461.

10. DAVID CHRISTIAN, MAPS OF TIME: AN INTRODUCTION TO BIG HISTORY (2005); FRED SPIER, BIG HISTORY AND THE FUTURE OF HUMANITY (2d ed. 2015).

11. Anne H. Osborne et al., *A Humid Corridor Across the Sahara for the Migration of Early Modern Humans Out of Africa 120,000 Years Ago*, 105 PNAS 16,444 (2008).

12. PETER BELLWOOD, FIRST MIGRANTS: ANCIENT MIGRATION IN GLOBAL PERSPECTIVES (2013).

13. Jan Selby & Clemens Hoffmann, *Water Scarcity, Conflict, and Migration: A Comparative Analysis and Reappraisal*, 30 ENV'T & PLAN. C: POL. & SPACE 997 (2012).

14. Tom I. Romero, II, *Bridging the Confluence of Water and Immigration Law*, 48 TEX. TECH L. REV. 779 (2016).

15. Larson, *supra* note 3.

16. JAMES N. GREGORY, AMERICAN EXODUS: THE DUST BOWL MIGRATION AND OKIE CULTURE IN CALIFORNIA (1989).

17. *Id.*

18. Rhett Larson, *Tarzan to the Terminator: Western Water's Story through the Lens of the Los Angeles River*, *in* 3 POWER & PLACE: CULTURE & CONFLICT IN THE BUILT ENVIRONMENT 40 (2018).

19. JAMES N. GREGORY, AMERICAN EXODUS: THE DUST BOWL MIGRATION AND OKIE CULTURE IN CALIFORNIA (1989).

20. Rob Picheta, *An Ancient Turkish Town Could Disappear Underwater in Weeks*, CNN, Aug. 27, 2019; Suzy Hansen, *In Turkey, a Power Play Will Leave Ancient Towns Underwater*, NAT'L GEOGRAPHIC, Oct. 25, 2018.

21. Nabila Shaikh et al., *Schistosomiasis in the Senegal River Basin*, 2 LANCET S27, May 1, 2018.

22. Khaled Diab, *Hope for the Egyptian Nubians Damned by the Dam*, GUARDIAN, Apr. 21, 2012.

23. GARRETT HARDIN, FILTERS AGAINST FOLLY: HOW TO SURVIVE DESPITE ECONOMISTS, ECOLOGISTS, AND THE MERELY ELOQUENT (1985).

24. David Grey & Claudia W. Sadoff, *Sink or Swim? Water Security for Growth and Development*, 9 WATER POL'Y 545 (2007).

25. Tennessee Valley Authority v. Hill, 437 U.S. 153 (1978).

26. Jean Ash, *Damming the Yangtze*, 13 F. FOR APPLIED RES. & PUB. POL'Y 78 (1998).

27. DAI QING, THE RIVER DRAGON HAS COME! THE THREE GORGES DAM AND THE FATE OF CHINA'S YANGTZE RIVER AND ITS PEOPLE (1998).

28. EARLE RICE, JR., THREE GORGES DAM (2018).

29. *Id.*; *see also* Jeffrey Ball, *Under Pressure: Bathers Duck Weak Shower Heads*, WALL ST. J., Nov. 13, 2009.

30. QING, *supra* note 27.

31. *Id.*

32. Jessica Macy Yu & Michael Martina, *China Braces for "Severe" Flooding on Yangtze River*, REUTERS, Apr. 1, 2016; Z.E. Kundzewicz et al., *Flood Risk and Its Reduction in China*, 130 ADVANCES IN WATER RESOURCES 37 (2019).

33. Brooke Wilmsen, *After the Deluge: A Longitudinal Study of Resettlement at the Three Gorges Dam, China*, 84 WATER DEV. 41 (2016).

34. *Millions Forced out by China Dam*, BBC NEWS, Oct. 12, 2007; Wang Hongjiang, *Millions More Face Relation from Three Gorges Reservoir Area*, XINHUA, Oct. 16, 2007.

35. Lisa See, *Waters of the Three Gorges Dam Will Wash Over World Culture*, L.A. TIMES, June 8, 2003.

36. Peter Bilson Obour et al., *The Impacts of Dams on Local Livelihoods: A Study of the Bui Hydroelectric Project in Ghana*, 32 INT'L J. WATER RESOURCES DEV. 286 (2016); Sunardi Sudianto et al., *Rebuilding Livelihood of the Rural and Peri-Urban Resettlers in Post-Involuntary Displacement of Saguling Dam Construction*, 5 J. ASIAN DEV. 13 (2019); Iman A.I. Ahmed, *The Merowe Dam in Northern Sudan: A Case of Population Displacement and Impoverishment*, *in* REFUGEES AND FORCED MIGRATION IN THE HORN OF EASTERN AFRICA (Johannes Dragsbaek Schmidt et al. eds., 2019), 131–53.

37. Li Heming et al., *Reservoir Resettlement in China: Past Experience and the Three Gorges Dam*, 167 GEOGRAPHICAL J. 195 (2001).

38. Grey & Sadoff, *supra* note 24.

39. *Id.*

40. *Id.*

41. Fiske v. Framingham Manufacturing Co., 29 Mass. 68 (1831).

42. Convention on the Law of the Non-Navigational Uses of International Watercourses, May 21, 1997, 36 I.L.M. 703 [hereinafter Watercourse Convention].

43. Rob Picheta, *Indonesia Will Build Its New Capital City in Borneo as Jakarta Sinks into the Java Sea*, CNN, Aug. 26, 2019.

44. Christina Nunez, *Sea Level Rise, Explained*, NAT'L GEOGRAPHIC, Feb. 19, 2019.

45. John Podesta, *The Climate Crisis, Migration, and Refugees*, BROOKINGS INST., July 25, 2019; *see also* Laura Parker, *143 Million People May Soon Become Climate Migrants*, NAT'L GEOGRAPHIC, Mar. 19, 2018.

46. *Id.*

47. Picheta, *supra* note 43.

48. *Id.*

49. Holly A. Michael et al., *Science, Society, and the Coastal Groundwater Squeeze*, 53 WATER RESOURCES RES. 2610 (2017).

50. Nahian Ahmed et al., *Understanding the Political Ecology of Forced Migration and Deforestation through a Multi-Algorithm Classification Approach: The Case of Rohingya Displacement in the Southeastern Border Region of Bangladesh*, GEOLOGY, ECOLOGY & LANDSCAPES (2018).

51. Jane M. Cohen, *Are We Killing the Rain? Meditations on the Water Cycle and, More Particularly, on Bioprecipitation*, 37 WATER INT'L 670 (2012).

52. Guangyu Wang et al., *Integrated Watershed Management: Evolution, Development and Emerging Trends*, 27 J. FORESTRY RES. 967 (2016).

53. Alden R. Hibbert, *Water Yield Improvement Potential by Vegetation Management on Western Rangelands*, 19 J. Am. Water Res. Ass'n 375, 378–79 (1983).

54. *See generally id.* at 379.

55. Charles A. Troendle et al., *The Coon Creek Water Yield Augmentation Project: Implementation of Timber Harvesting Technology to Increase Streamflow*, 143 Forest Ecology & Mgmt. 179 (2001).

56. *See* Diane E. McConkey, *Federal Reserved Rights to Instream Flows in the National Forests*, 13 Va. Envtl. L.J. 305, 310–11 (1994); *see also* Brandon Loomis, *Reduction in Tree Cover Over Rivers Could Mean More Water Flow*, Ariz. Cent., Oct. 30, 2015.

57. *Id.*

58. *Id.* The ultimate effectiveness of watershed management in addressing wildfire concerns is the subject of intense scholarly debate. *See generally* Wildfire Policy: Law and Economics Perspectives (Karen Bradshaw Schulz & Dean Lueck eds., 2012).

59. *Id.*

60. Cohen, *supra* note 51.

61. *See* Diane E. McConkey, *Federal Reserved Rights to Instream Flows in the National Forests*, 13 Va. Envtl. L.J. 305, 310–11 (1994); *see also* Loomis, *supra* note 56.

62. Claudia Radel et al., *Migration as a Feature of Land System Transitions*, 38 Current Opinion in Envtl. Sustainability 103 (2019).

63. Paul Summerfelt, *Will AZ Learn or Burn? Can AZ Learn to Burn?: The Flagstaff Experience*, 48 Ariz. St. L.J. 157, 176 (2016).

64. Annette Fredette, *4FRI and the NEPA Process*, 48 Ariz. St. L.J. 139 (2016).

65. Karen Bradshaw & Dean Lueck, *Contracting for Control of Landscape-Level Resources*, 100 Iowa L. Rev. 2507, 2537–40 (2015).

66. Diane Vosick, *Democratizing Federal Forest Management Through Public Participation and Collaboration*, 48 Ariz. St. L.J. 93 (2016).

67. *Id.*

68. *Id.*

69. Andrés Martínez Moscoso & Rhett Larson, *Forestry Management and Water Law: Comparing Ecuador and Arizona*, 44 Water Int'l 337 (2019).

70. Andrés Martínez Moscoso, El Derecho al Agua en el Ecuador: Un Análisis desde la Ciencia Política y el Derecho Público (2017).

71. H. Michael Rauscher, *Ecosystem Management Decision Support for Federal Forests in the United States: A Review*, 114 Forest Ecology & Mgmt. 173 (1999).

72. Elizabeth Long, Wyoming v. USDA: *A Look Down the Road at Management of Inventoried Roadless Areas for Climate Change Mitigation and Adaptation*, 40 Ecology L.Q. 329, 341 (2013); *but see* Bradshaw & Lueck, *supra* note 65 (discussing the incentives some forest landowners have to invest in watershed protection).

73. *Id.; see also* Emery Cowan, *How Good Earth's Plans Have Played Out*, Ariz. Daily Sun, Sept. 26, 2015.

74. Rhett B. Larson, *Orphaned Pollution*, 45 Ariz. St. L.J. 991 (2013).

75. Andrés Martínez Moscoso & Rhett Larson, *Forestry Management and Water Law: Comparing Ecuador and Arizona*, 44 Water Int'l 337 (2019).

76. *Id.*

77. Moscoso, *supra* note 70.

78. Erin O'Donnell, Legal Rights for Rivers: Competition, Collaboration and Water Governance (2019).

79. Joseph Sax, *The Public Trust Doctrine in Natural Resource Law: Effective Judicial Intervention*, 68 Mich. L. Rev. 471 (1970); Illinois Central Railroad Co. v. Illinois, 146 U.S. 387 (1892).

80. Ruth Langridge & Christopher Ansell, *Comparative Analysis of Institutions to Govern the Groundwater Commons in California*, 11 Water Alternatives 481 (2018).

81. Robert Muggah, *The World's Coastal Cities Are Going Under: Here's How Some of Fighting Back*, World Econ. F., Jan. 16, 2019.

82. Nicholas Burns & David Miliband, Opinion, *Syria's Worsening Refugee Crisis Demands Action from the West*, Wash. Post, July 9, 2015; Griff Witte, *New U.N. Report Says World's Refugee Crisis Is Worse than Anyone Expected*, Wash. Post, June 18, 2015

83. Patrick Boehler & Sergio Peçanha, *The Global Refugee Crisis, Region by Region*, N.Y. Times, Aug. 26, 2015.

84. *See* Deidre McPhillips, *The Tragic Numbers Behind Syria's Refugees*, U.S. News, Dec. 19, 2016.

85. *Id.*

86. *Id.*

87. Lara Saade & Cynthia Delgadillo, *Syrian Refugees Living in Jordan and Lebanon: Young, Female, at Risk*, World Bank (Dec. 16, 2015), http://www.worldbank.org/en/news/press-release/2015/12/16/syrian-refugees-living-in-jordan-and-lebanon-caught-in-poverty-trap [https://perma.cc/8FQY-33LU].

88. Omar Dahi, *The Refugee Crisis in Lebanon and Jordan: The Need for Economic Development Spending*, 47 Forced Migration Rev. 11 (Sept. 2014).

89. *Id.*

90. *Id.*

91. *Id.* at 12.

92. *See* Mohamed F. Hamoda, *Water Strategies and Potential Water Reuse in the South Mediterranean Countries*, 165 Desalination 31 (2004).

93. Hatem Jemmali & Caroline A. Sullivan, *Multidimensional Analysis of Water Poverty in MENA Region: An Empirical Comparison with Physical Indicators*, 115 Soc. Indicators Res. 253, 277 (2014); Eran Feitelson & Jonathan Chenoweth, *Water Poverty: Towards a Meaningful Indicator*, 4 Water Pol'y 263, 271 (2002).

94. Aleena Farishta, *The Impact of Syrian Refugees on Jordan's Water Resources and Water Management Planning* (May 2014) (unpublished M.S. thesis) (on file with the Columbia University Academic Commons), https://academiccommons.columbia.edu/catalog/ac:175300.

95. Stephen J. Klingseis, *Syrian Refugees: Are They a Non-Traditional Threat to Water Supplies in Lebanon and Jordan?* (Sept. 2016) (unpublished M.A. thesis) (on file with the Naval Post Graduate School), https://www.hsdl.org/?view&did=796642.

96. Taylor Luck, *In Jordan, Tensions Rise Between Syrian Refugees and Host Community*, THE WASH. POST, Apr. 21, 2013, https://www.washingtonpost.com/world/middle_east/in-jordan-tensions-rise-between-syrian-refugees-and-host-community/2013/04/21/d4f5fa24-a762-11e2-a8e2-5b98cb59187f_story.html?utm_term=.61a0b211f3f0 [https://perma.cc/KA6F-AMGD]; Tim Midgley et al., *Under Pressure: The Impact of the Syrian Refugee Crisis on Host Communities in Lebanon*, WORLD VISION INT'L (July 12, 2013), http://wvi.org/europe/publication/under-pressure-impact-syrian-refugee-crisis-host-communities-lebanon.

97. Peter Schwartzstein, *Syrian Refugees in Lebanon Camp Reliant on "Hell Water" that Reduces Metal to Rust*, GUARDIAN, May 26, 2015, https://www.theguardian.com/global-development/2015/may/26/syrian-refugees-lebanon-shatila-camp-hell-water [https://perma.cc/Y9J7-2W7F].

98. Khaled A. Alqadi & Lalit Kumar, *Water Policy in Jordan*, 30 INT'L J. WATER RES. DEV. 322, 323 (2013).

99. For more information about the project, *see A Holistic Water Solution for Underserved and Refugee Host Communities in Lebanon and Jordan*, ARIZ. ST. U., https://sustainability.asu.edu/sustainabilitysolutions/programs/solutionsservices/holistic-water-solutions/ [hereinafter *A Holistic Water Solution*]. The Holistic Water Solutions Initiative is made possible by the support of the American people through USAID. The views and information expressed in this book are solely my own and do not necessarily reflect the views of USAID, the U.S. Government, Arizona State University, or the other partners in the Project.

100. For more information about H2O for Humanity, *see* H2O FOR HUMANITY, http://www.h2oforhumanity.com/ (last visited Sept. 17, 2017).

101. *Id.*

102. For more information about Zero Mass Water, *see* ZERO MASS WATER, https://zeromasswater.com/technology/homeowner/.

103. *See A Holistic Water Solution, supra* note 99.

104. *Id.*

105. For more information on GreenCo, *see* GREENCO WATER, http://greencowater.com/.

106. For more information on the René Moawad Foundation, *see* RMF, http://www.rmf.org.lb/. For more information on Mercy Corps in Jordan, *see* MERCY CORPS: JORDAN, https://www.mercycorps.org/countries/jordan.

107. Abraham H. Maslow, *A Theory of Human Motivation*, 50 PSYCHOL. REV. 370 (1943).

108. Oliver-Leighton Barrett, *Central America: Climate, Drought, Migration and the Border*, CTR. FOR CLIMATE & SEC., Apr. 17, 2019.

109. Tom I. Romero, *Bridging the Confluence of Water and Immigration Law*, 48 TEX. TECH L. REV. 779 (2016).

110. JAMES N. GREGORY, AMERICAN EXODUS: THE DUST BOWL MIGRATION AND OKIE CULTURE IN CALIFORNIA (1989).

111. BLAKE GUMPRECHT, THE LOS ANGELES RIVER: ITS LIFE, DEATH, AND POSSIBLE REBIRTH (1999).

112. *Id.*

113. Adam Nagourney, *Frank Gehry Draws Ire for Joining Los Angeles River Restoration Project*, N.Y. TIMES, Sept. 23, 2015.

114. JOHN STEINBECK, EAST OF EDEN (Penguin Classics, 2016).

Chapter 8—Water Security and Technological Innovation

1. Larry W. Mays, *A Brief History of Water Technology During Antiquity: Before the Romans*, *in* ANCIENT WATER TECHNOLOGIES (Larry W. Mays ed., 2009), 1–28.

2. Jim Lochhead & Jennifer Pitt, *Killing the Colorado*, PROPUBLICA, June 16, 2015.

3. Tina Loo, *High Modernism, Conflict, and the Nature of Change in Canada: A Look at Seeing Like a State*, 97 CANADIAN HIST. REV. 34 (2016).

4. Rhett B. Larson, *Innovation and International Commons: The Case of Desalination Under International Law*, 2012 UTAH L. REV. 759 (2012).

5. SAINT BASIL OF CAESAREA, HEXAEMERON, HOMILY IV § 7 (1963).

6. Joanna Allhands, *Even If It Is Google or Microsoft, Should Data Centers Use that Much of Our Water?*, ARIZ. REPUBLIC, July 2, 2019.

7. SETH M. SIEGEL, LET THERE BE WATER: ISRAEL'S SOLUTION FOR A WATER-STARVED WORLD (2015).

8. *Id.*

9. Tony Allan et al., *The Water-Food-Energy Nexus: An Introduction to Nexus Concepts and Some Conceptual and Operational Problems*, 31 INT'L J. WATER RESOURCES DEV. 301 (2015).

10. SIEGEL, *supra* note 7.

11. *Id.*; *see also* Karin Kloosterman, *Launching Little Pigs to Fix Leaky Pipes*, ISRAEL 21C (Dec. 9, 2009), https://www.israel21c.org/launching-little-pigs-to-fix-leaky-pipes/.

12. Elisabeth Leamy, *It's Time to Replace That Old Toilet. Here's How Much You Could Save*, WASH. POST, Feb. 20, 2018, https://washingtonpost.com/lifestyle/home/its-time-to-replace-that-old-toilet-heres-how-much-you-could-save/2018/02/19/ebf235f4-1034-11e8-9570-29c9830535e5_story.html?noredirect=on.

13. SIEGEL, *supra* note 7.

14. *Id.*; *see also* Emily Harris, *Israel Bets on Recycled Water to Meet Its Growing Thirst*, NPR, June 21, 2015, https://www.npr.org/sections/parallels/2015/06/21/415795367/israel-bets-on-recycled-water-to-meet-its-growing-thirst.

15. SIEGEL, *supra* note 7.

16. James Crook & Rao Y. Surampalli, *Water Reclamation and Reuse Criteria in the U.S.*, 33 WATER SCI. & TECH. 451 (1996); Stuart J. Khan, *The Case for Direct Potable Reuse in Australia*, 38 WATER: J. AUSTRALIAN WATER ASS'N 92 (2011).

17. Janet C. Neuman, *Beneficial Use, Waste, and Forfeiture: The Inefficient Search for Efficiency in Western Water Use*, 28 ENVTL. L. 919 (1998).

18. Rhett Larson & Brian Payne, *Unclouding Arizona's Water Future*, 49 ARIZ. ST. L.J. 465 (2017).

19. Rhett Larson & Kelly Kennedy, *Bankrupt Rivers*, 49 U.C. DAVIS L. REV. 1335 (2016).

20. *Id.*

21. Salman M.A. Salman, *Downstream Riparians Can Also Harm Upstream Riparians: The Concept of Foreclosure of Future Uses*, 35 WATER INT'L 350 (2010).

22. *Id.*

23. Stephen McCaffrey, *Some Developments in the Law of International Watercourses*, *in* PROMOTING JUSTICE, HUMAN RIGHTS, AND CONFLICT RESOLUTION THROUGH INTERNATIONAL LAW (M. Kohen ed., 2007), 782–800.

24. Salman, *supra* note 21.

25. Rhett B. Larson, *Augmented Water Law*, 48 TEX. TECH L. REV. 757, 765–67 (2016).

26. *Id.*

27. IPCC, Climate Change 2007: Working Group I: The Physical Science Basis, "FAQ 3.2 How Is Precipitation Changing?"

28. *Id.*

29. Arnett S. Dennis, *Weather Modification by Cloud Seeding*, 24 INT'L GEOPHYSICS SERIES 670 (1980); *see also* Xueliang Guo et al., *A Numerical Comparison Study of Cloud Seeding by Silver Iodide and Liquid Carbon Dioxide*, 79 ATMOSPHERIC RES. 183 (2006).

30. *Id.*

31. *Id.*

32. Morteza Khalili, Sr. et al., *Results of Cloud Seeding Operations for Precipitation Enhancement in Iran during 1999–2007, Planned & Inadvertent Weather Modification/Weather Modification Ass'n* (Apr. 22, 2008), http://ams.confex.com/ams/17WModWMA/techprogram/paper_13 9149.htm; Cinnamon P. Carlarne, *Arctic Dreams and Geoengineering Wishes: The Collateral Damage of Climate Change*, 49 COLUM. J. TRANSNATIONAL L. 602 (2012).

33. Andrew Freedman, *Back in Business? The Government Takes Another Look at Weather Modification*, 59 WEATHERWISE 24 (2006); Anil Acharya et al., *Modeled Streamflow Response Under Cloud Seeding in the North Platte River Watershed*, 409 J. HYDROLOGY 305 (2011).

34. Noah Byron Bonnheim, *History of Climate Engineering*, 1 CLIMATE CHANGE 891 (2010); *see also* James R. Fleming, *The Climate Engineers*, 31 WILSON Q., Spring 2007, at 46.

35. Erica C. Smit, *Geoengineering: Issues of Accountability in International Law*, 15 NEV. L.J. 1060, 1086–87 (2015).

36. Larson, *supra* note 25.

37. *Id.*

38. Se. Colo. Water Conservancy Dist. v. Sheldon Farms, Inc., 529 P.2d 1321, 1323–24 (Colo. 1974).

39. *Id.* at 1325.

40. Larson, *supra* note 25.

41. *Id.*

42. *Id.*

43. Andrew Reeves, *Desalination: The Techno-Evolution Still Leads Back to a Simple Solution*, ALTERNATIVES J., Aug. 2018, at 32.

44. Stephen McCaffrey, *The Coming Fresh Water Crisis: International Legal and Institutional Responses*, 21 VT. L. REV. 803 (1997).

45. Walid A. Abderrahman, *Energy and Water in Arid Developing Countries: Saudi Arabia, a Case Study*, 17 INT'L J. WATER RESOURCES DEV. 247 (2001).

46. Tamim Younos & Kimberly E. Tulou, *Overview of Desalination Techniques*, 132 J. CONTEMP. WATER RES. & EDUC. 3 (2005).

47. *Id.*

48. Larson, *supra* note 4.

49. *Id.*

50. Robin Kundis Craig, *Water Supply, Desalination, Climate Change, and Energy Policy*, 22 PAC. MCGEORGE GLOBAL BUS. & DEV. L.J. 225 (2010).

51. Larson, *supra* note 4.

52. *Id.*

53. Emery Cowan, *Little Colorado River Fight Hits Home*, ARIZ. DAILY SUN, Feb. 19, 2016.

54. Treaty Between the United States of America and Mexico Respecting the Utilization of the Colorado and Tijuana Rivers and of the Rio Grande, U.S.-Mex., Feb. 3, 1944, 59 Stat. 1219 (1944).

55. Larson, *supra* note 4.

56. *Id.*

57. Treaty of Peace Between the State of Israel and the Hashemite Kingdom of Jordan, Isr.-Jordan, Oct. 26, 1994, 2042 U.N.T.S. 393 (1994).

58. Larson, *supra* note 4.

59. United Nations Convention on the Law of the Non-Navigational Uses of International Watercourses, 36 I.L.M. 703 (1997).

60. Larson, *supra* note 4.

61. Karin Aggestam & Anna Sundell, *Depoliticizing the Water Conflict: Functional Peacebuilding in the Red Sea–Dead Sea Water Conveyance Project*, 61 HYDROLOGICAL SCI. J. 1302 (2016).

62. Andrew Hodges et al., *The Economics of Bulk Water Transport in Southern California*, 3 RESOURCES 703 (2014).

63. Suzanne Timmons Lewis, *Domestic Solutions to the International Problem of Water Scarcity: Singapore, a Case Study*, 42 GA. J. INT'L & COMP. L. 247, 256 (2013).

64. Elizabeth Weise, *In a Drought, Should We Drink Sewage? Singapore Does*, USA TODAY, June 2, 2015.

65. *Id.*

66. Jeremy Leong, *Singapore: Review of Major Policy Statements*, 11 SING. Y.B. INT'L L. 277 (2007).

67. Rhett B. Larson, *Inter-State Water Law in the United States of America: What Lessons for International Water Law?*, 2.3 BRILL RES. PERSP. IN INT'L WATER L. 1–82 (2017).

68. *See generally* RHETT LARSON, THE CASE OF CANADIAN BULK WATER EXPORTS (2015), https://www.policyschool.ca/wp-content/uploads/2016/03/canadian-bulk-water-exports.pdf.

69. Sandra Zellmer, *The Anti-Speculation Doctrine and Its Implications for Collaborative Water Management*, 8 NEV. L.J. 994, 1001 (2008).

70. INT'L JOINT COMM'N, PROTECTION OF THE WATERS OF THE GREAT LAKES 44 (2000).

71. Larson, *supra* note 25.

72. *See* Larson, *supra* note 68.

73. Gabriel Eckstein & Renee Martin-Nagle, "Bulk Water Transfers: Panacea or Temporary Patch?," presented at 2015 World Water Congress in Edinburgh Scotland, http://aquadoc.typepad.com/waterwired/2015/06/gabriel-eckstein-renee-martin-nagle-presentations-bulk-water-transfers-un-watercourses.html (abstract and presentation notes).

74. Larson, *supra* note 68.

75. Larson, *supra* note 25; *see also* Cynthia DeLaughter, *Priming the Water Industry Pump*, 37 Hous. L. Rev. 1465, 1491 (2000).

76. Eugene Kontorovich, *Economic Dealings with Occupied Territories*, 53 Colum. J. Transnat'l L. 584 (2015).

77. *Id.*

78. *See, e.g.*, Robert A. Pulver, *Liability Rules as a Solution to the Problem of Waste in Western Water Law: An Economic Analysis*, 76 Cal. L. Rev. 671, 695 (1988).

79. Douglas A. Kysar, *Sustainable Development and Private Global Governance*, 83 Tex. L. Rev. 2109, 2116–17 (2005).

80. Christine A. Klein, *Water Transfers: The Case Against Transbasin Diversions in the Eastern States*, 25 UCLA J. Envtl. L. & Pol'y 249, 252 (2007).

81. Pulver, *supra* note 78, at 695; *see also* James S. Lochhead, *An Upper Basin Perspective on California's Claims to Water from the Colorado River Part II: The Development, Implementation and Collapse of California's Plan to Live Within Its Basic Apportionment*, 6 U. Denv. Water L. Rev. 318, 367 (2003).

82. *See generally* Alexandra Campbell-Ferrari, *Managing Interstate Water Resources: Tarrant Regional and Beyond*, 44 Tex. Envtl. L.J. 235 (2014).

83. Andrew Hodges et al., *The Economics of Bulk Water Transport in Southern California*, 3 Resources 703 (2014).

84. *Id.*

85. *See, e.g.*, Troy A. Rule, *Airspace in the Age of Drones*, 95 B.U. L. Rev. 155 (2015).

86. What follows is largely adapted from Rhett Larson, *If There Is Water on Mars, Who Gets to Use It? The Future of Human Colonies on the Red Planet Depends on the Answer to that Question*, Slate, Nov, 2, 2015.

87. Larson & Kennedy, *supra* note 19.

88. Francis Lyall & Paul B. Larsen, Space Law: A Treatise (2d ed. 2017).

89. H.R. 2262, 114th Cong. (2015–2016) (enacted): U.S. Commercial Space Launch Competitiveness Act (Nov. 25, 2015).

90. Dave Mosher, *Elon Musk and Jeff Bezos Have Profound Visions for Humanity's Future in Space. Here's How the Billionaires' Goals Compare*, Business Insider, June 9, 2019.

91. Lee Anne Fennell, Slices and Lumps: Division and Aggregation in Law and Life (2019).

92. Richard Thaler & Cass Sunstein, Nudges (2008).

93. Johanna Koehler et al., *Pump-Priming Payments for Sustainable Water Services in Rural Africa*, 74 World Dev. 397 (2015).

94. Mary Ellen Hannibal, The Spine of the Continent: The Most Ambitious Wildlife Conservation Project Ever Undertaken (2012).

Conclusion—Achieving Water Security

1. Zhi Li et al., *Drought Promoted the Disappearance of Civilizations Along the Ancient Silk Road*, 75 ENVTL. EARTH SCI. 1116 (2016); Daniel Kaniewski et al., *Drought and Societal Collapse 3200 Years Ago in the Eastern Mediterranean: A Review*, 6 WIREs CLIMATE CHANGE 369 (2015); Larry C. Peterson & Gerald H. Haug, *Climate and the Collapse of Maya Civilization*, 93 AM. SCIENTIST 329 (2005).

2. Marla Senise, *What Did Bruce Lee Mean: "Be Like Water"?*, HUFFINGTON POST, Aug. 2, 2014, https://www.huffingtonpost.co.uk/maria-senise/what-did-bruce-lee-mean-be-like-water_b_5431446.html?guccounter= 1&guce_referrer=aHR0cHM6Ly93 d3cuZ29vZ2xlLmNvbS88&guce_ referrer_sig=AQAAAB5RmW-3co0oIRxfuNmeZs 9gfKkWP07 eEYOzanSCJqRuUJNTdY8U2qb8u 1Hzn4h3F7ghKq0OCz8lx12z ByyLaF96dkqnZfNtj9GU8pmUZ- PgLRaA2Dwv- bgCv2HUhTIJMaxJp_ fYLT1r8yEolj-3CQmQRJdt4d46sXmTY-lDOXGy.

3. Much of the following is taken from Rhett B. Larson, *Global Climate Change and the Reallocation of Water, in* THE OXFORD ENCYCLOPEDIA OF ENVIRONMENTAL SCIENCE (David McQueen ed., 2019), 1–34.

4. For a general discussion of adaptive management in natural resource law, *see* J.B. Ruhl & Robert L. Fischman, *Adaptive Management in the Courts*, 95 MINN. L. REV. 424 (2010).

5. For a general discussion on management of extremes and avoiding assumptions about the stationarity of natural systems, *see* Robin Kundis Craig, *"Stationarity Is Dead"—Long Live Transformation: Five Principles for Climate Change Adaptation Law*, 34 HARV. ENVTL. L. REV. 9 (2010).

6. Much of the following information on the Aral Sea and its governance is taken from Dinara R. Ziganshina, *Central Asia: The Aral Sea Basin, in* RESEARCH HANDBOOK ON INTERNATIONAL WATER LAW (Stephen McCaffrey et al. eds., 2019), 414–30.

7. Colorado River Compact, 70 CONG. REC. 325 (1928); Arizona v. California, 373 U.S. 546 (1963).

8. Treaty Respecting Utilization of Waters of the Colorado and Tijuana Rivers and of the Rio Grande, Between the U.S.-Mex., Feb. 3, 1944, T.S. 994.

9. Eric L. Garner & Michelle Ouellette, *Future Shock? The Law of the Colorado River in the Twenty-First Century*, 27 ARIZ. ST. L.J. 469, 472–73 (1995).

10. Rhett B. Larson, *Law, Science, and the Colorado River*, 59 JURIMETRICS 83 (2019).

11. A. Dan Tarlock, *Toward a More Robust International Water Law of Cooperation to Address Droughts and Ecosystem Conservation*, 28 GEO. ENVTL. L. REV. 261 n.44 (2016).

12. Claudia Paul-Wostl, *Transitions Towards Adaptive Management of Water Facing Climate and Global Change*, 21 WATER RESOURCE MGMT. 49, 51 (2007).

13. Rhett B. Larson, *The New Right in Water*, 70 WASH. & LEE L. REV. 2181, 2263–65 (2013).

14. Gabriel Eckstein, *Water Scarcity, Conflict, and Security in a Climate Change World: Challenges and Opportunities for International Law and Policy*, 27 WIS. INT'L L.J. 409, 456–57 (2009) (citing U.N. Dev. Programme, Adaptation to Climate

Change—Integrating Adaptation into Development, http://www.undp.org/climatechange/adapt/mainstream.html) (using the "do development differently" language).

15. Eckstein, *supra* note 14.

16. *See, e.g.*, Robert Alexy, *Jurgen Habermas's Theory of Legal Discourse*, 17 CARDOZO L. REV. 1027, 1032 (1996); Rebecca Hollander-Blumoff, *Crime, Punishment, and the Psychology of Self-Control*, 61 EMORY L.J. 501, 553 (2012); Tom C.W. Lin, *The New Investor*, 60 UCLA L. REV. 678, 696 (2013).

17. J.B. Ruhl, *General Design Principles for Resilience and Adaptive Capacity in Legal Systems: With Applications to Climate Change Adaptation*, 89 N.C. L. REV. 1373 (2011).

18. Robin Kundis Craig et al., *Balancing Stability and Flexibility in Adaptive Governance: An Analysis of Tools Available in U.S. Environmental Law*, 22 ECOLOGY AND SOC'Y 1–3 (2017).

19. U.S. DEPARTMENT OF THE INTERIOR, ADAPTIVE MANAGEMENT TECHNICAL GUIDE 4 (2009).

20. Barbara Cosens, *Legitimacy, Adaptation, and Resilience in Ecosystem Management*, 18 ECOLOGY AND SOC'Y 3–9 (2013).

21. Rhett B. Larson, *Global Climate Change and the Reallocation of Water, in* THE OXFORD ENCYCLOPEDIA OF ENVIRONMENTAL SCIENCE (David McQueen ed., 2019), 1–34.

22. Ruhl, *supra* note 17.

23. Larson, *supra* note 3.

24. *Id.*

25. *Id.*

26. *Id.*

27. *Id.*

28. Joseph Sax, *The Public Trust Doctrine in Natural Resource Law: Effective Judicial Intervention*, 68 MICH. L. REV. 471 (1970).

29. Michael C. Blumm & Rachel D. Guthrie, *Internationalizing the Public Trust Doctrine: Natural Law and Constitutional and Statutory Approaches to Fulfilling the Saxion Vision*, 45 U.C. DAVIS L. REV. 741 (2012).

30. Robin Kundis Craig, *Adapting to Climate Change: The Potential Role of State Common-Law Public Trust Doctrines*, 34 VT. L. REV. 781 (2010).

31. Larson, *supra* note 3; *see also* Arizona Center for Law in the Public Interest v. Hassell, 837 P.2d 158 (Ariz. App. 1991).

32. Waweru v. Republic, 1 K.L.R. 677 (C.C.K. 2006) (Kenya).

33. Larson, *supra* note 3.

34. Prince Edward Island v. Canada (Minister of Fisheries & Oceans), 256 Nfld. & P.E.I.R. 343 (Canada, 2005).

35. Larson, *supra* note 3.

36. Rhett B. Larson, *Inter-State Water Law in the United States of America: What Lessons for International Water Law?*, 2 BRILL RES. PERSP. ON INT'L WATER L. 1–82 (2017).

37. Larson, *supra* note 3.

38. Barton H. Thompson, *The Public Trust Doctrine: A Conservative Reconstruction and Defense*, 15 SE. ENVTL. L.J. 47 (2007).

39. Daniel C. Esty, *Toward Optimal Environmental Governance*, 74 N.Y.U. L. REV. 1495 (1999); *see also* Ronald H. Coase, *The Problem of Social Cost*, 3 J.L. & ECON. 1 (1960).

40. MAUDE BARLOW & TONY CLARKE, BLUE GOLD: THE FIGHT TO STOP THE CORPORATE THEFT OF THE WORLD'S WATER (2005).

41. Gary D. Libecap, *Chinatown: Owens Valley and Western Water Reallocation—Getting the Record Straight and What It Means for Water Markets*, 83 TEX. L. REV. 2055 (2005).

42. Dustin Garrick et al., *Water Markets and Freshwater Ecosystem Services: Policy Reforms and Implementation in the Columbia and Murray-Darling Basins*, 69 ECOLOGICAL ECON. 366 (2009).

43. Tom Tietenberg, *The Tradable Permits Approach to Protecting the Commons: What Have We Learned?*, *in* THE DRAMA OF THE COMMONS (E. Ostrom et al., eds., 2002), 197–224.

44. Robert H. Cutting & Lawrence B. Cahoon, *Thinking Outside the Box: Property Rights as a Key to Environmental Protection*, 22 PACE ENVTL. L. REV. 55 (2005).

45. Anthony S. Keim, *Drought and Water Policy in Australia: Challenges for the Future Illustrated by the Issues Associated with Water Trading and Climate Change Adaptation in the Murray-Darling Basin*, 23 GLOBAL ENVTL. CHANGE 1615 (2013); *see also* Peter Drahos et al., *Nodal Governance*, 30 AUSTRALASIAN J. LEGAL PHIL. 30–58 (2005).

46. Cameron Holley & Darren Sinclair, *Governing Water Markets: Achievements, Limitations, and the Need for Regulatory Reform*, 33 ENVTL. & PLAN. L.J. 301 (2016).

47. Dustin Garrick et al., *Understanding the Evolution and Performance of Water Markets and Allocation Policy: A Transaction Costs Analysis Framework*, 88 ECOLOGICAL ECON. 195 (2013).

48. Holley & Sinclair, *supra* note 46.

49. Rhett Larson & Brian Payne, *Unclouding Arizona's Water Future*, 49 ARIZ. ST. L.J. 465 (2017).

50. *Id.*

51. G.A. Res. 70/1, Transforming Our World: The 2030 Agenda for Sustainable Development (Sept. 25, 2015).

52. Franny J. Crosby, *"Give," Said the Little Stream*, *in* THE CHILDREN'S SONGBOOK (The Church of Jesus Christ of Latter-day Saints, 1989), 236.

53. QUR'AN 21:30.

Bibliography

Introduction—Understanding Water Security

J.A. Allan, Virtual Water—The Water, Food, and Trade Nexus: Useful Concept or Misleading Metaphor?, 28 Water International 106 (2003).

Robert Glennon, Unquenchable: America's Water Crisis and What to Do About It (Island Press, 2010).

David Grey & Claudia W. Sadoff, Sink or Swim? Water Security for Growth and Development, 9 Water Policy 545 (2007).

Bruce Lankford, Karen Bakker, Mark Zeitoun, & Declan Conway (eds.), Water Security: Principles, Perspectives and Practices (Routledge, 2013).

Raul Pacheco-Vega, (Re)theorizing the Politics of Bottled Water: Water Insecurity in the Context of Weak Regulatory Regimes, 11 Water 658 (2019).

Sandra Postel, Replenish: The Virtuous Cycle of Water and Prosperity (Island Press, 2017).

Marc Reisner, Cadillac Desert: The American West and Its Disappearing Water (Penguin Books, 1986).

Steven Solomon, Water: The Epic Struggle for Wealth, Power, and Civilization (Harper, 2010).

Farhana Sultana, Water Justice: Why It Matters and How to Achieve It, 43 Water International 483 (2018).

Patricia Wouters, Sergei Vinogradov, & Bjørn-Oliver Magsig, Water Security, Hydrosolidarity, and International Law: A River Runs Through It, 19 Year Book of International Environmental Law 97 (2008).

Chapter 1—Water Security and Climate Change

Eric Biber, Climate Change and Backlash, 17 N.Y.U. Environmental Law Journal 1295 (2009).

Daniel M. Bodansky, Jutta Brunnée, & Ellen Hey, Oxford Handbook of International Environmental Law (Oxford University Press, 2007).

Robert D. Cooter, The Strategic Constitution (Princeton University Press, 2000).

Robin Kundis Craig, The Social and Cultural Aspects of Climate Change Winners, 91 Minnesota Law Review 1416 (2013).

Michael B. Gerrard & John C. Dernbach (eds.), Legal Pathways to Deep Decarbonization in the United States (Environmental Law Institute, 2018).

Rhett B. Larson, Water Security, 112 Northwestern Law Review 139 (2017).

Richard Lazarus, Super Wicked Problems and Climate Change: Restraining the Present to Liberate the Future, 94 Cornell Law Review 1153 (2009).

J.B. Ruhl, The Political Economy of Climate Change Winners, 97 Minnesota Law Review 206 (2012).

Dan Tarlock, The Potential for Local Governments in Watershed Management, 20 Pace Environmental Law Review 149 (2002).

Donald Worster, A River Running West: The Life of John Wesley Powell (Oxford University Press, 2002).

Chapter 2—Water Security and Public Health

Sumudu Atapattu, The Right to a Healthy Life or the Right to Die Polluted? The Emergency of a Human Right to a Healthy Environment under International Law, 16 Tulane Environmental Law Journal 65 (2002).

Rita R. Colwell, Global Climate and Infectious Disease: The Cholera Paradigm, 274 Science 2025 (1996).

Peter H. Gleick, Basic Water Requirements for Human Activities: Meeting Basic Needs, 21 Water International 83 (1996).

Lisa Heinzerling, Climate Change, Human Health, and the Post-Cautionary Principle, 96 Georgetown Law Journal 445 (2008).

Rhett B. Larson, Law in the Time of Cholera, 92 Notre Dame Law Review 1271 (2017).

Sharmila L. Murthy, The Human Right(s) to Water and Sanitation: History, Meaning, and the Controversy over Privatization, 31 Berkeley Journal of International Law 89 (2013).

Hari M. Osofsky, Learning from Environmental Justice: A New Model for International Environmental Rights, 24 Stanford Environmental Law Journal 71 (2005).

James Salzman, Drinking Water: A History (Overlook Duckworth, 2013).

Margaret J. Vick, The Senegal River Basin: A Retrospective and Prospective Look at the Legal Regime, 46 Natural Resources Journal 211 (2006).

Gilbert F. White, David J. Bradley, & Anne U. White, Drawers of Water: Domestic Water Use in East Africa (University of Chicago Press, 1972).

Chapter 3—Water Security and Human Rights

Ali Ahmad, Islamic Water Law as a Comparative Model for Maintaining Water Quality, 5 Journal of Islamic Law and Culture 159 (2000).

Maude Barlow, Blue Covenant: The Global Water Crisis and the Coming Battle for the Right to Water (The New Press, 2007).

Asit K. Biswas, Water as a Human Right in the MENA Region: Challenges and Opportunities, 23 International Water Resources Development 209 (2007).

Erik B. Bluemel, The Implications of Formulating a Human Right to Water, 31 Ecology Law Quarterly 957 (2004).

Peter H. Gleick, The Human Right to Water, 1 Water Policy 487 (1999).

Rhett B. Larson, The New Right in Water, 70 Washington & Lee Law Review 2181 (2013).

Stephen McCaffrey, A Human Right to Water: Domestic and International Implications, 5 Georgetown International Environmental Law Review 1 (1992).

Michael Rouse, Institutional Governance and Regulation of Water Services: The Essential Elements (IWA Publishing, 2013).

Anna F.S. Russell, International Organizations and Human Rights: Realizing, Resisting or Repackaging the Right to Water, 9 Journal of Human Rights 1 (2010).

Barton H. Thompson, Water as a Public Commodity, 95 Marquette Law Review 17 (2011).

Chapter 4—Water Security and Racial Discrimination

Anna Clark, The Poisoned City: Flint's Water and the American Urban Tragedy (Metropolitan Books, 2018).

David Groenfeldt, Water Ethics: A Values Approach to Solving the Water Crisis (Routledge, 2013).

Mona Hanna-Attisha, What the Eyes Don't See: A Story of Crisis, Resistance, and Hope in an American City (One World, 2018).

Laura Pulido, Flint, Environmental Racism, and Racial Capitalism, 27 Capitalism Nature Socialism 1 (2016).

Jason Robinson, Barbara Cosens, Sue Jackson, Kelsey Leonard, & Daniel McCool, Indigenous Water Justice, 22 Lewis & Clark Law Review 841 (2018).

Greg Ruiters, Environmental Racism and Justice in South Africa's Transition, 28 Politikon: South African Journal of Political Studies 95 (2001).

Farhana Sultana, The Right to Water: Politics, Governance and Social Struggles (Routledge, 2012).

Dorceta E. Taylor, Toxic Communities: Environmental Racism, Industrial Pollution, and Residential Mobility (NYU Press, 2014).

Ingrid Waldron, There's Something in the Water: Environmental Racism in Indigenous and Black Communities (Fernwood Books, 2018).

Edith Brown Weiss, Intergenerational Equity: A Legal Framework for Global Environmental Change, in Environmental Change and International Law (Edith Brown Weiss ed.) (United Nations, 1992).

Chapter 5—Water Security and Gender Inequality

Vivienne Bennett, Sonia Dávila-Poblete, & María Nieves Rico (eds.), Opposing Currents: The Politics of Water and Gender in Latin American (University of Pittsburgh Press, 2005).

Anne Coles & Tina Wallace (eds.), Gender, Water and Development: Cross-Cultural Perspectives on Women (Berg Publishers, 2005).

Lee Anne Fennell, Ostrom's Law: Property Rights in the Commons, 5 International Journal of the Commons 9 (2011).

Naila Kabeer, Gender Equality and Women's Empowerment: A Critical Analysis of the Third Millennium Development Goal, 13 Gender & Development 13 (2005).

Kathleen O'Reilly, Sarah Halvorson, Farhana Sultana, & Nina Laurie, Introduction: Global Perspectives on Gender-Water Geographies, 16 Gender, Place & Culture: A Journal of Feminist Geography 381 (2009).

Elinor Ostrom, Governing the Commons: The Evolution of Institutions for Collective Action (Cambridge University Press, 1990).

Aparna Polavarapu, Procuring Meaningful Land Rights for the Women of Rwanda, 14 Yale Human Right & Development Law Journal 105 (2011).

Marni Sommer & Murat Sahin, Overcoming the Taboo: Advancing the Global Agenda for Menstrual Hygiene Management for Schoolgirls, 103 American Journal of Public Health 1556 (2013).

Farhana Sultana, Water Politics: Governance, Justice and the Right to Water (Routledge, 2019).

Inga T. Winkler, Margaret L. Satterthwaite, & Catarina de Albuquerque, Treasuring What We Measure and Measuring What We Treasure: Post-2015 Monitoring for the Promotion of Equality in the Water, Sanitation, and Hygiene Sector, 32 Wisconsin International Law Journal 547 (2014).

Chapter 6—Water Security and Armed Conflict

Sunil Amrith, Unruly Waters: How Rains, Rivers, Coasts, and Seas Have Shaped Asia's History (Basic Books, 2018).

Joseph W. Dellapenna & Joyeeta Gupta (eds.), The Evolution of the Law and Politics of Water (Springer, 2009).

Peter H. Gleick, Water and Terrorism, 8 Water Policy 481 (2006).

Shafiqul Islam & Lawrence E. Susskind, Water Diplomacy: A Negotiated Approach to Managing Complex Water Networks (Routledge, 2012).

Flavia Rocha Loures & Alistair Rieu-Clarke (eds.), The U.N. Watercourses Convention in Force: Strengthening International Law for Transboundary Water Management (Routledge, 2013).

Miriam R. Lowi, Water and Power: The Politics of a Scarce Resource in the Jordan River Basin (Cambridge University Press, 2009).

Stephen C. McCaffrey, Christina Leb, & Riley T. Denoon (eds.), Research Handbook on International Water Law (Edward Elgar Publishing, 2019).

Oscar Olivera & Tom Lewis, Cochabamba! Water War in Bolivia (South End Press, 2004).

Aaron T. Wolf, Shared Waters: Conflict and Cooperation, 32 Annual Review of Environmental Resources 241 (2007).

Mark Zeitoun & Joeroen Warner, Hydro-Hegemony—A Framework for Analysis of Transboundary Water Conflicts, 8 Water Policy 435 (2006).

Chapter 7—Water Security and Mass Migration

Peter Bellwood, First Migrants: Ancient Migrations in Global Perspectives (Wiley-Blackwell, 2013).

Omar Dahi, The Refugee Crisis in Lebanon and Jordan: The Need for Economic Development Spending, 47 Forced Migration Review 11 (2014).

Jeff Goodell, The Water Will Come: Rising Seas, Sinking Cities, and the Remaking of the Civilized World (Little, Brown and Company, 2017).

James N. Gregory, American Exodus: The Dust Bowl Migration and Okie Culture in California (Oxford University Press, 1991).

Andrés Martínez Moscoso, El Derecho al Agua en el Ecuador: Un Análisis desde la Ciencia Política y el Derecho Público (Universidad de Cuenca, 2017).

Andrés Martínez Moscoso & Rhett Larson, Forestry Management and Water Law: Comparing Ecuador and Arizona, 44 Water International 337 (2019).

Fred Pearce, When the Rivers Run Dry: Water—The Defining Crisis of the 21st Century (Beacon Press, 2007).

Dai Qing, The River Dragon Has Come! The Three Gorges Dam and the Fate of China's Yangtze and Its People (Routledge, 1998).

Tom I. Romero, Bridging the Confluence of Water and Immigration Law, 48 Texas Tech Law Review 779 (2016).

John R. Wennersten & Denise Robbins, Rising Tides: Climate Refugees in the Twenty-First Century (Indiana University Press, 2017).

Chapter 8—Water Security and Technological Innovation

Walid A. Abderrahman, Energy and Water in Arid Developing Countries: Saudi Arabia, a Case Study, 17 International Journal of Water Resources Development 247 (2001).

Karin Aggestam & Anna Sundell, Depoliticizing the Water Conflict: Functional Peacebuilding in the Red Sea–Dead Sea Water Conveyance Project, 61 Hydrological Science Journal 1302 (2016).

Robin Kundis Craig, Water Supply, Desalination, Climate Change, and Energy Policy, 22 Pacific McGeorge Global Business & Development Law Journal 225 (2010).

Charles Fishman, The Big Thirst: The Secret Life and Turbulent Future of Water (Free Press, 2011).

Rhett B. Larson, Innovation and International Commons: The Case of Desalination under International Law, 2012 Utah Law Review 759 (2012).

Larry W. Mays (ed.), Ancient Water Technologies (Springer, 2010).

Stephen McCaffrey, The Coming Fresh Water Crisis: International Legal and Institutional Responses, 21 Vermont Law Review 803 (1997).

Salman M.A. Salman, Downstream Riparians Can Also Harm Upstream Riparians: The Concept of Foreclosure of Future Uses, 35 Water International 350 (2010).

David Sedlak, Water 4.0: The Past, Present, and Future of the World's Most Vital Resource (Yale University Press, 2014).

Seth M. Siegel, Let There Be Water: Israel's Solution for a Water-Starved World (St. Martin's Press, 2015).

Conclusion—Achieving Water Security

Maude Barlow & Tony Clarke, Blue Gold: The Fight to Stop the Corporate Theft of the World's Water (The New Press, 2005).

Barbara Cosens, Legitimacy, Adaptation, and Resilience in Ecosystem Management, 18 Ecology and Society 3 (2013).

Robin Kundis Craig, "Stationarity Is Dead"—Long Live Transformation: Five Principles for Climate change Adaptation Law, 34 Harvard Environmental Law Review 9 (2010).

Gabriel Eckstein, Water Scarcity, Conflict, and Security in a Climate Change World: Challenges and Opportunities for International Law and Policy, 27 Wisconsin International Law Journal 409 (2009).

Dustin Garrick, Stuart M. Whitten, & Anthea Coggan, Understanding the Evolution and Performance of Water Markets and Allocation Policy: A Transaction Costs Analysis Framework, 88 Ecological Economics 195 (2013).

Cameron Holley & Darren Sinclair, Governing Water Markets: Achievements, Limitations, and the Need for Regulatory Reform, 33 Environmental and Planning Law Journal 301 (2016).

Rhett B. Larson, Global Climate Change and the Reallocation of Water, in The Oxford Encyclopedia of Environmental Science (David McQueen ed.) (Oxford University Press, 2019).

Claudia Pahl-Wostl, Transitions Towards Adaptive Management of Water Facing Climate and Global Change, 21 Water Resource Management 49 (2007).

Brian Richter, Chasing Water: A Guide for Moving from Scarcity to Sustainability (Island Press, 2014).

J.B. Ruhl, General Design Principles for Resilience and Adaptive Capacity in Legal Systems—With Applications to Climate Change Adaptation, 89 North Carolina Law Review 1373 (2011).

Index

Figures are indicated by *f* following the page number.

For the benefit of digital users, indexed terms that span two pages (e.g., 52–53) may, on occasion, appear on only one of those pages.